T4-AIK-050

DEVELOPMENT ECONOMICS

PARI KASLIWAL

UNIVERSITY OF CALIFORNIA – LOS ANGELES

SOUTH-WESTERN College Publishing

An International Thomson Publishing Company

To the memory of my father

Acquisitions Editor: Kenneth King
Production Editor: Robin Schuster
Cover Design: Tin Box Studio/Sandy Weinstein
Internal Design: ©Micheal S. Yamashita

HS64AA
Copyright© 1995
South-Western Publishing
Cincinnati, Ohio

All Rights Reserved
The text of this publication, or any part thereof, may not be reproduced
or transmitted in any form or by any means, electronic or mechanical,
including photocopying, recording, storage in an information retrieval
system, or otherwise, without the permission of the author.

ISBN: 0-538-84745-X

1 2 3 4 5 6 MT 9 8 7 6 5 4

Printed in the United States of America

Library of Congress Cataloging in Publication Data

Kasliwal, Pari.
    Development economics / Pari Kasliwal
       p.   cm.
    Includes bibliography references and index.
    ISBN 0-538-84745-X
    1. Development economics.   2. Economic development.
      I. Title.
HD75.K367   1995
338.9—dc20

                                   94-33092
                                      CIP

IP

International Thompson Publishing
South-Western is an ITP company. The ITP trademark is used here
under license.

CONTENTS

Preface

This text grew out of a course I taught over the past decade to undergraduates at U.C.L.A. My particular pedagogic orientation, was not available in the standard textbooks. Meanwhile, there was ample time for my class notes to grow and cover my requirements. I have found this pedagogic approach, complemented by materials from supplementary reading, especially suited for undergraduates with a wide range of backgrounds and economic preparation.

This text is explicit in its application of the apparatus of economic analysis to the context of developing countries. Most other texts, in striving for realism, tend to smother the analysis in a barrage of words and description. The analysis here is direct and simple: mostly in diagrammatic form, rarely as equations. The text is designed for economics majors who take development as an elective course after completing introductory requirements such as micro- and macroeconomics. As such, this turns out to be a course in applied economics, complementary to sub-fields such as labor economics, public finance, international trade and finance, political economy, etc. Lessons from there can be directly applied to the development context. Conversely, this course provides a broad survey that helps combine the various fields together into an integrated whole. Applications of standard economic analysis are highlighted throughout this text. For instance,

the income and substitution effect is put through its paces while discussing the 'demand for children' in the Population chapter; general equilibrium analysis is contrasted with partial equilibrium in the chapter on International Trade; the arithmetic of present value and internal rate of return is reviewed in the analysis of Human Capital; and so on.

This text may also be distinguished in its reliance on 'stylized facts'. (Roughly these might be defined as just the first one or two significant digits of pieces of data). Instead of attempting to 'establish' such facts at this basic level, this introductory text makes sure to transmit the broad facts of the development experience, such as, for example, the striking rural/urban migration in developing countries. The focus is on examining the competing basic theories that aim to explain these facts. Subtle econometric exercises to establish the facts are better left to more advanced courses oriented. Yet students are encouraged, indeed required, to play with the detailed raw data from a current source such as the World Development Report . This annual publication is indispensable as auxiliary material since no textbook data could possibly remain current too long; nor could it hope to match the WDR's comprehensiveness of data coverage.

This text makes free use of cross-sectional data to transmit the broad generalizations that apply across the developing world. In contrast, another school of thought extols in-depth historical case studies of particular countries. In my teaching experience I've found that the average student is surprisingly more comfortable with case studies than in making the simplest analytical generalization. Yet it is the latter which is at the heart of the scientific approach. Students must be persuaded that recognizing patterns and extracting conclusions from empirical evidence is the main objective. This may even be considered courageous, since such conclusions are especially tenuous in the field of social science.

Inevitably, the particular focus, is bound to slight some or another. The reader must be forewarned about the parameters that circumscribe this work. Within development economics we focus squarely on the economics whereas various texts deal more concretely with the mechanics of development. Even the economics tends towards basic theory that cannot serve as a practitioner's guide. Nevertheless the student will be well advised to get this one-shot overview of the entire theoretical terrain before setting out to plow one of the of the many diverse fields of development.

PEDAGOGIC CONCERNS

The above noted emphases are likely to appeal to a specific kind of audience. American undergraduates typically have a limited exposure to geography and international matters. It is not enough to teach the general approaches to development theories; they must first be introduced to the diversity of problems among the 100 plus countries of the developing world. For instance, one must rectify simplistic notions such as "everyone is starving" in these countries, or that all have borrowed "a lot". Accordingly, each chapter contains a case study which illustrates the issues — ranging from profound to peripheral concerns — existing in the diverse real world context.

The pedagogic concern of this text is designed for students at a particular stage of academic development — typically economics majors at the junior undergraduate level. The author's eyes are fixed firmly on this audience, and not constantly looking over one's shoulder to colleagues at the frontiers of research. Thus the text makes no attempt at accuracy of chronology or citation — it only cites those articles that are particularly good surveys for the beginning student, or the names that are important in a doctrine-historical sense.

This introductory text remains utterly conventional in coverage and approach. This is less a "message" book than one text that aims to impart basic "lessons". Its building block approach only hints at the subtleties which may only serve to divert and confuse the novice. The pedagogic task is to nail down basic concepts within the student's head. Hopefully these will remain long after the details are forgotten. For instance, the chapter on capital prominently displays the statement "output growth is the rate of capital accumulation times the efficiency of its use." Each of these two items is then subtitled with bold letters in separate sub-sections that follow. To some this tautological statement may seem worthy of emphasis. Yet, not stating it in this bold way risks losing that conceptual clarity as in more sophisticated texts.

The concern for pedagogy is also reflected in the text's calculated use of jargon. Too free use can easily put off even the most dedicated student. An unfamiliar term tends to slow down the reader who must immediately look it up, or be intimidated into assuming a fancier concept than it actually is. On the other hand, knowledge of such terms is part of the required competence after completion of the course. In order to serve both ends the text takes care to explain each term the first time it comes up. Such technical terms are repeated in a kind of drill to ensure an eventual familiarity with these handy tools of our trade.

A final pedagogic aim is to escape the tyranny of the traditional literary style wherein 'everything is stated', but in sequential linear form. Instead one can work with the strength of today's student; the visual intelligence which can grasp the entire concept at a glance. Thus this book takes care about seemingly minor details such as ensuring that certain integral ideas fall in a single block, without the break entailed in flipping a page. Likewise, an abundance of diagrams aim to capture the eye, rather than masses of grey text which tend to glaze it over.

PLAN OF THE BOOK

Development economics as a discipline is perhaps unique in the degree to which 'everything is tied to everything else': Population growth, agriculture, technological progress, capital accumulation, poverty, education, etc., are all tied together in an interrelated network. Thus there's an unavoidable arbitrariness in the ordering of chapters. Yet the architecture of this book has involved a studied choice of where and how much to present certain topics.

An extended introductory part lays out the broad facts and issues of development economics. Then follows an introduction to the major theoretical strands that purport to explain those facts. The two major schools of development thinking are: the neoclassical paradigm versus the 'development economics' which dominated in the early years. The contrast between the two schools is highlighted through all succeeding chapters. Also included in this part of the book are the particular issues of equality and population which are of special concern in development.

The second part turns to growth models — following the presumption that quantitative growth is a crucial complement to the qualitative task of development. A production function approach delineates different theories of growth, from the Classical model through Structuralist models, to modern Neoclassical growth models.

The third part begins a detailed study of the prominent inputs that enter into the production functions. Separate chapters examine the theory and policy relating to each of those factors

in turn: Capital, Labor, Human Capital and Technology. Up to this point the book stays within the context of a closed economy merely as a convenience to keep the analytical issues simple.

Part four makes the transition to an "open economy" context which is more realistic in today's world. It addresses the question of what is the qualitative impact of international trade on overall economic growth. The opening chapter offers a capsule course in the pure theory of trade, as well as the empirical facts and theories relating trade with development. This is followed by separate chapters on trade policy for both exports and imports.

The fifth part turns to an examination of policy by taking a theoretical look at policy itself. This analysis is in two parts: one a normative analysis of 'what should be', the other a positive analysis of 'what is'. The former comprises the standard tools of applied welfare analysis, while the latter is the new political economy theory that examines the different underlying visions of a government role. The two succeeding chapters focus on policy for the specific sectors of agriculture and industry. Last, but not least, comes a chapter on macroeconomics policy, which departs from the preceding focus on 'real' determinants of growth. This relatively new addition to the development agenda derives from the painful lessons of the past decade as macroeconomic instability often became a major obstacle to development.

ACKNOWLEDGMENTS

In the end some acknowledgments are due. For meting out criticism and encouragement at just the appropriate moments along the way, and for his inspired efforts on this book, special thanks to my editor, Ken King. My thanks also to legions of students at U.C.L.A. who read progressive drafts of this text with varying degrees of interest. I've also benefitted enormously from incisive and detailed comments of anonymous referees. Valerie Bencivenga was most detailed and supportive.

Thanks also to my friends and colleagues Daniel Heymann, Ajit Jha, Jorge Palamara, and Vivek Moorthy for extensive discussions on many and diverse subjects over the years. I also thank Professors Axel Leijonhufvud and K. Velupillai for their friendship and support, even as their rarified domain of high theory remains far removed from the mundane concerns of applied economics and undergraduate pedagogy. The usual caveat applies: They have no responsibility for any errors in this text. For the latter pair in particular, such failings are despite their best efforts to straighten out my mind over the years!

Pari Kasliwal
1994

PART 1

INTRODUCTION AND BASIC ISSUES

Chapter 1

What Is Development Economics?

The world today is in the throes of a vast historical change, as momentous as the Industrial Revolution in eighteenth century Europe. Since the end of World War II many underdeveloped countries in the Third World have taken charge of their own destinies, touching off a profound transformation of our world. More than 100 nations of Africa, Asia, and Latin America have embarked on an intensive, often passionate pursuit of the economic development that will improve the living standards of their peoples. The striking impact of these continuing efforts is, of course, obvious within the developing world, but it is somewhat muted and distant to observers in the developed countries. Thus, students here face both a challenge and a unique privilege—to be able to study this historical phenomenon as it unfolds in the world around us.

Development economics is intellectually stimulating as it is momentous and current. The study of development in the Third World is a complex, interdisciplinary effort. The disciplines of sociology, public health, geography and urban planning, history, political science, anthropology, and the like are all intimately related with the economics of development. For instance, it is plausible that social attitudes or *culture,* normally taught in sociology departments,

may be of primary importance for development. Yet, courses in development economics usually concentrate just on the theoretical and empirical issues of economics. This exclusive focus should not be seen as a rejection of noneconomic aspects; rather, both types of aspects constitute two sides of the same coin. Consider a concrete example, that a people's ingrained cultural attitudes may affect their savings behavior. Clearly, the deeper cause is rooted in the culture, but the proximate indicator is the savings rate, an economic variable. Similarly, the root cause of a country's production and trade opportunities may lie in its geography, but the proximate indicator is its balance of trade. Because these various causal factors are reflected in measurable variables, performing an economic analysis ensures and enforces logical consistency in any explanations offered. It is therefore imperative that all students of development get the economic analysis correct.

Theoretical ideas of development economics have developed in response to actual needs, which reflect an ever-evolving reality. There is a growing recognition not only that development provides solutions, but also that each solution, in turn, gives rise to new problems! As perceptions about the importance of these problems change, so does the focus of **theory.** The discipline of development economics keeps reinventing itself to cope with emerging issues, such as the debt problem that plagued much of Latin America in the 1980s. In development economics, theory should be closely interrelated with practice or **policy.** (Sad to say, economists sometimes spin complex theories with little relation to reality, with very damaging effects.) Ideally, the task of theory is to suggest explanations for the observed facts; the theory implies certain policies will be most effective; policy makers then try out these precepts in a real world context; the impact of policy, in turn, alters the facts; the experience gained goes to further modify theoretical ideas. Thus, development economics is in a crucial way an empirical discipline.

Throughout the text, facts about the development experience are interwoven with the theories offered to explain them. Starting immediately below is a broad-brush sketch of the aggregate facts—the setting of development economics. (In the following chapters finer details are presented for each topic. For instance, the chapter on capital includes disaggregated data about savings rates and capital flows.) After this chapter presents these broad facts, it outlines some major issues of development, presenting them in the form of stark dichotomies. The purpose is to introduce the reader to the nature of the debate about today's most prominent problems. The chapter ends by elaborating the various (competing) theories that purport to explain development. The focus has moved from the early **development economics school** that dominated in the 1950s and 1960s, to the resurgence of the **neoclassical school** today. Other heterodox theories broaden and extend the scope of the development discipline.

THE SETTING

Our subject is the vast expanse of the "Third World", which encompasses most of the world except the developed countries that have attained high standards of living. The latter group is rarely referred to as the "First World"; instead, it is better known as the O.E.C.D. (Organization of Economic Cooperation and Development). This group includes the high-income countries of Europe, North America, and Japan, as well as Australia and New Zealand. (The rationale for a separate "Second World" disappeared when the Communist bloc began to crumble.) The Lesser Developed Countries (LDCs) can be defined in measurable terms: those with per capita income below $7,000 in 1993. More than 80% of the world's population lives in about 140 countries classified as LDCs. As individual countries within this group become richer, they surpass the threshold and can no longer be considered "developing." Thus, Spain, Israel, Greece, Cyprus, Singapore, and Hong Kong have escaped this classification in recent years. Taiwan and South Korea are now in the process of graduating, as are some oil-rich countries in the Middle East.

The start of the present development epoch dates from about 1950, when most LDCs gained independence from their colonial bonds. They then began a process of economic growth and social development unprecedented in their history. In the first twenty-five years of this epoch, up to 1975, per capita incomes of the LDCs grew at an annual rate of 3.4%, exceeding the growth rate of the developed countries. This rate was certainly much higher than their own experience of less than 1% annual growth over the previous century. However, the growth rate slowed to 2.5% in a recent twenty-five year period, 1965–90. By all measures, social progress also improved steadily. Secondary school enrollments, for example, nearly doubled, to about 40%. Although these overall figures appear respectable, the disaggregated data show diverse experiences, both across countries and across time periods.

The group of LDCs is so large and exceedingly diverse that no single generalization—or explanatory theory—can succeed in characterizing it adequately. The empirical data reveal striking contrasts between different sets of countries regarding their initial conditions and the principal problems they face. It may therefore be useful to think of subgroups of LDCs that share major characteristics. Some well-known categories of the LDCs are described below.

Newly Industrialized Countries (NICs) This group includes South Korea, Taiwan, Singapore, Hong Kong, Mexico, and Brazil. With annual growth rates that often exceed 6% over a sustained period, these rapidly developing countries will soon reach or surpass the per capita income of, say, Spain. Among this group, the most striking example is "the gang of four" East Asian countries noted above, although Malaysia and Thailand are not far behind. These NICs derive their growth mainly from an export orientation based on manufacturing. This effort began by capitalizing on their cheap labor, then moved in progression to higher grade production that uses advanced technology and highly educated labor.

Most Latin America Countries This group emerged as a distinct category when its members became deeply involved in a severe debt crisis for almost the entire decade of the 1980s. This region was especially affected because it had had rather free access to world capital markets in the late 1970s. Then, in the face of such external shocks as the sharp jump in oil prices, many countries chose to borrow to maintain high levels of consumption. By the early 1980s, though, it became apparent that this borrowing could not be sustained. All these countries were then obliged to embark on a wrenching policy of adjustment to restructure their economies and pay back the debt. Throughout the 1980s, real-growth policies were suspended while the region

put its financial house back in order. By the beginning of the 1990s, Mexico, Chile, and Bolivia had made a dramatic turnaround by implementing drastic stabilization policies, and totally restructuring their economies. Meanwhile, other countries, such as Brazil and Peru, are mired in a macroeconomic disequilibrium because they are unwilling or unable to endure the rigors of a drastic stabilization.

Countries in and around the Sahel Chad, Sudan, Ethiopia, Somalia, and the other countries in the sub-Saharan or Sahel region of Africa comprise the most destitute group among all LDCs. The decade-long drought during the 1980s created chronic problems of food shortages and sheer survival. These natural disasters have been exacerbated by such "unnatural" problems as wars, political turmoil, and ill-advised economic strategies. An ecological disaster now looms, for example, because traditional pastoral lifestyles are being replaced by more sedentary agriculture in an area where weak soils cannot sustain the continuous, intensive cultivation needed to support rapidly growing populations. The disastrous state of agriculture has forced much of the population to move to the cities. Unfortunately, industrial development remains so negligible that it cannot provide significant urban employment opportunities. Nor does there appear to be an immediate hope for vastly expanding exports, as has occurred even in rural Asia. Thus, Africa's economic prospects appear bleak unless there is a major breakthrough in the form of a new development approach that places particular emphasis on the agricultural sector.

Sub-Saharan Africa's losing race of food production versus population growth is illustrated in Table 1-1. It shows the growth rate of agriculture in the 1965–84 period and an index of food production per capita (base 1974–76 = 100). Most countries in this region showed a decline in food output per person, with some declining substantially. The GNP growth rates over the same period are shown for the sake of

Table 1-1   Food growth versus overall economic growth

	Annual growth rates GNP	Agriculture	Index of per capita food output (1982–84)
Cameroon	5.7	3.6	83
Ivory Coast	4.7	2.1	110
Ethiopia	2.2	.1	100
Ghana	.8	.9	73
Kenya	5.9	4.3	82
Liberia	1.9	4.4	91
Malawi	4.8	2.7	100
Nigeria	5.1	1.5	96
Senegal	2.3	1.5	66
Tanzania	3.2	1.5	100
Zaire	1.3	2.0	92

Sources: *ILO World Labour Report*, 1987; and *World Development Report*, 1986.

comparison. It is significant to note a strong correlation between agricultural growth and growth of the overall economy.

Capital-surplus oil exporters   These countries differ from other developing countries in that they do not lack capital but are still underdeveloped in various ways. They are members of the Organization of Petroleum Exporting Countries (OPEC), which enjoyed a sharp increase in revenues after the oil crisis of 1973. They then embarked on a very rapid pace of development, starting from an extremely underdeveloped base. Libya, for example, was one of the poorest countries in the world 25 years ago. The capital-surplus oil exporters are generally situated in the Middle East, and like Saudi Arabia, Kuwait, and the United Arab Emirates, are generally underpopulated. Although their sole export is petroleum, they can afford to import everything else. In contrast, the capital-short OPEC countries resemble other LDC categories in most ways. This group includes Mexico, Nigeria, and Indonesia, which have large populations and must therefore pay attention to industrial and agricultural growth.

Table 1-2 shows the wide chasm between the high incomes of many OPEC countries and their still-lagging levels of development. Unlike the simple income measure, the concept of development is related to well-being, defined more broadly in terms of health, education, and nutrition. All these dimensions are combined in a single measure called the Human Development Index (HDI). The rankings for this group of countries are tabulated for both the material measure of per capita income and the HDI measure of human development. Kuwait, for instance, ranks sixteenth in per capita income among all countries of the world but only forty-fifth in terms of human development. Such a large difference in the two rankings is common among the OPEC countries. The last two columns of the table show a couple of specific items that indicate human development. (Adult literacy is particularly low because women in these countries have traditionally been excluded from education for religious and cultural reasons.)

Continental groups   Grouping countries by continent can also be quite useful, as long as you remember that any generalization is subject to many qualifications and exceptions. Sweeping generalizations that link entire continents to a certain bundle of characteristics are provided simply

Table 1-2 Disparity between income and human development

OPEC country	HDI rank	Per capita GNP rank	Difference	Life expectancy	Adult literacy
Kuwait	45	16	-29	73	73%
Qatar	47	18	-29	69	82%
U.A.E.	59	14	-45	71	55%
Saudi Arabia	67	33	-34	65	62%
Libya	74	36	-38	62	64%
Oman	82	37	-45	66	35%
Iraq	85	46	-39	65	60%
Algeria	95	58	-37	65	57%

Source: *UNDP Human Development Report*, 1992.

as an aid to visualization. Clearly, the situations of individual countries will vary widely, and the student is expected to learn progressively more of these details. As a first step, Table 1-3 provides a quick summary of the common problems shared by the many countries within each continent.

These broad generalizations by continent help us visualize the situation of a given country, even where we lack detailed or specific knowledge. For instance, if your were asked to describe the economic situation of Zaire, of which you know nothing (except that it is located in Africa), the following might be adequate as a starting point: "It is a country rich in natural resources, but with very poorly developed human resources. In recent years it has been losing the race of expanding its food output to keep pace with its population growth. It is racked with the chronic political and fiscal crises that follow a harmful history of being colonized."

Before concluding these broad generalizations, let's examine briefly two important features that can also serve to characterize the various countries in the Third World: colonial heritage and country size.

Colonial heritage Opinions regarding the impact of the colonial experience are predictably

Table 1-3 Comparing development problems across continents

	Asia	Africa	Latin America
Natural resources	x		
Colonial past	x	x	
Human capital		x	
Food/population balance		x	
Political stability		x	
Macroeconomic/debt problems		x	x
Inequality			x

divided along ideological lines. Leftists, as well as Third World nationalists, denounce the experience as inflicting lasting physical and psychological damage, which has impaired development. In contrast, conservatives point to the beneficial effects of being exposed to Western know-how and institutions. In a backhanded sort of way, colonialism has even been lauded because the very opposition it engendered often fostered a sense of nationalism. This kind of consciousness, which unified nation-states, is credited for fueling the former colonies' constructive push for nation-building as soon as they gained independence.

The controversy about the benefits or harm of being colonized rages on unresolved, mainly because the argument is about the counterfactual. How would those countries have done if they had never been colonized? No one can say. The observed effect, which varies enormously from quite beneficial to extremely deleterious, is much clearer. Lloyd Reynolds (1983) claims that the economic—as opposed to political or social—benefits depended primarily on the identity of the colonizer. (Note that Reynolds refers pointedly to beneficial effects, not necessarily to benevolent intentions!) Reynolds ranks the colonizers in descending order as follows: Japan, the United States, England, France, Spain, Holland, Belgium, and Portugal. The last two were particularly harmful to indigenous peoples, because they populated their colonies with their own nationals while neglecting the education of locals. At independence, these expatriates departed, leaving the country devoid of the indigenous skills required for development.

Another stylized aspect of colonial economies was the type of development that did occur. In most colonies the pattern of investment and infrastructure was specifically oriented toward exporting. In many cases, colonies took the form of export enclaves—mines and plantations—from which resources could be extracted easily and repatriated to the home country. Thus, primary production was typically emphasized over industry. In addition, many colonial powers

deliberately fostered the import of manufactured goods from the home country. Quite possibly, this hindered the colony's industrialization.

Most of Latin America is nominally free from such a colonial heritage, having achieved independence from Spain and Portugal in the early nineteenth century. Yet many Latin Americans complain about the neocolonial burden they have borne right up to modern times. The economic power that the industrial countries wielded over them has been considered so harmful that their nominal independence was not very meaningful. This domination is said to have had a lasting effect on economic structure and performance. In the "southern cone" countries of Argentina, Chile, and Uruguay, foreign investment took an indirect form of "portfolio investment" rather than direct foreign control. Foreign purchases of stocks and bonds of local companies, mainly by the British, allowed an indigenous entrepreneur and middle class to thrive. In Central America and the Caribbean, on the other hand, there was mainly foreign direct investment from the United States, which wiped out local entrepreneurship and thereby eliminated the middle class. Thus, sharp class warfare between a tiny oligarchy and the masses continues to this day. This kind of historical experience provided the intellectual roots of **dependency theory,** which was initiated and actively cultivated by Raul Prebisch and others in Latin America, particularly over the period 1950–80. We discuss this theory later in this chapter.

Country size Population size and density serve to distinguish certain types of countries. For China, India, Bangladesh, and others, the sheer size of their populations may pose unique problems, since certain economic characteristics may grow disproportionately with size. (If everything grew proportionally there would be no essential difference between a small and a large country.) On the plus side, scale economies in some activities may improve national productivity. Counterbalancing this, however, are inefficiencies that arise from centralized control over a large territory. Other differences include: (1) Foreign involvement is much less important than in small countries, where external trade and finance play a crucial role. This kind of insulation makes the large country's economy less vulnerable to foreign shocks. (2) Of necessity, self-sufficiency in food production plays a central role in large economies. Unlike small countries that tend to specialize their pattern of production, large countries find it impractical to rely on substantial food imports in exchange for other exports. Fortunately, the largest countries have essentially solved the mismatch of food to population in the 1980s. This was achieved both by raising food yields and by controlling population growth. (3) The large countries' huge population nevertheless require continued emphasis on labor-intensive methods and an emphasis on rural production and employment.

DEVELOPMENT ISSUES

This introduction moves from a broad overview of the facts of development to the substance of the debates. To begin, it may be worthwhile to sample a range of issues presented in the form of sharp dichotomies. These are deliberately exaggerated to help you understand the kind of distinctions made in later analyses. Similar development dichotomies offered by P. Streeten (1983) were sometimes criticized as being too simplistic, since real-world issues rarely involve such black-and-white choices. Yet, as a pedagogical matter, sketching the extremes can be a mind-expanding exercise.

GDP versus equity Gross domestic production and social **equity** are two independent goals that are often loosely associated with the mind and heart, respectively. Pursuing one may lead to conflict with the other. This is obvious when there is a one-for-one diversion of resources from one objective to the other. Funds redistributed toward the poor, for example, must be taken away from such productive investments as dams and bridges. Another possible link is through savings. If it is true that rich people have a higher propensity to save, income inequality serves to boost overall capital accumulation and, thus, economic growth. Also, redistributions may impede growth by blunting work incentives; shirkers see no need to work because they will be bailed out anyway. The more productive members may also cut back efforts, since their earnings are taxed heavily to improve equality.

The opposing argument is that a more equitable society enhances feelings of belonging, and thus enhances the participation and productivity of the poor. A more equal distribution of income is also likely to promote social cohesion and stability, which in turn are conducive to growth. Thus, social spending becomes a kind of "investment." This kind of debate is familiar in all societies, developed and developing. However, the arguments may become muddled, since politicians are often less than honest and deny there is any conflict between the two goals. If, in fact, there is no ultimate conflict in goals, the argument becomes a minor difference of means. Thus, conservatives argue that the primary focus must be on growth, since the wealth created will eventually "trickle down" to the masses.

Growth versus efficiency A naive reading of neoclassical economics may suggest a congruence between these two objectives. But what if free market policies that assure (static) **efficiency** do not lead to the maximum (dynamic) growth rate? It may be possible that the growth process requires major changes in the basic economic structure. Neoclassical economic theory assures us that a perfectly free market will attain maximum efficiency, defined as the maximum output that can be achieved with given resources and technology. However, maintaining a laissez-faire policy at all times would preclude the large gains that can accrue from major structural changes. A good example of this is the extremely rapid growth South Korea achieved via interventionist government policies. A wide array of interventions surely moved South Korea's economy away from the static efficiency promised by free market theory. Far from being bad "distortions" to the price system, its policy choices have been beneficial.

The lessons of development have altered the terms of the debate. In place of a crude face-off between interventionism versus free markets, there is now substantial agreement that some government involvement is imperative and desirable. The only issue is what constitutes "good" policy. Neoclassicals concede that government is crucial in setting up an environment conducive to growth. Meanwhile, interventionists have learned that government policies work better through price instruments than through wholesale abrogation of markets.

Absolute versus relative poverty   In the developed countries the term *poverty* usually refers to conditions of **relative poverty.** By the standards of the developing world, people in such a condition would be considered fairly well-to-do and not a problem. Nevertheless, relative poverty does cause serious problems, which place demands on policy. For instance, the Blacks in South Africa are objectively better off than most other Africans; yet the stark contrast between their incomes and those of their white compatriots constitutes an unacceptable situation. Continued development and redistribution are required to address the feeling of being "poorer." By contrast, absolute poverty has deeper ethical implications. In countries where people may be literally starving to death, national policy must address this problem in a direct way.

Figure 1-1 depicts two income distributions. Both display the same relative degree of inequality, but each is located at different income levels. In country *A,* where a significant proportion of the population is tenuously existing below subsistence, the major problem is **absolute poverty.** Redistributive strategies would not really be feasible in this case, because there are so few rich people to tax in the first place. Country *B* has a small fraction of its population living below subsistence but is fairly rich on the average. Although absolute poverty is not a significant concern, the existence of relative poverty may nevertheless pose a serious problem since it creates feelings of deprivation and poor morale.

Closed economy versus international participation
Modern advances in transport and communications have obliged all countries to become increasingly interdependent. Yet, just a few generations ago the dominant paradigm of development economics was the **closed economy.** That theory envisaged that the typical LDC could enhance growth by insulating itself from international influences, rather than participating freely in such interchanges.

However, today's mainstream economics must concern itself with the **open economy.** In particular, the smaller countries are vulnerable to outside forces beyond their control. Issues of international debt, labor migrations, and the flow of technology and goods reflect the extensive interdependence among nations. Often such influences are perceived as a painful surrender of national autonomy, which leads to the question of "how" and "how much" LDCs should integrate themselves into the global economy. Leftist ideology still values self-sufficiency and remains suspicious of a reliance on trade, which is viewed as subjugation to the capitalist powers. The rift between the earlier closed economics and today's open economics is also reflected in the structure of this course. The first half of this text presents the theory that is relevant to largely closed economies. The latter half turns to an explicit consideration of development of an open economy.

Growth versus stability   The development discipline of even a decade ago concerned itself largely with growth, to the exclusion of considerations of economic stabilization. The **supply side** of roads and bridges, the optimum allocation of scarce resources, and so on. In the face of such obvious macroeconomic problems as the chronic

Distribution

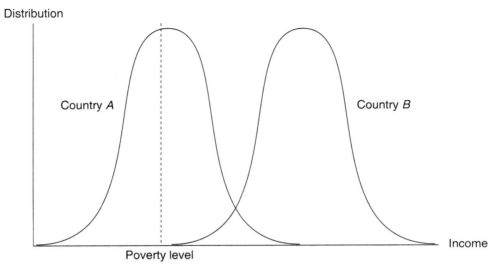

Figure 1-1 *Relative versus absolute poverty*

inflation in Latin America, however, development economists are increasingly focusing on stabilization policies that control the **demand side.** By analogy, when there is a fire, all efforts to build homes become secondary to fire fighting. Nor could construction proceed smoothly if fire were an ever-present hazard. For this reason, development economics is now becoming more concerned with the stabilization issues that have been dominant in the developed countries.

Growth versus limits to growth Throughout history there have been persistent doubts about the ecological **limits to growth.** Because rapid growth uses up inherently limited natural resources, surely such growth would be forced to cease. These arguments contrast slow, "organic," and therefore **sustainable development** to rapid growth. If this rapid growth damages crucial environmental components, spoiling the water and disrupting the ecosystem, they are bound to lose their capacity to produce. Some think the conflict between unlimited growth and resource depletion may be resolved if technical progress eases the environmental constraint. Then growth can continue, but

in altered form. Only if the unchanged techniques continue to be used, will environmental constraints necessarily become binding. Still, the antigrowth forces are urgently warning that they see an oncoming ecological disaster. In the past, they hold, technological leaps have only "staved off disaster" because growth proceeded in fits and starts. Yet, it remains a matter of faith that technological change will always save us in the future. (The relation of growth to the environment is studied in a later chapter on population.)

Growth versus development *Growth* simply means quantitative increases in per capita GNP, whereas *development* is a more qualitative concept. In its widest sense *development* implies that citizens receive greater life-sustenance, feel increased self-esteem, and enjoy greater freedom to choose among a variety of **options.** On the other hand, merely quantitative growth may bring with it increased pollution, cultural turmoil, and a perception of reduced autonomy in the face of modern, impersonal systems. If a given growth strategy does not lead to development, then there is a danger that it might be repudiated. Furthermore, a narrow-minded pursuit of current growth may limit sustained growth by irreversibly damaging the environment. For instance, the destruction of Brazil's tropical jungles in the name of growth may ultimately be seen as very costly once the jungles are all gone. This kind of growth without development cannot be sustained. In this light, critics of growth have argued for a strategy that directly addresses the broader agenda of development.

To repeat, the ultimate goal of development differs starkly from growth per se. Compared to quantitative growth, development is a complex and multifaceted qualitative achievement that is much harder to define or measure. Indeed, we can observe the example of various countries that remain underdeveloped even as their measured income has grown enormously. Their attainment of pure growth is missing fundamental changes in economic structure—items such as an improved income distribution or basic social and human development. Professor Amartya Sen (1983) defines development as an improvement in functional capabilities, the society's ability to perform essential tasks. Another definition of development refers to the **sustainability** of a continued process of growth and change. Many features such as capabilities and sustainability are notably absent in the dramatic growth of most of the oil-rich countries. For example, Libya might still be considered an underdeveloped country despite its high per capita GNP growth, since it has not learned to achieve sustained growth without oil.

In the early days of this development epoch, up to the 1960s, development was often viewed as more or less equivalent to Westernization or **modernization.** A prominent protagonist of this school, Peter Bauer argued that for LDCs to flourish they must come to resemble the already industrialized countries (1971). Such ethnocentric and unilinear ideas were soon forcefully challenged, however. The focus moved to a quest for notions that would be more widely acceptable. A specific requirement

was to define the fuzzy notion of development in an objective way, so that it could be measured. {See Srinivasan, 1994} Proposed indicators aimed to measure progress toward a "good society." These would take into account improvements in the quality of life, provision of basic needs to the poorest, as well as moves toward an equitable and meaningful participation by all members of society. Various alternative measures of well-being have been suggested, such as the Physical Quality of Life Index, and the Human Development Indicator (HDI).

An alternative **dependency theory** views development in terms of power relationships. This school argues that true development must result in greater autonomy for a society, in both its external and internal relations. According to this view, the capitalist West dominates the "world system" to keep the Third World shackled in a peripheral and subordinate position. Similar relationships also prevail within the developing country itself, as dominant elites subordinate the peripheral groups within the society. Thus, development would require a fundamental restructuring of international political economy relationships, as well as domestic ones. An example of a policy derived from this view would use a special sort of education to teach new values that reinforce cooperation and fight elitism.

A concrete description of what constitutes one ideal form of development is provided in a newspaper column, which talks

. . . about an environmental and egalitarian utopia. There are few cars and no smog. There are no graffiti. . . streets are cleaned, trash is picked up. Everything is recycled, nothing wasted. Some communities get electricity from windmills and cow-dung slurries that generate combustible methane. Small dairy herds have been established and new fields planted to make the island self-sufficient in agriculture and break its dependence on cash crops for export.

There is no underclass of destitute people, no one begging for food or sleeping on the streets, no barefoot children with bellies swollen with malnutrition. The infant mortality rate is virtually tied with that of the United States and is much better than in America's inner cities. There is free medical and dental care for everyone, and the number of doctors per capita is one of the world's highest.

Women have the right to choose abortion and the right to eighteen weeks paid maternity leave. They constitute 56 percent of all working professionals. There are more female than male doctors and judges.

Most urban neighborhoods have free day-care centers and preschools, and education is free through university and graduate school levels; literacy is 98 percent.

That island is Cuba.

The last sentence will signal how controversial "development" can be. Cuban policies are strongly criticized for violating human rights and for leading to economic stagnation. Even if the policies are evaluated on their own terms, it is doubtful whether reality matches the above description. Yet the normative *ideals* of this kind of socialist "Ecotopia" are clearly stated: Equality, social welfare, women's rights, anticonsumerism, self-sufficiency, "small is beautiful," sustainable development, the use of renewable sources of energy, reducing waste to protect the environment, and so on. There is a stress on developing the community's capabilities, as espoused by A. Sen. All these features comprise an alternative vision of the goals for development. (See the comprehensive review by Ingham, 1993.) These features are also commonly supposed to be the antithesis of capitalism, as illustrated by a trivial example: reducing waste serves to reduce total output and thereby tends to depress GNP, at least as measured in the conventional way.

Despite the sharp contrast between development and growth, these two are not necessarily always in conflict. Growth might be *a necessary but not sufficient condition* for development. In practice, structural changes are easier to make in the context of a growing economy, rather than otherwise. Consider by way of analogy projects of urban renewal; these are difficult to undertake in the absence of quantitative growth. However, if a town is growing, its new parts can be specifically planned for new uses, while the older parts are

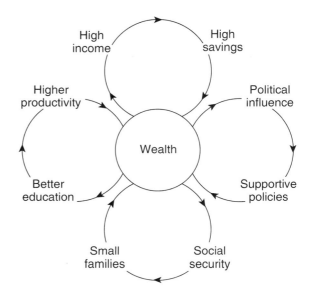

Figure 1-2 *Virtuous or vicious cycles*
Source: Adapted from Killick, 1984.

redesignated for industrial or other uses. Simply put, it is usually easier to add something new than to change what already exists. In the context of the development of entire countries, overall growth also facilitates development from a political standpoint, since development inevitably involves massive structural changes that lead to a reshuffling of relative incomes. As a rule of thumb, it is easier for people to slice up a larger pie than to redistribute a pie of fixed size. In the latter zero-sum game, the political forces that resist change are strongest.

Vicious or virtuous cycles Other contrasting visions of development relate to the debates discussed above. The neoclassicals envision a smooth process of growth and structural change mediated by the free market. In contrast, the development school expects sharp discontinuities that may make it impossible for poor LDCs to get from here to there. Such "traps" may seem familiar to any student who has ever heard, "You can't get a job without experience," and "You can't get experience without a job!" In the same way, **vicious cycles** may keep LDCs trapped in poverty. Conversely, countries fortunate enough to have escaped poverty may now benefit from an interlocking set of self-reinforcing **virtuous cycles,** as shown in Figure 1-2.

The poorest LDCs may face an analogous set of vicious cycles, which operate in reverse to keep them mired in poverty. The problem for development strategy is how to break out of such low-income traps. We examine each of these cycles in the appropriate context later in the text. The low income $\rightarrow$ low savings trap, for example, will be discussed in the chapter on capital. The cycle of poverty $\rightarrow$ political powerlessness locks the disadvantaged groups into their place, for example, and the cycle of poverty $\rightarrow$ old age insecurity $\rightarrow$ need for large families operates through the population mechanism. Although the **development economics school** has always highlighted "structural constraints" that create vicious cycles, the neoclassical school is only now recognizing various dynamic processes that lead to the same result. Otherwise, in smoothly operating free markets, traps should not arise. Breaking out of these traps, whatever their cause, requires concerted government interventions.

The issue of vicious or virtuous cycles can also be related to the mathematics of dynamic systems. When there is negative feedback, cycles tend to be damped, leading to equilibrium, whereas positive feedback reinforces each round of the cycle, leading to an explosive dynamic.

DEVELOPMENT THEORIES

A lively debate continues about which theory is appropriate to explain the facts and address the issues of development. The mainstream theories emphasize the tangible inputs and constraints that influence growth. By contrast, a less-established heterodoxy emphasizes intangible elements, such as culture and attitudes.

Mainstream theories echo the old refrain "no such thing as a free lunch," based on the implicit assumption that there is an objective limit on how much can be produced with the country's given resources and technology. In Figure 1-3 the so-called **production possibility frontier** indicates the combination of goods that can be produced (of goods A and B, say). If the economy is inside this frontier at x, **neoclassical economics** assures us that free market policies will help it advance up to the frontier at y, say.

A different dynamic focuses on pushing out the frontier itself as fast as possible through technical advance. Such a move from Y to Z may be considered the domain of the development economics school. As we shall detail below, this school emphasizes various structural constraints that limit growth, rather than a lack of markets per se. The distinguished economist J. Schumpeter pondered the sources of endogenous technological progress. He argued that entrepreneurs provide the driving force needed to push the production frontier outward. This creative urge is mediated by such institutional features as society's culture, morale, and attitudes, which determine how effective individual efforts are in generating growth. The focus is on an intangible resource, the body of useful knowledge available to a nation.

Another Austrian economist, von Hayek, argued that competition prompts an ongoing process of discovery that expands the stock of knowledge. An intangible source, the competitive process itself is posited as a basic source of growth. This contrasts with the **structuralist** prescriptions of the 1950s, which relied largely on adding the tangible input of capital. However, that emphasis on marshalling domestic or external capital resources very soon ran into diminishing returns. Similarly, when the focus shifted to another missing component, human capital, many LDCs became overrun by unemployed university graduates. Apparently it is not sufficient to just pile on more education. It is pertinent to ask: Was Europe's Industrial Revolution prompted by having many engineers, or did the process of development itself generate the needed engineers?

The focus on tangible inputs derives from an intuitive idea: If the poor countries are poor, isn't it because they lack something? Filling that gap should therefore eliminate the problem. But such a focus on missing inputs confuses cause with effect. The rich man is not rich because he has a Cadillac; he has the Cadillac because he is rich. A similar erroneous lesson was derived from the postwar reconstruction of Europe. That effort seemed to require only an infusion of capital; so the casual inference was drawn that development needed only capital mobilization put to rational use by means of economic planning. However, since the start of the modern development epoch, this optimistic recipe has provided rather disappointing results for most LDCs. This can be attributed to the LDCs' lack of other intangible elements. In contrast, Europe's institutional structure and management capabilities had largely survived the ravages of war. Thus, the input of capital alone could prompt the remarkable postwar growth of Europe.

The above skepticism about tangible inputs extends to other single variable explanations, such as attributing economic success exclusively to political stability, or resource endowments, or education. For each case cited to support these arguments, there are various counter-examples. Politically volatile Brazil and resource-poor South Korea have both grown quite successfully. In a way, the idea that growth requires bountiful natural resources resembles old mercantilist thinking: Because the wealth of nations is a given, the only way a nation can enrich itself is at the expense of others. Neoclassical comparative advantage theory could also be interpreted as a kind of limit: If a country is "stuck" with meager resources, it can advance only to the extent it can gain from trade. Resource-poor countries have sometimes used this as an excuse for their lack of growth. Yet, what you have is less important than what you do

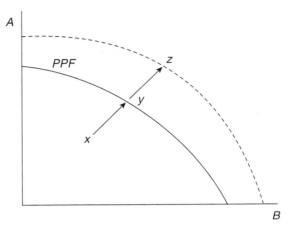

Figure 1-3   *Neoclassical versus development economics view of growth*

with what you have. Despite their natural riches, countries such as Zaire, Ghana, and even India have been left at a level far below their potential.

In a course such as this it is natural to ask: Is there really a development theory distinct from regular economics? Development economists may feel inclined to answer in the affirmative. (Our livelihood depends on it!) But is development theory anything other than regular economics applied to a different context? Certainly, this difference is not trivial; the circumstances and constraints that prevail in the developing world can be so *extremely* different from those in the "First World" that just impressing these facts on the First-World student would justify a separate course. Moreover, the issues of development range so widely that this course may be viewed as a useful survey in applied economics; it serves to synthesize subject matter as diverse as labor, microeconomics and macroeconomics, trade theory, and public finance.

However, the debate about a separate development theory goes deeper than this. Theorists early in this development epoch felt strongly that the discipline of development economics was different in an essential way. They argued that the developing economies have specific structural constraints that inhibit development of the LDCs. They sought to build an analytical structure that incorporated these constraints; this structure would constitute a separate theoretical rubric from standard economics.

Today the main schools of thought unite in denying any separate identity to development economics. Neoclassical theory claims to provide all the necessary explanatory power for any economy, developing or otherwise. Similarly, on the left, Marxian analysts claimed a universal application for their discipline. Of course, these theories constitute the extremes. By distilling the insights of each side, modern structuralists, such as Lance Taylor of MIT, highlight the structural constraints within an essentially neoclassical analysis. On the other side, Professors Bardhan of Berkeley and Roemer of Davis use the strengths of neoclassical economics to work out a neo-Marxist analysis of development. They retain the Marxist insight of conflict between economic classes, so that standard theory is updated by the "new political economy" associated with Buchanan and Tullock.

Structuralist Versus Neoclassical Economics

Toward the end of the twentieth century, the **neoclassical school** is reasserting dominance over the **structuralist** or **development economics school** that was so influential in the middle of the century. The neoclassical school of free markets and laissez faire opposes the government interventions favored by the earlier structuralist thinking. This argument, couched in theoretical and empirical terms, is a recurring theme throughout this book. The argument has two distinct components, disagreement about the *assumptions* of theory, and rejection of the *implications* of policies, even when there is no conflict about underlying theory. The first component is an aspect of **positive economics,** a

scientific question that can be resolved by reference to data, while the second is an aspect of **normative economics** relating to outcomes—a difference in tastes or values that cannot be resolved by argument. We briefly examine the theoretical differences below, but a fuller examination of the conflicting views is taken up in each of the chapters to follow.

The neoclassical school holds that prices are a crucial influence on economic behavior, subject to that famous qualifier "other things being equal." These other things include such variables as income, tastes, habits, and the given information. By contrast, the structuralists tend to stress the importance of just these other variables, in comparison to price. To understand the essential difference, recall an example from microeconomics principles: Does the demand for umbrellas depend more upon price or on days of sunshine? If you think it is the former, neoclassical analysis is appropriate; if the latter, structuralist economics is more appropriate. These alternative approaches can be simply distinguished in Figure 1-4.

Neoclassical analysis assumes agents are fairly responsive to prices (indicated by the rather elastic slope of the demand curve) in comparison to changes in other variables (shift of D curve). The development economics school argues that structural constraints are far more relevant to the LDC context. Simply letting prices adjust will do nothing to relax these constraints. Throughout this course, we highlight the contrast between the two schools in various areas—structuralist versus neoclassical growth models, the human capital model versus manpower planning, export-led growth versus export pessimism, and so on. As a concrete example of the contrast, consider the case of individual savings. Neoclassicals focus on the effect of price (i.e., the interest rate) on individual savings choice, while structuralists place greater emphasis on other factors, such as the accessibility of banks or the age profile of households. For instance, older families tend to have higher savings to provide for their impending retirement years.

The neoclassicals admit that free market policy becomes inappropriate in situations of **market failure.** In the absence of a free market equilibrium, the promised efficiency does not obtain. Market failures occur, for example, in the case of monopolies or such external effects as pollution. In her book *Aspects of Development and Under-Development* (1979), Joan Robinson argued that such conditions are widespread in the developing world where markets are also underdeveloped. Thus, structuralist models would be more relevant there than in developed countries. But the neoclassicals make a strong rejoinder: Even where market failures are widespread, it does not follow that government interventions are justified, since **government failures** often make the cure worse than the disease. Further, they challenge the statistics indicating widespread market failures. In a famous book *The Poverty of Development Economics* (1983), Deepak Lal attacks the claim that underdeveloped countries suffer from unique kinds of market failures, saying this is an empirical rather than a theoretical question. The debate about structuralist ideas continues in the development context and mainstream economics.

A prominent example of development economics theory is the Lewis model, which claims that underemployed rural workers are paid more than their marginal product. (This model is discussed in detail in a later chapter.) This apparent violation of neoclassical economics in the labor market is supposed to occur because traditional agricultural production is typically organized to use the extended family instead of wage labor. It would hardly be appropriate to pay family workers their marginal product, which is below the minimum required for subsistence; nor would a viable society be structured in a way that permitted large numbers of its members to starve. In other words, the problem might lie with a simplistic form of economic theory. A vigorous defense of the development economics school is provided by Toye (1985) and by Griffen. The tone

of these papers indicates some of the passion of the debate. However, despite their shrill tone, supporters of the conflicting positions have been forced to concede many of each others' points. As a result, their substantive differences have been greatly reduced in theory, if not in policy.

Another rationalization for a separate development economics is H. Chenery's argument (1983) that profound **structural change** can cause long lags in adjustment. In contrast to the standard neoclassical presumption, this view assumes the economy is in a state of transition or **disequilibrium** for years, even decades. A prominent contemporary example is the set of formerly communist European countries that are engaged in the major restructuring needed to become free market economies. In LDCs, the structural transformations involve a reallocation of such resources as capital and labor, a shift from agriculture to industry, and a significant increase in exports as a share of total output. These same shifts occur more gradually and automatically—though not without pain—in more advanced countries. The current transition from an industrial to a service economy is a good example.

Neoclassicals perceive structural changes in a different way—as effects, not a cause of development. Hence, nothing can be gained by forcing structural changes. If "everything is efficient" and always in equilibrium, we couldn't do better by using government intervention. Orthodox neoclassicals will say: Don't intervene to instigate a growth industry; don't try to change the existing comparative advantage; and don't attempt to alter the existing income distribution. Even where this is desirable, the available instruments tend to have deleterious side effects. To many activists in developing countries this attitude seems very defeatist. Yet, A. Harberger, a renowned development practitioner, advocates just this form of modest development policy. Although he admits that market failures are widespread, he still argues in favor of continuously seeking small improvements in

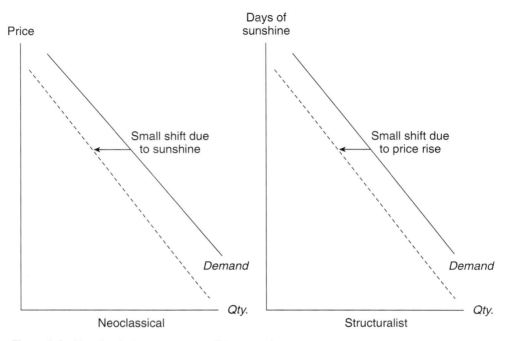

Figure 1-4   *Neoclassical versus structuralist economics*

efficiency, eschewing large discontinuous structural changes. (In graphical terms, this may be visualized as advancing upwards by scaling local hills rather than aiming to climb the highest mountain.)

Theories inspired by Marxism reject the neoclassical orthodoxy for a different set of reasons. Such theories give prominence to the power relationships between economic groups. Rejecting the neoclassical faith in mutual gains from trade, they stress that one party's gain is another (weaker) party's loss. Such gains and losses, combined with the corresponding political strengths, will dictate economic policy, since economic actions have both causes and consequences in politics. **Dependency theory** is a related school that was prompted by the Latin American disappointment with the benefits of trade promised by neoclassical theory. This thinking, which originated in the worldwide Great Depression of the 1930s and spread over

the developing world after World War II, presents a persistent opposition today.

In the face of all these challenges, there has been a powerful resurgence of neoclassical ideas with the support of international institutions, such as the World Bank. The reappraisal in the past twenty years was aided in no small measure by the visible example of various success stories that relied on free market policies (e.g., Taiwan and Hong Kong). Other successful countries, such as South Korea, pursued much more interventionist policies but their use of price rather than quantitative policies, as well as their outward orientation, stood in sharp contrast to either the radical or structuralist schools.

Neoclassical thinking has been criticized for its underlying assumptions that stress **methodological individualism.** These assumptions are based on Western cultural norms that glorify the role of the autonomous and idiosyncratic decision maker. The social aggregate is supposed to be nothing but the sum of these individuals interacting with each other through an impersonal market. For its role in combining and reconciling individual choices, the free market process is also viewed favorably. However, in traditional societies interpersonal interactions are usually not based on such individualistic principles. For example, the landowners of Guatemala have well-defined group interests that differ from those of the peasants. Clearly such groups interact through non-market modes in accordance with their (political) power. In such cases, the neoclassical paradigm would appear inappropriate. A policy of economic "liberalization," for example, would merely shift the gains and losses of different groups, with consequences that can be quite at odds with the predictions of neoclassical theory.

We now turn to differences in goals, rather than theories. A. O. Hirschman (1981) pointed out that normative, rather than analytical differences, might animate the development debate.

1. Many analysts may reject neoclassical economics because they perceive this framework places paramount emphasis on efficiency, as opposed to such goals as equity.

2. Another distinct goal is national sovereignty. But free trade along neoclassical lines is seen to inevitably reduce the scope for national autonomy.

3. Those favoring nationalistic values also tend to approve of centralized control; thus they distrust private enterprise and the consumer sovereignty that flourish within decentralized free markets. (One historical example is the Peronist regime in Argentina during the 1950s and 1960s; another familiar example is the dominant ideology of Mexico until the 1980s.) The desire for national autonomy remains particularly strong in nations that were long under the colonial yoke. Yet, all the countries in the world are now obliged to admit limits on the ideal of sovereignty.

4. A free trade strategy is also deplored because of its perceived stress on exports of low-tech primary goods. Instead, many LDCs want their development to be based on advanced manufacturing capabilities.

Possibly the most important normative objection to neoclassical economics arises from fears of the adverse distributional consequences that may flow from it. Proponents counter that neoclassical policies do not inevitably lead to greater inequality. They point to the empirical example of improved equity in many rapidly growing countries. Neoclassical theory makes a sharp separation of production from distribution. It says, in effect, organize production along efficient neoclassical lines; then redistribute to get any desired income distribution, simply making sure that the set of taxes/transfers used does not distort economic incentives. In practice, critics counter, this neoclassical policy is quite unrealistic. The initial arrangements of production, they hold, are the dominating determinants of the income distribution that is likely to prevail. Later redistributions are technically difficult and politically implausible. These critics tend to dismiss as excuses the arguments that the redistributive tools are too distortionary. They suspect that the neoclassicals' primary concern is really efficiency, not distribution. In effect, they deny a separation between positive and normative economics.

Convergence of Competing Theories

Given the skepticism about a separate body of development theory, a hybrid is increasingly used in the LDC context. Paul Streeten (1983) cites another reason for this confluence between the different economics schools: Whereas many problems of the South are now seen to be shared by the North, not all LDCs face common problems. There has thus been a great deal of cross-learning between the developed countries and the LDCs. (A generation ago, the college economics syllabus in a developing country would have appeared very different from that in a developed country. However, in present times both are beginning to appear remarkably similar.) Three examples of this cross-fertilization may be cited.

• Development economics was responsible for highlighting the fact that labor markets are often segmented. Instead of a unified wage, vast wage disparities seem to persist. The existence of a dual labor market is so obvious in LDCs that it must be explained adequately by economic theory. This feature is now incorporated into mainstream theory in the form of the "efficiency wage theory" developed by Mazumdar (an LDC economist) and Stiglitz (a U.S. economist). As we detail in the chapter on labor, these observed disparities in wages are explained by a more elaborate model of the labor efficiency required in different work settings.

• The LDCs have always operated within an open-economy context, but the significance of this fact was highlighted in recent years by the macroeconomic experience of many LDCs following the debt crisis. The insights gained have led to variuos changes in macroeconomic theory in general. These important modifications to the mainstream macroparadigm are relevant also to the advanced economies, as shown by the work done by Professor Rudi Dornbusch of MIT and others.

• The discipline of **political economy** has been revived and updated as a mainstream idea. No longer is it confined to the special case of "class conflict" defined by Marxian analysis. Standard theory now incorporates an analysis of conflict between economic actors based on differences in their economic **interests** and political power.

In recent years the open economy, macroeconomic approach has provided novel insights that displace the closed-economy emphasis that was common in such developed countries as the United States. Macroeconomic theory is in a state of flux for both the developed and the developing world. The worldwide debt crisis of the 1980s, in particular, led to new views about stabilization policy. Lately the same set of issues relating to liberalization and stabilization have arisen in many countries, including Eastern Europe and the former Soviet Union. The "macro" rubric focuses on monetary and fiscal policies, while development economics deals with "real" issues of restructuring the economy to correct distortions in relative prices. Such micro concerns are now combined with macro issues in the form of *adjustment policies*. There is a two-way influence, since the real structure may lead to macro problems, which can prompt basic changes in the development strategy itself. For example, much of the radical restructuring of policy in Latin America and South Asia came about as a reaction to the fiscal crises that arose from their previous policy choices.

With the renewed recognition of the importance of political economy, development economics has also moved closer to the standard economics of the advanced countries. Without this recognition, the positive theory that purports to explain "what is" was seen as doing a poor job. Today economists acknowledge that any policy action is bound to create winners and losers who possess varying degrees of political power. Thus, economic policies will be adopted or thwarted by interest groups that exercise power as mediated by the existing political institutions. All these considerations are now combined in the discipline of political economy, which as a result does a better scientific job of explaining observed outcomes.

The Expanding Scope of Development Economics

The development of poor countries is nothing if not about the creation of "something out of nothing." The process of development depends importantly on intangible factors, not just the material inputs emphasized in standard theory. The list of necessary inputs has now been expanded beyond labor and capital to include human capital and an all-encompassing item called "technology." Intangible elements, such as social organization, attitudes, morale, and the like, obviously play a very large role. The previous resistance to intangible elements stemmed from a belief that economics, as a scientific discipline, must be based on objective, not subjective, factors. Yet, the intangibles referred to here cannot be dismissed as merely subjective feelings; rather, these elements can serve to objectively alter material output.

When we relax the narrow parameters that circumscribe the scope of the development discipline—at least as defined by economists—we are impelled to ask more basic questions. For example, what really are the key determinants of development performance:

policy, interests, institutions, or culture?

Many in the economics discipline used to omit the last three items almost by definition, simply because these were not considered aspects of economics. Fortunately, such a dogmatic segmentation is now beginning to wither. At the end of the twentieth century, the discipline of development economics is poised at the cusp of an arc that will incorporate these other elements. This introductory text concentrates just on the analysis of policy and interests; beyond admitting their paramount importance, the text does not discuss institutions and culture. Despite our raised consciousness about the development problem seen as a whole, a segment of the neoclassical school still stubbornly denies any role for the other variables (cf. Balassa, 1988). It argues, in effect, that only policies matter. A country has just to adopt the correct set of economic policies to prompt a dramatic spurt of development. What remains is then only a technocratic discussion about what constitutes "correct" policy.

The empirical evidence is very important in addressing this controversy. There is abundant evidence that the highly distorted policy regimes of the 1960s and 1970s gained a lot from policy reforms. A pioneering study by the National Bureau of Economic Research (NBER) in the early 1970s highlighted the huge costs of distortions in various developing countries. That study led to a sharp switch in the conventional wisdom. Now there are many examples of countries that turned to high growth by eliminating excessive controls and distortions. An example is Chile since the mid-1980s. Once again, it is important to stress that the answer is not merely a perfect free market, but rather a policy structure that ensures the proper incentives. In support of this contention, one may cite Korea's dramatic growth during a highly interventionist regime (See Amsden, 1989). Meanwhile the economy of many colonies remained stagnant, even though they had essentially free markets prior to their independence. A final note on the policy question is the complementarity between micro and macro policy reforms. The micro set of reforms corrects the incentive structure, while macroeconomic policy aims to provide a stable economic environment in which to form long-term expectations.

The dominant role of **culture** is obvious even to the most casual observer of development. It operates through various channels: through a society's taste for consumption versus leisure, through social attitudes towards inequality, savings and risk-taking; and through institutions that administer fairness and social justice. How could anyone possibly deny the role of this crucial determinant? The opposition stems partly from a belief that such explanations are a cop-out; anything that cannot be explained is simply attributed to culture. Moreover, cultural aspects cannot easily be measured. Yet, it would be a serious mistake to claim that if something cannot be measured it must be "unscientific."

The opponents of cultural explanations of development also point to sharp changes in performance that result from policy changes that alter incentives. Considering that China has had the Confucian culture for centuries, they argue, this cultural aspect cannot possibly be used to explain China's dramatic growth spurt in recent decades. Yet, a cross section of many Southeast Asian countries shows undeniable evidence that Chinese expatriate communities do strikingly better than indigenous populations. Obviously, such performance must be attributed to cultural aspects. Opponents of a cultural explanation find a surprising source of support from indigenous chauvinists who bridle at criticism of their cherished cultural values. In locales as diverse as Fiji, Malaysia, or East Africa, for instance, indigenous populations have been perturbed by the economic success of outsiders. Although this divergence in performance is often explained away as an "unfair" advantage, the only exogenous difference is really the cultures. A recent resurgence of intellectual interest in this subject may be marked in Harrison's book, *Who Prospers?* (1992). His examples may not be totally convincing, but there may still be a nugget of truth in the cultural explanation for economic performance. Thus, there may be a role for a "cultural policy" that aims to alter the least functional aspects of age-old cultures.

An entirely different view shifts the focus from governments not knowing the right policies, to governments not wanting certain policy outcomes. In other words, the interests of powerful groups dictate actual policy rather than the national interest. Recent advances in the theory have turned this new political economy into an accepted part of the standard economic paradigm. Various studies in this mode—notably by Bates on Africa—purport to explain how the operation of political economy causes the persistence of policies that are clearly inferior overall. But note that this is only "positive" theory, which explains why policy choices are what they are. How is one to infer from this a workable "normative" policy for reform?

Instituting beneficial policy reforms in the face of powerful entrenched interests may be a job for politics, which involves leadership, public persuasion, and initiatives. Yet, politics is constrained to work within the existing political and social institutions. One must face the question of who will implement the beneficial policies: "Who will bell the cat?" The narrow interest groups in power are precisely the ones who decide current policy. Due to this dilemma, the issue of political economy was largely left to academics. The august World Bank, normally at the forefront of the development discipline, had tended to downplay this aspect, at least until 1990, when it began recognizing problems of governance. This diffidence is understandable since the World Bank must deal officially with governments; it would hardly seem politic to offer advice of the form: "Mr. President, if you would only remove yourself and your clique from power, our positive analysis predicts that your country's growth would blossom . . . ."

The political economy approach is argued to be particularly relevant because development entails drastic redistributions of income, which result from major structural changes. Thus, the economics of development must pay special heed to the interaction of economics and power relationships that emerge from, or impede, the process of change. For example, the growth of income in new sectors can trigger an even larger growth in wants through the demonstration effect. The increased dissatisfaction is instrumental in creating new political constraints. Thus, the path of economic development is affected step-by-step by politics, which is itself affected by the political situation. A well-known example can be cited:

$$\text{Politics in} \longrightarrow \text{Development}$$
$$\text{Pinochet's Chile} \qquad \text{strategy}$$

A tough authoritarian regime can manage to suppress real wages for extended periods, allowing the use of a stricter strategy than otherwise possible (see Ffrench-Davis, 1983). According to the precepts of political economy, such a regime may represent the interests of one social group against other labor interests. Thus, it would be disingenuous to claim that neoclassical policies are "purely economic"; such policies also constitute a subset of political economy. The connection between politics and economics continues full circle. An example of the opposite causation is:

Economic development ⟶ Political
in Iran   upheaval

In this case the pattern of Iran's economic development up to the mid-1970s was considered quite successful—at least, according to one definition of success. Yet, this strategy so drastically altered existing social relations and shredded the social fabric that it led to the violent overthrow of the Shah's regime in the Iranian revolution. A more general lesson is that change that is either "too rapid" or "too slow" can trigger instability. But what is the appropriate pace? This may be defined in relation to social expectations that develop with a separate dynamic of their own. The chapter on inequality presents such a dynamic postulated by Hirschman.

We can cite various examples of the interplay of economic policy, performance, and social expectations. Mexico in the 1970s was a prime case of surging expectations, prompted by the discovery of vast new petroleum reserves. The government was tempted (obliged?) to undertake "populist" policies, which led the country deep into debt and touched off the consequent crisis of the 1980s. An opposite example—of beneficial expectations—is provided by India's relatively successful first decade of development in the 1950s. This success may be attributed, at least in part, to the confidence of the early post-independence years, which allowed a political consensus to pursue long-term development strategies. The subsequent deceleration of growth led to widespread opposition by the end of the second development decade. Such political forces have limited the kinds of strategies

Table 1-4 Development debate: Point-Counterpoint

Structuralist model	Chapter	Neoclassical reaction
Redistributive policy	3	Poverty reduction policy
Cultural determinants of fertility	4	Economic determinants of fertility
Dual economy model	5	Agricultural responsiveness (14)
2-gap model of foreign exchange constraint	6	
Financial repression to promote investment	7	Financial liberalization
Efficiency wage theory	9	
Migration and unemployment	9	
Industrial sector planning	15	Liberalization, privatization
Import substituting industrialization	12	Export-led growth
Structural inflation	16	Monetarist discipline

that are feasible. In many LDCs an uneven distribution of the benefits of growth was initially tolerated as an indication of national progress. But later a building cynicism and impatience with the "trickle down" effect has often led to violent protest and forced changes in the development strategy, as happened in the Philippines in the 1980s.

The debate about development theory has prompted a succession of changes in the conventional wisdom. Of course, no final word is in yet, so the process of thesis, antithesis, and synthesis will continue. Segments of this debate will be highlighted throughout the text, as shown in Table 1-4. The specific topics are listed along with the chapters in which they occur.

SUMMARY

This introduction addresses the question, what is development economics? This subject is obviously of great topical interest in current affairs, and it is also intellectually challenging. In its broad interdisciplinary sweep, development economics encompasses most of social science and more. However, this text limits its focus on economics, which constitutes a crucial and essential component of development studies.

Theory and the empirical facts of development are closely interrelated. Hence, we must examine the development experiences of a diverse array of countries dating from the 1950s. We observe varying initial conditions, principal problems faced, and policy choices that were made. To encompass this wide diversity, one must make broad generalizations—despite obvious caveats. The experience is summarized in terms of familiar geographical groupings, which highlight the problems commonly shared among groups of countries.

Next, we presented various development issues as mind-expanding exercises. These were deliberately presented as sharply contrasting dichotomies, to prepare us for the theoretical debates. Examples include the contrast between growth and development, relative poverty versus absolute poverty, growth versus equity, and so on.

The main theoretical debate in recent decades has been between the neoclassical and structuralist schools, both of which stress tangible inputs and constraints to growth. The former paradigm extols the virtues of free markets, while the latter emphasizes various market failures that are supposedly widespread in the developing context. Thus, a separate kind of development economics, which highlighted the role of structural constraints, was prominent early in this development epoch. However, obvious policy failures have led to a revival of market-based approaches combined with an outward orientation. The continuing debate has narrowed the divergence between the competing schools.

Newer heterodox theories, by contrast, go beyond tangible factors to stress intangible elements such as social organization, culture, and institutions that constrain development. Most prominent among these is political economy theory, which holds that development can be impeded by the interplay of groups that advance their self-interest, over the national interest.

KEY TERMS

Development economics	Absolute poverty	Structuralist
Culture	Closed economy	Positive economics
Theory	Open economy	Normative economics
Policy	Supply side	Market failure
Development economics school	Demand side	Government failure
Neoclassical school	Limits to growth	Structural change
Development	Sustainable development	Disequilibrium
Dependency theory	Modernization	Methodological individualism
Equity	Vicious cycle	Political economy
Efficiency	Virtuous cycle	Interests
Relative poverty	Production possibility frontier	Culture
		Adjustment policies

Chapter 2

Measurement of Levels, Growth, and Change

Development economics aims to be a science that explains actual experiences of development. Accordingly, its theories must be based on facts of the real world. This chapter presents measurements and data that can give objective form to our discussions. Among the most relevant measures are the levels of output and growth rates. We introduce each of these while pointing out possible shortcomings. Note, however, that this text often relies on "stylized facts," which may be defined as numerical data that include only the first or second significant digit. (At this introductory level it appears somewhat superfluous to try to establish ever more detailed facts.)

The succeeding sections present the different types of data available: **time series** and **cross sectional data.** Time series data are used to follow the temporal progression of change within a given country; cross-sectional data are relevant for making contemporaneous comparisons across countries. The last section of this chapter lays out the stylized facts of structural change that occur as an economy develops. These provide a description of qualitative changes in the composition of the economy, in contrast to the quantitative measures of aggregate output level or growth rate.

INCOME LEVEL

Looking at any data involves the use of measurement. In each chapter that follows we always start by introducing objective measures that will make the concepts more concrete. For example, in the employment chapter we first offer a definition of unemployment that allows precise measurement of this concept. In the present context the concept of development is made objective. Various measures can be used for evaluating performance and making comparisons across time and across countries. However, all measures are bound to have problems, particularly as development is a multi-dimensional concept; so any single measure is therefore only arbitrary. (By way of analogy, consider the idea of human size; "bigness" can be measured by either height or weight or girth.) Despite such unavoidable imperfections, the measure of gross domestic product per person, GDP/Capita, continues to be widely used because it is the handiest measure of income.

1. Various biases are inherent in any GDP measure:

Much production of goods and services is not traded in the market, and thus does not get included in the calculation of \$GDP. Typical examples are household production for one's own consumption, such as occurs on farms, and housewives producing services in their homes. The result is a downward bias in measured GDP, particularly as the least developed countries initially start with a wide range of nonmarket activities that are excluded.

Excluding of negative externalities tends to overstate the real standard of living. The onset of development is accompanied by many visible "bads" such as pollution and congestion. Measured growth tends to be overstated because the expanded output is duly counted into GDP accounts, but the accompanying negative externalities are not. In effect, some of the negatively valued terms in the GDP summation are left out:

$$GDP = p_1 q_1 + p_2 q_2 + \cdots p_n q_n$$

Finally, the GDP computation is based on prevailing prices P, which provide a very imperfect measure of an economy's true welfare. Even if there's a perfectly competitive market in which prices equal marginal cost, prevailing prices still do not measure welfare. Suppose, for example, that water-scarce Saudi Arabia, where one gallon currently sells for one dollar, suddenly discovered

a huge gusher of water. The market price would surely go down, so the measured $GDP valuation, P times Q, may possibly also decline. Since output has actually increased, the total value would increase unambiguously only if evaluated at initial prices. Figure 2-1 shows welfare (the area under the demand curve that exceeds production cost) increasing even as supply shifts so far that water becomes a "free good." The prevailing prices in any economy depend on a variety of reasons. Observed prices in LDCs are often weighted in favor of manufactured goods and biased against agricultural products. Use of such "market prices" tends to further bias the measured GDP.

2. To make comparisons across time, **nominal income** must first be corrected for the rate of inflation to obtain **real income.** This is done by replacing current values (all the p_t included in the GDP summation of the pqs) by the corresponding base year prices (p_0) so as to provide a common basis of comparison. However, the consumption bundle itself tends to change as the country develops over time. This creates a different problem for comparison; for example, mechanical calculators or slide rules being

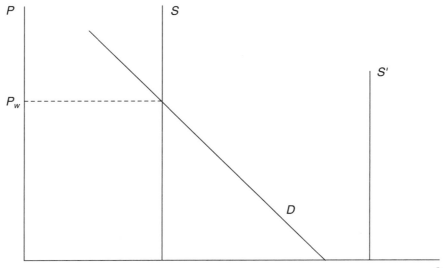

Figure 2-1 *Market valuation for GDP accounting*

displaced by computers as prominent components of national output. Further, as the quantity of computers rises their supply price has dropped dramatically; thus, this product of P and Q, which is the dollar amount included in nominal GDP, may either rise or fall. This issue, in general falls under the rubric of the "index number" problem.

3. For purposes of comparison, the income statistics must be converted from various national currencies into a common unit, say U.S. dollars, using the **exchange rate.** This conversion generally causes a downward bias in stated GDP as detailed below. The prevailing exchange rates for developing countries tend to be undervalued relative to their domestic purchasing power. An ongoing project for **real income comparisons,** by Irving Kravis and colleagues, tracks the actual purchasing power across countries. Their finding is that the poorer the country the more its real GDP is understated; purchasing power can be as much as five times higher than indicated by the dollar conversion using market exchange rates.

GDP accounting has another controversial aspect. Recall that the computed aggregate aims to avoid any double counting of intermediate activities. But do the activities of middlemen (such as wholesalers, agents, banking, and insurance intermediaries) actually add value, or are these merely redistributions? According to the labor theory of value, only workers and peasants are considered to be productive. Following this belief, Marxist regimes of the past took steps to eliminate the "parasitic" middleman. This invariably resulted in a drastic drop in total output, as such activities are also productive in an indirect way. There are many examples in which socialist governments banned farm middlemen with the hope that all returns would remain with the producers. But they soon found out that this middle activity of finance, distribution, or insurance is indispensable. In effect, one learns that grain is not simply grain; the middlemen add value in the process of converting—converting countryside grain to city grain, grain in normal times to grain in uncertain times, and so on. These kinds of service activities

can account for more than 25% of GDP, and this function grows in importance as the economy becomes more complex.

There are other reasons why $GDP/capita can be an inaccurate measure of the well-being of a typical person. If we look at the composition of GDP we might find a large component of investment, for instance, which points to higher living standards in the future but not in the present. Nor does measured GDP capture the contribution of certain nonproduced "goods" that nevertheless improve well-being. Principal among these is **leisure,** of which there's an abundance in poor countries. Furthermore, increases in **life expectancy** and declines in infant mortality must certainly be seen as a boon; yet both of these act to worsen the GNP/capita measure by increasing its denominator. For all these reasons new measures have been suggested to better capture well-being; e.g., the **Physical Quality of Life Indicator (PQLI).** Whereas this measure includes life expectancy, literacy, infant mortality, and so on, there is still a problem of how each is to be weighted in a composite index. Such direct measures of societal welfare are usually related to the level of GDP; but not always. Socialist countries such as Cuba and, at one time, Nicaragua, have by direct efforts actually attained a higher PQLI even at low levels of GDP/capita.

GDP/capita is a reasonable measure of the static level of development. A country's state of development might instead be better indicated by its **dynamic capability** to sustain continued growth by improving technology. Then the GDP growth rate better measures capability in the development process rather than level of GDP. Countries such as Libya, for example, have rocketed to a high level of GDP/capita through their discovery of oil. There is little evidence of further sustained growth of capabilities in non-oil sectors. Another case of stalled GDP growth is that of Argentina, which demonstrates that a wealth of resources can lead to a focus on the redistribution of unearned income, or rents. In such an environment this country's economic development remained stalled for generations.

So far we have not distinguished between two closely related measures of national income. **Gross domestic product (GDP)** is the total of goods and services produced domestically. However, in an open economy context, many international flows of income alter the actual availability of goods and services. Earnings from foreign investments, or remittances sent home by expatriate workers, can cause income to be higher than domestic product. **Gross national product (GNP)** measures the total that accrues to the nation whether or not it is produced here. Often GNP and GDP are so close that the difference between them may be ignored, but for specific countries the distinction can be quite large. All the Mediterranean countries that get substantial remittances from Europe have a GNP higher than GDP. For the opposite case consider the heavily indebted countries that are now repaying past borrowings. Their GNP is lower than GDP.

International Comparisons Project (ICP) The United Nations, through various technical agencies, sponsors the project for making real income comparisons across countries. This massive statistical effort to restate incomes every five years has widened its coverage to encompasses sixty-four countries as of 1993. Its methodology is to convert incomes in national currencies to an "international $" based on **Purchasing Power Parity (PPP).** Thus, the restated per capita incomes become comparable across countries. Table 2-1 gives results for a representative sample of LDCs in 1990. (Note that the first column contains GNP as against GDP in the second column, which makes them slightly incommensurate.) Income in terms of purchasing power is invariably higher than indicated by the conventional conversion using prevailing exchange rates. The corrective multiple can be as high as five times! The size of this error tends to decline with increasing income level.

The reasons for the systematic bias in income valuations may be easily understood. Note that market exchange rates are determined by the exchange of traded goods. A country with low productivity in the traded goods sector will have a correspondingly low wage in terms of the exchange rate. That sets the prevailing wage throughout the economy and, thus, its income

Table 2-1   Real Income Comparisons

| | 1990 per capita incomes | | |
	$ GNP	International $ GDP	Multiple
Bangladesh	210	1050	5
Pakistan	380	1720	4.6
Ghana	390	1720	4.4
Indonesia	570	2350	4.1
Philippines	730	2320	3.2
Ivory Coast	750	1540	2.1
Morocco	950	2670	2.8
Peru	1160	2720	2.3
Jamaica	1500	3030	2.0
Botswana	2040	4300	2.1
Malaysia	2320	5900	2.5
Venezuela	2560	6740	2.6
Brazil	2680	4780	1.8
Hong Kong	11490	16230	1.4

Source: *World Development Report,* 1992, Table 30.

level. Meanwhile productivity in nontraded goods usually diverges much less across countries. Yet these goods are also valued at the same market exchange rate, leading to an undervaluation of total income. The underlying wage differentials will persist as long as labor mobility is constrained and productivity remains low in the traded goods sector. Thus, producers of services, such as barbers, chefs, and cab drivers, are paid far less for the same services produced in advanced countries. The standard income measures tend to be even more exaggerated since market exchange rates fluctuate for all sorts of reasons. Variations in the real exchange rate can further increase the purchasing power error by a factor of two or three (see the last chapter). For instance, in certain countries at certain times, one may be able to buy nontraded goods for as little as one-fifteenth of its dollar price in the United States; say, a $30 dinner in a gourmet restaurant for $2!

As an illustration, consider Bangladesh's income of 6,300 Takas per capita. At the going exchange rate of about Takas 30 = $1, this translates to $210, which appears to be an unbelievably low income. Sure, Bangladesh is poor, but how could anyone possibly survive on $210 a year? The answer is, obviously, that most **nontraded goods** can be purchased at lower prices than, say, in the United States. The higher purchasing power implies a more meaningful real exchange rate of, say, 6 Takas = $1. After this correction Bangladesh's income in international dollars appears as a far more plausible $1,050 per capita.

An underestimate of real income is generally most exaggerated at the lowest levels of per capita income, as seen in Table 2-1. However, the undervaluation may also vary widely even within the set of the poorest countries. The ICP estimates of 1986 real income for a set of countries include three of the poorest. Table 2-2 shows how the ICP estimates of per capita income (and ranking among a set of 114 countries) may deviate sharply from the standard $GDP estimates in the *World Development Report* (WDR).

The quest for an objective study of development has led, in stages, to seeking ever more meaningful measures. Earlier development economists would have been happy to obtain any income measures of reasonable accuracy; now, as the world learned to collect and compile these routinely, our standards have risen. The standard GDP measure is flawed for making income comparisons not only across rich and poor countries, but also among the poor countries. Thus, we move to a more ambitious agenda for measuring not just income, which is merely an instrument, but to some measure of the ultimate goal, which is an improved quality of life.

HUMAN DEVELOPMENT

Clearly, the achievement of a high level of income is not the sole aim of development. More fundamental is the desire for human development, defined as people having wider choices. While income certainly expands individual choices, the quality of life depends on many other variables not necessarily related to income, such as health, education, and a good physical environment, as well as freedom of action and expression. The student faces this very issue when making personal decisions about careers. High

Table 2-2 Per capita income and rankings using alternative methods

	WDR$	ICP$	WDR rank	ICP rank
Bangladesh	150	647	113	86
Ethiopia	110	310	114	113
Zaire	170	210	108	114

Source: Adapted from Stern, 1989.

pay is only one element in this choice; others are location, leisure time for cultural and family activities, the scope for personal development, and more. In deciding between alternative prospects, the student does, in fact, weight such factors, though perhaps only implicitly. Similarly, a country's focus on human development can be made objective through an explicit index that is a composite of various indicators of social development:

life expectancy
mean years of schooling
adult literacy
per capita income

The methodology for constructing a composite index deals with three issues: (1) separate the ends from the means in picking relevant indicators, (2) translate these indicators to a common denominator, and (3) weight them appropriately in a composite index.

In considering the objective, the index must take care to include only true ends rather than means. The income indicator continues to be included even though it is argued to be a mere means, not an end in itself. Still, income serves as a measure of all the purchasable commodities that expand human choices—although we all know things that money cannot buy! The next issue is to decide which indicators to include in the construction of an index, and what weight to give each. While the HDI includes the above-listed indicators, it does not include infant mortality, level of nutrition, or unemployment, to name only a few. Srinivasan (1994) echoes the standard criticism that all the components are so correlated with each other, that the choice of included indicators is somewhat arbitrary.

Third, the method for translating selected indicators to a common denominator is simple, if ingenious. For each indicator a modified scale is constructed whose end points are defined by the best and worst performance achieved by any country. For example, the lowest life expectancy, 42 years, occurs in Sierra Leone; accordingly, this country is assigned a score of zero on the modified scale. Japan has the highest mean life expectancy of 78 years, so its score on the modified scale is set at unity. Each other country falls somewhere in between, and is assigned a score proportionate to its distance from the end points on this scale from zero to one. This measure informs at a glance a country's "distance" from the best achievable performance on any given dimension of development. For instance, Peru's literacy index of .83 means that it has traversed 83% of the distance from the worst to the best among all countries; it has 17% more to go. Since these numerical proportions have no dimensionality—such as years, calories per day, and so on—the various indicators can be combined as a simple or weighted average. The resulting HDI composite is a single number which allows one to directly rate countries, without having to resort to complex multidimensional exercises.

Table 2-3 presents the HDI computed by the United Nations Development Program. This detailed table is provided here because it may be harder for the student to gain access to the *Human Development Report* than, say, the *World Development Report,* which is widely available for reference in libraries.

Certain features are strikingly evident in these numbers. First, there's an obvious correlation between level of per capita income and human development. The richer the LDC, the higher seems its HDI. At least partially, this follows from the fact that income is included in the HDI index. However, the HDI would be superfluous if it merely duplicated the rankings by income. Thus, the exceptional cases are of specific interest. HDI rankings deviate most from income rankings for two categories of countries: Countries with a socialistic orientation generally attain a higher level of human development than is usual for their income level. China is the most remarkable example, as its world ranking by HDI is 51 places ahead of its ranking by income (see HDR rankings table in previous chapter). At the other extreme lie the OPEC countries, which earn fairly high incomes from oil. Yet their

Table 2-3   HDI values and ranking for developing countries

1	Hong Kong	.91	34	Dominican R	.59	67	Haiti	.28
2	Uruguay	.88	35	Tunisia	.59	68	Tanzania	.27
3	Trinidad	.88	36	Jordan	.58	69	Zaire	.26
4	S. Korea	.87	37	Mongolia	.58	70	Laos	.25
5	Chile	.86	38	China	.57	71	Nigeria	.25
6	Singapore	.85	39	Lebanon	.57	72	Yemen	.23
7	Costa Rica	.84	40	Iran	.56	73	Liberia	.22
8	Argentina	.83	41	Botswana	.55	74	Togo	.22
9	Venezuela	.82	42	Algeria	.53	75	Uganda	.19
10	Kuwait	.81	43	Indonesia	.52	76	Bangladesh	.19
11	Mexico	.80	44	Gabon	.50	77	Cambodia	.19
12	Mauritius	.79	45	El Salvador	.50	78	Rwanda	.19
13	Malaysia	.79	46	Nicaragua	.50	79	Senegal	.18
14	Colombia	.77	47	Guatemala	.49	80	Ethiopia	.17
15	U.A.E.	.74	48	Honduras	.47	81	Nepal	.17
16	Panama	.73	49	Viet Nam	.47	82	Malawi	.17
17	Jamaica	.73	50	Morocco	.43	83	Burundi	.17
18	Brazil	.73	51	Lesotho	.43	84	C. Afr. Rep.	.16
19	Turkey	.72	52	Zimbabwe	.40	85	Mozambique	.15
20	Thailand	.72	53	Bolivia	.40	86	Sudan	.15
21	Cuba	.71	54	Myanmar	.39	87	Bhutan	.15
22	Syria	.69	55	Egypt	.39	88	Angola	.14
23	Saudi Arabia	.69	56	Congo	.37	89	Mauritania	.14
24	S. Africa	.67	57	Kenya	.37	90	Benin	.11
25	Sri Lanka	.66	58	Madagascar	.33	91	Chad	.09
26	Libya	.66	59	New Guinea	.32	92	Somalia	.09
27	Ecuador	.65	60	Zambia	.31	93	Mali	.08
28	Paraguay	.64	61	Ghana	.31	94	Niger	.08
29	Korea DR	.64	62	Pakistan	.31	95	Burkina Faso	.07
30	Philippines	.61	63	Cameroon	.31	96	Afghanistan	.07
31	Oman	.60	64	India	.31	97	Sierra Leone	.06
32	Peru	.59	65	Namibia	.29	98	Guinea	.05
33	Iraq	.59	66	Ivory Coast	.29			

Source: *Human Development Report,* 1992; includes only developing countries with a population greater than one million.

human development still lags markedly despite rapid progress over the past two decades. For example, the United Arab Emirates, Oman and Iran, each lag at least 45 places in world rankings of HDI than would be warranted by their income levels.

Use of the HDI: The foregoing section introduces the human development index, which includes indicators of social progress with the standard economic measure of per capita income. We now turn to examine some of the ways this concept may be used or extended. Note that this index is useful not only to address the issue of poverty in developing countries, but also for policy-making in the advanced countries. Its application in the context of LDCs will be demonstrated in the following chapter on poverty. The indicator can be used for policy purposes both for following trends over time, and for making cross countries comparisons.

The HDI measure may be extended in three important ways. The first is to make some allowance for the level of *income equality* prevailing in a country. The issue of equity is examined in detail in the following chapter. For current purposes, it is enough to say that the HDI index so augmented would be a more comprehensive and accurate indicator of overall *social* well-being. A second extension accounts for the existing *status of women*. The well-being of the female half of the world's population suffers in comparison to its male compatriots. These disparities are more prevalent in some cultures than in others. For instance, in the more fundamentalist Islamic countries the education of women is slighted. Thus, overall well-being in such countries may be lower than would seem to be indicated by the existing numbers.

Finally, due weight must be given to political freedoms and human rights as indicators of individual and social well-being. Previously such issues were considered only for their instrumental value: Do authoritarian regimes give rise to greater economic benefits? However, when the ultimate goal is defined more broadly, these other indicators should be included directly as components. Even a casual examination of HDI trends shows that wars and civil strife result in severely retarding human development. Many modern examples can be cited: Uganda, Afghanistan, Mozambique, Nicaragua, and, most recently, Angola have seen a sharp decline in their level of human development. (See HDR 1992)

The trends of HDI over a twenty-year span from 1970 to 1990 are revealing. In the aggregate there is good news in the form of a shrinking gap between the already **developed countries (DCs)** and the lesser developed countries (LDCs). This effect is only to be expected. Since "basic needs" are indeed basic, the advanced countries will ultimately get to fulfill them 100%, and go no further. Thus the LDCs as a group are bound to catch up. Table 2-4 shows progress on various indicators. The solid arrow shows the beginning and end points for the group of LDCs that comprise the South. The difference shows the advance over the 1970–90 period. The dotted arrows show the corresponding advance for the developed countries of the North. For all these indicators, the South is seen to be catching up.

In contrast to the indicated progress of the whole group, the HDI advance varies sharply across individual countries of the South. As noted earlier, the OPEC group managed to advance dramatically by using oil wealth. Another group composed of the East Asian economies aimed specifically for improvement in human resources—and succeeded spectacularly. For instance, Hong Kong, South Korea, and Singapore are not very far behind Spain and Italy. At the other extreme lie mainly countries from sub-Saharan Africa, whose economic growth rate have been low or negative over the past generation. Their agonizingly slow progress toward improving human development remains a serious problem. This issue is discussed in detail in the section on poverty reduction in the next chapter.

Table 2-4 The closing gap in human welfare between North and South

Life expectancy	———— 22.8 ————>
	.... 11.7 ....>
Adult literacy	———— 49 ————>
	.... 33 ....>
Infant mortality	———— 123 ————>
	.... 61 ....>
Nutrition	———— 34 ————>
	.... 25 ....>

SCEPTICISM ABOUT DATA

This section on the importance of data closes with a cautionary note: The student must acquire a healthy scepticism about the numbers themselves—an issue apart from the problems of interpretation noted above. When viewing authoritative sources such as the *World Development Report* one can easily be impressed by the apparent solidity of the columns of numbers. But real world data can be anything but. The numbers may be entirely arbitrary, pulled together to fulfill some requirement, tainted for various political motives, or seriously flawed by simple errors near the point of collection. In many cases the numbers are just estimates which depend crucially upon assumptions and projections based on uncertain theories.

In a revealing portrait of the actual situation within a typical developing country in Africa, Klitgaard (pg. 59) cites a telling example. In 1986 the World Bank's estimate for 1988 exports by Equitorial Guinea was $42m, the U.N. estimated $34m, and the IMF $30m. The high estimate exceeded the low estimate by 44% Nor are past numbers any more solid. In the balance of payments accounts (to be discussed in our last chapter), a catch-all category is "errors and omissions." In Equatorial Guinea in 1985, this category totalled $9m in comparison to exports and imports of $23m and $33m respectively. As a result, a large chunk of the balance of payments deficit could not be explained.

Despite all the inaccuracies, however, the data may still be useful for indicating trends. But then the direction of the error must not jump erratically from year to year. Klitgaard (pg. 220) cites another example from Equatorial Guinea: According to figures presented at a ministerial meeting, GDP for 1987 had grown by an implausible 12% over the previous year. It was soon noted that this number was not adjusted for inflation. But the only price numbers available were for the capital city, where the price index had dropped by 13%. That would imply real GDP had grown over 20% Later almost half of the dubious GDP jump was attributed to the number cited for Public Administration. Its 1987 figure appeared to be $6 million larger than the 1986 figure, which was smaller than the 1985 figure by roughly the same amount. Instead of such a drastic flip-flopping, it was far more likely that the 1986 number was suspect.

Such data problems can cause quandaries in the context of both theory and policy, as we shall see in succeeding chapters. Often population numbers are deliberately obscured since this is a sensitive political issue, especially where ethnic or group rivalries are rife. Uncertainty about numbers can also spark fierce debate among academics. For instance, determination of the main sources of growth for East Asia's economic "miracle" depends critically on measurements of inputs and outputs. It is possible that a rapid expansion of labor force participation may explain much of the measured output growth rather than just advances in productivity. Thus, the reliability of data can have large and obvious implications for policy.

ECONOMIC GROWTH

We move now from the qualitative concept of development to a focus on purely quantitative indicators of economic growth. In fact, the *growth rate* might be a better indicator of success than the *level* of income. On the face of it this provocative suggestion may appear strange. Surely, happiness or utility depends on the level of income or consumption. How then can we claim that it depends on the growth rate rather than income level? In response, note first that total utility must be the sum of the utility in all future periods. Thus, output growth will obviously raise the levels of future consumption that enter into that sum. (Of course, utility in each future period must be appropriately discounted so that the present is valued higher than the future.) However, our claim is not merely that growth is desired because of the higher future incomes it will bring.

Instead, we are saying something rather less obvious: that a country with a higher growth rate than another is to be considered more successful right now, regardless of levels of income. The rationale is that countries can derive a certain sense of achievement from present performance. In the classroom this is analogous to the recognition awarded for "the most improved performance," as opposed to the best student.

Note one relevant caveat: the maximization of economic growth obviously cannot be an unlimited goal. There is such a thing as "too much growth." Growth requires investment, which requires saving, which is nothing but refraining from consumption. In fact, societies must make a choice between present and future consumption to determine the "optimal" rate of growth. (This topic is examined in a later chapter on modern growth models.) In authoritarian regimes this choice may be based on a leader's own interests. For instance, in Roumania in the 1980s, Ceausescu went for all-out growth by cutting current consumption, which caused severe hardship to much of the population.

The power of the growth objective lies in the enormous impact of **compound growth** over time. The size of this effect may not be fully appreciated. An annual growth rate of a mere 1.5% is able to transform an initial per capita income of $400 to a level of almost $8,000 over the course of 200 years. After World War II the growth rate of the industrial countries speeded up to about 2.5% annually, enabling them to reach a level of around $15,000 per capita. The LDCs as a group have grown at a faster average rate of about 4% per capita in recent times. The varying impact is apparent from examining Table 2-5, which indicates the number of years it takes to double the level of any quantity at various annual growth rates.

Despite the generally faster growth of LDCs, early fantasies about "closing the gap" have faded. Given the extreme disparities in initial levels, the catching up process can take generations, even centuries. LDCs must therefore place primary emphasis on their own growth, without comparisons with income levels in the DCs. There's a common saying that "comparisons are odious" in the context of valuing individuals. Likewise for countries, success may be measured by the *rate of growth* relative to potential, rather than the *level of income* per se. However, even the achievement of robust growth of average incomes may not be enough to satisfy social objectives. Development must aim to alleviate the condition of absolute poverty for the segment of population that lies below the poverty line.

For many countries secular growth is a relatively novel idea, whereas many people in the advanced countries have casually come to expect progress year after year. Taking a historical view, for millennia there have been ups and downs in per capita income while the long-term trend remained essentially flat. **Cumulative growth** began only with the industrial revolution in Europe around the seventeenth century. For someone in Chad, for instance, the idea of progress is not at all obvious. Only after a nation gets on the "escalator" of progress do people learn to expect growth to continue indefinitely. The problem for development economists is to determine how to get stagnant countries to reach a turning point.

An influential idea of the 1950s was that a specific series of steps was necessary for development. Walter Rostow used the metaphor of "take-off" in an elaborate explanation of the "stages of growth." By contrast, our purpose here is merely a description of the general transitions that occurred in history. Of course, an

Table 2-5 How growth rates affect levels

Annual growth rate	Years to double
1.5%	46.5
2.5%	28.0
5.0%	14.2
10.0%	7.3

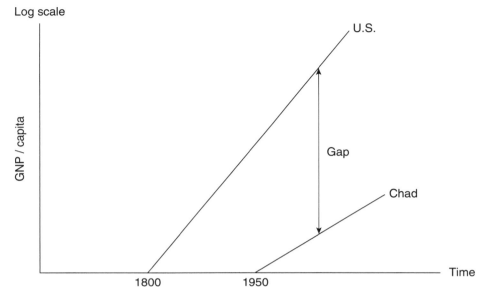

Figure 2-2   *Growth paths*

understanding of the preconditions would help policy makers to secure rapid economic growth. For the moment we focus just on quantitative growth, which abstracts from the complex notion of development.

In Figure 2-2, growth of output is shown in terms of the logarithm of GNP on the vertical axis. Whereas an exponentially growing series appears as a curving path, the "logs" of that data trace out a straight line. For constant growth rates, the straight lines have a steeper slope the higher the growth rate.

For the least developed of the LDCs—say, for example, Chad—the long delay before the growth process even starts results in a huge income gap compared to the already developed countries. Even if Chad were to grow at the same rate as the United States, the **absolute gap** will widen while its relative standing is maintained. There is hope for closing the income gap only if Chad sustains a growth rate much higher than that of the United States. Thus, in all cases of vast initial disparities, the gap is initially bound to widen. As a simple example consider an LDC with per capita income of $400 versus the United States with $16,000. If the former grows at 10% and the United States grows at 5%, their incomes will become $440 and $16,800 in a year. The absolute gap widens from $15,600 to $16,360. The LDC would be able to catch up only if it maintains its faster pace over an extended period of time.

The **transition to development** has been compared to stepping on an escalator. The developed countries completed their transitions in the nineteenth century, while the LDCs have been making their transitions at different times during this century. These turning points may be identifiable in hindsight; but the real question is to define the preconditions which might provide guidance for countries that are just starting.

CASE STUDY: DETERMINING GROWTH RATES FROM RAW DATA—CAMEROONS

	1981	1982	1983	1984	1985	1986	1987	1988	1989
GDP (Tril. Fr.)	1.98	2.30	2.78	3.21	3.84	4.17	3.97	3.70	3.50
GDP deflator	63.5	71.9	80.7	89.6	97.7	98.1	100	100.9	98.8

The development discipline is especially concerned with growth rates: with statements like "variable X grew at an average annual rate of such and such." To clearly understand the meaning of this statistic, let's work out numerically a concrete case starting from raw data. We pick the Cameroons, a nation in West Africa that has been unusually successful in comparison to its neighbors.

First, we obtain basic economic data so we may determine, say, the average growth rate of GDP. A widely available source is the *World Development Report* (WDR) published by the World Bank. Note, however, that each of its annual issues presents cross-sectional data for just one year. To compute growth rates we require a single source that ensures consistency across years of historical data. The *International Financial Statistics* (IFS) from the I.M.F. provides this. However, it reports more financial rather than "real" economic variables. For the latter we may use the *STARS* computer data base, also from the World Bank, to extract the desired series for the period of interest.

Next, we translate the nominal GDP (given in local currency at current prices) into real GDP. We must divide by the price index—in this case the GDP deflator set at a base year of 1987. After accounting for inflation, which was especially rapid in the early 1980s, real GDP growth appears much slower than the sharp rise of nominal GDP:

What would you say is the annual growth rate over the given time period? Various answers are possible based on different measures of "average" growth:

Point to point compound growth rate Taking into account just the beginning and end values, we can compute the compound growth rate over eight years:

$$3.12 \, (1+g)^8 = 3.54$$

This growth rate, $g = 1.59\%$, is subject to the obvious criticism that it relies exclusively on the end points, which may be chosen arbitrarily. If instead of ending the series in 1989 we consider only the 1981–86 period, the growth rate would be a sharply higher $g = 6.37\%$. Of course, one must pick the time interval appropriate to the context; but beware of dishonest motives that can make the statistics appear good or bad as needed.

	1981	1982	1983	1984	1985	1986	1987	1988	1989
Real GDP	3.12	3.20	3.44	3.65	3.93	4.25	3.97	3.67	3.54
Annual % growth		2.56	7.5	6.1	7.67	8.14	–6.59	–7.56	–3.54

Average annual growth rate   The arithmetical mean of the eight annual growth rates is $g = 1.78\%$. This simple average assigns equal weight to each year's data. Thus, if there is any "outlier" among the data, its contribution to the overall average gets diluted over the number of years spanned.

Econometrically estimated growth rate   Another measure combines data points so that outliers get the most weight in an "average," since these points may contain revealing information about the true relationship. A trend line is estimated so that the sum of square deviations around this line is minimum. This fitted line is well known as a "regression." With compound growth, the data traces an exponential curve. The log of such data falls along a straight line whose slope represents the growth rate. Since regressions are set up to compute a straight line, we must first convert the raw data into logs:

Actual data X grows exponentially: $X_t = X_0 \, e^{gt}$
Log X traces a straight line with slope g:
$$log X_t = log X_0 + g \, t$$

The graph below displays the level of GDP translated onto a log scale. We use a computer to estimate a regression line on the log levels. This is the straight line which best "fits" this data. The estimated value of its slope (i.e., the growth rate) turns out to be $g = 1.39\%$ over the full 1981–89 period—compared to a robust 6.35% average growth rate over the shorter 1981–86 period.

To perform this regression, the dependent variable, comprised of the logged time series, is regressed against the "explanatory variable," time, and a constant term. The slope of the regression line is the estimated time trend. Of the three proposed measures of growth rate, this one must be considered most appropriate from a statistical point of view. It does not arbitrarily assume that outlier points arose from some typographical or other error. Instead of smoothing them out by averaging, the regression estimate takes this data seriously as arising from the underlying probability distribution.

Notice how all these methods give different values of average annual growth rate. Clearly

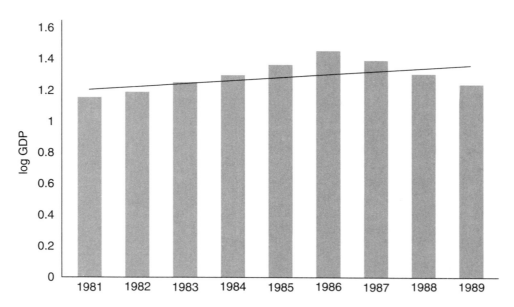

Estimated and actual GDP growth

the regression estimate is the least arbitrary; but even so, interpreting the meaning of the statistics introduces variables. The humped growth path of Cameroons in the 1980s—rapid growth in the early part followed by a sharp slump later—obviously cannot be represented by a single statistic. Nor is it possible to judge whether this performance was good or bad. One must further examine population growth over that period (about 3 percent per annual) to realize that per capita incomes fell over the decade of the 1980s.

STRUCTURAL CHANGE

We now turn to view certain "stylized facts" of development. (Stylized facts are truisms that are so obvious they can be stated baldly; they do not really need to be established by complicated econometric or statistical exercises.) The process of development involves important qualitative changes in the structure of output, and not just of a high quantitative rate of growth. Lloyd Reynolds examines the historical experience of such structural change in *The Spread of Economic Growth to the Third World 1850–1980*. He distinguishes sharply between the kind of economic dynamics before the turning point and the cumulative process of development that follows it.

We digress to offer a brief cautionary note about the lessons of history. The experience of the already developed countries certainly provides valuable lessons to assess prospects for LDC development. But such evidence must be interpreted carefully—the rich countries are observed to have a different economic structure; but do not causally attribute their level of prosperity to these visible differences. One must distinguish between **causality** versus **correlation.** For example, owning more cars is not the cause of wealth, it is the effect of wealth. Similarly, even the correlation between education and higher incomes must be interpreted carefully. Is expanded education a cause or an effect of increased wealth?

In our examination of historical growth patterns we focus mainly on correlations rather than on any causal explanation. Reynolds has labeled the growth that occurs before the turning point as **extensive growth.** (This term is used because land for cultivation is extended by clearing the jungle or bush.) During the process, while everything grows proportionately, few qualitative changes occur. Following the turning point there is a transition to intensive growth during which per capita incomes rise cumulatively.

A common characteristic of the extensive growth process is that production is carried out predominantly by the household. (The economics of household production is analyzed in chapter 14.) Generally, more than just the production of food is involved; such production also involves most household commodities—agricultural, manufactures, and services. Certainly, at low levels of income, food constitutes a high percentage of output and consumption. Another common characteristic is that existing industry is mostly of the handicrafts mode; there is little factory production since specialization is limited by the size of the market. Self-sufficient "autarkic" production implies minimal trade (both local and international), which requires a low level of commercialization and monetization.

Before the start of intensive growth, savings and investment stay at a level that just allows replication of the customary level of output. Why the average rates for savings remain so low for extended periods of history is something of a puzzle. Curiously, this phenomenon coincides with the observation that high savings (and investment) rates are certainly possible even when a country is perilously close to subsistence. The historical record notes many instances of disasters that wipe out a traditional society's assets; following that, their savings rate shoots up to allow asset stocks to regain their former level. So why doesn't the society maintain that rate in normal times to build up an even higher capital stock, and therefore output?

Instead of the common characteristics just described, the defining feature of extensive growth according to Reynolds is that population growth just matches the growth of food output. This resembles the Malthusian idea that the food/population ratio stays at a subsistence level in the long run. In the modern era, a slight difference is that population growth is exogenous, while output expands at approximately the same rate to match the population. As noted, "extensive" growth involves expanding cultivation by extending the frontier, while the qualitative techniques of production remain unchanged.

Extensive growth continues quantitatively without much change in the qualitative nature of the economy. Eventually the economy reaches its extensive frontier. Then some qualitative changes in productive methods become necessary. That marks the transition to modern **intensive growth.** As population continues to increase, the extra labor must work on the same plot of land. Thus, newer methods, such as a shift in the type of crops, are required to obtain higher yields per acre. At an early historical stage of development, the transition was typically seen as livestock and pasture activities giving way to the intensive cultivation of crops.

$$\frac{\text{Output}}{\text{land}} \uparrow \quad \text{and} \quad \frac{\text{Output}}{\text{acre}} \uparrow$$

In terms of growth accounting, the growth up to the extensive margin stems from proportionate increases in all productive factors, including labor. However, when the expansion of cultivable land becomes constrained, further output growth must come from improvements in productivity. Such induced technical change is a separate contribution to sustained growth apart from increased factor inputs. Improvement of the output/land ratio, or yield, exceeds growth in the population/land density; so the output/per capita begins to rise. A surplus can now be accumulated to finance further growth since income growth exceeds population growth, so the per capita income rises.

Another defining characteristic of the process of intensive growth is that exports grow faster than overall output, so that the ratio of exports to income rises. Prior to 1950, LDCs typically exported primary goods— mineral and agricultural products—whereas manufactured goods are increasingly the focus of export-led growth. Intensive growth also brings a change from handicraft to factory modes of production. This transition occurred earlier in larger countries, such as India and China, that could reap economies of scale. Industries that rely extensively on scale economies, such as textiles or iron and steel, initially face serious competition of cheaper imports from the established large producers. Even if a country possesses the potential for attaining comparative advantage, that particular infant industry must initially be protected from cheap foreign manufactures. Such a policy of import-substituting-industrialization (ISI) by means of trade barriers was adopted by many developing countries.

Intensive growth in recent years is also distinguished by a marked increase of government intervention in economic affairs. This tendency arose naturally in the newly independent countries as political forces demanded concerted national efforts toward development. In addition to the above-noted protection to domestic industry, government intervention is widespread throughout the economy and takes various forms. The neoclassical prescription to abolish this complex of interventions ("distortions") is somewhat naive in its presumption that a free market is sufficient for economic growth to take off. At the same time, excessive distortions have clearly been a major cause of much LDC stagnation, as we will study later in the chapter on policy.

A different kind of justification for a governmental role is that public involvement must inevitably become larger as an economy grows. This justification stems partly from the supply side as government aims to enhance growth by expanding public infrastructure; there is also a contribution from the demand side. As per capita incomes rise, consumers naturally desire a larger fraction of publicly provided goods in their consumption set: more highways, expanded water supply and other utilities, and so on. The *World Development Report* of 1988, which focussed on public finance, has characterized this requirement as a:

". . . fundamental structural change comparable in scope with such other basic transformations as industrialization and urbanization. The long term evolution of public finance in the industrial countries provides a reference point for the experience of the developing world."

Table 2-7 below contrasts the time series experience of various advanced industrial countries (including socialistic Sweden) with the present cross-sectional situation for various LDC groups. When interpreting such data, be aware of a cautionary note: Public expenditure data can be problematic because "public" is defined in different ways. For instance: Are state and local figures included with central government accounts, as sometimes occurs? Should public sector enterprises be included? And so on.

Thus far we have merely described the sequence of structural changes that seem to invariably accompany economic development. A natural question to ask is one of causation:

Does structural change $\xrightarrow{\text{cause}}$ economic growth?

Or economic growth $\xrightarrow{\text{cause}}$ structural change?

This section focuses on the latter issue of how economic growth in itself predictably generates a series of structural changes. Past the turning point, different sectors grow at disproportionate rates, so the economic structure undergoes a series of fairly generic changes. "Structure" is defined by the concrete measure: The fractional share in GNP of major sectors such as **agriculture, industry,** and **services.** (These coincide roughly with the categorization of primary, secondary, and tertiary sectors, respectively.) A numerical example shows how differential rates of growth in various sectors propel structural change.

Table 2-7 Percentage share of public expenditures in GDP

	Germany	Japan	Sweden	U.S.	all advanced countries	LDCs middle income	lower income
1880	10	11	6	8			
1960	32	18	31	28			
1985	47	33	65	37	28	26	18
$GDP/per capita in 1986:				$12,960	$1,200	$250

Analysis: Differential sectoral growth amounts to structural change

Suppose a leading sector of the economy, industry (In), which comprises 30% of output, grows at 10%, while agriculture (Ag), which comprises 70%, grows at 2%. The overall rate of output growth is then a weighted average of the two. This phenomenon can explain why the least developed countries tend to grow at a low overall rate. Even if their small industrial sector were to grow very rapidly, it would not contribute much to their overall growth rate because its share is so small.

$$\hat{Y} = 70\%\left(\hat{Ag}\right) + 30\%\left(\hat{In}\right)$$
$$= .7(2\%) + .3(10\%) = 4.4\%$$

Due to these differential growth rates, the sectoral shares will gradually change:

	Ag	In
initial levels	$Y_i = 70 + 30 = 100$	
after 10 years	$70(1.02)^{10} + 30(1.10)^{10}$	
final outputs	$Y_f = 85.3 + 77.8 = 163$	
final shares	$52\% + 48\%$	

In this view, structural change is an effect—not a cause—of growth. But that just pushes the question one level deeper: Why does the industrial sector generally grow faster than agriculture? A partial explanation is that these growth rates are crucially influenced from the demand side. As income increases the share of income allocated for foodstuffs typically drops, while demand for manufactured goods increases. **Engel's curves** depict commodity demand as a function of income (as distinct from demand curves which relate quantity demanded to price, while holding income constant).

The income elasticity of demand is low for the basic necessities of life—after all, how much more potatoes are you going to eat if your income rises? An income elasticity below unity (say, .6) means that if income were to grow by 5%, demand for such goods would grow only .6 x 5% = 3%. Demand for manufactures or for recreation, on the other hand, is much more income elastic. It typically exceeds one; thus, 5% income growth will result in growth of such demands that exceed 5 %. For such reasons the pattern of production must change with growing income. (Note that this analysis applies strictly within a closed economy—or the world as a whole—in which the composition of output must match the composition of consumption.)

Separate from the demand effects are important supply side effects that influence changes in the production structure. As an economy grows, the extension of the market allows increased specialization in the production process; in turn, this prompts induced technological change and economies of scale, and so on. In particular, the manufacturing sector tends to enjoy increasing returns to scale, whereas constant returns to scale usually prevail in the agricultural

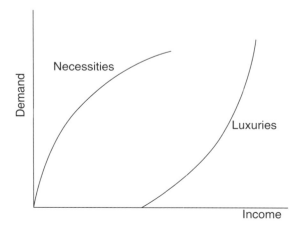

Figure 2-3 *Engel's curves*

sector. These supply and demand effects taken together combine to alter sectoral shares in a predictable pattern over the growth process.

The following section describes the time sequence of structural change as a country develops from a primarily agricultural to a primarily industrial economy.

Cross-sectional versus time series data The available data can be of two types. Cross-sectional data describes the contemporaneous state across a range of different countries at a point in time, whereas the process of development over time is described by time series data for a given country. The latter is typically harder to get since most countries, and especially LDCs, did not collect data on a consistent and continuous basis in the past. By contrast, cross-sectional data is now compiled across a wide range of countries with a somewhat greater consistency enforced by international organizations. The *World Development Report* of the World Bank is a very good source that provides the latest annual data, giving us a worldwide snapshot at a point in time.

The two types of data are suitable for very different purposes. In-depth research, such as country studies, calls for time series data, while broad comparative studies utilize cross-sectional data. Our study of structural change in the following section presents a concrete example of the use of time series data. Where the appropriate data type is unavailable it may be possible to use the other type, but with caution. For instance, to examine the question of structural changes one would use time series data from similar historical episodes. Lacking that, one may look at a cross-sectional sample of countries at widely disparate stages of development to infer the progression that a country may follow over time. But it is important to note that all countries need not follow along the same path that the developed countries followed. There need not be a linear succession of "stages of growth" as propounded by Rostow.

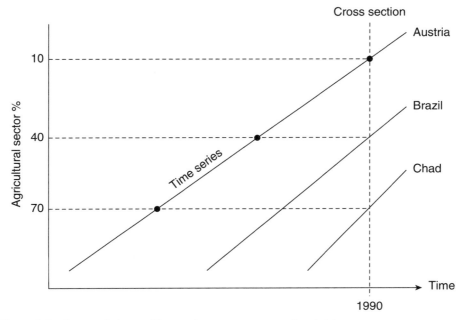

Figure 2-4 *Structural change: Time series versus cross-sectional data*

Gerschenkron hypothesized instead that there may be an advantage to being a follower nation. The technological gap facing lagging nations allows them to access existing know-how and skip intervening stages, thereby progressing at a much faster rate. This may explain why the growth rates of follower nations have, in fact, generally been faster. However, not all developing nations have grown faster. It is crucially important to study why some countries have benefited from the Gershenkron effect, while others have not. Recent research by D. Dollar finds that certain abilities are a prerequisite to the ability to utilize the available technology. Thus, LDCs that have built up their human capital are observed to advance at the fastest pace.

Contemporaneous cross-sectional data across countries depict the approximate progression of structural change at different income levels—aside from the caveats just noted. Such structural change takes place in step with income growth, and not as in neoclassical theory—with relative prices being the determining factor. A structuralist view also confers a special importance on certain sectors, contrary to the neoclassical approach that treats all sectors alike. However, all agree that the infrastructure sector (which includes roads, communications, education) must be developed first as a precondition for advances in other sectors. Government intervention is needed because infrastructural development cannot occur by itself no matter how free the price system. Such a focus on structural changes and constraints is associated with the work of H. Chenery of Harvard, as articulated in his study *Patterns of Growth* (1962).

Turning our focus to specific sectors, we first examine the pattern of change that occurs in agriculture.

Table 2-8   Changing role of agriculture in developing countries

		(percentages)		
	Rural popl / total popl		Agr. output / GDP	
	1975	1990	Avg. 70s	Avg. 80s
Africa				
Tanzania	93	67	46	54
Malawi	94	88	38	37
Nigeria	83	65	24	34
Kenya	89	76	32	28
Ghana	68	67	54	53
Zambia	63	50	24	24
Egypt	56	53	25	18
Tunisia	53	46	15	11
Asia				
Bangladesh	91	84	55	48
Pakistan	73	71	29	24
Indonesia	81	69	32	25
Philippines	64	57	28	24
Thailand	86	77	30	20
Latin America				
Jamaica	55	48	74	68
Costa Rica	60	53	20	21
Brazil	55	25	74	68
Mexico	37	27	11	8

Source: *World Development Report* and *Human Development Report*, 1992.

Table 2-8 tells a remarkably consistent story across a representative sample of LDCs. These countries are listed in the table in ascending order of per capita income within each regional group. At a glance we can see that the more developed a country, the smaller its relative involvement in agriculture, both in terms of output and of rural population. Another robust "stylized fact" emerges if these countries are rearranged in order of their growth performance. The largest declines in agricultural share occurred in the fastest growing countries. For instance, Thailand's agricultural (or rural) share dropped sharply as its GDP grew rapidly. Meanwhile, Ghana's economy was virtually stagnant over this period, and its structure of production remained essentially unchanged. However, population movements are a less reliable indicator of economic progress. We emphasize below that rapid urbanization has often occurred in spite of poor development performance. In Table 2-8, Zambia may be cited as one such example.

Studies of economic structure use cross-sectional data on various countries at different stages of the development process. Data from a point in time (as in Table 2-8) may suggest the time series pattern that a typical LDC takes over the course of its development. But be warned about the hazards in drawing conclusions from this observation. Viewing such patterns of structural change, some LDC policy makers confuse cause and effect. They jump to conclude that industrialization causes growth; then they implement specific policies to promote industry. However, Engel's analysis highlights that income growth may cause industrial growth, rather than the other way around.

Yet in the early years of this developmental epoch, industrialization was considered the sine qua non of development. A strategy of forced industrialization was chosen by many LDCs, notably Brazil, India, Argentina, and Egypt. To initiate industry in the face of cheap imports, a policy of import-substituting industrialization was adopted. This ISI strategy favored the artificial stimulation of industry by restricting imports. Inevitably this came at the expense of the agricultural sector, as resources were extracted by sheer force or by setting prices that depressed the relative price ratio P_{agr}/P_{ind}. Such thinking prompted the policy of punitive taxation on agriculture, as in Stalin's Russia or Mao's China during the years of their "Great Leap Forward."

By the decade of the 1970s, however, the strategy choice of ISI had suffered many disappointing experiences. Various aspects of the strategy can be blamed: (1) Excessive government intervention tended to disrupt the efficiency of the price system. (2) The antitrade policy particularly damaged the possibility of export-led growth. (3) Gradually it was realized that industrial production is not a substitute for agricultural production, but complementary with it. For example, countries such as Ghana and Tanzania realized quite belatedly that, at the very least, agricultural health is a necessary condition for overall growth. China's disastrous experiences of the late 1950s, and India's famines of the mid 1960s, convinced policy makers that no industrial progress would be possible if the agricultural sector could not feed everybody. The agricultural economy also plays an important role in generating a surplus for investment in the industrial sector as well as a source of demand for its output. The proper way to make the transition is highlighted by the successes of Japan and South Korea, both of which based their industrialization on a vital agricultural sector.

When categorizing sectors, agriculture must be separated from mining, as both are included in the "primary sector" based on natural resources. An important distinction is that agricultural output is regenerated year after year, while mineral output is eventually depleted even as it provides a stream of economic rents in the present. Industry includes both manufacturing as well as other activities such as utilities. The special status of this sector has been removed, as can be seen in many LDCs that now consider other goals as indicators of development besides crude industrial capacity. These include social indicators, market integration, natural resource exploitation, and so on.

The process of structural change involves increased market integration, both domestic and international. **Specialization** in production reaps increasing scale economies and is accompanied by increased middleman activity. Specialization causes rapid growth of the tertiary sector, which is made up mainly of services. As production becomes more specialized the share of trade in GDP is bound to increase. While the volume of exports grows, so do imports to provide the needed raw materials and capital goods. In addition to this quantitative change, qualitative changes occur in the pattern of trade. As production and consumption diversify, there is an increase in trading partners as well as in numbers and types of goods traded. Such a process of continuous change is consonant with dynamic comparative advantage, as we see later.

Major shifts in manpower accompany the process of structural change, as shown in the pre-vious table. Invariably these take the form of increased **urbanization.** In the early years of this development era, around the 1950s, this kind of shift was welcomed as a harbinger of "moderniza-tion." Along with this attitude came an optimistic belief that industrialization would serve to absorb labor from the agricultural sectors with low pro-ductivity, and direct it to the urban industrial areas with high productivity. Thus, an urbanized population was considered indispensable. (We study these issues in greater detail in later chap-ters on labor markets and agriculture.) In recent years, however, the error in such concepts has been exposed as many Third World countries experienced exploding urban populations, with concomitant problems of housing, transport, education, health, unemployment, and more. Thus, instead of viewing urban growth in a posi-tive light, modern policy is now mainly directed at stemming the tide of rural to urban migration.

Exercise

To familiarize yourself with data available in the World Development Report, use a recent issue to extract relevant data. From the set of developing countries whose population exceeds 1 million, determine the five countries with the fastest growth of per capita income and five with the slowest growth. Fill in all the entries in the table below. Then write a one-page essay to compare and contrast these two groups.

	A	B	C	D	E	F	G	H	I

Fast growth group

1. _____

2. _____

3. _____

4. _____

5. _____

Slow growth group

6. _____

7. _____

8. _____

9. _____

10. _____

    A.   Growth rate of per capita income 1975–93

    B.   Population growth rate

    C.   Growth rate of industrial production

    D.   Growth rate of agricultural production

    E.   Savings rate in 1993

    F.   Share of industry/GDP

    G.   Export growth rate

    H.   Literacy rate

    I.   Urbanization rate 1970, 1990

SUMMARY

This preliminary chapter introduces some basic tools used in the development discipline. Measurement of facts is indispensable to advancing scientific discourse. The role of empirical data is stressed, and various alternative measures are examined critically.

Measures of level, growth, and structural change are among the most relevant. An obvious measure of the level of development is GDP per capita. We review the conventional measures of GDP, as well as criticisms of the concept. A particular shortcoming for the case of poor countries is the severe downward bias of measured income when comparisons are made across countries. The income comparison project (ICP) aims to correct this by making income in local currencies comparable in terms of an "international dollar" that better reflects actual purchasing power.

An alternative gauge of development is to measure the well-being of individuals directly, rather than indirectly through income. A human development indicator combines measures of health, longevity, and education.

In studying growth, the student is reminded of the power of compound growth. Even apparently small differences in growth rates translate to large differences over the course of years, altering the gap between the rich and poor countries. The absolute gap can grow even if the poor countries grow at a faster rate. In any case, the process of equalizing incomes may take generations, if not centuries. Thus, it is preferable to gauge performance by growth rates rather than by comparing the achieved level of income with rich countries.

Another important descriptor of development is structural change. Differential rates of sectoral growth cause predictable changes in their shares of overall output. Economic structure is defined by the ratios of sectoral output to total GDP. As development proceeds, the share of agriculture tends to drop and the other sectors, industry and services, grow at a faster rate. The government's share, in particular, tends to rise. This kind of progression is explained by Engel's curves, which indicate that demand for agricultural goods rises only slowly with income, in sharp contrast to manufactured goods.

KEY TERMS

Time series data	International Comparisons Project (ICP)	Causality
Cross-sectional data		Correlation
Nominal income	Purchasing Power Parity (PPP)	Extensive Growth
Real income	Nontraded goods	Intensive growth
Exchange rate	NICs	Agriculture
Real Income Comparisons	Developed Countries (DCs)	Industry
Leisure	Compound growth	Services
Life expectancy	Stages of growth	Engel's curves
Political freedom	Cumulative growth	Specialization
Estimated growth rate	Economic structure	Urbanization
Physical quality of life indicator (PQLI)	Primary sector	Take-off
	Transition to development	Absolute gap
Gross Domestic Product (GDP)	Secondary sector	Human rights
Gross National Product (GNP)	Average annual growth rate	

Chapter 3

Inequality

Most societies today profess that the promotion of equity among their citizens is a major objective. This is perhaps a stronger imperative in the developing world, which only recently has been exposed to the possibilities of social progress and individual freedom. Thus, at least as an ideal, many LDCs seek to advance the interests of the disadvantaged masses. Whereas **equity** means justice in a broad sense, in economics it translates to equality of opportunity and, ultimately, to greater equality of outcomes. Different countries place different weights on this objective of greater **income equality** vis a vis economic growth. Of course, it would be preferable to have both, but when a choice must be made between these distinct aims, the Right end of the political spectrum prefers the growth objective while the Left focuses on income equality. A neoconservative school gives primacy to a third objective, personal liberty, which implies neutrality between the two. Such a regard for the status quo does not seem to resonate much in the LDCs. Socialist countries, such as Cuba and Vietnam, avowedly place equality first. They have succeeded in attaining a high degree of equality, but their overall growth stagnates lower than its potential. Brazil is a prominent counter example; it has stressed growth while its progress toward equality was left to an uncertain trickle-down effect.

This chapter studies the equity problem in four sections. First we will review the theoretical basis for seeking a more equal distribution of income. We will give this concept an objective form by presenting various measures. Applied to survey data, the measures help gauge the actual extent of income disparities in the LDCs. The data indicate vast disparities within and across countries and also highlight prominent trends over time. From this rather formal and static theory, we move to a more realistic, dynamic framework. Any policy that aims to alter income distribution invariably has complex interactions with economic growth. Thus we are led to analyze the issue of growth versus equality. After theory, we turn to an analysis of policy. Archetype policies are laissez-faire, direct redistributions, and a detailed welfare state. In recent decades, however, the early focus on redistribution has been discarded. Instead, there is a new focus on directly addressing the worst manifestations of poverty.

The new focus of alleviating poverty rather than adjusting income equality amounts to a major paradigm shift. The early development economics school expected that growth would automatically reduce income inequality. The Left, on the other hand, relied on income redistributions. Both of these views are now in disfavor. The former because income disparities have persisted while the poverty problem looms large despite growth. As for the latter, countries that opted for a redistributive strategy have generally suffered a major drop in growth. The reorientation toward poverty alleviation focuses on providing basic needs only to those below the poverty level. This new approach is not merely altruistic; It also promises to boost economic growth as the poor and dispossessed become active participants in the process of development. The last section of this chapter summarizes an important United Nations study that highlights various poverty processes and their close relation to the overall growth strategy.

THEORETICAL BASIS

The idea of equality has historical roots that date at least from the time of the French Revolution at the end of the eighteenth century. (Note the middle item of its famous slogan: "Liberte, Egalite, Fraternite.") In tracing the intellectual roots, we may note a few distinct historical stages.

1. Even in absolutist times there were ideals of fairness and justice that prescribed normative laws for kingdoms. These values were also thought to have instrumental value to the extent that they promoted harmony and stability and, thereby, prosperity.

2. With the coming of the European enlightenment arose the more sophisticated idea of a **social compact:** All segments of society are bound together by an implicit contract that guarantees each of them certain rights along with their responsibilities. The cooperation of the classes at the bottom of the social pyramid was elicited not merely by brute force, but by the promise of minimum social benefits. Around the same era, a separate Liberal tradition sought to strive for "the greatest good for the greatest number."

3. In modern times we often tend to think in terms of democratic political structures.

Where they exist, the poor (who constitute a majority) assert their power to require more equality. But how are the rules instituted in the first place and by whom? For the answer to this we must more closely examine the history of equality.

The English **utilitarians** in the nineteenth century first put the idea of equality into a concrete form amenable to economic analysis. Their idea was to add up individual happiness, or utility, to come up with aggregate social utility. On reflection, this concept has deep theoretical problems. Since we cannot directly distribute happiness per se, we must redistribute the income that helps raise individual utility. But how do we distribute these incomes to attain the greatest overall happiness? Even if we make the large assumption that each person derives equal utility from the same income, it is still possible that an unequal distribution of income gives rise to the largest sum of societal utility! If individual utility is a rapidly increasing function of income, say $U = Y^2$, then greatest utility is gained by concentrating all the income in just one individual. To illustrate, note how total utility from \$6 of combined income is greater if it is distributed in an unequal manner between two individuals.

$$U_1(6) + U_2(0) = 6^2 + 0^2 = 36$$

versus

$$U_1(3) + U_2(3) = 3^2 + 3^2 = 18$$

Only if utility is a slowly increasing function of income (for example, if marginal U decreases with rising Y), does it make social sense to equalize incomes. This implies equality only with a special assumption about individual utility functions. A more serious problem with the utilitarian idea is its assumption that interpersonal comparisons of utility are possible. Of course, there is no objective way to compare my pain with your pain (or happiness). Yet the utilitarians made the enormous assumption that utility could be viewed as a cardinal number and could, in effect, be measured,

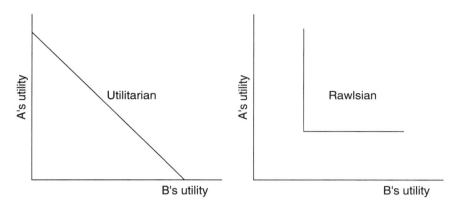

Figure 3-1 *Social welfare functions*

added, and so on. Thus they came up with a utilitarian **social welfare function** shown in the left panel of Figure 3-1, in which society balances more utility for one individual against less utility for another—the same way an individual utility function balances the utilities from the consumption of two different goods.

The idea that utility is not comparable across individuals was emphasized by Vilfredo Pareto at the turn of the century. Given this restriction, how could one even talk about aggregate social utility? The philosopher John Rawls gave a justification based on the social arrangements a person would choose before knowing what his or her actual status would be. In that case, each individual will agree to a rule that society must provide for the poorest of its citizens. Thus **Rawlsian social welfare** is based on the well-being of the poorest member of society as seen in the right panel of Figure 3-1. If the richer member's utility were to increase, the function shows that social welfare would be unchanged since the poorer member's utility has not changed.

To implement such ideas of social welfare is another matter altogether. Unlike the Rawlsian assumption, societal decisions about **redistributions** are made by individuals who know where they stand in the current income distribution. Even if these individuals agreed with the Rawlsian

concept, it would be hard to elicit the truth for the purposes of redistribution. Taxpayers tend to understate income, while potential beneficiaries magnify their pain. A greater difficulty is that social utility cannot simply be the sum of individual utilities. Suppose one person lost a lot of utility (in the extreme, gave up life itself), while those remaining enjoyed huge gains in utility. The loser certainly would not agree that this is a social improvement. Thus an accounting of total utility depends on who you ask since there is no way to make interpersonal comparisons of utility, nor any way to add up individual utilities to get social welfare. To talk at all about a redistributive policy, we are obliged to assume a **benevolent dictator** to impose evaluations. The dictator must be omniscient to be able to know each individual's utility function; benevolent, because the aim is to maximize the utility sum; and a dictator, so as to be able to force this distribution scheme on the losers.

Let us assume the existence of a benevolent dictator who deems equality to be a primary goal. This is plausible since equity in the form of universal education, basic health, and social welfare for all must surely constitute a primary goal of development. Amartya Sen is the chief proponent of this view (1982). This goal is achievable as seen from the example of various LDCs.

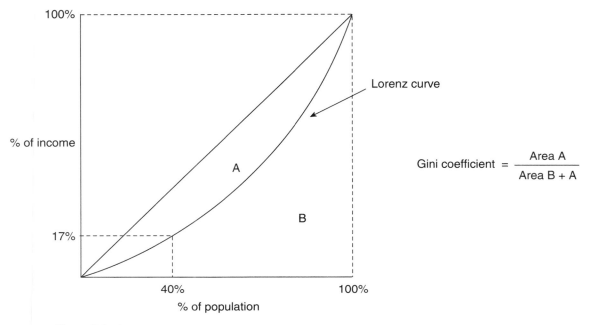

Figure 3-2   *Lorenz curve*

Socialist countries have been very successful in attaining such explicit and narrowly defined goals. Alternatively, equity may be favored on instrumental grounds—as a means to advance output growth rather than just as an end in itself. A properly educated and healthy workforce appears to be an essential condition for enhanced productivity. Thus it is possible that a redistribution of the pie may help to increase the total size of the pie. In practice, however, aiming for income equality often is thought to reduce output growth—the empirical evidence is mixed. Where income distribution interacts with growth, the analysis becomes far more complex than the problem of redistributing a pie of fixed size. Before moving to such analysis, let us first introduce the needed measurements.

Measures of Inequality

As always, when we introduce a new concept we strive to present a suitable measure that makes the

concept objective. At the same time, we point out its failings. A useful depiction of income inequality is the **Lorenz curve** diagram shown in Figure 3-2. Population is ordered in terms of its income; then the cumulative percent of persons is charted against the cumulative percent of national income received. The shape of this curve indicates the degree of inequality. For a country like Guatemala, with extremely unequal income distribution, the curve would be sharply concave. At an extreme, the Lorenz curve would closely follow the horizontal and vertical axes. The lowest 99% of the population gets a tiny proportion of total income, while the top 1% gets all the rest. It is often desirable to summarize the entire distribution by a single parameter, for example, the share of income going to the poorest 40%.

Another statistic is the **Gini coefficient,** which measures how far the Lorenz curve lies from perfect equality. This coefficient lies between 0, which indicates perfect equality, and 1, for perfect inequality.

A problem with the measure is that many patterns of income distribution can give the same Gini coefficient ratio of areas. Other measures of inequality have been suggested, the standard deviation of the (cumulative) distribution of income. But the alternative measures may give rise to contradictory rankings of equality: One measure might rank country X as having high equality, whereas another measure ranks it as the worst. Which of these statistics are we to believe? Clearly the choice of measure must depend on the objective for which it is used. Note that, as a practical matter, data on income distribution often are fragmentary and out-of-date.

Whichever measure of income distribution is chosen, one must exercise great care in interpreting purported indications of inequality. Accordingly we distinguish between individual and group disparities such as those that arise from an inequality between regions. The relevant income unit must be the family, however, since individual disparities arise naturally from income changes over the life cycle. One might account for this by using average lifetime income per household member as the basic unit for comparison. For similar reasons nonworking spouses also are not necessarily poor. The recent women's rights movement, however, highlights the possibility that a high degree of inequality often exists within the family. Research shows that in many societies women work much harder than the men, but receive a smaller share of family earnings. From an early age such intrafamily disparities show up starkly as male/ female differences in a wide range of statistics on infant mortality rates, nutrition, and school enrollments.

The student must also be cautioned against automatically assuming a Western-style nuclear family unit comprised of just mom, dad, and their kids. In the LDC context there is often a tradition of the extended family, whose members might not even be legally related. These traditional relationships operate under such a complex set of rules as to be almost incomprehensible to the Westerner. A detailed network of privileges and obligations is inculcated in each individual from a very early age. "Who gets what from whom" and under what conditions may be very difficult to specify. Thus we might find ourselves unable to state categorically that so-and-so gets so much net income. (Rather than a formal study of anthropology, it might be more interesting for the student to read literature or view movies from non-Western societies to appreciate the nuances of such social networks.)

Moving from the level of individuals or households to the level of the group, measured income disparities must be interpreted carefully. Income disparities may derive mainly from regional or group differences, with the latter defined by race, tribe, or caste. For example, northeast Brazil is dramatically poorer than the wealthy southern region around Sao Paulo. Such inequality problems call for policy responses quite different from those needed to address disparities in personal income. A legitimate question to ponder is: Why stop at the national boundary? Why focus so much on equality within a country while ignoring vast differences across countries? The idea of sovereignty has such a powerful hold that many world citizens tend to ignore huge inequalities across countries while railing against societies that have much smaller internal disparities by comparison.

Regional disparities may be illustrated by an example from India where such disparities have widened over time as the leading region grew faster than the others. In 1960, incomes in the state of Punjab in the prosperous northwest were 91% higher than Bihar in the east. Twenty-five years later this disparity had become 240% higher due to Punjab's higher economic growth rate. What should be done about this kind of income inequality? This is not an income distribution problem, but rather one of unequal growth. Instead of finding Punjab at fault, the remedy is to boost Bihar's particularly slow growth. As it is, the central government already redirects some resources from the Punjab to

Bihar, so the Punjabis might be justified in asking why they are penalized for their high productivity. The main lesson here is that the mere existence of inequality does not necessarily mean that the situation must be—or can effectively be—remedied by a redistribution of income.

Instead of a fiscal redistribution, the suggestion is to boost growth of overall income in the lagging region. This issue is appropriately studied under the rubric of regional economics. This subdiscipline makes the assumption that factors of production are more mobile across regions than across national borders. One policy implication is to promote migration away from the lagging region or reduce its population growth rate. Another policy is to induce capital flows into the backward region. It is a puzzle why capital is not automatically attracted by the region's low wages. A classic example occurred in Italy. For generations, the southern region of Italy lagged behind the vibrant north. Labor continued to migrate north while capital and industry were reluctant to move south, despite inducements offered by the government. (See discussion in the IMF Survey 7/12/93).

Group disparities also derive from distinctions that exist worldwide between races, tribes, and castes; this syndrome makes this delicate subject even more politically sensitive. One careless statement and you could easily be accused of racism or worse. The key issue is one of fairness: To what extent is the plight of the poor group the fault of the rich group? In other words, is each group getting its just rewards in a fair game? To consider one striking example, the poorest white worker in Zimbabwe may earn several times the national average level of income. Is this person really more productive than the majority of Zimbabwe's population? Again, such questions require a group focus rather than an individual focus. An important lesson from history is that simple **expropriation** from the high income group is often like "killing the goose that lays the golden eggs." Thus notions of justice built on a purely individual basis contrast with a reality of social actions

and reactions that have a group basis. If the problem arises from group inequities, however, solutions also must also be found at the group level. This was certainly the lesson in parts of East Africa that chose to expel their energetic Asian minority. In parts of Southeast Asia the distribution of income is at odds with the distribution of political power: The Malays versus Indians and Chinese in Malaysia, the ethnic Chinese versus indigenous populations in Indonesia and the Philippines, and so on.

The impetus toward equality does not derive simply from envy and greed. At issue are deeper questions about society and ethics: Is perfect equality to be desired even in a perfect world? With the vast range of talents and inclinations inherent in humanity is it really desirable to equalize everyone along that one dimension? Why shouldn't an indolent tribe continue its cultivation of the leisurely arts while another cultural group is driven by a work ethic and a taste for material goods?

Modern life introduces another complication. Certain professions have become internationalized, causing the incomes of entire groups to equalize across countries. For instance, airline and shipping crews, petroleum and petro-chemical engineers, and research scientists are quite mobile and earn international salaries. A specific example is that of Philippine immigrant nurses working in America. International salaries may appear shockingly out-of-line with salaries that prevail in many poor countries. Do the dictates of equity require that these salaries therefore be drastically taxed away in the LDCs? Do the extra rewards derive from the country's supply side that provided the education and nuturing, or from the extended demand side?

The last few paragraphs have teased out some (normative) insights for policy in instances in which we face significant measured inequality. The important lesson is that *we mustn't always rush to remove inequality the moment we find it.* A further cautionary note relates to the implications drawn from measured disparities: Given any measured income distribution, note that a particular household may well be moving up or down the scale. Thus inequality of results can coexist with **equality of opportunity.** So long as opportunity and access remain truly open to all, it may be tolerable, perhaps even desirable, to allow some degree of inequality so as to promote motivation and entrepreneurship.

Finally, it is useful to distinguish income from consumption levels. If high income earners also have high savings rates, then income inequality per se could be favorable for long-term economic growth. This would be the happy result if the rich do not indulge in wasteful consumption, but instead accumulate productive assets that add to the national capital stock—provided, of course, the capital stays at home. Now, as the economy works with more capital per worker, the wage rate or marginal product of labor rises. At the same time the larger capital stock serves to depress the return on capital. Such effects work to reduce

inequality over the long run. One hopeful note is that the LDCs as a group— except for much of Africa—have managed to achieve a relatively large savings ratio. This is bound to improve incomes and consumption in the future, even as present levels of consumption continue to appear bleak by the standards of the already developed countries.

GROWTH VERSUS EQUALITY

We now examine the connection between equality and growth in its generality. This issue is illustrated in Figure 3-3, which depicts the income distribution of society split among two groups of earners, starting at an initial distribution at point *I*. The groups are defined, for simplicity, as the rich group, comprising of the top 50% of the population with the higher income, and the lower 50% called the poor group.

Figure 3-3 shows the relation between **redistribution and growth** for various possible policies.

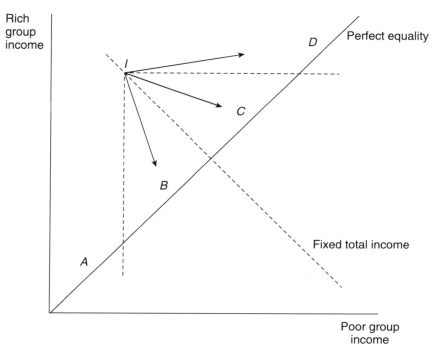

Figure 3-3 *Income growth versus increased equality*

The initial distribution at point I depicts income biased in favor of the rich group. A redistributive policy would aim to move in the direction of the income equality (45°) line, which signifies constant total income. Since redistributive policies generally tend to alter total income, the end result would move away from the starting total. A redistributive policy that moves toward region A is definitely inferior. It makes the rich group poorer, while the poor also get poorer. In region B the poor group gains by less than the rich group loses, so total income drops. Above the $(-45°)$ line of constant total income there is the possibility for growth with redistribution as total income rises. Only those distributions that move into region D are Pareto superior because each group has at least as much income as before.

An extreme normative preference for equality can prompt policies into region A where the aggregate income is drastically cut. The radical redistributions that occurred under Pol Pot in Cambodia can be characterized as such. More common redistributions into region B also aim to tax the rich to give to the poor, but suffer some loss of total income as societal resources are spent just to effect the transfer—think of this as the **cost of fairness.** Total income is lower, since the arrow points below the –45° line.

The cost of achieving fairness arises from various sources. A major loss comes from the distortionary effect of taxes. Neoclassical economics teaches us that a free competitive market is most efficient, so any intervention is bound to reduce efficiency. Another cost arises from the possibility of government failure. We cannot assume that government acts with mechanical certainty to reach desired outcomes. Even assuming the best of intentions, the social planner faces a very difficult computational problem to sort through the complex of interacting policies (as discussed in the following section). Policy design is particularly difficult since it must set up incentives for diverse economic agents, each of whom is maximizing individual self-interest. Finally, the most obvious cost of redistribution is the direct expenditure on the bureaucrats needed for its administration. Real resources must be diverted from other productive uses—just as expenditures on health and welfare must reduce government infrastructure investments on roads, bridges, industry, and so on. The economy thus pays a cost in the form of lost growth to move to regions A and B of Figure 3-3.

By contrast, policies that aim for redistribution with growth lead to regions C and D. A country that could progress far into region D and also reach complete equality would be practically dead. But such policies are the hardest to accomplish technically, even if they are the easiest to implement politically. Such redistributions meet the Pareto criterion that no one's income is going down while others' are improving. Redistributions to the area D are therefore the easiest for all groups to accept politically.

Certain growth strategies involve a curved arrow as the income distribution gets worse before it improves. In the kind of growth that proceeds through a leading sector, the rich group's income increases before the poor group's income also begins to increase. This kind of arrow would be shown at the upper end of region D. This sequential process corresponds with Kuznets' hypothesized U-curve, discussed later.

Policies that aim to move us from the initial distribution toward greater equality are limited in practice. Suppose the redistribution is achieved by taxing the rich to give to the poor. One might expect that a higher tax rate will raise revenues. But when the tax rate is raised, rich producers tend to slacken their efforts, so tax revenue does not remain proportionate to the tax rate. In the extreme, a 100% tax rate will elicit zero revenue. The resulting Laffer curve of taxation in Figure 3-4 shows how it becomes progressively harder to raise revenues just by increasing the tax rate on the rich; beyond a certain point this kind of policy becomes counterproductive.

The Laffer curve may come as a surprise to those account types in finance departments who assume that tax revenue T rises linearly with the

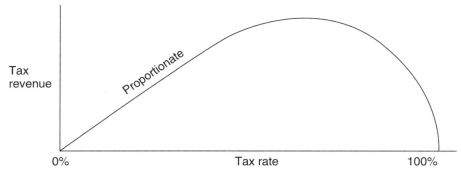

Figure 3-4 *Laffer curve*

tax rate *t*. Economists, on the other hand, understand clearly that the tax base, income Y, is itself a decreasing function of the tax rate.

Accountants: $T = t . Y$ Economists: $T = t . Y(t)$

While the end points of Laffer curves are known, their exact shapes remain indeterminate. Yet the concept is useful to show the limits of taxation for the purpose of redistribution. In Figure 3-3 we could determine such limits, or the maximum possible combinations of total income and equality. This frontier would depict what is possible, not what is desired. There may be an unfortunate trade-off as total income shrinks the closer we approach equality. But this supposed conflict between growth and equality is now being disputed. This effect may just be an artifact of our simplistic static construct. Instead, a redistribution that radically alters morale and behavior of the poor could have a far greater dynamic impact on long-term growth compared to the immediate negative static effect. More on this when we examine policies.

The connection between growth and equality springs primarily from the problem of **incentives.** Why should anyone work if material equality is guaranteed to all regardless of effort? The very same mechanism operates on the poor (as a lack of incentives) just as it does for the rich. If the masses are effectively excluded from

the fruits of development, they are unlikely to be enthusiastic participants in it. The effect of redistributions also depends on whether the policy primarily serves to empower the poor or take from the rich. The former might have a positive supply-side effect, while the latter negativly affects supply.

A policy of equality is also connected with growth since a growing pie eliminates much struggle over how the pie should be sliced. In the absence of growth, any redistribution of shares is a **zero-sum game**—for one to gain another must lose and the losers tend to resist such policy. Thus Pareto redistributions are easiest to make in political terms, but Pareto-improving growth is the hardest to attain technically.

Another phenomenon stemming from subjective feelings of deprivation was dubbed the *tunnel effect* by Albert Hirschman. Imagine multiple lanes of stalled traffic inside a tunnel, where the view ahead is blocked. As one of the lanes begins to move forward, everyone cheers. But if everyone else continues to move while your lane remains stalled, you are likely to suspect foul play. You might even try to impede the "unfair" advance of others.

Another connection between growth and distribution is through the short-term impact of macroeconomic policies. This issue becomes relevant when a country conducts an adjustment program to attain macroeconomic equilibrium under the terms of I.M.F. conditionality that follow a financial crisis. In the short term such programs again appear to pit equity against growth. But in the long term there is no necessary conflict between these objectives. (see chapter 16)

The empirical evidence about equality and economic growth was first highlighted by Simon Kuznets. He noted that as a country's income grows there is an initial tendency for equality to drop; only later does equality begin to improve. Over time this creates the **Kuznets' U-curve** as seen in Figure 3-5. (Also called an inverted U-curve if drawn for inequality.) But this is just a hypothesis about the development process, not an established fact. Recent studies have cast doubts on the reliability of the statistical evidence, with crucial implications for policy. The absence of a U-curve would imply that a transitory worsening of income distribution is not an essential feature of growth. Thus trickle-down policies would be unacceptable because they are unnecessary.

The empirical pattern between income equality and the level of income presents a convenient way to test alternative theories of growth. Structuralist theory offers an explanation for Kuznets' U-curve. It posits that growth invariably proceeds through leading sectors that advance first. Income inequality worsens in the initial stages due to the higher productivity of labor in these sectors. Later on the higher wage spreads throughout the economy to the other sectors. This is the genesis of the **trickle-down effect.** This equalizing effect is reinforced by the increased provision of public goods. (This is an integral part of the process of structural change noted earlier.) As per capita incomes rise, so does the demand for public goods—typically infrastructure such as roads, communications, education, and social security. Since this consumption is shared fairly equally, this adds a progressive element to overall consumption standards.

This structural explanation can be illustrated by a simple exercise. Suppose a country starts out with a substantial income equality of $30 per month. A tiny fraction of the population earns a higher income of $100, but this has a negligible impact on aggregate income, so equality is high as measured by the fraction of total income earned by the poorest 40% of the population. This measure starts near .4 in the Year 0. Figure 3-6 shows its progression over time.

As the leading sector advances, it employs one-third of the population at some point. Aggregate income rises to ($100*.33) + ($30*.67). The income of the poorest 40% remains unchanged in absolute terms, but its relative share drops to just 23% of total incomes in Year 1. The leading sector then expands further to employ two-thirds of the population. Aggregate income rises to ($100*.67) + ($30*.33), so the income share of the poorest 40% drops further to 21.8% in Year 2. Only when the leading sector encompasses the entire population in Year 3 will the equality measure return to .4.

The Lewis model of growth implies this pattern for developing countries. The leading sector, industry, advances to use up the labor from the rural sector. A familiar contemporary example of such a pattern in developed countries might be the computer industry, which initially brought enormous wealth to a few, while the economic benefits spread with the passage of

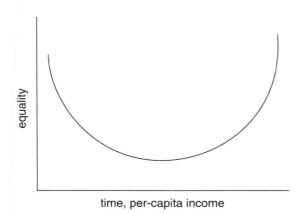

Figure 3-5   *Kuznets' U-curve of equality*

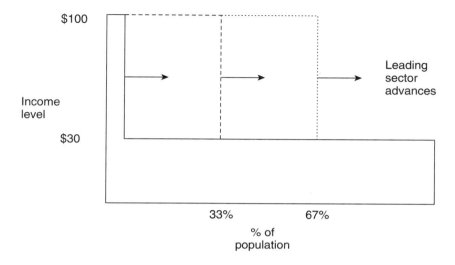

Figure 3-6 *Growth through a leading sector*

time. In the last century, a similar pattern also occurred with the development of railroads. Such a trickle-down pattern is observed in the historical time-series experience of countries that are now developed.

The horizontal axis of the Kuznets' U-curve can represent the passage of time as income distribution evolves in a single country. The same pattern might also represent a cross-section of countries, at a given point. In this case the poorest countries are arrayed toward the left side of the curve. As noted, the U-curve of income equality is consistent with the Lewis Model, which will be discussed later. In contrast, neoclassical growth theory implies that the share of total income going to wage earners should remain level, or even rise slightly with development. (This is one of the "stylized facts" of growth highlighted in chapter 6, on growth theory.) The flat line of income distribution predicted by neoclassical economics contrasts with Kuznets' conjecture of a U-shaped curve and also with the Marxist expectation of ever-declining equality. Marx's theory predicted that the working class would be oppressed more and more by capitalists,

so inequality was bound to keep worsening until the inevitable revolution erupts. What happens afterward is of less concern. Marx is reported to have remarked, "Anyone who makes plans for after the revolution is a reactionary."

POLICIES FOR EQUALITY

No matter how it is measured, and how those measures are interpreted, inequality remains unacceptably high in many developing countries. Political imperatives require that policy seek to redress this problem. We will examine some of the prominent approaches that are suggested: (1) Laissez-faire, or a perfectly free market, (2) simple redistributions of income and assets, and (3) more complex redistributive schemes, or the detailed welfare state of some advanced countries.

Laissez-faire The standard neoclassical prescription for most ailments is to "get prices right." Bringing factor prices in line with their scarcity would result in a **functional distribution of income** as each factor of production earns the value of its marginal product. But this has dubious consequences for improving income equality.

Approving a functional distribution in effect promotes efficiency as the primary concern, while the resulting income distribution is relegated to a secondary place. "Efficiency" in the neoclassical sense means that all possible gains from trade have been exploited in a Pareto-optimum equilibrium.

Figure 3-7 illustrates the differing objectives of efficiency and income equality. The final distribution reached on the efficiency frontier depends on the initial distribution of factors of production. It is possible to achieve both objectives in two different ways: A one-time **asset redistribution** that shifts the initial point then allows neoclassical policy to take us to the desired point on the frontier, or starting from the initial distribution of assets, the economy operates normally to get to some point on the efficiency frontier. After that, an appropriate income redistribution would take us to another desired point on the frontier. To avoid distorting incentives, the redistribution is affected by **lump-sum transfers.** Such a system encourages people to continue making efficient decisions; only later are they hit with a redistributive tax. While this is a fine theoretical idea, it is unrealistic in practice because people

cannot be fooled very often. They begin to understand the system of taxes/subsidies and adjust their economic decisions accordingly.

Neoclassical economic theory proves that a competitive market allows us to reach a **Pareto-optimal** equilibrium. In Figure 3-7, at each point on the frontier, no one can be made better off without making someone else worse off. But the resulting income distribution (A) depends on the location of the initial distribution of assets (I). The initial distribution might be extremely skewed in a society where the poor own nothing but their individual labor, while a single person owns all the capital. Operation of a free market provides a high return to the owner of the scarce factor and prompts a move from any initial point to the efficient frontier. In the figure this northeast move (I to A) is a Pareto improvement, while the frontier itself is Pareto efficient. Yet this equilibrium is not necessarily equitable. Thus movements toward efficiency are orthogonal to distributional concerns. An emphasis on efficiency is indifferent between any point on the frontier and any other. A lump-sum redistribution of income that does not distort incentives allows a

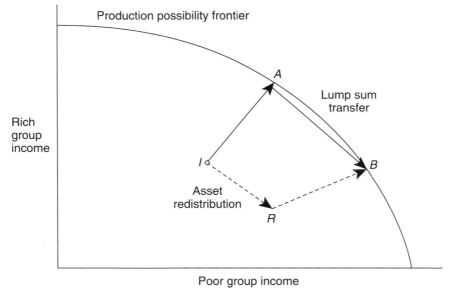

Figure 3-7   *Non-distorting redistributions*

Table 3-1   Income disparity versus wage disparity

Rich group		Poor group	
K = $100,000	L = 1	K = $100	L = 1
r = 10%	w = $2,000	r = 10%	w = $2,000
income = rK + wL	= $12,000	= 10 + 2,000	= $2,010

move from *A* to *B*. Alternatively, a redistribution of assets can take us from *I* to *R*, from which point free market forces can again take us to the frontier at the desired distribution *B*.

The neoclassical prescription does have merit in situations where the labor market is seriously distorted. Often, a small segment of the labor force gets an artificially high wage while vast other segments remain unemployed. The removal of such a nonmarket wage would surely increase the employment offered by firms, and thereby reduce the inequality between a "labor aristocracy" and the unemployed. (This is an improvement at the lower end of the Lorenz curve.) But reverting to a free market situation in LDCs also implies a higher return to the scarcest factor, capital, which would widen the gap between all workers and the rich capitalists (worsening the upper end of the Lorenz curve).

A recent neoclassical perspective on inequality turns away from the broader perspective just highlighted, toward a microapproach to determining the main effects on incomes. Broad concepts such as trickle-down or the Kuznets' U-curve—whether valid or not—may not be very useful except as descriptive devices. The new approach, pioneered by Gary Fields of Cornell, instead relies on detailed studies of the labor force obtained from household surveys. Such surveys provide information in specific settings about who earns how much from what activity over the course of a year. It may then be possible to fashion micropolicies that affect opportunities and earnings through a variety of instruments available to the government.

Simple Redistribution   A simple redistributive strategy appears most direct to the layperson, but turns out to be rather impractical in most developing countries. Before we examine this proposition we need to clarify a basic distinction of wage versus asset income. It is crucial to note that the distribution of total incomes depends far more on unequally distributed assets rather than from inequality of wages. A simple numerical illustration (Table 3-1) shows how even with equalized wage rates *w* the total incomes can diverge sharply due to differential holdings of capital *K*. Per capita incomes tend to diverge even further since poorer groups usually have a larger number of dependents per family.

Unequal endowments of assets contribute far more to disparities in total income than wage differences per se. Thus to reduce income disparities, a society must reduce the highly skewed distribution of assets, which include physical capital and human capital. In agrarian societies the main physical asset is, of course, land, followed by livestock and other forms of wealth. We shall examine the possibilities of land redistribution later, and trace the productivity impact of smaller landholdings in a later chapter. A more sophisticated—and also feasible— approach is to equalize human capital endowments by expanding education. Education, especially of women, in turn affects fertility decisions and family size. Chapter 4 examines this aspect in greater detail. We now begin to see how the entire complex of development efforts is intimately intertwined with the issue of income distribution. We shall also examine this inter-connectedness in the context of poverty reduction in a following section.

The distribution of incomes and assets have a close dynamic relationship over time. (Refer back to the vicious cycle diagram in the introduction.) Even if income distribution started out fairly equal, divergent savings rates can cause differential accumulation of assets; this causes interest income to diverge even as wages continue to be equal. Yet accumulation is hardly something a society wants to discourage, no matter how much income inequality is deplored. Further, differing rates of return on assets can cause a divergence even if asset holdings are equal in size. Thus to ensure absolute equality, one must be prepared to redistribute over and over again. This formed part of the underlying Communist rationale for public ownership of all assets, as well as maintaining essentially equal wages—at least in theory.

The major asset holding in agrarian developing countries is land. But redistributing this asset would require a major shake-up of the social and political status quo, which is hard to do short of a violent revolution. In instances when significant **land reform** has occurred, however, it has proved enormously beneficial for subsequent industrial development. This has been demonstrated by the post-war examples of Taiwan and Korea following the breakup of their feudal landholdings under Japanese occupation. Japan itself instituted a major redistribution of land in the late nineteenth century, which, in turn, led to a far more equitable distribution of incomes and reoriented incentives in favor of growth.

Note, however, that a pro forma land reform is not guaranteed to provide all these great results. If the initial redistribution is not buttressed by ongoing support to generate a sustained flow of income, the static distribution is bound to degenerate over time. Peru's socialist government in the 1970s instituted a program of land reforms that ended in failure since lacking complementary inputs such as know-how, credit, and marketing, the productivity of the redistributed land suffered a drastic decline. Other countries, such as Mexico, have taken steps to prevent redistributed land to revert back to concentrated ownership. Laws are enacted to prohibit the new recipients from freely disposing of this property as they so choose.

Welfare State   The **welfare state** approach follows the example of complex budget schemes used in advanced countries. This model of redistribution, however, is infeasible in the Third World context. Massive problems of poverty and inequality cannot be addressed in this way because the typical LDC government's budget is chronically subject to severe pressures even for performing such basic tasks as external defence and law and order. Draws upon the budget must come in that order of priority. The next priority must be expenditures for national development, such as building general infrastructure projects. Thus the addition of yet another huge budgetary task, redistribution, can hardly be accommodated easily. This quandary brings to mind that famous problem: With limited resources what would you rather do—provide a hungry man with a fish, or give him a net to continue to catch fish?

In short, only a small part of the budget remains for the purpose of fiscal redistributions. The government's budget is comprised of both taxation and expenditure decisions. It is difficult to significantly expand revenues on the taxation side since the fiscal apparatus in LDCs tends to be rudimentary. The easy sources of revenue already have been overtaxed, while other sources, such as a personal income tax, require far more sophisticated administrative arrangements than typically are available. The various types of taxes affect different social groups in different ways as shown by their **tax incidence.** Direct taxes on income and wealth can be the most **progressive**—they apply more than proportionately on the rich. These are also the hardest to administer and suffer from the Laffer curve effect mentioned earlier. The so-called indirect taxes on consumption (sales tax), production (excise tax), or trade (tariff) are far easier to apply. Unfortunately, these taxes also tend to be the most **regressive.** But since developing countries are obliged to rely more heavily on the latter type of taxes, the overall effect of their tax systems are at

Table 3-2 Taxes and expenditures as a share of household incomes

Income group (percentage)	Britain		Sri Lanka		Iran		Chile		Colombia	
0–20	100+		12		9		18		15	
		100+		20		15		73		73
21–40	43		15		7		17		10	
		70		17		8		60		17
41–60	39		15		7		16		10	
		27		17		8		46		13
61–80	38		17		7		17		11	
		17		15		5		34		11
81–95	39		19		8		17		12	
		14		12		5		28		14
96–100	41		29		9		24		25	
		8		3		22		8		6

Note: Top number is percent of income paid in taxes. Lower number is percent of income received from government expenditures.

Source: *ILO World Labour Report 1987*, pp 88–90.

best neutral. In short, they have little scope for income redistribution through their tax systems, which is reinforced by the reality that a poor country has few rich people available to tax.

LDC governments may be better able to influence income distribution through expenditure decisions. Outlays on projects/programs can be designed to target specific groups rather than influence the individual income distribution as such. Without the benefit of computers, individual identification numbers, or trained personnel, the latter approach is simply not possible in the typical developing country. It is easier to target poor groups through projects such as the building of productive facilities in the poorer areas. Such public works serve a developmental as well as redistributive role. In general, the redistributive aim may be attached to a higher priority task. As another example, the armed forces employ large numbers of poor recruits in addition to their primary purpose of national defence. Similarly, industrial projects are promoted in backward regions. All of these are illustrations of policy that plays a dual role.

Table 3-2 shows the role of tax and expenditure policy for redistribution in a sample of LDCs in the early 1970s. The comparable figures for Britain serve as an example of data for advanced countries. To interpret this table, consider the case of Sri Lanka: The lowest income group paid 12% of its income as taxes, and received 20% of its income through various government expenditures. Iran had the least developed tax system as it gathered the smallest fraction of GNP for public purposes. We may infer some generalizations about the role of fiscal policy in redistributing incomes:

(1) The role of tax and expenditure policy tends to be rather limited;

(2) Generally the more developed the country, the larger the degree of public sector involvement; and

(3) Expenditure policy can be more progressive than tax policy. For this set of LDCs, however, the progressivity of both taxes and expenditure is smaller than for Britain. In Iran, before the revolution, public expenditures were in fact sharply regressive as the richest 5% got the largest proportionate benefit from government expenditures.

In recent years direct policies of income redistribution have had disappointing results. The adverse affect on incentives, and hence on growth, has been too high. At the same time the commitment has been too low for the painful process of asset redistributions. These redistribution attempts have a heavy political cost and are virtually impossible to implement in reformist regimes. Historically, significant redistributions have taken place only in very turbulent and exceptional times. For instance, the breakup of large landholdings in Taiwan and Korea took place under Japan's stringent occupation before and during World War II.

Absent such extraordinary upheavals, the status quo continues as the distribution of assets remains highly skewed in many countries. For example, 90% of the land in Colombia is owned by just 10% of the population. Even in India, where the goal of land reform was loudly professed for decades, the impact has been negligible. Such widespread failures have led to a much less ambitious policy objective of poverty reduction. The abstract goal of achieving equality of incomes has been replaced by a stronger policy commitment to reduce poverty. The social philosopher, John Rawls, also provides a theoretical justification for improving the condition of the very poorest members of a society.

POVERTY REDUCTION

The issue of equity and social justice has undergone a major change in emphasis in the past few decades. The former concern for reducing income disparities in general has turned to a specific focus on alleviating absolute poverty. Such poverty can be quite varied in its manifestations, but not difficult to identify. In the simplest terms, the absolute poor have no day-by-day assurance whether they can work or be able to eat. For such people the key economic strategy is to ensure household food security. The absolute poor in rural areas typically operate as household units that take a unified view of production/consumption decisions regarding foodgrains, vegetables, livestock, and wage labor. (See chapter 14.) Occasionally there might be a remittance from a relative in the city or possible government relief. There even may be a savings decision to make if there is a surplus on a good day. This stark decision process applies to the entire household—children as well as adults.

For all these social and ethical imperatives, policies of **poverty reduction** take on a special significance in LDCs. Absolute poverty literally can be life threatening; it is not just a problem of contending with relative poverty. In general, growth-oriented policies have not made an appreciable dent on the poverty problem. As populations have grown the number of poor has also tended to grow, in a representative sample of LDCs shown in Table 3-3. Meanwhile the proportion of poor in the population generally has fallen as average income levels rose. Table 3-3 tabulates changes in the rural poor over the period 1965–1988.

Such numbers indicate a general decline in the proportion of poor in the rural population even as their absolute numbers have increased in step with increasing population. The situation is worse in some LDCs as quantitative economic growth has not even reduced the proportion of the poor. The main problem is rather the qualitative nature of that growth. Thus even a strategy that successfully generates growth of aggregate incomes, ironically may foster pressures to change policy. Particularly in urban areas, poverty is more visible and certainly more politically potent. Also, the absolute gap between the richest and poorest can widen. In light of such trends, development thinking has been obliged to shift its main focus away from sheer growth toward policies specifically aimed to raise the standard of living of the poorest of the poor. This applies especially to the least developed of the LDCs, mostly in the Sahel regions of sub-Saharan Africa. One hopeful sign is that various other Third World countries, such as those of south Asia, are steadily graduating out of this category.

Table 3-3 Change in absolute poverty

Changes in absolute poor over 1965–1988			
	Change in numbers (million)	Proportion of population (percent)	Per capita income growth rate % p.a.
Africa			
Egypt	+3.7	17 → 25%	4.2
Ethiopia	+0.6	65 → 43%	–.1
Malawi	+2.9	85 → 90%	1.0
Zambia	+1.5	52 → 80%	–2.0
Latin America			
Bolivia	+1.4	85 → 97%	–.8
Brazil	–1.6	66 → 73%	3.5
Guatemala	+1.3	84 → 74%	.9
Venezuela	+0.2	52 → 80%	–1.0
Asia			
Bangladesh	+36.7	83 → 86%	.4
Indonesia	–7.7	47 → 27%	4.4
Malaysia	–2.0	59 → 22%	4.0
Sri Lanka	+4.9	13 → 46%	3.0

Source: *State of the Rural Poverty* by International Fund for Agricultural Development, and *World Development Report*, 1993.

Different countries have adopted different strategies for poverty reduction. Brazil is often cited as an example of a country that promoted all-out growth, while relying on the hope that some benefits would trickle-down to the poorest. On the other hand, socialist Cuba applies an explicitly redistributive strategy by controlling incomes at the source. It also delivers a wide range of basic needs as described in the introduction. Let's view these strategies starting from an initial income distribution *A*. Figure 3-8 shows how the entire income distribution (using any one of the measures mentioned earlier) can be shifted to *C*, thereby raising the average income level and also the low end of the distribution. By contrast, a socialist strategy aims to narrow the distribution (*B*) without necessarily altering the average level of income.

The Poverty Problem

The new focus on poverty reduction has induced a policy reorientation to directly tackle poverty rather than to address income inequality as such. The new approach is evaluated in the 1990 *World Development Report*. This policy effort requires a detailed analysis of the varied causes of poverty in the specific situation of different countries. Such a comprehensive study was undertaken by the United Nations agency, The International Fund for Agricultural Development (IFAD). The agricultural focus of this study is consistent with the finding that over 80% of worldwide poverty is situated in rural areas (as examined in chapter 14). This study isolated ten proximate causes of poverty creation in the developing countries. Of course not all factors apply in the case of each LDC, nor do they apply with equal intensity.

The dynamic processes may work to perpetuate poverty in the form of vicious cycles. Many of these processes cause low incomes in general, but become critical for those segments that fall below the poverty line. For instance, an economywide recession lowers all incomes and thereby pushes more people into poverty. By

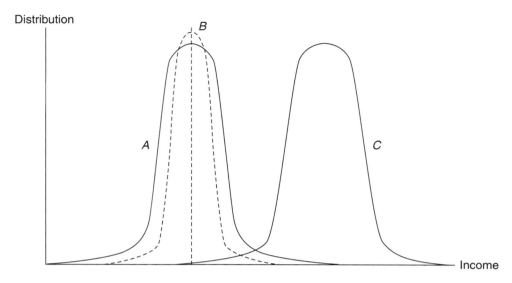

Figure 3-8 *Alternate strategies for poverty reduction*

contrast, other processes exacerbate poverty while raising incomes at the upper end of the income spectrum. The ten specific poverty processes may be categorized under five heads: policy, natural/environmental, cultural/institutional, political, and international. Clearly, each category calls for a different policy orientation. For instance, an environmental cause, such as rapid population growth, requires a corrective policy that produces results only in the long term.

Perhaps the most regrettable cause of poverty is that induced by policy biases. Such errors of development strategy will be detailed in the relevant context in the chapters that follow. Prominent among them was an urban bias that damaged productivity growth and incomes in the agricultural sector (chapter 9). The subsidization of industry tended to encourage capital intensive technology with the side effect of reducing labor demand and employment (chapter 10). Agricultural pricing policies have also had adverse affects on rural incomes and poverty (chapter 14). Further price distortions occurred as a result of export taxes or, indirectly, through

overvalued exchange rates. More generally poverty is a by-product of dualism. This has deep historical roots in Latin America with its traditional division of large landholdings, "Latifundia," and a separate marginalized class of peasants. In many Latin American countries large-scale agricultural producers still control the bulk of land and labor resources. Africa traditionally has been much more egalitarian, but inequality arose from the colonial pattern of production in the agricultural sector and has expanded in the post-colonial period.

Unlike the policy effects, population growth appears to be a natural factor that perpetuates poverty (as the Malthusian basis of the Classical growth model). In the agricultural context this works through an increasing pressure on land as poor families tend to choose to have more children as a form of social security, and as a consequence, they cannot afford human capital improvements, so the cycle of poverty continues (chapter 4). Examples of such places include Egypt, along the banks of the Nile, and, until recently, on the crowded Indonesian islands of

Java and Bali. Rapid population expansion is also tied to a progressive degradation of the environment. This damages the carrying capacity for sustainable development. Existing poverty leads to a more rapid exploitation of renewable resources than nature's capacity to regenerate them. This takes the form of excessive deforestation in Nepal and overgrazing in large parts of sub-Saharan Africa and the horn of Africa. Ultimately, the damage can become irreversible, as soil erosion and even climatic changes occur. The most adversely affected are those poor people at the margin of subsistence who triggered the process in the first place.

Another source of poverty arises from the misfortune of certain countries to lie in geographical zones that are particularly prone to natural disasters. A prime example is Bangladesh with its periodic devastation by typhoons. Another example is the long-term decline of rainfall in parts of the Sudan. Even as these examples may seem entirely natural, however, there are economic forces at work. For instance, the pressure of population forced people to move onto low islands in Bangladesh that were always known to be vulnerable.

In the category of cultural and institutional determinants, a crucial poverty process arises through racial and ethnic biases. The raw numbers of income inequality and backwardness tend to obscure the fact that most such instances apply not to individuals per se, but to well defined groups in a historical inferior relationship. In much of Latin America the poverty problem applies almost exclusively to the native Indian population in societies largely controlled by those of Spanish extraction and Mestizos. In South Africa income classes also divide neatly along racial lines. Under the apartheid system, recently dismantled, the per capita income of Whites in Namibia was about $15,000; Blacks (in the rural areas "reserved" for the majority) was about $120.

Another cultural effect is the widespread prevalence of a gender bias, as noted earlier while interpreting measures of inequality. Among the poor, women tend to constitute the poorest group. This stems from dislocations that cause destitution and breakdown of the family structure, which traditionally provided some measure of social security. While many males migrate to find employment elsewhere, women are left to eke out a living as best they can. Meanwhile, society continues to act according to the old cultural values in its presumption that males are the nominal head of families. A reflection of this very syndrome may be seen in the struggle for womens' rights even in the United States. Employment and credit discrimination in favor of men used to be justified on the basis that they had to provide for families. Now that women are playing that role in increasingly significant numbers, that argument cannot be sustained. The underprivileged status of women operates as another process that perpetuates poverty, as this syndrome is passed on to their children.

Turning now to differences in individual power, we observe that exploitative intermediation can operate as a mechanism to perpetuate a poverty trap. In chapter 13 we will detail how market interactions are just one mode of economic transactions. Other modes are reciprocity, as within a family, or command, as in the feudalism of the past. The latter mode still prevails in certain parts of the world. It is reflected in a sharp difference in power between landlords and tenants or sharecroppers. Similarly, in a situation of monopolistic credit supply, moneylenders can force their clients into virtual bondage. Another modern category that flourishes is the government bureaucracy unrestrained by checks and balances that extracts large penalties from the poor—the group with the least power (see chapter 13 on political economy). Another political process operates in a situation of civil disorder. Political fragmentation and civil strife can obviously disrupt productive activities. It also obstructs the efforts of national and international aid agencies to provide aid to the most destitute. The recent situation in Somalia provided a striking example.

Finally, poverty may be aggravated by certain international processes. Individual countries may have little or no influence on these varied channels. Primary exporting countries may suffer severely from commodity price fluctuations (see chapter 11). Also, protectionism by importing countries against certain commodities can seriously affect the poorest producers. Tightening of sugar quotas, for instance, would directly impact Mautitius and the Dominican Republic, while Caribbean nations have recently been concerned that the European Union will switch to importing lower cost bananas from Latin America. A different channel operates through fluctuations in world interest rates, which have a significant impact on heavily-indebted countries.

The IFAD conducted in-depth surveys to gauge the operation of these various processes in a sample comprising fifty-eight developing countries. Their results, summarized in Table 3-4, indicate that African countries are most afflicted by the poverty processes.

Table 3-4   Poverty processes in developing countries

Causal factors identified
1 Domestic policy biases
2 Dualism
3 Population pressure
4 Poor resources/environment
5 Natural disasters
6 Gender bias
7 Cultural/ethnic biases
8 Exploitative intermediaries
9 Political strife
10 International processes

Number of factors with substantial impact in sample countries	
Africa:	Sudan 10
	Ethiopia, Kenya 8
	Mozambique, Morocco 7
	Chad, Ghana, Somalia, Zaire, Zambia, Zimbabwe 6
	Gambia, Egypt 5
	Guinea, Nigeria, Tanzania, Tunisia 4
	Angola, Botswana, Mali 3
	Cameroon, Madagascar 2
Latin America:	Haiti, Guatemala, Honduras, Peru 7
	El Salvador 6
	Brazil, Colombia, Ecuador, Guyana, Mexico 5
	Panama 4
	Costa Rica 1
Asia:	Philippines 7
	Pakistan 6
	Bangladesh, Indonesia 5
	India, Nepal, Sri Lanka 4
	Thailand 0

Providing Basic Needs

Increasingly LDCs are realizing that poverty is best addressed by a **basic-needs strategy.** The task for policy is to design a delivery system to provide the minimum acceptable set of basic needs. One choice may be to make direct **in-kind transfers** of necessities such as free health care, subsidized basic foods, fuels, and so on. But these expenditure programs restrict benefits to just the poor. Such problems may be avoided by a specially designed program. For example, a public health program of preventive medicine can benefit the entire population, but aids the poor more than proportionately. China is famous for its barefoot doctors who provide very basic health services. By contrast, modern facilities of curative medicine tend to be used more by the rich. For the latter kind of services, it is possible, indeed desirable, to require at least some partial payment instead of free provision to all. An analysis of such cost-recovery is deferred to a later chapter in the context of education.

When public projects are considered for adoption, there's invariably a pressure also to make them serve a redistributive function. Whatever the immediate objective—transportation, education, and so on—an additional demand is: What will this do for the poor? As a consequence, the limited funds do not necessarily go to build the bridge or dam that adds most to economic efficiency, but rather to one that helps certain disadvantaged groups. In social benefit/cost analysis (studied in chapter 13) the choices are influenced by weighing project benefits according to the impact on various income groups. Harberger challenges the efficacy of such **distributional weights** in his article "Distributional Weights or Basic Needs?" (1984). He argues that the goal is not primarily to raise the utility of the recipients of redistributive transfers. Instead, it is donors who maximize their own utility from seeing the poor receive basic needs.

Another example of such in-kind tranfers in LDCs is the provision of public housing in an effort to eradicate slums. Society views the very visible slums with distaste, so it provides public housing to the slum dwellers. Very soon, however, the beneficiaries subdivide or sublet their premises so that the new premises begin to look like slums. Again, this stems from a divergence between the objectives of donors and those of recipients. Thus for in-kind transfer programs to be successful, careful thought must be given to their design. Public programs that address the basic needs requirement but have no ready substitute in private expenditures are ideal. It is even better if the program serves to enhance productivity so as to provide redistribution-with-growth.

Finally, we note that the assurance of employment to all is now becoming a primary goal at par with economic growth or equality. In fact, this imperative has become so strong that many LDCs seek to design policy for increased employment even if such policy has no impact on the other objectives. Fortunately, the expansion of employment does have a positive effect on income distribution. In recent years governments have learned to combine employment schemes with in-kind payments, usually in the form of food. Such workfare schemes provide threefold benefits. First, they leave behind a legacy of public works, such as roads or canals, that add to the society's productive capital stock. Second, they address directly the twin problems of unemployment and malnutrition. Finally, they make it possible to precisely channel the limited resources available for redistribution—only those who are really destitute will opt to work for the very low wage offered by such jobs. This kind of policy is increasingly tried by many LDCs following the successful example of its implementation in Ethiopia during the 1970s and in Somalia in the 1990s.

Analysis: Redistribution through cash or in-kind transfers

To illustrate this distinction, consider an example from daily life. Are you more willing to donate $1 worth of food to a pan-handler or $1 in cash, which he might use to buy booze? If you opt for the former, you are really increasing your own satisfaction. Of course the recipient benefits too, but cannot maximize his utility freely as if he had gotten money. This is precisely the logic behind rules that make it illegal to resell ration-cards or food stamps.

Figure 3-9 analyzes this situation from the point of view of the recipient. Given the utility (or indifference) curves, which depict his preferences, a person with budget *B* will choose a consumption combination at *A*. At this point the poor person maximizes utility by allocating part of his income for basic needs such as food. But society views this level of consumption to fall short of its desired minimum standard. The donor may give an in-kind transfer of basic goods in order to bring the recipient up to the minimum level at *T*. This combination of food and booze, however, is not most desirable from the recipient's point of view. If he can resell a portion of the food and adjust his consumption, he can reach higher utility at point *R*. Again, consumption of basic needs falls below the societal norm, so the donor's aims are frustrated. If donors impose prohibitions against resale, the recipient is obliged to consume the in-kind transfer of amount *AT*.

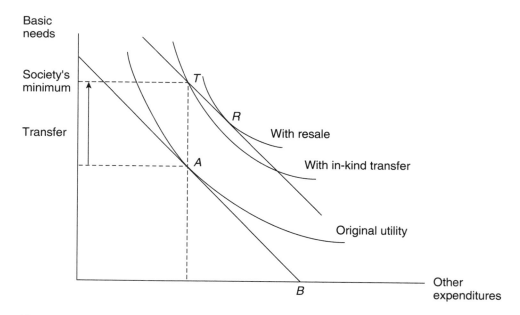

Figure 3-9   *In-kind transfers*

Note, however, that the recipient's remaining funds are interchangeable. Since the donor's conditions do not apply to these, the recipient can easily adjust purchases to partially undo the donor's desires. Many examples of such action-reaction between donors and recipients may be cited. For instance, society deems that childrens' nutrition is paramount and institutes a program of basic feeding in schools. In response, parents cut back somewhat on the child's diet at home. If you think this is callous, reconsider this issue from the household's point of view. The family with a limited budget makes the difficult choice of balancing food intake across all members of the family. The additional nutrition for the child at school is, of course, welcomed; the family proceeds to rebalance the diet of all family members to spread the benefit around. At its root, we observe a conflict between society's objectives and the family's perception of its own best interest.

CASE STUDY: GENERAL FOOD SUBSIDY IN EGYPT

The case of the general food subsidy in Egypt is instructive. This example from the 1990 *World Development Report* illustrates the various pros and cons of this common tool for dealing with poverty. While the professed aim is to aid the poor, the general food subsidy is actually provided to all. It takes the form of a price subsidy on bread and flour normally sold at private bakeries and stores. This arrangement has the advantage that no separate infrastructure is needed for public distribution.

Can this program be deemed successful? A likely answer may be . . . yes and no! In a narrow sense it certainly succeeds in alleviating hunger among the poor. This aim is achieved at a very high cost, however. Consider both the program's high absolute cost, as well as its low cost-effectiveness. The fiscal cost was as much as 15% of total public expenditures during the period 1975–84. To evaluate this, consider other pressing demands for these public funds: Roads, education, public health, and housing. By way of comparison, food subsidies amounted to about 6% of public expenditure in Jamaica and 1% in Colombia. While

there always needs to be a balance of spending priorities, the general food price subsidy was a poor use of the severely limited public budget in Egypt. In terms of cost-effectiveness only twenty cents of every dollar reached the lowest quartile of the income distribution.

The food subsidy could be made more effective by targeting. It could be specifically designated both by commodity and by location so as to reach the intended target. A subsidy on coarse flour would better reach the poor since the non-poor are unlikely to buy it anyway, despite its subsidized price. As it is, location does affect the incidence of the subsidy. The bread subsidy accrues more to urban dwellers since there are more bakeries in urban areas, while the flour subsidy accrues relatively more to rural residents who tend to bake their own bread. More directly, the rural population suffers from the price controls that keep farm prices below the world market prices. The International Food Policy Research Institute estimates that rural incomes fall by an average of $4 per capita due to this intervention.

Table 3.5   Transfers by general food subsidy in Egypt, 1981–82

Type of household	Annual transfer (Egyptian pounds)	As % of household expenditures
Urban		
Poorest quartile	15.4	9%
Richest quartile	18.1	3%
Rural		
Poorest quartile	11.9	11%
Richest quartile	15.2	3%

Table 3-5 shows how the food subsidy was distributed in a biased way that favored the urban sector. It was regressive in the sense that richer households got a larger absolute amount of transfer, even if it implied a larger percent of poor household incomes. If the aim was solely to provide food to the poor, all the utilization by the rich may be considered a fiscal waste.

An alternative method of subsidizing food for the poor is by a **public distribution system.** Every person is allotted a ration card, which entitles them to buy a limited quota of subsidized food from ration shops. People can buy more if they wish in the higher-priced open market. This arrangement is much cheaper on the public purse, even as more of the subsidy reaches the poor. In Egypt the rich are found to partake less than the poor from ration shops, as opposed to about 20% more from the general food subsidy. The ration program also has a down side: It makes heavy demands on limited administrative capabilities. There's the constant hazard of corruption allowing the subsidized ration goods to leak into the open market, as others try to beat the system through fraud and forgery. This system also has a distributional flaw as ration shops are most accessible in urban areas, so the benefits of such a system flow mainly to urban residents.

Last, but not least, are the political aspects of Egypt's food subsidy program. While the non-poor certainly were not the original intended beneficiaries, they have now become accustomed to this particular **entitlement.** They threaten to riot whenever there are plans to cut or eliminate the subsidy. The government conceded to this populist demand despite all its budget stringency for a very special reason: Egypt received huge aid flows from the United States during those years. The United States went along with the subsidy program as a necessary evil so as to consolidate political support within Egypt for the Camp David Accords. Thus we see that international and domestic political considerations combined to maintain a program that is seriously flawed economically from a fiscal point of view as well as distributional and efficiency consideration.

SUMMARY

Many societies deem that equity is an extremely important goal of development; In many cases even at par with the primary objective of growth. But a serious theoretical problem arises in defining precisely how society will make the decisions that affect the income redistributions. We are obliged to resort to the fiction of a benevolent dictator to impose this imperative. In order to discuss the concept of income distribution in a concrete manner, we introduce various inequality measures. While this allows us to make comparisons across countries and across time, we learn that such measures must be interpreted with caution. The mere existence of measured inequality does not mean that we must rush out to remove it.

In seeking greater equality there can be a trade-off with the objective of growth. We study this problem in some detail for various kinds of policies. Neoclassical economics is neutral in its prescriptions for achieving equity. On the other hand, familiar instruments, such as the Welfare state, are found to be not workable in the context of the LDCs or too expensive in terms of reduced growth. The currently favored prescription is for redistribution-with-growth. The disappointment with redistributive policies has prompted a major reorientation away from seeking pure income equality to a focus on the worst manifestations of poverty at the low end of the income spectrum. To solve such problems requires not just that the poor receive incomes per se, but rather that they be assured of certain minimum entitlements, broadly defined.

Processes that perpetuate poverty may result from (1) Mistaken policy; (2) Endogenous cycles of population growth and poverty that operate in a vicious cycle; (3) Cultural/institutional arrangements that perpetuate poverty; (4) Differences in power that could only be remedied by political means; and (5) International influences that can be ameliorated by international policy actions. The new focus on poverty reduction is to provide only the very basic needs. Where the government opts for direct provision of basic needs, care must be taken to see that such aid is directed only to the poorest.

KEY TERMS

Equity
Income inequality
Social compact
Utilitarian theory
Social welfare function
Rawlsian social welfare
Redistribution
Benevolent dictator
Lorenz curve
Gini coefficient
Regional disparities
Expropriation

Equality of opportunity
Redistribution and growth
Cost of fairness
Laffer curve of taxation
Incentives
Zero-sum game
Kuznets' U-curve
Trickle-down effect
Functional distribution of
    income
Lump-sum transfers
Pareto-optimal equilibrium

Land reform
Welfare state
Tax incidence
Progressive vs. regressive taxes
Poverty reduction
Basic-needs strategy
In-kind transfers
Distributional weights
Public distribution system
Entitlements

Chapter 4

POPULATION

IMPORTANCE FOR DEVELOPMENT

The development performance of a country depends obviously and crucially on its population size and rate of growth. The interaction between the two is complex and multifaceted. The size and growth rate of population affect the economic growth rate, while the level of development, in turn, influences the population growth rate. This chapter examines the various ways that the population level and growth rate will affect the growth of output, then details the stylized facts of population growth worldwide, and presents the contending theories that purport to explain the causes of population growth.

To begin, the most obvious developmental effect of a larger population is that a given output must be shared more widely, so per capita income will drop. In this view population is considered as mouths to feed rather than pairs of hands that will help expand output. One striking example comes from the economic history of fourteenth-century Europe. As the dreaded Black Death killed almost half the population in certain regions, those who survived had a noticeable improvement in their standard of living. The decline in aggregate GNP by as much as a third certainly qualifies as an economic catastrophe. Yet, it's also true that per capita incomes increased for the fewer mouths that remained to feed. But can that be termed development? Of course, in the modern context, nobody envisages reduced population levels, but the focus is certainly on reducing the **population growth rate** in the hope of advancing development.

Figure 4-1 depicts both aspects of a larger population: The lower per capita income that results—at constant output—and the increased production to be expected from a larger labor force. At the initial point A, output Y and population P are as shown. The slope of the dotted line to A indicates per capita income Y/P. If the same output had to be shared with a larger population at B, the per capita income would obviously drop. However, the added population also adds to output along the curved line. This production function shows how an increased labor input causes output to increase, but with diminishing productivity. Again, the level of per capita income at C is lower than before.

An obvious perspective on population is to view it negatively since per capita income becomes smaller with population growth, which enters the denominator of the output/population ratio. Yet, **population size** in itself sometimes has been viewed positively due to its link with overall output. Nationalists may consider the

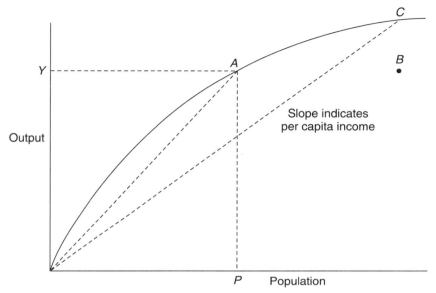

Figure 4-1 *Population and per capita income*

level of output to be more important than per capita figures (point *C* preferred to point *A* in the above diagram). India and China, for instance, are very poor countries in terms of per capita income, but giants in terms of economic size. Chairman Mao used to note that a large population allowed China to field a powerful military force. Another situation where unfettered population growth is viewed favorably is when contending ethnic groups vie for political influence; in these instances a larger size group is construed as winning.

Another influence on development is the effect of **population density** on productivity. As the ratio of population/resources increases, labor must inevitably run into diminishing marginal productivity as it is constrained to work with a limited land area or fixed resources, in general. (In Figure 4-1 this is seen as a flatter line of average income when population expands.) An opposing view is that a high population density of itself may serve to induce technological progress. If the necessity of population pressure sparks our ingenuity, it may become possible to continuously

improve the efficiency of resource use so that it would become irrelevant to emphasize the limit of resources. In fact, some of the most successful cases of development, including Japan and Holland, are famous for their marked lack of natural resources. At the same time, such well-endowed countries as Mexico, Zaire, and India performed far lower than their potential.

POPULATION VERSUS RESOURCES

A recent stance toward population growth is based on the view that our planet's resources are finite. Thus an exponential growth of population cannot continue indefinitely. It has become outdated to think in terms of a closed economy in view of the obvious interdependence between all nations within the world economy. The global implications of population growth were examined in the 1984 *World Development Report*. All countries are affected by this environmental limitation of **spaceship earth,** especially as population growth continues in large countries such as India and China, where the population/land ratio is already large. A small, intellectual school sustains a challenge to the very notion that the world's use of resources is anywhere close to the limit.

Some years ago a highly influential report, *The Limits to Growth* (1972), triggered a controversy about growth and the environment that continues to this date. This report, by a group of scholars called the Club of Rome, has been harshly attacked, particularly for its flawed methodology, which neglected a crucial role for prices in regulating scarcity. Nevertheless this report must be applauded as the first step that raised awareness of this issue. We start our elementary study by noting that any analysis of **resource depletion** and economic growth must recognize that natural resources usage depends on:

Resource = Population × Per capita × Intensity of depletion   size   income   resource use

This accounting identity, whether stated in terms of level or as rates of change, has to be true simply as a tautology. This relation still can provide us important insights. It summarizes the obvious role of three major variables of concern: economic growth, population growth, and environmental degredation. We will examine the behavior of each of these variables, keeping in mind that there may be important interactions between them. For example, we've already seen how the rate of population increase might influence output growth and vice versa. In a similar way the complex relationship between economic growth and resource usage is subject to much debate. The Club of Rome report was widely attacked because it took a rather mechanistic view of resource usage. By contrast, an economic view emphasizes how changes in relative prices would warn of impending scarcity.

In neoclassical theory, prices serve as an automatic mechanism to regulate the intensity of resource use on the demand side and also to prompt the supply side to expand available resources through exploration. As a resource becomes increasingly depleted, price rises would induce technological innovation (creation of substitutes) in both consumption and production. A familiar example is the increase in automobile fuel economy that was prompted by the 1973 oil crisis. Environmentalists who have learned from the economists to allow a role for prices may still remain pessimistic. Yet such expressions of concern in the past have all too often seemed to be crying wolf.

A true story: In 1980 the famous environmentalist Paul Ehrlich made a $1,000 bet with the pro growth economist Julian Simon: In a decade the prices of five metals (copper, chrome, nickel, tin, and tungsten) would rise. However, by 1990 the prices of all five had actually fallen, and Ehrlich was obliged to pay up.

A popular book by Julian Simon is entitled *The Ultimate Resource* (1981), referring to population. If there's any doubt about the author's orientation, it is immediately dispelled by the themes printed in big type on the cover: "Natural resources and energy are getting less scarce," "The world's food supply is improving," and "Population growth has long-term benefits."

Such sharply contradicting views of intelligent men spring from fundamentally different precepts about natural resources—in particular about nonrenewable resources. There's no argument about the use of inexhaustible resources—examples of which are solar, wind, and tide power, perhaps silicon from sand, and so on. But which resources are truly exhaustible? If we dig deeper into the earth, surely we can find more of each mineral (perhaps a million times more) than all that has been recovered in the history of mining. The issue is thus one of cost. The pro growth people have an abiding faith in technological progress to rapidly reduce the cost. For other deposits, such as hydrocarbons, the idea of limits may be more plausible.

Two fundamentally different ways of looking at resource usage are quantities versus prices. An engineering viewpoint, which emphasizes quantities, typically leads to the most alarming prospects for future resource depletion. This kind of projection, however, may be unduly pessimistic, even in its own terms, since quantitative plans may fail to recognize that intensity of resource use varies widely across countries. If all countries would adopt the least wasteful technology (even that currently available within the public domain), the pressure on exhaustible resources and the environment would be greatly relieved. A recent Sino-Japanese study quantifies the extent to which this is possible. The study found that China generates 24 times more carbon compunds and 184 times more sulfur oxides than Japan to produce the same amount of steel, electricity, cement, and paper.

In addition to the **technical diffusion** of already known technology, a continued process of **technical innovation** would further ease resource depletion. The antigrowth people, however, point to critical areas where the market does not work to this end. They are particularly concerned about irreversible changes. For instance, the extinction of species is forever. Thus resouce depletion becomes a risky matter: What if the faith in technology fails us in the future? From all these considerations there is a growing consensus about at least one aspect of this issue: LDC population growth must be controlled no matter how the other variables evolve over time.

The idea of limits to growth is perhaps most controversial in the political implications of suggested solutions. For any economic policy proposal, it is imperative to examine who wins and who loses from it. Even if there is widespread agreement that scarce global resources are being used up, the disparate remedies suggested would raise heated argument (see *The State of the World*, published annually by The Worldwatch Institute). The Third World takes the political position that rich countries must limit their profligate resource use (which the poor countries consider "waste"). In response, the rich countries urge LDCs to cut their population growth rates both for their own sake and for the sake of everyone else on the planet. They point out that unrestrained population growth encroaches on the habitat of disappearing wildlife, equatorial rain forests, and other forms of life. This issue is simple: What is more important—people or nature? Note the sharp tone in the exchange of letters between a British schoolboy and the prime minister of a developing nation, Dr. Matathir of Malaysia (*Wall Street Journal*, 4/4/88). In the starkest terms this can be seen as a plea by the rich for not despoiling the world playground. In response, a supposed champion of the poor claims that they have the right to do what they want (on their own turf) to better their own condition.

A Letter From a British Schoolboy, 10, Stirs Malaysian Leader's Sharp Reply

BY STEPHEN DUTHIE
Staff Reporter of THE WALL STREET JOURNAL

KUALA LUMPUR, Malaysia—The exchange of letters between British schoolboy Darrell Abercrombie and Malaysian Prime Minister Mahathir Mohamad was mercifully brief.

Darrell, a wildlife enthusiast from Surrey, England, wrote to Dr. Mahathir in mid-1987. His one-paragraph missive started friendly enough: "I am 10 years old and when I am older I hope to study animals in the tropical rain forests."

Then he got a little rough.

"But if you let the lumber companys {sic} carry on there will not be any left. And millions of animals will die. Do you think that is right just

Mahathir Mohamad

so one rich man gets another million pounds or more. I think it is disgraceful."

"Dear Darrell," Dr. Mahathir answered. Then he got rough. "It is disgraceful that you should be used by adults for the purpose of trying to shame us because of our extraction of timber from our forests."

Malaysia, like many other tropical lands, is being criticized for the rapid exploitation of hardwoods that, environmentalists contend, destroys forests and threatens endangered animal and plant species and the balance of nature. Malaysia, for one, is fighting back. Primary Industries Minister Lim Keng Yaik speaks of "trade competitors: in Europe who have recruited environmentalists and "blind idealists" in a "no-holds-barred attack on timber products and Malaysia's forest conservation and management policies."

But Darrell isn't a competitor or an idealist. "He just sort of dabbles at the moment in studying wildlife—you know, a kid's sort of interests." says Reginald Abercrombie, Darrell's father. He says Darrell was prompted to write to Dr. Mahathir by an article in the BBC Wildlife magazine about the plight of animals in heavily logged tropical jungles.

"He wrote the letter by himself, though his mother helped him a bit," says Mr. Abercrombie. "We were so flabbergasted at the response. We couldn't believe anybody would say that to a child."

Dr. Mahathir's rejoinder was largely a lesson on the tropical timber industry's importance to Malaysia. Logs and sawn-timber exports earned $2.35 billion for the country in 1987, the second most important export behind petroleum.

"The timber industry helps hundreds of thousands of poor people in Malaysia," with every man in the industry supporting, on average, a wife and three children, Dr. Mahathir wrote to Darrell.

As for Darrell's accusation of timber tycoons leveling the jungle and destroying wildlife, Dr. Mahathir noted that "without the rich man not only will the government get no tax, but there will be no logging and numerous people will be jobless. And "the tax the government collects will provide education, health and other services also for the poor."

"Are they supposed to remain poor because you want to study tropical animals? Is your study more important than filling the empty stomachs of poor people? Are Malaysians expected to lose millions of pounds so that you can study animals?"

Darrell's ancestors weren't spared either. Dr. Mahathir said Malaysia's former British rulers had "burnt millions of acres of Malaysian forests so that they could plant rubber [trees]." The natural forest and the wood in it "was totally wasted" and "millions of animals" died. "What your fathers did was indeed disgraceful."

But Dr. Mahathir provided Darrell with a solution. "If you don't want us to cut down our forests, tell your father to tell the rich countries like Britain to pay more for the timber they buy from us," he wrote. "Then we can cut less timber and create other jobs for our people."

Short of that, Darrell's elders "should not be too arrogant and think they know how best to run a country," Dr. Mahathir added. Instead, "They should expel all the people living in the [British] countryside and allow secondary forests to grow and fill these new forests with wolves and bears etc. so you can study them before studying tropical animals."

In a parting shot, Dr. Mahathir closed, "I believe strongly that children should learn all about animals and love them. But adults should not teach children to be rude to their elders."

Mr. Abercrombie says Darrell would just like to forget about the pen-pal skirmish.

But Dr. Mahathir's letter hasn't cooled Darrell's ardor for wildlife. His father says Darrell spends his spare time tending to his pet barn owl, which he hopes to breed and restock the nearby countryside.

Reprinted by permission of The Wall Street Journal© 1988. Dow Jones & Company, Inc. All rights reserved worldwide.

POPULATION GROWTH

The foregoing discussion argued the importance of population in development—either as a constraint or as a boon. Thus we are left to study the determinants of population growth, whose components are summarized in the following expression:

$$\text{Population} = \begin{bmatrix} \text{Birth rate} - \text{Death rate} \pm \text{Migration} \end{bmatrix}$$
growth

$$\begin{array}{cc} \text{Fertility} & * & \text{Proportion of women} \\ \text{rate} & & \text{in childbearing age} \end{array}$$

Salient facts about today's global population include: The level of world population stood at 5.7 billion in 1994 and is projected to reach 10 billion by the middle of the 21st century; only then will it (hopefully) begin to drop. The growth rate of the world's population used to be less than half of 1% per annum for millennia. In this century the average growth rate shot up to over 2.5%. Recently the growth rate has abated from 1.9% in the 1970s to 1.7% in the 1980s, and a projected 1.6% in the 1990s.

Population growth is mainly a problem in the Third World, but its effects inevitably will be felt worldwide. The overall growth rate of 1.7% per annum is split as 2.1% in the LDCs and about .6% in the DCs. The fastest growth occurs in the poorest regions, as seen in Table 4-1 of the changing population shares by region.

The three proximate determinants of population growth are **birth rates, death rates,** and **migration rates** (immigration, and emigration). For the largest countries the last item may be considered negligible—after all, emigration of even a million people from China would hardly make a dent in its population level. But in selected countries, migration can be quite important. Significant examples of emigration are from Mexico to the United States, and from North Africa to Europe; meanwhile, immigration makes a significant qualitative and quantitative impact in the sparsely populated oil-rich countries of the Middle East. The poor overpopulated countries have the strongest pressures to emigrate, while immigration is important for the richest countries, which have low population growth rates. Some of the very lowest rates of population growth—even declines —occur in Japan as well as eastern and northern Europe.

The most general determinants of population size remain the birth and death rates. We show the net effect of these two factors in the next section. Then, assuming that the main concern is population limitation, we turn our focus on the most significant controllable variable, the birth rate.

Table 4-1 Population shares and growth by region

| Region | Share of global population | | Annual growth rate |
	1950	1990	1980–91
China	22.1%	21.5%	1.5%
India	14.2	16.1	2.1
Asia-other	18.9	26.8	
Africa	8.8	12.1	3.1
Europe	22.8	14.8	.9
Latin America	6.6	8.5	2.0
North America	6.6	5.2	1.0
Global Population	2.5 billion	5.3 billion	1.7%

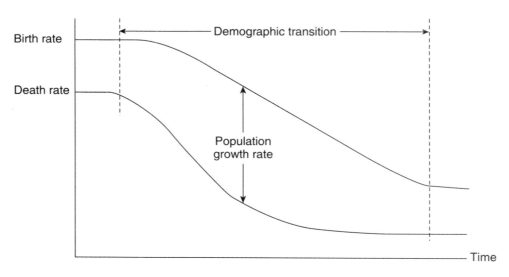

Figure 4-2   *Demographic transition*

Demographic Transition

With the onset of development, easily implemented techniques of public health, such as the control of malaria and the virtual eradication of smallpox, immediately translated into lower death rates, particularly of infant mortality. Also, as life expectancy increases, the population expands even if the birth rate is unchanged. With the progress of development, the death rate drops rapidly; however, the birth rate drops only very gradually. (Figure 4-2) People are slow to change their reproductive behavior, and the birth rate may even rise initially as improved prenatal care increases survivability after birth. The wider gap between birth and death rates causes a large jump in the population growth rate. The period over which all these effects occur is called the **demographic transition.** This pattern is commonly observed in both cross-sectional data as well as in time-series data.

These dramatic effects in today's LDCs contrast with the milder experience of the advanced countries, which made their transition in the 18th and 19th century. The European demographic transition was far less pronounced since birth rates did not start so high and death rates declined only slowly. Thus the transition took longer—almost a century rather than decades—while the population growth rate never shot up so dramatically. Another difference is that the lowered death rate in Europe was caused more by general improvements in living standards—including nutrition and sanitation—rather than by specific medical advances, such as antibiotics or control of epidemics.

Another demographic effect of rapid population growth is that the age distribution skews toward larger numbers of younger people in relation to the total population. The **dependency ratio** is defined as the number of dependents as a fraction of the total population. This increased ratio in the LDCs causes job creation and education to become critical problems. A younger population may cause society's savings rate to drop just when large investments are needed for job creation and infrastructure. By contrast, slow population growth in the developed countries skews their age distribution toward an older mix. Their dependency ratio also rises, but in a different way. An aging population brings the issue of social

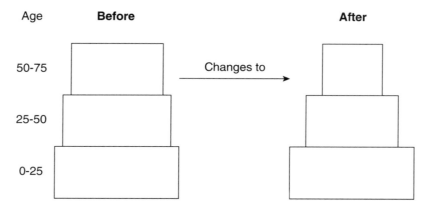

Figure 4-3 *Changing age profile of population*

security to the fore. For instance, the slowed rate of population growth in the United States will mean that when today's youth reaches retirement age, there will be fewer than three active workers per retiree to provide social security. The change in age composition due to population growth can be depicted by the **population pyramid** for the case of developing countries.

Figure 4-3 shows how birth and death rates can alter the shape of the pyramid over the next generation. Rapid population growth results in a much higher proportion of younger people. More than one third of the population is below 15

years old! In fact, first-time visitors to developing countries often notice children everywhere. In a couple of decades the girls in this group will come to maturity, and there will be a high proportion of women of childbearing age in the population mix. This altered age distribution ultimately results in a **population momentum.** The large group of young women ensures that the birth rate remains high even if the fertility rate drops appreciably. This factor is now the largest contributor to the population growth rate, as highlighted in a U.N. conference on population held in Cairo in 1994. The number of women of reproductive age

Table 4-2   Fertility rates and population doubling time

	Fertility rate (births per woman)	Doubling time (years)
Taiwan	1.6	66
Cuba	1.8	72
Sri Lanka	2.3	49
Chile	2.6	44
Turkey	3.6	32
Cambodia	4.6	27
Congo	5.6	28
Libya	6.4	21
Kenya	6.5	19
Yemen	7.7	20
World		**57**

Source: Population Reference Bureau, 1993

has grown to more than one billion in 1993 from 600 million in 1980. Their numbers are projected to reach 1.5 billion by the year 2010.

The population size may end up about one-third larger years after a country has settled at the replacement rate of fertility. The example of China may be cited: Even though it cut its **fertility rate** to about the replacement rate, China's population will continue to grow. The population momentum has an easily understood consequence in the time it takes for population to double. Table 4-2 presents this doubling time, given current fertility rates, for a sample of LDCs.

The projected population increases appear ominous, especially when presented concretely as the number of years for population to double. Fortunately, these increases are mitigated by the dramatic drop in fertility rates in recent years. Even as the drops are expected to continue, birth rates are high and sometimes even rising. While each woman will have fewer children, women of childbearing age constitute a high percentage of total population. The fertility rate in LDCs dropped from 6.0 births per woman in 1965–70 to 4.2 in 1985 and is projected to drop to 3.5 by 1995. To evaluate these numbers, note

that the magic number for stabilizing the population level is supposed to be 2.1 births per woman. The significant decline in fertility rates from the mid-1970s to the early 1990s is highlighted for a broad range of LDCs (see Robey et al, 1993). The numbers in Table 4-3 are obtained from periodic World Fertility Surveys conducted first in 1972 and again in 1984. These surveys for forty-four developing countries are buttressed by some national surveys. Among the most populous countries, the decline in China and Indonesia are particularly notable.

EXPLAINING FERTILITY RATES

We now turn to study the determinants of fertility, the key component of population growth that can be influenced by policy. Before rushing to suggest policy prescriptions, one must first understand the body of theory that aims to explain fertility. Such theories date back from classical times. Modern theories offer far more hope since they postulate that population growth is not endogenous, but can be controlled by appropriate policy. The competing modern explanations provide divergent implications for policy based on structuralist or

Table 4-3 Fertility decline in LDCs

	Mid '70s	Early '90s
Latin America		
Colombia	4.6	3.8
Dominican Republic	5.5	3.3
Paraguay	6.8	4.6
Africa		
Cameroon	6.2	5.9
Kenya	8.2	5.3
Egypt	5.2	4.5
Asia		
Pakistan	6.2	5.1
Thailand	4.5	2.1

Source: Robey, et. al., 1993

neoclassical views. The various explanations are detailed in the following:

1. The classical explanation for population growth was the **Malthusian mechanism** postulated in the late eighteenth century. In earlier times it appeared that societies passively allowed their numbers to increase, so that population was limited mainly by the availability of food. This naturalist explanation implies that population will tend to expand (geometrically) up to the point of mere subsistence. The dismal consequence is that per capita income remains stagnant forever. This pessimistic vision may indeed have been accurate for large parts of the underdeveloped world, including India and China, until quite recently. Any increase in output inevitably prompted a spurt in population due to increased birth rates and declining mortality rates. Reproductive behavior became instilled in culture and tradition. Ecological conditions were also such as to favor large families, since family wealth was tied to the benefits of childrens' labor and the support they provided in old age.

2. Modern theories of fertility snap the automatic connection between increased output and population growth. Now the fertility rate is seen to depend on various exogenous variables, some of which are controllable by appropriate policy. Thus the theoretical controversy about fertility has a counterpart in policy debates. The main contenders are cultural determinants of fertility versus a neoclassical approach that emphasises that parents are rational actors in deciding how many children they want. Since these preferences are essentially fixed, changes in the demand for children derive mainly from changes in opportunities or technology. Such opportunities include information about contraception or the costs and benefits of having or curtailing births. The alternative view is that preferences can change drastically over a short period of time.

The worldwide push for **family planning** began in the 1950s. This approach originally focused on the supply side, assuming that families wanted to have fewer children, they just did not know how. This may be characterized as a technocratic or logistical effort to moderate fertility rates. Many LDCs used national and international funds to publicize the benefits of smaller families and the facts about birth control, and to distribute the physical means such as contraceptives, clinics, and so on, to reduce the birth rate. While worldwide results generally have been modest, a notable exception is Indonesia's successful program, which drastically reduced fertility rates in the crowded islands of Java and Bali. (See the case study on page 88.)

Some evidence in support of the family planning approach was cited in the 1984 *World Development Report*. Detailed, up-to-date monitoring is done by the Population Council and the UN Population Fund. Forty years of efforts in over 100 LDCs has provided a wealth of experience and data about family planning programs. The performance of all these countries' programs can be rated from good to almost nonexistent across various groups of countries. The success record presented here is just a broad generalization, which is, of course, subject to many individual exceptions.

Good	Fair	Poor	Nonexistent
Asia	Latin America	Sub-Saharan Africa	Rich Arab countries

The family planning approach has now broadened its focus from merely reducing the gap between achieved and desired births to actually influencing the desired level. Contrary to the neoclassical presumption, preferences are neither immutable nor adequate as a characterization of the various motivations that move human behavior. Instead, Pollack and Watkins (1993) point out that ideas, aspirations, and attitudes are all important. And these are determined by social factors. Moreover, abrupt changes in the **cultural environment** can affect individual behavior. One need look no further than the remarkable change in attitudes toward cigarette smoking in the United States. In one short decade smoking went from being chic to quite the opposite. It is

Analysis: Demand for children as an economic good

Neoclassical economics analyzes the **demand for children** as well as other goods in the consumption bundle of parents. The impact of income depends on whether children are considered normal or inferior goods. Demand for inferior goods falls when income rises. A glance at the data on fertility rates reveals that richer people (and countries) tend to have fewer children. Yet it would be hasty to conclude that children are inferior goods.

Figure 4-4 shows how demand for children is the net result of both an **income** and **substitution effect.** If children are a normal good, an increase in parents' income from *A* to *B* would increase the number of children demanded from *C* to *D*. The higher income is shown by an outward shift of the budget line, which becomes tangent to a higher utility curve. Separately, if the opportunity cost of having children rises, the budget line becomes flatter. This higher price for children leads households to substitute other goods for children. It is possible that the positive income effect may be swamped by the negative substitution effect. The combined effect would be a drop in the number of children desired from *C* to *E*. Note that the substitution effect does not always overwhelm the income effect. For example, in recent years the rising prosperity in some of eastern China has raised the net birth rate due to a strong income effect.

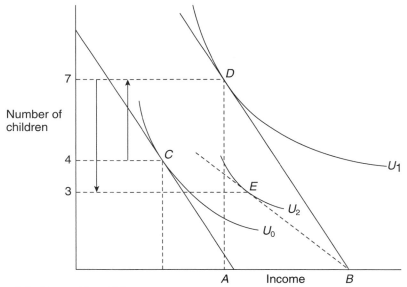

Figure 4-4   *Demand for children*

Casual observation may confirm that the high cost of child raising is a major deterrent to having more children. The most prominent component of this cost is not the direct financial cost; instead it is the opportunity cost of a mother's time spent on child raising. The fertility rate is observed to drop as mothers become more educated. In a cost/benefit calculus, LDC families used to have many children as a form of insurance benefit. But as infant mortality has declined in recent decades, there is less need to have extra children to ensure that some will survive.

quite implausible that this behavioral change was caused mainly by changes in costs and benefits or even the information about smoking.

Culture is the codification of rules of behavior that serves to reduce the domain of choice. A perfectly good reason for this is the operation of **bounded rationality,** as expounded by the Nobel laureate economist Herbert Simon. Instead of computing every decision every time from first principles, the individual can just follow the rules of thumb previously established by society. Thus culture defines the boundary between choice and non choice behavior. But culture itself may change by the diffusion of ideas. This process may be done by opinion leaders or trendsetters, who are perhaps influenced by exposure to other groups. The broadened role of family planning can be construed as a kind of cultural policy.

The mixed record of family planning efforts around the world may appear somewhat puzzling. If such policies are indeed so beneficial, why are they not adopted more enthusiastically? Real success only occurs when the skills of sociologists, publicists, and marketing people are added to the previous technocratic approach. Moreover, the effect of opportunities and preferences are found to be intertwined. Expanding the opportunity for birth control will have no relevance if fertility is not a choice variable. Likewise, fertility choice has no relevance if the techniques of birth control are unknown or unavailable. If some find it hard to believe that fertility was ever outside the calculus of choice, consider this recent interview with a woman in Mali who has heard about the contraceptive pill but has not used it.

Q: . . . how many children more would you like to have?

A: Ah! That is for God to decide.

Q: You yourself, how many would you like to have in your whole life?

A: I don't know the number . . . It's when God stops my births.

Q: How many boys and how many girls would you like to have?

A: It's God that gives me children, since it is God that gives or not. You can't make a choice about children.

Source: Pollack & Watkins, 1993

This interview, which is by no means atypical, shows how the rational actor concept must be limited to within the domain of choice. Then the neoclassical approach certainly has a role.

3. By the 1970s an explicit economic explanation was developed to explain choices regarding fertility. Instead of assuming that families will automatically have fewer children if only they could, the focus was turned to the demand for children based on the costs and benefits facing the parents.

The **Human Capital model** was developed by T. W. Schultz, Gary Becker, and others at the University of Chicago. A landmark conference on new economic approaches to fertility in 1972 laid the theoretical foundations that later had a significant influence on development practice. The crucial insight is that number of children is a choice amenable to microeconomic analysis in the same way as any choice subject to given constraints. Household decision makers (parents) make the fertility and even mortality (through health) choices by weighing the pros and cons of having a child. The demand for children is, in general, a function of income and relative prices.

Effect of Market Failures

Within the human capital framework, various market failures may be seen to affect fertility. For instance, even capital market imperfections can have an indirect effect on increasing desired fertility. Many LDC households do not have an easily accessible method for savings, especially in remote areas, so the most convenient means to provide for old age support is through investment in children. Thus, even rudimentary arrangements for social security can noticeably affect fertility. Also, if children start going to school, the benefit to parents of their children's labor is reduced. Then parents begin to view children less as investments than as consumption goods; quality is substituted for sheer quantity of children. For example, having just one child that goes to college is preferred to five that remain illiterate. Rising family incomes prompt increased expenditures on health, nutrition, education, and so on. In sum, demand for children declines with development. This causal relationship from level of development to slower population growth can explain why the birth rate eventually falls in the demographic transition.

Another kind of market failure arises when individual costs and benefits diverge from social costs and benefits. Then measures to bring down the birth rate run into the **free-rider problem,** which occurs when an individual gains from an action where society largely bears the burden. Despite being aware of the social consequences, individuals are prompted to say: "Even if I behave responsibly, others will not. They will have extra children, while I'll be stuck with the bill. So I might as well go ahead and have more kids of my own." This logic applies to other individuals as well. So everybody tends to have more children even though everybody loses in the end. Figure 4-5 depicts the benefits and costs in the two situations: where the costs of extra children are just private costs and where the full social cost is considered.

China has attempted to eliminate free riders by guaranteeing that the childbearing restraint will be forced on everybody else. In effect, the right social decision is made by forcing the individual costs to equal social costs. China has implemented this by raising the individual cost of having extra children through user costs of public services or fines. Singapore focuses more on raising benefits to families that choose to have fewer children.

These arguments blame the excessive fertility choice on two market failures—the lack of information in developing countries and the free-rider problem. A third possible market failure is the lack of a readily accessible method for storing household savings. Then parents may choose to have more children as a form of saving. If the

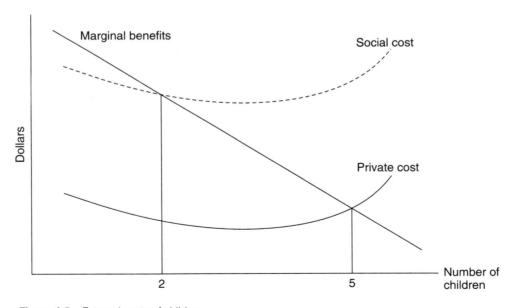

Figure 4-5 *External costs of children*

long-term capital market is imperfect or nonexistent, children appear to be the most convenient investment. Thus individual decisions that appear quite rational in the highly constrained LDC context, can result in bad social choices. Given all these plausible structural explanations, the neoclassical model of rational choice nevertheless remains a useful framework for organizing our theoretical thoughts.

The past forty years of population control efforts have taught us several important lessons. Most significantly, the old Malthusian mechanism of endogenous population growth has broken down for most parts of the world. Currently, population growth is seen to depend on variables that are more or less controllable. While the family planning approach succeeds on occasion, one reliable mechanism for reducing fertility appears to be a rise in per capita incomes. This process, however, may operate too slowly while population spurts sharply during the demographic transition. Thus population control remains a continuing problem for most LDCs. This requires a wide range of efforts that influence the family's demand for children and women's opportunities.

The Crucial Role of Women

In the area of family and fertility choices, the crucial importance of the **women's role** is obvious. Women must be seen as actors in this crucial decision, not merely as a means to an end in the top-down approach that has dominated in the past. Various Third World surveys establish that as many as 40–75% of women of childbearing age desire to have no more children—except in Africa and the Middle East. In certain countries 20–30% prefer to postpone pregnancy, if they could, by a year or more. Furthermore, in almost all these countries, the number of women who want no more children exceeds those using some form of contraception. Such an unmet need supports the supply side argument that lack of information and means is a significant factor explaining high birth rates. This variable is clearly most important among the direct influences on fertility:

- Contraceptive use

- Marriage age

- Spacing between children

- Abortion

The recent experience in the Cameroons is instructive. Like other sub-Saharan African countries, its fertility rate in 1990 was at a high level of 5.8 births per woman. This was down from the even higher rate of 6.4 in 1978. During the boom years of high petroleum prices, this country actually subsidized larger families. The subsequent austerity required the ending of these subsidies. Many families continue to prefer many children, and half of all women marry before their nineteenth birthday. Still, about 1/8th of the women in a 1991 survey said that they wished to have no more children—after already having four or five. If just these married women had access to contraception, the fertility rate would instantly drop to 5.2 (see Populi, Sept. 1993). Many other women want to wait at least two years between children. Satisfying this demand would mean an increase in contraceptive use from 16% to 38%. All of these are softer alternatives to the harsh imperative of "have fewer children": delayed marriage, greater spacing between children, and influencing parents after they already have many children.

Among the indirect influences on fertility are womens' education, family wealth, and cultural/religious beliefs. The level of women's education, in particular, is found to be crucial in limiting births. Education may serve to empower women in general. Even within the narrow domain of the family there can be conflicting interests since women bear far more of the burden of childbearing while men enjoy more of the benefit. Education may also raise womens' awareness of family costs and benefits. Alternatively, the costs and benefits themselves

Table 4-4 Correlation between basic education and population growth

	Population growth rate 1970–80	Per capita GNP growth
Female school enrollment rates	–0.31	+0.49
Literacy rate	–0.47	+0.54

may change as women get educated, as was analysed using the tools of neoclassical economics.

Cross-country evidence for a sample of ninty-four countries shows a negative correlation between population growth and female school enrollment rates for 10–14 year-olds. Table 4-4 is from Rosenzweig.

The educational variables also display a strong positive correlation with per capita GNP growth. Note again that correlation does not indicate causality or its direction. While education may cause lower fertility rates and higher economic growth, it's also true that higher income growth leads to increased education. This two-way causality is likely to be marked with respect to literacy rates in general, but the role of female education is specifically stressed. A study in Indonesia provides more details about this effect. A basic education of girls for just six years does not reduce fertility by much. But education to the ninth grade has a significant impact—most directly by delaying the marriage age by 2.2 years (McMahon and Boediono 1992).

CASE STUDY: INDONESIA'S SUCCESSFUL FAMILY PLANNING PROGRAM

Over twenty years ago the Indonesian government became persuaded that population control would be a critical component of its development strategy. This was a major departure from the thinking of the previous president, Sukarno, who favored a large population for nationalistic reasons. The Suharto regime initiated a family planning program in the face of religious opposition rooted in the majority of the population, which is Moslem. Given these inauspicious initial conditions, it was a pleasant surprise that the program has been so successful as to serve as a model for others in the developing world.

Starting from 1970 Indonesia's fertility rate has fallen from 5.6 births per woman to 3.0 in 1991, a decline of some 45%. This may indeed be attributed to the family planning effort since contraceptive use has risen from 10% to about 50% over this period. This is likely to rise further, so that in fifteen years, the birth rate is targeted to drop to the replacement level of 2.1—eventually leading to ZPG or zero population growth.

Indonesia's achievement is remarkable since it occurred largely without the coercion that marked the other prominent population control success story, that of China. In the early years there was indeed some pressure by overeager officials aiming to reach targets. They organized safaris of health workers who raided remote villages to force contraceptive use on an unprepared population. To a much larger extent, however, the program has accentuated the positive: The benefits accruing to "a small, happy, and prosperous family." This has been a massive exercise in public persuasion and communication that worked to influence the demand side. This stands in contrast to the neoclassical paradigm that assumes that preferences are fairly fixed and unchangeable. Instead, much is owed to the disciplines of mass communication and marketing. The minister of population, Suyono, has a doctorate in sociology with a specialization in communications.

The special design features of this program include many elements of what is known as KAP (knowledge, attitudes, and practise).

1. The program aimed at persuasion and communication. Since a large fraction of the population was then illiterate, this required a vast multimedia public relations campaign. Influential people in the community, especially the Moslem clergy, were drawn in. Once they were convinced, they have continued the work apart from the government.

2. It specifically targets younger women. The marriage age was raised from 18 to 22 years, and from 1994 the minimum education requirement has been raised from 6 to 9 years. The aim is to delay the start of new families by getting women to work or stay in school so as to delay the start of family. Young couples are also encouraged to have a "honey-year"—like an extended honeymoon—before they take on family burdens by having their first child.

3. There is a major expansion of trained midwives who serve multiple roles—mainly as obstetricians, but also as family planning advisors and promoters of womens' health in general. Significantly, these are women who eliminate the inhibitions of dealing with doctors, who are mostly male.

4. As noted earlier, the program does accentuate the positive. It relies to a small extent on providing material incentives to reduce family size. Like in neighboring Singapore, civil servants are rewarded if they have three or less children, while farmers are also offered appropriate benefits.

5. The program utilizes a range of contraceptive methods without emphasizing any single one: pills, IUDs, implants, condoms, and sterilization. The latest technology is the drug Norplant, which is implanted beneath the skin on the arm. This prevents pregnancy for up to five years and can be removed if desired.

It is just as important to examine the features not emphasized by the program. First, condoms are less popular than in other comparable programs due to a social stigma that associates condoms with illicit sex and prostitution. The program focuses on the family in family planning. Issues such as teenage sex or AIDs prevention remain outside the program, even though these are becoming a growing concern. Finally, in sharp contrast to China, abortion is illegal except in certain cases involving the health of the pregnant woman. Despite all this, an estimated million abortions do take place annually. The overall lesson is that attention paid to social, cultural, and religious concerns has contributed to the program's success.

A related lesson of the Indonesian experience is the idea that economics is not the sole determinant of behavior. A significant fraction, 22%, of the people practicing contraception were willing to pay for it at private clinics. Such self-reliance, or *mandiri*, is partly explained by suspicion about the government and partly by the psychological notion that people value things more when it costs them rather than receiving benefits for free. But there is a more general lesson for development. By analogy with immunization programs, which similarly provide both private and social benefits, it is not inevitable that government must provide all public goods. Once people become convinced of the private benefits, they will choose to participate themselves. Social and cultural constraints will adjust accordingly, albeit slowly. Such changes can be expedited through an integrated social/political program, not just by economic programs that insert the correct incentives by getting prices right.

SUMMARY

Population has an obvious and critical impact on development. An increased population level implies a smaller per-person share of a given output. Or population growth may influence the growth rate of output. An emerging concern is about the imbalance between a growing population and limited resources, or the environment in general. The rate at which exhaustible resources become depleted depends on the combined effect of population growth, income growth, and the intensity of resource usage. Thus long-term sustainability of growth depends on population control as well as technological advances that economize on resource usage. A minority view challenges the standard conclusion that population growth is necessarily detrimental. It argues that population pressures may instead serve to stimulate technical progress.

The chapter enumerates salient facts about population growth and its global effects. For individual countries, population growth depends on migration as well as birth and death rates. In modern times the last two variables have changed in such a way as to cause a demographic transition with an unprecedented acceleration of population growth rates. The consequent spurt in population levels exerts enormous demands on developmental resources. It also sets up a population momentum as female reach childbearing age a generation later. Since the age profile is predetermined, the main controllable factor in birth rates is the fertility rate.

Population control policies must focus accordingly on the fertility rate, or number of children born to each woman. Various theories aim to explain fertility, each with its own implications for policy. The family planning approach assumes that a lack of contraceptives or information causes achieved births to exceed the family's desired number of births. A cultural approach argues that desires are importantly influenced by social mores, which can be changed by some kind of cultural policy.

By contrast, the neoclassical school deems that parental demand for children is determined by the usual calculus of costs and benefits as for any good. In backward economies children serve as a form of investment and social security for old age. In more advanced economies, children are viewed as consumption goods. While increasing per capita income is an important variable that acts to decrease the demand for children, this effect takes too long to be relied upon. Instead, government may have a role if there's a divergence between private versus social costs and benefits. The example of Indonesia shows that government's role is less to provide birth control means than to persuade and support individual decisions to act in the common interest.

KEY TERMS

Population growth rate	Demographic transition	Human Capital model
Population size	Dependency ratio	Free rider problem
Population density	Population pyramid	Diffusion of knowledge
Resource depletion	Population momentum	Womens' role
Technical diffusion	Fertility rate	Demand for children
Technical innovation	Malthusian mechanism	Income effect
Birth rate	Family planning approach	Substitution effect
Death rate	Cultural environment	
Migration rate	Bounded rationality	

PART II

GROWTH THEORY

The arguments so far have made clear that the ultimate goal of economic development is distinct from the purely quantitative idea of growth. Nonetheless, growth is seen as a necessary complement to development process, which makes it imperative to study growth theory. A series of models is presented that focuses just on output growth while abstracting from all the complexity associated with development, a broadly defined concept. Over the years, a progression of theoretical ideas sought to pinpoint the essential ingredients for growth. All these models share a basic similarity—the sources of growth are encompassed within a production function framework:

$$\text{Growth of INPUTs} \xrightarrow{\text{cause}} \text{OUTPUT growth}$$

The best known growth models are discussed in chapters 5 and 6. Their main characteristic features may be summarized as:

The earliest growth model of classical economics was quite pessimistic about prospects for sustained long-run growth. This is a consequence of the assumption of strictly limited natural resources. By contrast, modern growth models are much more hopeful since they are based on factors that can be augmented rather than limited factors such as land or natural resources. They also differ in assuming that population will not grow inexorably to defeat the goal of raising per capita living standards.

The early growth models of the modern epoch may be considered structuralist as each highlights critical constraints in the LDC context. The Lewis model follows its classical roots in focusing on the low productivity of agricultural labor. It argues that this chronically underutilized resource in LDCs can be put to productive use in a capitalist sector that serves as the focus of capital accumulation. More generally, the Lewis model highlights the dualism of LDC economies as two or more sectors, such as agriculture and industry are segregated structurally. The Harrod-Domar model singles out capital as the crucial missing component. Growth is attributed primarily to capital accumulation, while other variables are relegated to a secondary status.

Neoclassical growth models since the 1960s dispense with the special constraints assumed by the structuralist school. The original Solow model aimed to explain the growth of industrial countries with well-functioning markets. Thus no factor can be singled out as uniquely responsible for growth; instead the various factors can substitute for each other within a production function. As the economy grows and changes, input prices are continually adjusted by market forces. Production techniques adapt to the changing availability of input factors. Growth can proceed without the need for government interventions in the markets for labor or capital.

	Circa	Characteristic features
Classical		
Ricardian	1800	Constrained natural resources
		Unchecked labor growth
Lewis	1950	Surplus agricultural labor shifted to industry
Modern		
Harrod-Domar	1940	Capital accumulation
Solow	1960	Substitutable factors
		Exogenous technical change
Latest variant	1980	Endogenous technical change

The most recent theoretical focus is on building purer neoclassical models to remove ad hoc assumptions incorporated in the original Solow model. They dispense with the rather simplistic saving function assumed. Instead, they derive choices about production, consumption, and saving more fundamentally within a framework of intertemporal choice. They also aim to explain the process of technical advance that was previously assumed to spring from random exogenous forces. Recent growth models aim to explain such innovations as arising endogenously from investments in human capital or increasing scale economies.

Chapter 5

Classical Growth Models

RICARDIAN GROWTH

The first theoretical model that aimed to explain economic growth of countries was developed by David Ricardo, Thomas Malthus, and Adam Smith in the late eighteenth century. This classical model has two essential ingredients.

1. **Natural resources** are considered the main constraint to growth. This classical idea, the **Ricardian model,** was particularly appropriate in Britain, which is an island with limited cultivable land. The most productive land is brought into cultivation first, then the lesser productive, and so on. The marginal productivity of labor declines as more land is brought into production. In contrast, most modern theorists implicitly believe that technology will "bail us out" as we approach the limits of natural resources. Recently, some economists have returned to Ricardian thinking. For example, following the 1973 oil crisis, the idea of limited natural resources made a reappearance.

2. The other main ingredient is the **Malthusian idea** that population expands endogenously with output. Whenever output grows, population also will expand until average consumption drops to the level of subsistence. In other words, whenever an economy produces too much, people will procreate to expand their numbers until they revert to subsistence level (the level necessary for sheer physiological reproduction). Thus, over the long run, standards of living are doomed to stagnate. For this reason economics used to be labeled the dismal science. This theory is not just an antiquated relic, irrelevant for current purposes. It appears to operate even in modern times in parts of Asia and Africa where population has grown at roughly the same rate as output. Thus the per capita consumption in these countries shows no strong trend over the long term, staying at a level close to subsistence. China's growth experience, even up to the middle of the twentieth century, might also be explained by this model.

These two assumptions are an integral part of the classical growth model. The **production function** indicates that output Y is a function of capital K, labor L, and land D. Capital and labor are assumed to grow endogenously, while land is fixed in supply.

$$Y = fn\,(K, L, D) \quad \text{where}: \frac{dY}{dL} > 0, \quad \frac{d^2Y}{dL^2} < 0$$

Note that increases in labor L lead to increases in output Y (the first derivative is positive), but as labor keeps growing, the increments to output are at a decreasing rate (the second derivative is negative), since the labor must work with a fixed land area. Inevitably the increased supply of labor results in a diminishing marginal product.

The major implication of the classical growth model is depicted in Figure 5-1 of output with respect to labor. Over time, output expansion slows due to **diminishing marginal productivity** of labor on the fixed land. Whereas output growth slows, the minimum consumption required for subsistence increases proportionately to the labor force. Assume an expanding economy is initially at L_1, Y_1. The distance between Y_1

and Y_2 is the surplus split between landowners and capitalists. This profit encourages capitalists to accumulate and invest more, which induces technological advance. More labor is employed, but the extra output increasingly goes for subsistence. Ultimately profits also are squeezed, so investment ceases. Then all of the surplus accrues as rent to the owners of the scarce factor, land. Thus growth of the economy can cease even before we get to point Z, the **stationary state,** where the output line and **subsistence consumption** line intersect.

Classical economics envisaged an absolute limit to per capita output growth. Even if technological advance did take place, this would shift the entire curve upward but the economy would still reach a stationary state, albeit at a higher output level Z. Given its assumptions, the Ricardian model has a clear implication: In the long run, labor's per capita consumption must revert to subsistence level.

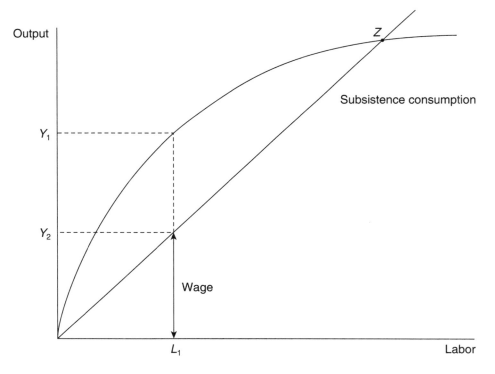

Figure 5-1 *Classical growth model*

The classical pessimism is not easily removed. Even if there is another sector not subject to diminishing returns, there is still no escaping the dismal stationary state. A manufacturing sector that does not seem inherently limited might seem to offer hope. Yet, overall growth still grinds to a halt due to the diminishing marginal productivity of increasingly more labor working the fixed area of land. As the demand for food rises with population, its price will rise relative to manufactured goods. And since the subsistence wage must be paid in food, manufacturing profits will be squeezed until investment ceases.

Food sector	~ diminishing marginal productivity on land
Manufacturing sector	~ constant returns to scale

One possibility to escape from classical stagnation still remains. If food can be imported at a fixed price, the industrial sector (which does not suffer from diminishing returns) may expand essentially without limit to raise the country's standard of living. Thus, strictly speaking, the Ricardian model applies only to closed economies, or better yet, large economies where the influence of the rest of the world must necessarily be small. Two current examples as India and China.

Clearly, the classical projections run contrary to the experience of modern economic growth (past the point of extensive growth mentioned in chapter 2). Perhaps the most important reason for this happy circumstance is that the Malthusian mechanism no longer applies. Population does not automatically grow as a consequence of income growth. As we saw in chapter 4, rising income levels usually lower the demand for children, not raise it. Another important way to escape the bare subsistence level of the stationary state is for agricultural productivity to continually grow at a rate faster than population growth. In other words, agricultural

productivity and population run a race in which the former wins. Empirically, such a process appears to be a precondition for sustained industrial growth to occur.

Once again, note that the classical model does not rule out the possibility of **technical progress.** It just maintains that such progress cannot exceed the pace of population expansion in the long run. Adam Smith noted three different channels for progress.

1. The expansion of markets allowed more specialization, and thereby economies of scale. This was based on the rather obvious benefits of the Commercial Revolution that sparked England's economic progress in the seventeenth and eighteenth centuries.

2. The increased specialization of function could provide a slow, but steady, source of improvements.

3. Irregular spurts of scientific and technical advance, such as the steam engine and iron production, were certainly important contributors to economic growth.

All three modes of advance are visible in the context of today's developing countries. For instance, the extension of markets, both domestic and internationally, is a stylized fact of the structural transformation. Large discontinuous advances in technology also are evident; but in the modern context such technological leaps most often come from the already advanced countries. Also evident in the LDCs is a gradually increasing specialization of function that leads to a more professional attitude at work. The important difference in modern times is that these very channels of technical advance can add up to more than the rate of population growth.

THE LEWIS MODEL

A prominent structuralist model of the development economics school is the **Lewis model** of surplus labor dating from the early 1950s. This model makes the classical assumption that limited land causes diminishing marginal product for agricultural labor. It discards the Malthusian assumption that population will grow endogenously to reach the limit of food production. Instead, surplus labor can be diverted to a capitalist sector that accumulates capital to allow unlimited growth. The latter sector is usually interpreted as an industrial sector that does not suffer from diminishing returns.

The Lewis model (1954) was based on the observation that most LDCs have a conspicuous "reserve army of the underemployed" that can be put to work in a dynamic new sector to generate growth. The **underemployment** in LDCs is quite different from the familiar unemployment of DCs. Even though most people in LDCs appear to be doing something, they are working far below their potential. Unemployment, per se, is unlikely since LDCs typically lack welfare or other safety nets. In such a context, a person who is literally unemployed probably would starve. But the underemployed in LDCs do manage to survive somehow—implying that they must not be totally without income.

Underemployment is defined more precisely as a low marginal product of labor (MP_L). For the extreme case, where $MP_L = 0$, an underemployed worker may be removed from the labor force without any drop in output whatsoever.

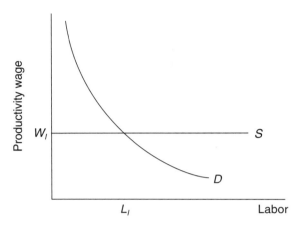

Figure 5-3   Industrial sector: labor market

Lewis notes that the agricultural sector has lots of such **surplus labor.** When the marginal worker is transferred from agriculture to the more productive industrial sector, aggregate output is bound to increase. This transfer will continue over time as industrial demand for labor expands to soak up the surplus labor.

Figure 5-2 depicts productivity, wages, and employment in the traditional agricultural sector. The prevailing wage W_A exceeds the marginal product of labor when the number of workers in agriculture is L_A. All those whose wage exceeds marginal product are surplus labor and could be transferred to the industrial sector without any rise in wages. The flat labor supply to the industrial sector is shown in Figure 5-3. Industrial demand for labor has the normal downward slope like any other demand curve.

The constant wage in agriculture is termed the **subsistence wage.** This wage rate does not need to be precisely the minimum required for physiological subsistence. It may be fixed at some higher accustomed standard of living called an institutional wage. The important point is that this wage level is not set by the precepts of neoclassical economics. Given these structuralist assumptions, the Lewis model gives rise to certain implications that can be seen in Figure 5-4. This

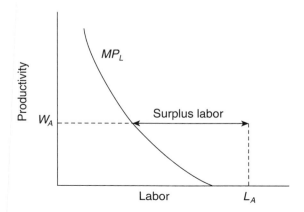

Figure 5-2   Agricultural sector: labor market

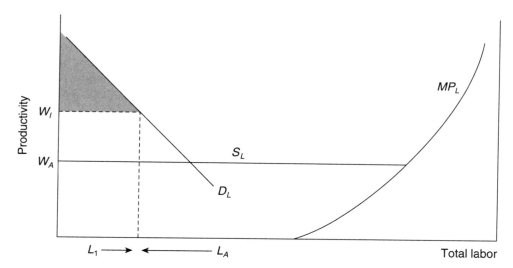

Figure 5-4 *Lewis model*

figure is constructed by flipping agriculture's labor curve and attaching it to the right side of the industrial sector curve. We can see how labor employed in industry L_I and agricultural labor L_A add up to the country's total labor force. As industry expands, wage remains constant until all the surplus labor is absorbed; only then will wage begin to rise for the whole economy.

Perhaps the most important contribution of the Lewis model is its elaboration of a **dual economy.** An economy may be split into various sectors that are somewhat insulated from each other. For example, factor prices of labor or capital may differ significantly across sectors. Originally Lewis postulated a modern capitalist sector distinct from a family-run sector. These days the sectors are loosely associated with industry and agriculture respectively—even though the capitalist sector may include commercial agriculture, while family may include urban inform sector industry. This idea may be generalized to modern and traditional sectors, variously defined.

The Lewis model implies that LDC growth is indeed quite hopeful. Industrialists are expected to make ample profits (shaded area above the cost line in Figure 5-4). This encourages them to accumulate capital and expand industry so the demand for labor increases. The model implies a steady accumulation of capital, at least until surplus labor is exhausted. After that, the growth process reverts to essentially neoclassical growth. So long as the wage rate remains low, the capital/labor ratio utilized in industry also remains constant. Thus the rate of return on capital stays high, thereby encouraging continued investment for K accumulation.

Rather strong policy implications follow from the Lewis model.

1. The industrial sector must be especially encouraged, possibly by attracting foreign capitalists who invest in view of the low wage rate. Alternatively the government might intervene to stimulate domestic industry that is initially protected from import competition. In other words, industry could start by *import-substituting-industrialization.*

2. Savings, which provide for investment by capitalists, should be especially encouraged. An important inducement is to assure a

high rate of industrial profit by ensuring that wages indeed remain low, at least until all the surplus labor is consumed. In general terms this is done by extracting resources from the agricultural sector (by taxation or low food prices) and diverting these toward industry. Lewis also explicitly recognized the possibility of state-capitalism, and the state-bearing direct responsibility for investment.

3. To the extent possible, the rate of population growth (and so labor force growth) must be controlled to keep it less than the rate of employment creation by industrial expansion. If labor grows faster than its potential absorption into industry, the turning point of increasing wages or reduced unemployment never will be reached. Note the resemblance with the hopeless race of the classical model in which population grows endogenously to outstrip the rate of agricultural growth.

The Lewis model was particularly appealing in the 1950s in view of the observed labor surplus, combined with the obvious missing component of industrialization in LDCs. By the 1960s, doubts began to arise. Today the model has been largely superseded, but the theoretical legacy of structuralist thinking remains. An invaluable contribution is the idea that LDC economies generally do not have unified markets. Two or more sectors can operate simultaneously under very different conditions in sharp contradiction to the tenets of neoclassical theory.

While structuralist analysis postulates failures in particular markets—as in the Lewis model—the neoclassical assumptions continue to apply elsewhere. Other economists have elaborated a more complete Lewis model, taking into account the endogenous changes in the price of factors, as well as quantities produced by the two sectors. The Lewis model also may be credited as the point of departure for models that explain the labor migration from rural to urban areas. (The Harris-Todaro model is elaborated in chapter 9 on LDC labor markets).

Critique

Any critique of a model is based either on assumptions being false or the model's implications not conforming to reality.

The classical model showed how industrial growth may still not save a country from the stationary state since stagnating agriculture can force up the relative price of food. Then industry would need to pay its workers a rising wage, which would choke profits and stop accumulation. By contrast, the Lewis model implies no significant loss of agricultural output when surplus labor moves away. Food prices remain low, and industry continues to make profits and expand. While Lewis expected no drop in agricultural output, no one anticipated big increases in agricultural productivity either.

The unexpected **Green Revolution** around the 1970s raised the marginal productivity of labor in agriculture as shown in Figure 5.5. This increased wage levels independently of industrial activities. New technology utilized new seeds, fertilizers, pesticides, and multiple-cropping to effectively relax the constraint of limited land. The Lewis model had led to an attitude of benign neglect of agriculture. The new lesson learned from this period was that agricultural development could not be ignored. Agricultural health appears to be an essential precondition for industrial development. Even worse was an active bias against agriculture that led to taxation of this sector with the proceeds transferred to industry. (Chapter 14 notes that such taxation stands in sharp contrast to subsidization of the agricultural sector in the developed economies.)

The historical experience of industrial growth shows that even after two generations of development this sector has not significantly used up the surplus labor available in LDCs. Even as industry grew—quite successfully in some cases—the demand for labor increased very little to D'. People did migrate to the cities as implied by the Lewis model, but not all ended up with industrial jobs there. An unfortunate consequence of such

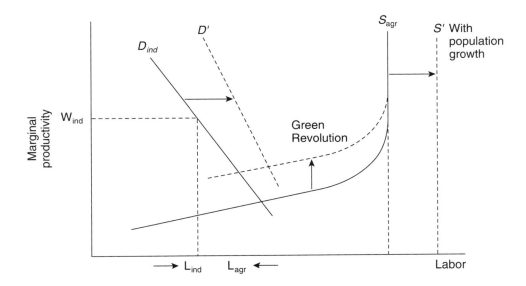

Figure 5-5 *Dynamics of the Lewis model*

a pattern of growth is manifested in the excessive urbanization of all developing countries. The rate of *labor absorption* in other production activities falls short of its release from agriculture. The root cause may be the use of laborsaving technological methods for various reasons. As governments aimed to encourage industry, they often overdid the incentives to investment. The artificially-cheapened capital induced firms to use excessively capital-intensive techniques. Moreover, industry based on technology imported from the developed countries usually is laborsaving and thus inappropriate for the LDCs with surplus labor. (We will study this tendency for excessive capital intensity in greater detail in chapter 10 on technology.)

Lewis took a rather benign view of the dual economy. But the resulting worsening of the income distribution is now increasingly viewed as a serious problem for development. It was anticipated that inequality would follow a U curve pattern over time as the industrial sector started its expansion from a tiny base (see chapter 3 on inequality). At the beginning everyone starts out

approximately equal—equally poor—receiving just a subsistence wage. As industry expands, so do profits of capitalists; thus income inequality is bound to worsen initially. Ultimately, when all surplus labor is absorbed, equality can improve as wages finally begin to edge up and capitalist profits are squeezed. Putting their faith in this model, developing countries started out with a generous tolerance for a transitory inequality. But bitter experience has exposed the generally disappointing employment record of industry. Not only was the return to equality delayed, the extent of inequality was exacerbated by widening wage differentials.

The Lewis model assumed that the industrial wage would (and should) remain a bit higher than the subsistence wage in agriculture, such that:

$$W_{ind} - W_{agr} = \text{Wage gap}$$

A small wage differential (shown in Figure 5-4) is needed to compensate for the higher cost of living in cities, especially since the migrant loses all the ancillary services available in the village. But in empirical reality, the **wage gap** has varied dramatically over time and across countries. During the 1960s and early 1970s, industrial wages soared in relation to agricultural wages in much of the developing world, so the wage gap widened well before full employment was reached. Various explanations (detailed in chapter 9) are offered for this wage gap: (1) The human capital or skill levels of urban labor must be higher than those of their rural counterparts. Yet, even for identical skill categories, the wage gap can be enormous. (2) The urban sector can appropriate more of the national income since labor unions, or urban politics in general, tend to be organized more effectively. (3) Industry tends to have a higher capital intensity, which raises the marginal product of its labor. But this poses a puzzle for neoclassical theory—why should employers agree to raise industrial wages if surplus labor still exists? (4) The latest explanation is that high wages serve to secure a higher level of effort. This efficiency wage hypothesis (elaborated in chapter 9) by Stiglitz and Mazumdar (1976) first noted that labor effort is differentiated even if labor is homogenous. Once employers hire a worker they willingly pay a higher wage to elicit the effort, even if other labor is available to work for less.

Wage differences can be very large, both between the rural and urban sectors, and between organized and traditional sectors. Such dualism can be characterized variously as a dichotomy between rural-urban, agriculture-industry, or traditional-organized. Basically two entirely different kinds of economies are coexisting within the same country. This is in contrast to the standard neoclassical presumption that wages should tend to equalize in coincident labor markets.

Turning now to tests of assumptions in the Lewis model, does agricultural labor really have a zero marginal product or is it just a low marginal product? A zero MP_L means that removing a laborer from the fields will not result in decreased output. Theodore Schultz (University of Chicago) examined this question using data from a historical situation where supposedly a lot of underemployment or surplus labor existed. In India during 1918–19, a significant fraction of the labor force was decimated by an influenza epidemic. Total output declined somewhat, which appears to suggest that MP_L certainly was positive. But this reduced productivity may only have been a short-term disruption effect, since after an adjustment period output recovered to its former level.

In contradiction to the assumption of zero marginal product is the observed rural wage labor in many poor agrarian economies. If there is so much surplus labor, how can a rural proletariat (wage labor) with positive marginal productivity possibly exist? A possible resolution to this puzzle is by carefully defining the marginal product of labor. During the agricultural seasons for sowing and harvesting labor may indeed be scarce, while a surplus exists in the off-seasons. Similar doubts about the definition of MP_L are raised in studies of productivity and farm size. Smaller farms were found to be more productive per acre of land even though they operate at an accounting loss, for example, someone must be getting paid more than his or hers marginal product. Note, however, that such farming typically involves the entire household or extended family. This feature may explain the apparently low MP_L: Women are simultaneously engaged in various family activities such as child care. This kind of unpaid household production tends to be omitted from calculations of output, thus biasing the measures of productivity downward.

In any case, whether the MP_L is low or zero, standard economics has had a hard time explaining why the subsistence wage is higher than MP_L. Instead it appears that such labor is being paid the average product of labor. Since farm production is undertaken by family units, not by profit-maximizing employers, they are bound to have social and family motivations. A subsistence wage greater than MP_L therefore can exist. This is a good example of how strictly neoclassical economics runs into problems if it does not consider unique features of the LDC context.

Alternate growth models aim to highlight other key elements of reality in the developing countries. The Harrod-Domar model, advanced at about the same time, also assumed that capital is the main contributor to growth. The Lewis model can be interpreted as an elaboration of the Harrod-Domar model in a situation of widespread underemployment.

SUMMARY

The classical model explains economic growth from the vantage of economies that are mainly engaged in traditional agricultural production. The two main inputs are land and labor. While land is a fixed factor, labor continues to grow—so its marginal productivity drops. Given the Malthusian assumption that population grows endogenously in step with output growth, the inevitable implication is a stationary state in the long run. Population is expected to continue to grow such that per capita income reverts to the level of mere subsistence. Even in modern times, the very poorest of the LDCs appear to have followed the classical model fairly closely until quite recently.

The Lewis model is classical in many ways, but it has one crucial difference. It drops the Malthusian assumption of endogenous population growth. Instead, population is assumed to grow at some exogenously-given rate. The low marginal productivity of rural labor is now seen in a positive light since it assures a pool of surplus labor that can be diverted to an urban industrial sector. The low wage rate allows industry to make large profits and accumulate more capital for continued expansion. Ultimately, when all the surplus labor is absorbed, wages will begin to rise in both sectors.

The Lewis model may be criticized for various failures in the LDC development experience. Industrial wages are observed to rise even before much rural surplus labor is absorbed. While industrial job creation has been disappointing, the labor migration from rural to urban areas continues. This excessive urbanization has led to a new set of LDC problems. A more serious criticism is directed against this model's implied bias against agriculture and in favor of industry. Such a policy bias has apparently held down overall economic growth in many LDCs. In recent years, policy has been revised to restore incentives to agriculture and stem excessive urbanization. Also, the Lewis model's neglect of the possibility of technical progress in agriculture was confounded by the later spectacular successes of the Green Revolution.

The Lewis model must be credited for recognizing the importance of dualism in developing countries. This generalized phenomenon applies to the agricultural sector, labor markets, and technology, and has major ramifications for equity and growth.

KEY TERMS

Natural resources	Factors of production	Underemployment
Ricardian model	Capital accumulation	Surplus labor
Malthusian idea	Savings function	Subsistence wage
Production function	Intertemporal choice	Dual economy
Inputs	Stationary state	Green Revolution
Output	Subsistence consumption	Labor absorption
Diminishing marginal	Technical progress	Wage gap
productivity	Lewis model	Mazumdar

Chapter 6

Modern Growth Models

The world has now experienced more than three centuries of growth across a wide range of countries and initial conditions. These experiences include the Industrial Revolution in Europe, which started it all, long periods of stagnation as in the protectionist era between the world wars, imperialism and colonialism, episodes of growth based on primary exports (for example, the oil-exporting countries), and most recently, the dramatic growth spurt of the East Asian manufacturing exporters.

The cumulative lessons of history allow us to update growth concepts beyond the classical ideas. Growth theory must relate to the stylized facts of the empirical reality. The critique of classical models already show how a theory stands or falls based on how well it explains the facts of growth experience. But what are the facts? In reality there are widely diverse countries, whose individual experiences are explained by a multitude of variables. The highly abstract growth models are based on a small handful of variables, by contrast, and must be judged by how well they explain the gross stylized facts of growth.

As noted earlier, population does not grow uncontrollably in modern growth. Contrary to the Malthusian assumption, the rate of population growth declines with increases in per capita income, while it may be considered exogenous in the short run. Another gross characteristic is the changing pattern of income distribution. A **stylized fact of growth** over the long run is that the share of national income going to the various factors has remained roughly constant over time—approximately 2/3rd going to labor and 1/3rd to capital.

A final issue is whether the growth rates of various countries tend to converge in the long run. It is apparent that these rates can diverge for substantial intervals. This issue may be split into two parts. One, does convergence actually occur; two, what might explain convergence if it did occur? The **Gershenkron hypotheses** is that relative growth rates depend on the existing technological gap between the countries that developed early and those that lagged behind. Growth models that aim to explain the LDC growth experience therefore must explicitly account for the international context. This element is incorporated in some of the modern endogenous growth models to be examined later.

Whether convergence even exists is an empirical question that can be addressed by examining growth across a diverse group of

Table 6-1 Convergence and divergence in growth rates

Country deciles	1960 income ($1000)	Growth rate of per capita GDP
1	5.5	2.1%
2	3.4	2.3
3	2.0	3.1
4	1.4	2.8
5	1.1	2.7
6	.9	1.6
7	.6	1.4
8	.5	1.3
9	.4	.8
10	.3	1.4

Source: D. Dollar, 1992.

countries. A conditional kind of convergence is observed: Lagging countries can indeed grow at a faster rate, provided they have a minimum capability to access and absorb the knowledge available from more advanced countries. This capability is measured in terms of national expenditures on education, while access depends on the degree of openness. An empirical study by David Dollar (1992) demonstrates this extension to Gershenkron for a cross-section of over 100 countries split into deciles. Ranked at the top are those countries that started their growth process earlier and, therefore, have reached a high level of per capita income. Table 6-1 shows that middle income countries tend to have higher growth rates than high income countries, while the lowest income countries grow at the slowest rate. This explains the stylized fact of the least developed countries (mostly in Africa) also having the lowest growth rates in the world. Meanwhile the newly industrialized countries (NICs, mostly in Asia) are catching up with the advanced countries in terms of per capita income.

HARROD-DOMAR MODEL

Land and agriculture started to lose their predominant economic role once the growth of agriculture forged decisively ahead of population growth. From the era of the Industrial Revolution, as industry provides seemingly unlimited growth based on capital accumulation rather than on limited natural resources, a new view has evolved about the determinants of economic growth. Freed from the constraint of diminishing marginal productivity of limited land, capital is considered the most significant input for increasing output. There is new hope for growth of per capita incomes since an unchecked Malthusian population growth will no longer eat it all up. The Harrod-Domar model of the 1940s incorporated these new elements to generate ever increasing output. The Harrod-Domar model formalizes the two crucial assumptions:

1. Production depends on capital.

$$\Delta Y = \frac{1}{v} \Delta K$$

where $v = \dfrac{\Delta K}{\Delta Y}$ = **Incremental capital output ratio (ICOR)**

2. Capital accumulation depends on income.

Savings $S = s \cdot Y$ where s = savings propensity

The first equation indicates that an increment in the capital stock K generates a given increment to output. The effectiveness of capital is reflected in the ICOR parameter v. For income to grow by 3 units in a country with a characteristic $v = 4$, investment must be 12. Notice that a role for labor is not even mentioned since it is not a limiting constraint. By analogy, note that air is essential for any production, yet its usefulness would be acknowledged only if air were lacking.

The second equation says that capital is accumulated through domestic savings, which is simply a certain fraction, s, of output. The simplifying assumption that investment is funded solely by domestic savings implies: $S = I = \Delta K$. Substituting these factors in the first equation we see that

$$v \, \Delta Y = s \cdot Y$$

Thus, the growth rate of GNP is

$$\boxed{\dfrac{\Delta Y}{Y} = \dfrac{s}{v}}$$

This equation indicates that the higher the savings rate, the greater the growth rate of output generated by productive investment. A high ICOR, on the other hand, reduces the rate of growth, and so on, a lot of investment is needed to achieve a given growth. A small value for v means that the country is an efficient user of capital.

The Harrod-Domar model is used widely as a quick and easy exercise for growth planning. Suppose s and v are known constants, how much investment is needed for a desired amount of economic expansion? Once growth targets are set, planners utilize the country's ICOR to determine the level of investment needed. Note that the ICOR applies marginally to new investments and does not necessarily equal the average COR that applies for the already existing capital stock.

Further elaborations of this theory aim to explain how each variable s or v might be affected by various policy actions.

Critique

Some implications of the Harrod-Domar model appear to conflict with real-world empirical evidence. A major problem is the implication that output must grow at the same rate as capital over the long term. This can be inferred from the fixed relationship between capital and output: $Y = 1/v \; K$. The constant capital/output ratio implies that the percent changes in capital stock and output must be equal. However, for a wide cross-section of LDCs, $\hat{Y} > \hat{K}$. Growth accounting studies find that, roughly, net capital growth is $\hat{K} = 2\%$, while $\hat{Y} = 4.5\%$. Therefore it is invalid for Harrod-Domar to assume that increased capital is the only source, or even the primary source, of growth. Obviously other important sources of growth are subsumed in the parameter v. For example, there can be increments in productive labor, skills, technological improvements, and so on. Studies in the 1960s empirically determined the sources of growth for the United States to be roughly as follows, with the residual attributed to technological progress.

$$\hat{Y} = \text{due to } \hat{K} + \text{due to } \hat{L} + \text{residual}$$
$$4.0\% \;\; = \;\; 1.7\% \;\; + \;\; 1.3\%$$

The Harrod-Domar model has the strong implication that other factors do not matter for growth. At the start of the development epoch following World War II, physical capital was considered particularly scarce in comparison to other factors. But what precisely is meant by "scarcity"? According to basic economics principles, a scarce good is anything that has a positive price. Other factors, such as labor, are also observed to have a positive price, yet physical capital was assumed to be somehow more productive in relation to its price. If all markets operate efficiently, the ratio of marginal productivity of a factor to its price should become equalized, so no factor can be singled out as scarce. Thus the early development economists must have assumed that markets failed to fulfill this condition. Recall Lewis' assumption that labor isn't very productive in relation to its exogenously-set price. Consider a numerical illustration where

$$\frac{MP_K}{P_K} = \frac{9}{\$3} \qquad \frac{MP_L}{P_L} = \frac{2}{\$1}$$

In a normally operating price system, such a situation could not possibly persist. Firms that are able to substitute between the factors, K or L, would increase their demand for capital and thereby raise its price or, equivalently, drop their demand for labor and so depress the wage rate. Eventually the two ratios must be equalized. Any presumption of capital scarcity must be taken as just reflecting some market failure. It has been suggested, for example, that individuals undervalue the benefits from an increased capital stock in contrast to society as a whole, which places a higher value on future output. An alternative explanation is that instead of a scarcity, there is actually a shortage since capital is artificially priced too low.

The Harrod-Domar model also is criticized because its implied growth is seen as inherently unstable. This is in contrast to the stationary state of the classical model. Various economists in the early 1950s worried about the feature of the Harrod-Domar model; though this must be seen as a problem with the model rather than the real world. This problem was easily fixed by the neoclassical model, which dispensed with the unrealistic assumption of a fixed K/L ratio. Once the intensity of factor use is allowed to respond to changes in the scarcity of factors, the indicated instability disappears.

This instability arises from the mismatch between the rates of growth of capital and labor force. Recall that modern growth models differ from the classical model in assuming that L grows exogenously—it is independent of income growth. But how will an annual population growth rate of 3% mesh with a 2% rate of growth of the capital stock? If these two rates diverge, a mismatch must emerge between capital stock and the labor required to run the machines. There is no reason for the labor growth rate to equal output growth s/v, except by coincidence. Thus the L growth must also differ from K growth, causing one of two things to happen: (1) unemployment, or (2) a change in the capital/labor ratio. Such conditions of unbalanced growth should cause chronic cycles.

Growth in the Harrod-Domar model is depicted in Figure 6-1. It is drawn on a per-person basis. (Population and labor force are obviously distinct, yet our analysis proceeds on a per-person rather than per-laborer basis due to the close relationship between these two variables.) The vertical axis may be interpreted as output per worker and the horizontal axis as capital stock per worker: the K/L ratio. The production function shows output increasing linearly with K. Implicitly this assumes that there is unemployed labor sitting around below the point of full employment. There is a fixed relation between labor and machines—for example, one-to-one. Beyond full employment there is no more labor to be matched with additional machines, so output produced levels as shown by the kinked line OY. Savings remains a fraction of such output as indicated by the dotted line OS. This is drawn proportionately below the output curve according to the savings rate, say $s = 20\%$.

Recall that modern growth models assume that labor grows exogenously at a rate $n\%$ per year. For balanced growth, the K/L ratio must remain constant, so growth of the capital stock must not outpace growth of the labor force. Capital also must grow at the same rate n, so investment must be $\Delta K = I = nK$ as indicated by the straight line $I = nK$, along which the K/L ratio remains constant. Also, for equilibrium we must have savings equal investment. Such balanced growth can only occur at point 0 or B. While 0 indicates zero output, an equilibrium at B is also implausible since it lies beyond F, the full employment of labor, implying that a sizable por-

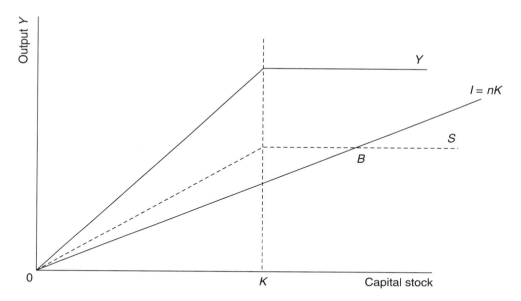

Figure 6-1 *The Harrod-Domar model*

tion of capital is left unused. If savings lie below the required investment, however, the economy will move toward the other equilibrium at 0, which is implausible.

Thus the only way to have stable growth would be if $n v = s$. The investment line must coincide precisely with the (dotted) savings line, which is a very unlikely circumstance. The Harrod-Domar model implies that the growth process must be chronically unstable, but in our experience such crises are not endemic even though labor and capital growth continue at quite different rates. Still, these theoretical difficulties aside, the Harrod-Domar model does provide an approximate picture of the initial growth process when labor is almost a free good. Another structuralist model, which explicitly defines a labor market surplus, is the Lewis model.

The Two-Gap Model

The basic Harrod-Domar model has been extended to the case in which an economy has

access to foreign capital. The foregoing analysis had assumed investment to be financed exclusively from domestic savings. Capital inflows from abroad allow a country to import more than it exports. The **Two-Gap model** basically is similar to the Harrod-Domar model, but makes the further assumption that the investment program requires a minimum import component in the form of machinery or intermediate goods. Thus the growth rate of output can be limited by two distinct constraints: the total amount of capital available for investment or the amount of foreign exchange available for needed imports.

As mentioned before, the early development economics school had a strong belief in structuralist ideas. All sorts of structural constraints were believed to be binding and immutable. One such constraint was the assumption that export revenues could not be increased. Thus, even if domestic savings provide ample capital resources, output growth might be restricted by the lack of foreign exchange for needed imports. Conversely, if a country has ample foreign resources but low domestic savings, growth might be restricted by the low level of total investment.

Let's work out how the output growth rate will be constrained by the smaller of these two gaps. To begin, use the national income identity $Y = C + I + (X - M)$ to get

$$(M - X) = (I - S) \qquad \text{where savings } S = Y - C$$

As an identity this equation is true by definition. But the equality just applies to realized quantities—there's no reason for planned quantities to match since separate sets of people make the decisions regarding investment, savings, export, and import. These people do not tally or coordinate their plans beforehand. Based on the investment requirement, the Harrod-Domar growth rate is limited by the available capital.

$$\boxed{\hat{Y} = s/v}$$

But output may also be constrained by an import requirement. Just as output growth requires investment, it is equally plausible that output growth may require imports in proportion to the output increment: $M = m \, \Delta Y$, with m defined as the propensity to import. Dividing both sides by output Y, we get $M/Y = m \, \Delta Y/Y$. Now the output growth rate, $\Delta Y/Y$, is also seen to depend on the import ratio $r = M/Y$. According to this import requirement, the growth rate is limited to

$$\boxed{\hat{Y} = r/m}$$

So which is it: Does the growth rate equal s/v or r/m? The investment requirement constrains the rate of growth according to the first constraint, the import requirement according to the second constraint. Notice that all these letters denote fixed parameters. s, v, r, and m are supposed to be given characteristics of a particular

economy—at least in the short run. The Two-Gap model claims that the applicable growth rate will be the smaller of these two rates. This model is thoroughly structuralist in its assumption of various rigid structural constraints: fixed export revenues X, fixed import requirements m, a fixed ICOR c, and the like. Neoclassicals attack all such assumptions of inelasticity, in which quantities supposedly do not respond to prices that reflect scarcities. (See the scathing critique in D. Lal's *The Poverty of Development Economics,* 1983.) Yet the Two-Gap model can serve as a quick and dirty calculation device to compute growth while assuming all other parameters remain constant.

SOLOW GROWTH MODEL

The neoclassical growth model was first formulated by Solow in the 1950s. It emphasizes that many inputs can be freely substituted for one another in a production function to generate output. The relative supplies of factors change with economic growth, leading to a change in their relative prices. In response, producers substitute between the various inputs. Thus the K/L ratio can change in the neoclassical model, unlike the Harrod-Domar model, which assumes it to be constant. Then growth can continue smoothly even if there's no perfect balance between labor growth and capital growth. Like most modern growth theories the neoclassical model assumes that population grows independently of income. But it differs fundamentally from the structuralist models of Lewis and Harrod-Domar, which assume that developing economies have imbedded in them certain structural flaws or constraints that cannot be overcome by the operation of free markets. Solow's neoclassical model consists of the following elements.

$$Y = F(K, L)$$

The production function summarizes supply conditions, in which output is a function of various inputs. This function has diminishing *MP* of each factor as well as constant returns to scale.

$$\frac{dF}{dX} > 0, \ \frac{d^2F}{dX^2} < 0 \quad \text{where } X \text{ represents each factor } K, \ L$$

Note that both capital and labor can be used to produce output, unlike the Harrod-Domar model in which capital is the only productive factor. If labor becomes abundant, production techniques switch to utilize more labor in relation to capital. The neo-classical model emphasizes that factor substitutability take place in response to changes in relative factor prices, P_k/P_L.

$$S = sY \quad \text{and} \quad S = I = \Delta K$$

In addition to the neoclassical features, the model retains a simple savings function, just like the Harrod-Domar model. Investment equals the available savings in a closed economy. In an open economy, of course, the amount of investment differs from saving by the extent of net foreign borrowing. Each year's investment contributes to capital accumulation.

Labor grows exogenously at rate $\hat{L}$

The neoclassical growth model makes the modern assumption that the rate of labor growth *L* is determined exogenously. If the capital stock grows at a faster rate, the *K/L* ratio would tend to rise. But as increasing amounts of capital are used by each worker, the marginal product of capital would diminish. Consequently output growth would slow, and capital accumulation also would decline. Ultimately, the growth of output and capital slows down so much that they match the exogenously-given rate of labor growth. An extremely important implication of the Solow model is that regardless of the savings rate,

output growth ultimately will just equal the rate of labor growth. Per capita income will stay constant as will the *K/L* ratio. This is a situation of steady state growth where *K* and *L* grow at the same rate.

$$\hat{K} = \hat{L} = \hat{Y}$$

Figure 6-2 illustrates these elements of the growth process. To show the relationship between the three variables, *K, L,* and *Y,* would require a three-dimensional figure. But we can reduce this to two dimensions by the expedient of considering the *K/L* ratio *k,* rather than capital *K.* On the other axis we depict how per capita output *Y/L* responds to changes in *k.* As the capital intensity increases, output grows, but at a diminishing rate due to the falling MP_K. The growth of savings also slows, as shown by the dotted line. This line is drawn below output at a fixed proportion that is the savings rate *s.* A third line, which is straight, is drawn to show the *K* increment needed to keep the *K/L* ratio constant. This level of investment is precisely where *K* grows at the same rate as *L.* The growing economy eventually gets to point *B,* where the level of savings equals this special level of investment. Then the amount of savings is just enough to provide the extra capital needed for the expanded population. Thus there is no further tendency for the *K/L* ratio to change.

Unlike the Harrod-Domar model, steady state growth continues without unemployment of either *K* or *L* since usage of these factors adjusts to take up the slack. (This issue of factor substitution will be examined more fully in terms of production isoquants in chapter 10.) Suppose, as is normal, that the growth rate of capital exceeded the growth rate of labor. At such a point *A,* the economy's *K/L* ratio would be increasing. But the use of more capital runs into diminishing MP_K, so that rate of growth of output slows. As the output levels out, so does the related *K* accumulation, even at an unchanged savings rate. Eventually a steady state is reached at point *B*. Unlike the Harrod-Domar model, stable growth is possible in the Solow model due to factor substitution, as well as the diminishing marginal productivity of capital.

At the steady state growth, $\hat{K} = \hat{L}$ so the K/L ratio stabilizes. This ratio is called the technique of production. The United States, for example, has a relative shortage of labor compared to capital so it tends to use *K*-intensive techniques. By contrast, in Mexico it makes sense to use the relatively abundant factor, labor. The technique uses changes in response to endogenous changes in relative factor prices, which, in turn, reflect changing relative scarcity of the factors.

$$\frac{P_K}{P_L} \xrightarrow{\text{influences}} \frac{K}{L}$$

In sum, the Solow growth model fits in with the rest of neoclassical economics. Unlike the earlier development models, it assumes no structural rigidities. Instead, the price system works in factor markets to induce substitution of one factor for another in production. Thus the unstable growth of the Harrod-Domar model is avoided. Yet the neoclassical model has an implausible implication: *Regardless of the rate of saving, the economy will ultimately settle at a constant level of per capita income.* Thus increased savings rates will only speed up growth temporarily. This conclusion arises since the more capital accumulates, the sooner it runs into diminishing marginal product of capital. The Solow model implies rapid growth only in the case in which the capital stock is small. Yet the empirical data presented earlier indicate the opposite for the poorest countries. Moreover, rich countries display no evidence that their level of per capita income is reaching some limit.

The strength of the Solow model lies in indicating the-long term determinants of economic growth. It cannot be used for the short term—less than two or three decades. This model

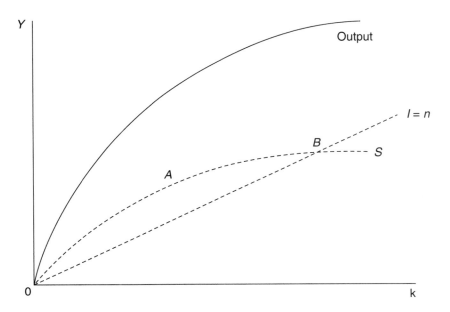

Figure 6-2   *The neoclassical growth model*

is best seen as an organizing principle for our thinking. It brings together the various necessary elements within a stylized market framework: the production function, factor accumulation, and technological progress. While the Solow model does not explain actual growth behavior of countries, it does point to some relevant empirical questions. Is there a systematic relation of growth rates to the level of income? Can the actual distribution of growth rates across countries be explained by the measurable parameters?

Critique

The Solow model has been criticized as inappropriate for the development context since it is based on neoclassical assumptions that rely on **efficient markets.** Structuralist economists (such as Lance Taylor at MIT and Hollis Chenery at Harvard) point to various market failures that occur in developing countries: (1) Prices do not adjust freely, and (2) economic agents respond slowly to the price changes that do occur. The latter criticism, dubbed the "dumb peasant" hypothesis, or elasticity pessimism, is pretty much in disrepute by now. The average person in LDCs, whose behavior is supposedly bound by tradition and customs, is found to be just as responsive to economic incentives as anyone else. The first objection, that market failures are widespread and due to lack of information, externalities, increasing returns to scale, and non-market modes of allocation, is more applicable. Further, when governments intervene, they often create even more distortions. Whatever their source, it is certainly true that factor markets can be seriously distorted in LDCs. Perhaps most critical are widespread labor market imperfections in which labor receives more than its free market wage. We examined this particular structuralist feature in the Lewis model of growth.

The idea that markets do not respond to price signals is superceded by the objection that markets cannot adjust in LDCs—at least not so easily as the neoclassicals presume. Adjusting the factor intensity of production in response to changes in prices may take a good deal of time. Thus, in practice, economies may be thought to operate more according to fixed K/L ratios. Technology is typically embodied in the existing stock of machinery. A change in factor prices would entail changing all the existing machinery, which is not an easy task. As a concrete example, consider the experience of airlines. Previous generations of jet planes normally were flown with a cockpit crew of three. Later, as the price of labor rose relative to capital, it became appropriate to raise K intensity. But this could only be done slowly over decades as the industry invested in new equipment: planes specifically designed to operate with just two pilots. In contrast, **disembodied technological change** works faster, since the use of new methods allows the K/L ratio to change even as the old machines continue to be used. Another example of such changed production processes is a switch from a single shift of labor to two shifts working in a factory with an unchanged capital outlay.

The neoclassical growth model also is criticized for its emphasis on equilibrium as factor usage is assumed to change smoothly in response to changes in factor prices. In reality the disequilibrium dynamic may be far more important. Economic growth is more plausibly characterized as a jerky process of technological advance by discovery and adaptation. This process is governed primarily by incentives for innovators and entrepreneurs, which, in turn, are a function of constraints embedded in the institutional framework of a society. Technological advances are depicted in Figure 6-2 as upward shifts of the entire production function rather than rightward movements along it.

Growth Accounting

The neoclassical model lends itself to separating the contribution to growth from each input in the production function. We first write out the neoclassical production function in its growth form, where the lowercase letters refer to growth rates.

$$y = \alpha k + (1 - \alpha) l + t$$

Here k = capital, l = labor, and t = technological growth rates. The rate of growth of output y is a weighted sum of the growth of inputs plus the growth of technology. The weights are respectively the share of each input in overall output. Such growth accounting exercises—both empirical and theoretical—will help address a variety of questions that are pertinent to development. First let us view the cross-sectional evidence in Table 6-2 that has been gathered from a number of studies.

We shall examine each of the ingredients for growth in the chapters that follow. From this summary take note of certain strong relationships that appear to hold between the various factors. It appears that the successful countries have relied on technological progress far more than just the accumulation of the measured factors.

The production function framework may be used theoretically to tackle various questions. For instance, one question raised was: How does population growth affect growth of per capita income? Unlike the Harrod-Domar model, which views labor as just mouths to feed, the Solow model recognizes that these mouths come attached to hands that produce. Thus population growth is not automatically bad for development. To analyze the relationship between population and per capita income growth, this equation may be rearranged so as to highlight the growth rate of per capita income.

$$y - l = t + \alpha k - \alpha l$$

This equation tells us how per capita income is affected by population growth, given the values of the other parameters and variables. (Here a simplifying assumption is that population and labor force growth rates are identical.) The equation can be manipulated to derive various implications. In case productivity is stagnant ($t = 0$), the resulting per capita income growth will be positive only if $k > l$. For example, if population growth is $l = 2\%$, the rate of capital accumulation k must also be at least 2% to maintain per capita income.

We can use this growth accounting framework for another exercise where capital accumulation is assumed zero ($k = 0$). In this case, the rate of technological progress required to keep per capita income constant would be $t > \alpha l$. In short, for per capita income to be maintained in the face of faster population growth, faster technological growth and/or faster capital accumulation is required. Clearly, income growth depends on the rates of growth of the factors, k and l, as well as t. But these are not always exogenously fixed. Rather, the rates of technical progress and capital accumulation t and k may themselves be dependent on l, the rate of population growth. Consider each case in turn—the rate of population

Table 6-2   Sources of growth, 1960–1987

	Output growth	Capital growth	Labor growth	Technology growth
Africa	3.3%	6.3	2.2	0.0
Latin America	3.6	6.3	2.6	0.0
South Asia	4.4	7.7	2.1	0.6
East Asia	6.8	10.2	2.6	1.9
LDC average	4.2	7.2	2.3	0.6
United States	3.0	3.4	1.8	0.5

Source: *World Development Report,* 1991.

growth alters the dependency ratio to increase either older people or youngsters as a fraction of total population. Such changes are likely to have an effect on savings rates, though in opposite directions.

Population growth also can alter technical progress through various channels. As we saw earlier in chapter 2, an increasing population on fixed land prompts a switch from extensive to intensive methods of cultivation. Esther Boserup (1981) has suggested that population growth also may induce improvements in productivity through scale economies and additional investment, as well as various other channels. In sum, population growth can affect overall growth adversely through lower savings and positively through productivity inducements. In many countries these effects cancel each other out, so the effect of population growth on overall growth is ambiguous in the cross-sectional and time-series experience.

RECENT NEOCLASSICAL GROWTH THEORY

The Solow model has been criticized for making some ad hoc assumptions. To fix these, modern growth theory makes two changes. In the Solow model the crucial role of technical advance was tucked away and labeled the "residual", defining, as it were our zone of ignorance. Modern theory is unwilling to leave out such an important component of growth. It assumes that endogenous technical progress is determined as a function of input, such as the investment in physical or human capital. Variants of this kind of model base the rate of technical progress on the level of educational achievement, or on **learning-by-doing.** A modern development is to assume **increasing returns to scale** in contrast to the previous assumption of constant returns to scale.

Modern growth theory eliminates Solow's simple assumption of savings being exogenously driven. Why must the savings rate stay constant over time? Indeed, why will people always have such a concern for the future (evidenced by high savings rates) when they continue to face a poverty-stricken present? Instead savings derive explicitly from an **intertemporal decision.** Agents choose a rational balance of present consumption foregone in exchange for higher future consumption. Current investments offer increased future consumption to compensate our natural impatience for immediate gratification. Beyond our lifetimes, such a trade-off may be phrased in intergenerational terms—How much are we willing to forgo to make our rich kids even richer in the future? Intertemporal analysis maximizes total utility summed across all present and future periods $U_{t=0}$, $U_{t=1} \cdots$

Since future utility is valued less than today's, this cannot be a simple sum of the utilities. Quantities in each future period must be discounted appropriately to make them all comparable in present value terms. Given an interest rate r, the discount factor for each period t is.

$$f_t = \frac{1}{(1+r)^t}$$

$$\text{Total } U = \Sigma f_t U_t$$

The economic problem is to decide how much to consume in present and future periods so as to maximize intertemporal utility subject to the constraint of resources. Utility derives from consumption, while production depends on the available factor inputs and technology as indicated by a production function. For present purposes, let us analyze a simple two-period case that illuminates how intertemporal tastes and productivity determine consumption, saving, investment and growth.

Analysis: Intertemporal choice

The amount of savings, and the productivity of investment, will determine output growth. The production possibility curve in Figure 6-3 shows the possible combinations of present and future goods that can be produced with the known technology. The slope of the PPC is such that a given amount of present goods provides a larger amount of future goods. The slope of indifference curves indicate that consumer preferences are normally biased in favor of present goods over future goods.

The consumer chooses the optimum combination to reach the highest utility curve U. The point of tangency on the PPC denotes desired consumption as well as the savings that generate future goods. Clearly, the higher the level of savings and investment, the higher the associated growth rate will be.

This framework can be manipulated for analyzing all kinds of intertemporal problems. Using this new tool, let us see what would happen if we acquire an enhanced taste for the future. The indifference curves would become flatter such that the savings S will increase.

As another example, an increase in investment productivity is seen to influence the amount of savings. The new choice results from an income effect combined with a substitution effect. The increased productivity (shown as a steeper PPC dotted curve) implies that we have become richer overall, inducing us to increase consumption in the present and in the future. The increased productivity also tends to cheapen the relative price of future goods. This prompts a substitution effect so we consume more in the future and less now. The two effects work in opposite directions. The income effect makes us save less in the present, while the substitution effect makes us save more. The net effect on savings, in general, is ambiguous.

The general equilibrium analysis is generally more complicated than familiar partial equilibrium analysis which uses demand and supply curves for present goods alone (see next chapter). We can use this rough and ready analysis of savings as an approximation since, in most cases, these two types of analysis give similar results.

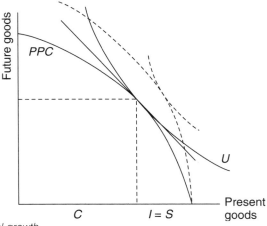

Figure 6-3 Intertemporal growth

ENDOGENOUS GROWTH MODELS

As noted, the Solow model has two major flaws: First, the empirical facts contradict the theory's implication of convergence. Growth in the rich countries has not slowed down, nor is the entire set of LDCs catching up in terms of living standards. Second, the assumption of exogenous technological advance is uncomfortable since this major contributor to growth is left unexplained outside the model. Endogenous growth theory addresses these difficulties as explained in Paul Romer's (1994) survey of theoretical progressions over the past decade. He starts with extensions of the Solow concept to explain the failure of convergence. Next he moves to a more fundamental issue: the market for production and dissemination of knowledge involves imperfect competition contrary to the assumed competition in the neoclassical model.

Convergence   Earlier empirical evidence was interpreted to infer that per capita incomes may roughly be converging. The British case is often cited as anecdotal evidence. Britain was the first to embark on modern growth and to attain a high level of income; Its subsequent growth has been slower, so late starters such as Italy have now attained that standard of living. However, on reconsideration of the empirical data convergence appears far more doubtful, especially in recent data that cover a wider sample including the developing countries.

The absence of convergence forces a rejection of the assumption of similar technical opportunities worldwide. The standard diagram of the Solow model below depicts the advanced U.S. and one LDC, the Philippines, marked off as A and B at their respective levels of per capita output. This neoclassical curve indicates that if the two countries are to grow at equal rates the U.S. must have a much larger investment rate. Using plausible parameter values, Romer shows that the U.S. with roughly ten times the output per person would need to have 30 times (!) the investment rate of the Philippines. In fact, the

investment rate is only about 20% of GDP in the U.S. compared to 15% in the Philippines.

A crucial feature of the Solow model is that marginal product of capital falls as capital accumulates. However, technical advance in the richer country can overwhelm the diminishing MPK to alter this characteristic result. It is certainly realistic to posit that the U.S. uses more advanced technology than the Philippines; and this technical advance may occur endogenously as a function of increasing income. In the Solow diagram this is seen as an upward shift in the U.S. production. Then the same growth of U.S. output (to point A' on the diagram) requires a far smaller investment rate, in line with observed values.

Three versions of the model attribute the boost in productivity to different reasons: (1) spillovers, (2) diffusion, and (3) human capital investment.

An early Romer model posited overall technical advance occurring due to knowledge spillovers from increases in the capital stock. Thus individual investments—or research expenditures—provide a positive externality as a technical boost for the entire economy. Such investments cause an outward shift of the aggregate production function in the above diagram. Overall productivity advances beyond the gains accruing to the individual firm doing the expenditure. Symmetrically, an increase in labor supply causes a negative spillover since it reduces the incentive for firms to make L-saving innovations.

Barro and Sala i Martin (1992) expressly posit that technology is not identical across countries. Given the existing technology gap a slow diffusion of knowledge takes place from advanced countries to the backward countries, leading to a slow convergence. The difference in technical levels removes the implausible Solow implication that MPK must be much larger in poorer regions.

A third mechanism can similarly counteract the effect of diminishing MPK in the advanced countries. Mankiw, Romer and Weil (1992) argue that the human capital factor provides a separate boost to growth within a production function. Growth occurs endogenously as advanced countries tend to accumulate human capital at a higher rate. Now even if the physical capital is mobile towards areas of high returns (productivity), the lack of human capital in poor regions will contain any tendency towards convergence. In sum, all such extensions allow the Solow model to escape the constriction of diminishing MPK. Thus it is possible for growth rates to be increasing rather than decreasing.

Imperfect competition in the market for knowledge contributes importantly to the possibility of endogenous growth. Romer argues that economics of knowledge admits the possibility of increasing returns, which is incorporated only awkwardly in neoclassical theory. The production and diffusion of knowledge occurs in a context of monopolistic competition. The process of discovery and innovation is motivated by temporary monopoly rents. Modern models are called neo-Schumpeterian as they highlight this feature.

The intrinsic nature of knowledge gives it a special status as an economic good. (1) It is a non-rival good; Unlike an apple, use by one does not diminish or preclude use by another. (2)

Knowledge can also be excluded to those who do not pay for it. Familiar examples are cable TV, which is an excludable, and broadcast TV is not. New knowledge is often an excludable good even as it remains non-rival in use. For this reason, a firm may be able to charge a monopoly rent by controlling access to knowledge. The most recent growth theory incorporates the newly developed aggregate theory in the context of imperfectly competitive markets.

The policy implications from such theory extend beyond the typical neoclassical prescription for increased physical capital, or human capital accumulated through schooling. Instead, an explicit technology policy is needed (as examined in chapter 10). For example, LDCs may only need to promote one advanced firm into domestic markets, for the knowledge spillovers to spread to all other firms in that industry. This places a new focus on multinational corporations (MNCs), or a feedback between trade policy and innovation. More generally, LDCs would have to examine the best institutional arrangements for gaining access to already existing from the advanced countries.

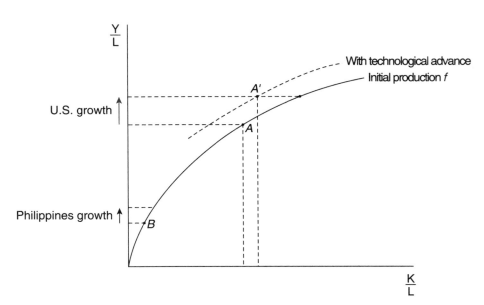

Figure 6.4 *Technological Advance counteracts diminishing Marginal Productivity of capital*

SUMMARY

In modern times, all growth models demote land from its preeminence as an ingredient of economic growth. This factor has been replaced by capital and, more recently, technology. Unlike land, each of these is an augmentable factor. The simplest formulation of this idea is the Harrod-Domar model, which assumes that output grows linearly with capital. In effect, other factors, such as labor, are supposed to be irrelevant. Thus the rate of output growth can be expanded by either faster capital accumulation through a higher savings rate or by allocating capital more efficiently. A variant of this model for the open economy is the Two-Gap model, in which foreign resources may be available to supplement domestic savings. But growth is constrained not just by the total available capital, but also by the foreign exchange assumed to be needed for capital goods that must be imported. The smaller of these two gaps is the limiting constraint on growth.

Solow's neoclassical growth model rejects the assumption of a zero marginal product for labor. Instead, capital and labor may be substituted for each other in the production function in response to changes in their relative price. But as the K/L ratio rises due to capital accumulation, the marginal product of capital drops. Ultimately the incremental output due to savings is canceled by the diminishing MP of capital. Long-run growth of per capita income can continue only if there is technological progress.

The neoclassical model lends itself to a so-called growth accounting that decomposes the output growth rate into parts that may be attributed to growth of various inputs (such as capital and labor) as well as to technological progress. Various empirical growth accounting exercises show that modern growth is increasingly attributable to the latter.

The modern endogenous growth model aims to remove the assumed exogeneity of technological progress. Many variants of this model explore various channels whereby technological advance may be explained from within the model itself. For example, if the specific form of accumulation is in human capital, then the enhanced skills will promote the adoption of new techniques. The new model also updates the original neoclassical model by deriving the rate of capital accumulation from more fundamental intertemporal choices.

KEY TERMS

Stylized facts of growth
Gershenkron hypotheses
Convergence
Incremental capital-output ratio
(ICOR)

Two-Gap model
Factor substitution
Balanced growth
Efficient markets
Embodied technical change

Learning-by-doing
Increasing returns to scale
Intertemporal growth or
decision

PART III

INGREDIENTS FOR GROWTH

The foregoing growth models highlighted the different ways that inputs can be combined to generate output. This new section begins a study of the various inputs into the production function. The prominent factors of production are capital, human capital, labor, and technology. In separate chapters we will examine each of them in their qualitative and quantitative aspects.

Two characteristics can distinguish the inputs: (1) whether they are **augmentable factors** and (2) the kind of **scale economies** they offer—increasing, constant, or decreasing returns to scale. Previously we touched on the role of fixed factors, such as land and natural resources, that are prominently in the Ricardian debate on population growth versus resources. In modern times the focus shifted to the aug-mentable factor, capital. However, even this focus is beginning to look old-fashioned as the possibility of increasing returns to scale offers most hope for continued economic growth. By contrast, the earlier presumption was always of decreasing returns or at, best, constant returns. The possibility of increasing returns appears most natural for the intangible factors, human capital and technology, as noted in the previous chapter. The fourth major input, labor, gains its importance not for what it can do (for output growth), but for what it is, since the very objective of development is to improve the well-being of people, not only as consumers, but also as workers.

The first chapter in this part starts on the most tangible of factors, capital.

Chapter 7

Capital

THE ROLE OF CAPITAL

It was long casually assumed that capital must be the most important input for modern growth. The development economics school of the 1950s assigned a preeminent role to capital, as in the Harrod-Domar model. The implicit faith was that development led to industrialization, which requires Capital formation. Mainstream ideas, however, have so evolved that capital accumulation is considered a necessary, but hardly a sufficient, condition for development. Nevertheless, capital remains an important ingredient that merits separate study. This chapter studies this factor in three parts: (1) the definition of capital, (2) the methodologies for the efficient **allocation of capital,** and (3) an examination of issues relating to **capital mobilization** from various sources, domestic and foreign.

As we saw earlier the presumed "scarcity" of capital may really have been a "shortage" induced by government policy that aimed to encourage capital investment. Historically the early days of (supply-side) development theory coincided with the Keynesian paradigm, which focused on investment as a demand-side stimulus to expand current output. The 1950s also was an era in which the Soviet Union was still considered a positive example for the LDCs. The Soviet-growth strategy also may be interpreted as structuralist, since it emphasized capital mobilization for industrialization.

India provided a prominent example of socialist-inspired countries that followed such a model in its initial development program of the 1950s and 1960s. The special status accorded to capital was matched by an emphasis on industrialization, in particular on heavy industrialization. As we shall see in a later chapter, this policy argued for investment in factories to produce "machines to make machines." This kind of capital-intensive strategy was expected to furnish a higher growth rate over the long run.

The modern vision of scarce resources ascribes no special merit to capital—or to any other factor, for that matter. Instead, a succession of different resources or constraints are expected to become critical as growth and structural change proceed over time. Viewed in a temporal sequence, the ratio MP/P for one resource or another might appear temporarily out of line (Harberger 1984).

As an example, consider a stylized sequence in a typical LDC. In the early years, a lack of capital may have appeared to be the most serious constraint to development as emphasized by Harrod-Domar. Then as a burgeoning population outpaced agricultural growth, food shortages might have become prominent around 1965; later, around 1970 as the maldistribution of income became critical, the social instability turned into a major constraint to development. (Even though income distribution is not a commodity as such, a lack of social harmony can limit growth in much the same way as scarcity of any material resource.) If this problem was resolved somehow, it would, in turn, highlight the next problem that arises in the growth process. With expanding production by 1980, infrastructure, such as transport and electricity, could become a constraint, and so on. . . .

1950	1960	1970	1980	1990
Capital	Food	Income distribution	Electricity	Human capital

In short, a scarce factor can be defined more broadly as any constraint that limits growth. Particular bottlenecks come to the fore and persist only for transitory periods. Meanwhile there is a high marginal benefit (or productivity) associated with the removal of that constraint relative to cost. This idea is related to the balanced growth concept propounded by the pioneering development economist A. Hirschman. Over the long run, however, the ratio of productivity to cost MP/C must equalize across all factors. If a particular factor has low productivity relative to its cost, people stop using it. Thus capital is also just one among many scarce factors. This has been confirmed by growth accounting studies mentioned in the previous chapter. Empirically, the rate of growth of output far exceeds the contribution of just capital growth. The neoclassical growth model notes that other factors also contribute significantly to growth—unlike the Harrod-Domar model, which may have had particular relevance only in the 1950s.

Measurement of Capital

As each new concept is introduced, we are careful to first consider its definition and measurement.

Capital is defined as a durable resource built up through investment so as to provide a stream of services into the future. It can take various forms as physical, financial (working), or human capital, while the stream of services that flow from it could be either productive or consumption services. For example, current investment in a refrigerator will return cooling services over an extended future. We concentrate here specifically on tangible physical capital, for example, industrial machinery or farm cattle. Note that financial capital can be just as productive in the growth process.

The measurement of capital is difficult because the concept itself is complex. In a naive view a given capital stock might be the sum of all past investments less depreciation. But this simple sum, or **book value,** does not distinguish between cost and the productivity of different vintages of machines. For example, a $1,000 machine from 1950 is considered equivalent to an inflation-adjusted $1,000 machine of 1990. In contrast to this backward-looking accounting view, an economic view is forward-looking: **Market value** of capital stock is defined by (the present value of) the stream of output that it is expected to produce into the future. Note that this value depends on future expectations that are subjective, even imaginative (Figure 7-1). If a machine's output is worthless, the capital value of the machine also will be zero, regardless of the cost of resources packed into its durable frame. Note also that this valuation is altered by changes in the interest rate, which is used to discount the future flows to a single present value.

Unfortunately, the correct theoretical measure of capital is difficult to implement in practice. For most kinds of assets, and for most countries, a stock market does not exist to determine market valuations. Therefore, we must fall back on computations of that faulty measure, book value. Even this exercise is not simple since one must sort out expenditures for investment from those merely for consumption. In national income accounting, for example, educational expenditure is customarily classified as consumption even though some

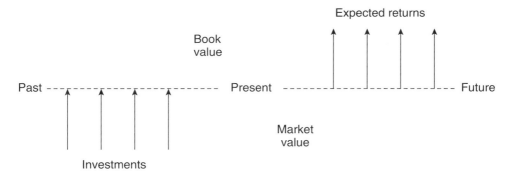

Figure 7-1 *Valuation of capital*

of it certainly builds the stock of durable human capital. Moreover, many personal expenditures on durable goods (such as cars) are not added into the national capital stock. Similarly, expenditures on research and development often are not properly counted as investment even though these increase future productive capacity. Accounting students will recognize this distinction as "expensing" versus "capitalizing" certain items of expenditure. Only in a few cases is it easy to clearly identify investment goods such as tangible machinery or power plants.

Similarly, indirectly productive activities may be difficult to distinguish from investments that are directly productive. For example, is a program for feeding the poor a productive "investment" that enlarges K stock? Feeding the undernourished may well increase overall productivity in the same way as expenditures on infrastructure. While much government expenditure is certainly essential, everyone is also aware of many government expenses that are patently wasteful and unproductive. Such expenditures in no way constitute investment and must correctly be classified as current consumption.

The important role of public investment in the overall capital expenditures must not be slighted. The distribution of investment between public and private must depend on their respective rates of return. However, public investment is largely a complement rather than substitute for private investment. For instance, if a particular region of the country lacks adequate public infrastructure, the private sector might not wish to build a factory there. In this way, the private rate of return depends on prior public investment. This crucial complementarity between projects must be kept in mind when we study project evaluation in the next section.

Finally, one type of capital that is often overlooked is **working capital.** This includes various uses of capital other than for fixed plant and machinery. In the planning of small ventures, or entire economies, a common error is to underfinance short-term working capital. This causes chronic problems for the production process. Significant subcategorizes are inventory and work-in-progress. Generally, as output expands, the capital tied up in inventory tends to become a smaller fraction of output. If output rises by 20%, it might be sufficient to increase inventories by only 15%. Consequently the inventory/output ratio tends to decline. Further innovations, as in the just-in-time production methods used in Japan, try to minimize this ratio. In developing countries, however, the production system is imperfectly integrated, so each producer needs a separate stock of inventory. Thus as industrial development proceeds, the capital/output ratio (COR) due to inventories can be expected to decline, even as it may rise for other reasons.

Another neglected component of working capital is that needed for the upkeep of existing capital stock. There are many horror stories of expensive facilities going to rot due to lack of minor maintenance funds even as the limited capital is lavished on capital-intensive projects. For instance, a $10 million-factory might produce an output of $1 million indicating ICOR = 10, while the same factory might produce twice as much by enhancing working capital by just $3 million. The improved efficiency would be indicated by a lower ICOR of 6.5.

We now proceed to evaluate the role of capital in growth. As in the Harrod-Domar model, we note that output growth can be decomposed into the efficiency of capital use times the quantity of investment.

Output growth rate	=	Efficiency of capital use	*	Quantity of investment

Table 7-1 Contribution of capital to growth in LDCs 1960–1984

Country	Growth rate of GDP per capita	investment ratio GDP	ICOR
Low growth			
Ghana	-1.7	6	12.1
Somalia	-1.0	13	8.6
Zambia	-0.5	14	7.9
Jamaica	.3	17	13.0
Chile	.6	12	7.4
Peru	.7	10	4.7
Mali	1.0	11	4.8
Argentina	1.3	14	7.0
Bolivia	1.3	9	4.0
Uruguay	1.7	6	5.3
Group average	**.4**	**11**	**7.2**
High growth			
Philippines	2.5	17	4.3
Malawi	2.6	17	4.3
Colombia	2.7	14	3.9
Turkey	3.1	14	3.6
Dominican Republic	3.3	13	3.1
Mexico	3.4	16	3.3
Malaysia	4.3	16	3.3
Brazil	4.4	19	3.7
Thailand	4.5	17	3.3
Greece	4.6	18	4.5
Hong Kong	6.1	27	3.9
Korea	6.4	17	2.7
Botswana	7.3	27	3.2
Singapore	7.4	24	3.3
Group average	**4.5**	**18**	**3.6**

Source: *World Development Report*, 1986.

Ample empirical evidence across cross-sections of countries confirms a positive relationship between investment and the rate of output growth. However, the efficiency of capital dominates the quantitative investment rate. Table 7-1 with a cross-sectional sample of LDCs confirms two important features.

1. Countries with high investment rates tend to have a more efficient use of capital. Various reasons for this will be examined later.

2. Variations in ICORs better explain growth performance than the investment rate. ICOR refers to overall efficiency, which subsumes the contribution of all factors to growth, not just capital alone. For instance, if skills are inadequate, even a high level of investment will not lead to much output growth.

ALLOCATION OF CAPITAL

This section addresses the first element in the previous equation. For an economy with a given amount of capital available for investment, how must the policy maker allocate it most efficiently? One obvious criterion would be to invest first in the activity with the lowest ICOR. In the following table, first fund the school project (ICOR = 2), then roads (ICOR = 2.5), and so on sequentially until all the capital budget is utilized. An appropriate procedure might seem to be: Rank projects in order of ICORs, then allocate capital starting from the best project.

Possible projects	ΔK	ΔY	ICOR
Steel mill	2000	400	5
Chemical plant	800	300	2.6
Roads	1000	400	2.5
Schools	400	200	2
Grain storage	300	100	3
Power plant	750	150	5

At first glance this method of capital budgeting may appear quite reasonable. Yet it is seriously flawed. A major flaw is its implicit assumption that all the other factors contribute nothing to productivity. If this method was applied mechanically, as in the example, the chemical plant would be ranked as the best investment. Suppose the planner neglected to consider the limited availability of chemical engineers; the project's output would ultimately turn out to be disappointing. Further, the planner might not account for complementarities that exist between projects. This makes it problematic to associate specific capital investments with specific increases in output. In the example given, the chemical plant might not work without the power plant, but the latter might not have been approved for funding. For such reasons the policy planner must consider all externalities—positive and negative—to determine which projects have the best net social value. This issue was emphasized by A. Hirschman (1958) in prescribing the appropriate sequencing of investment to build up a country's infrastructure.

Any project evaluation exercise gets even more complicated. The output from projects generally lags behind the preceding capital expenditure. For example, a hydro-electric project has a long gestation period so its investment does not yield full output until decades in the future: The apparent ICOR may appear very unfavorable until full output is reached. We must correct for this by distinguishing between average and marginal quantities. We must allow for unequal project lifespans as well as their varying time path of returns. Another complication is the presence of business cycles, which make it difficult to associate an increased output with a particular capital outlay. For example, in a recession year, output is low for any given K stock. Thus even a good project might show a bad ICOR if the whole economy is in recession. Similarly, when using historical data to estimate an economy's ICOR, it would be a mistake to simply relate the change in capital to change in income over a few years. Do not assume ceterus paribus; changes in other factors can shift the curve relating capital to output. In Figure 7-2, the apparent ICOR is indicated by AC, whereas it actually should be AB.

Project Evaluation

The simple methodology for project choice outlined earlier has many flaws as noted. The fundamental problem is that private costs and benefits often may differ from their social values. So as to allocate resources most efficiently at the national level, the tool of project evaluation makes appropriate allowances to reach the stated objective of maximizing net social benefit. The comprehensive approach called Social Benefit–Cost Analysis is widely utilized by the World Bank as well as developmental agencies in LDCs. This approach avoids the error of assuming that only capital has a cost. Instead it adds the scarcity cost of all inputs to determine total cost. This cost is juxtaposed against total benefits to determine net social benefit. The benefits also are corrected for possible externalities where social benefits may differ from perceived private benefits as reflected in market prices.

This methodology is called social because it utilizes social or **shadow costs** rather than market prices to value the inputs and outputs of a project. Put simply, the shadow cost is the true opportunity cost to society, while the prevailing prices in the market may not be. A complex set of adjustments must be made to apparent costs and benefits so as to derive the net societal benefit from a project as explained by one pioneer, Harberger, in *Reflections on Social Project Evaluation* (1987). The ranking of projects using this methodology truly would reflect the best net benefit to society. Typically such projects must be undertaken by the government since private entrepreneurs only respond to the observed private benefits and costs. In the example presented earlier, the shadow cost of scarce chemical engineers may be calculated at $100,000 each,

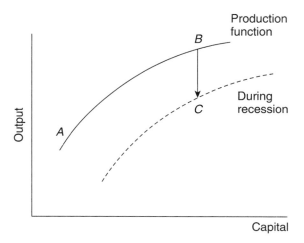

Figure 7-2 *Measuring the relation between capital and output*

instead of a market wage of $35,000. **Project evaluation** exercises typically require sizable corrections to be made for various prices. The most notable corrections are for the social cost of labor, capital, and foreign exchange.

Another example of project evaluation illustrates how choices are affected by the shadow wage rate applicable in a dual economy. Suppose a proposed project will hire eighty laborers, expanding industrial employment from L_0 to L_1 in Figure 7-3. At the going wage of $W_1 = \$15$, the labor cost in the organized sector will amount to $1,200 (the area of the rectangle BCL_1L_0). Should this project be undertaken if project output is estimated to earn just $750 in revenues? Any smart private entrepreneur will say: Definitely not! Yet this project is desirable from the social point of view. Labor's social cost, or the opportunity cost in alternative employment, is just the $W_A = \$6$ wage in agriculture. Then the social cost of employing the eighty laborers is only $6 x 80 = $480 (area of rectangle ADL_1L_0). According to this social B/C computation, the project would make a net social benefit even though it operates with a financial loss.

Benefit–cost evaluation typically must balance many more conflicting goals than indicated in this example. A project that aims to expand current output might possibly come into conflict with savings—and thus with growth of future output. Figure 7-3 shows how output would expand if the labor on that project is assigned a low social cost W_0, instead of the higher prevailing wage rate W_I. When the additional labor L_0L_I gets paid the industrial wage W_I, they are receiving more than the marginal value of their production. While output certainly increases (area of triangle ABD), the wage bill also increases by area $ABCD$. If laborers are assumed to consume substantially all their income, the resulting reduction in savings is area BCD. This drop in savings could be avoided if employment remained at L_O as dictated by the industrial wage W_I. So what are planners to do. Should they set the shadow wage rate at W_A to maximize current output, or should it be W_I to maximize saving? Or should it lie somewhere in between?

This introduction to benefit–cost analysis gives just a tiny taste of all its elaborations. We will resume the discussion in a later chapter on policy under the rubric of applied welfare analysis. There we will survey the vast literature on both theory and practice, as well as criticisms of this approach. Suffice to say that the practice of social cost–benefit analysis is now quite advanced. Practitioners have learned how to make adjustments for various situations where distortions or market failures cause prices to deviate from their true social values. The aim is always to pick the projects that will be most efficient for society as a whole.

ACCUMULATION OF CAPITAL

As noted, the rate of growth of output depends on efficiency of capital use multiplied by the rate of capital accumulation. We now examine the second aspect, the role of K accumulation through savings and investment. Various cross-

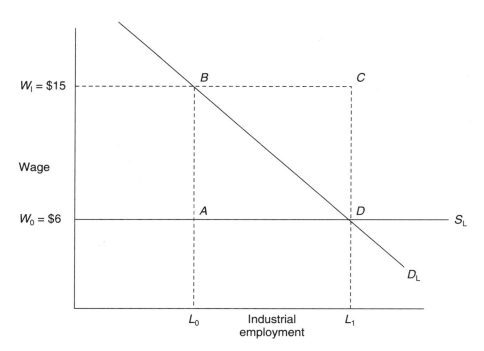

Figure 7-3 *Social benefit–cost analysis evaluation*

sectional studies indicate a fairly weak relation between growth and the investment rate (investment/GDP). Whereas output growth is affected more by the qualitative effectiveness of investment, the LDCs nonetheless have placed great emphasis on the quantity of investment. Students may relate to this by an analogy close to their own experience. To produce better grades, the student can either increase the time spent studying or increase the efficiency of the use of time. Which policy do you think is more likely? Not surprising, many find it easier to put in more hours rather than to upgrade the quality of their work.

LDCs historically have placed great emphasis on resource mobilization as a basis for their growth. Accordingly, we must study in some detail the sources of capital for a country's quantitative investment. The principal source is certainly domestic savings within most LDCs, and this primacy has grown over the years. To a certain extent, capital resources may be augmented by **foreign savings,** only part of which is aid that does not have to be repaid. Yet such funds may not be strictly additive to overall capital mobilization. The inflow of foreign funds may cause the domestic savings effort to slacken. Since all funds are fungible, a country may utilize foreign inflows to increase its consumption, not just investment. This results in a corresponding decrease in the domestic savings rate. We shall examine in turn each source of capital accumulation.

$$\Delta K = I = S \begin{cases} \text{Foreign} \begin{cases} \text{Aid} \\ \text{Direct investment} \\ \text{Loans} \end{cases} \\ \text{Domestic} \begin{cases} \text{Government} \\ \text{Private} \end{cases} \end{cases}$$

Foreign Capital

For LDCs over the long term, foreign savings have amounted to a small fraction of capital accumulation and a much smaller fraction of

their GDP. This average has been dropping over the past decade as many indebted countries actually returned net funds to their creditors. In earlier decades the developing countries got new loans that exceeded repayments, so net inflows were positive. Today the average transfer to LDCs remains at only about 2% of the recipients' GNP. Even these numbers represent gross savings; net inflows excluding interest payments are smaller yet. Net transfers of long-term loans to developing countries (in billions) have fluctuated drastically.

Table 7-2 shows a typical situation at the end of the 1980s for the financial flows between the World Bank and three prominent LDC clients. These countries were not among the seriously indebted and have a substantial long-standing relationship with the World Bank. Yet, as we see, their net inflows from this major source are small or even negative.

The simple lesson is that foreign sources of capital are generally small in comparison to domestic sources. They can nevertheless be quite important, since the ability to attract foreign funds, in itself, may constitute a good indicator of a country's effective use of funds. International financial institutions as well as private investors serve as external examiners that enforce prudence and consistency in a country's own financial plans. During the late 1970s, a lapse in such oversight allowed some countries to borrow excessively, which later plunged them into a severe debt crisis. Even though foreign funds constitute a relatively minor source of funds, the conditionality attached to them can be appreciated as an important benefit. (The issue of conditionality remains quite controversial. More on foreign capital flows, the debt crisis, and its macroeconomic consequences will follow in chapter 16.)

The extent of foreign financing for various LDC groupings is summarized in Table 7-3. Note that foreign financing comprises the difference between investment rate and the domestic savings rate.

Table 7-1

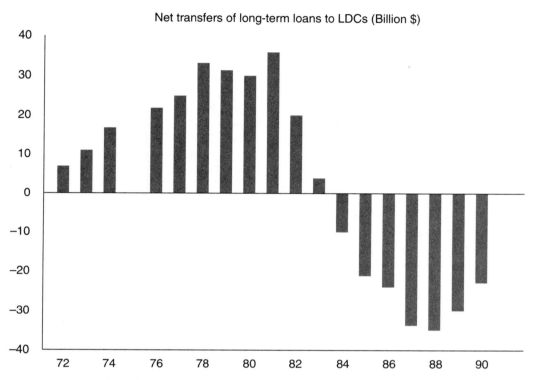

Net transfers of long-term loans to LDCs (Billion $)

Source: World Debt Tables.

Table 7-2 World Bank lending (millions of dollars)

	Pakistan	Turkey	Egypt
Commitments	$949	$709	$241
Disbursements	491	567	117
Repayments	82	488	143
Net disbursements	389	79	−26
Interest charges	104	523	132
Net transfer	285	−444	−158

Source: World Bank *Annual Report,* 1989.

Some results of the 1980s' debt crisis and its aftermath are obvious. Some of the most affected countries got into trouble largely of their own making. Easy access to the world's capital markets in the late 1970s tempted them to undertake large investments financed from abroad, while their domestic saving rates remained relatively low. For these LDCs I was greater than S by almost 4% of GDP in each of the six years preceding the debt crisis that began in 1982. Because of debt servicing difficulties, the foreign inflow dropped sharply so $I > S$ by only 1% as foreign lenders sharply cut back any new lending. Both the reduced investment (from 27% to 19% of GNP), and the resulting recessions depressed growth rate of output (from 4% to 2%) and the savings rate (from 23% to 18%).

Other countries—mainly in Asia apart from the Philippines—that had not relied so heavily on foreign borrowing were hardly affected by the debt crisis, and their growth rate continued. Both rich and poor countries were affected by the debt crisis, so there is no such sharp distinction between the performance of high/versus low-income countries. Yet the faster growth rate of low-income countries after 1982 largely reflects the robust growth of just two countries, India and China. They were largely unaffected by the external debt crises and also initiated beneficial internal policy reforms during the 1980s.

Foreign aid used to finance a large part of LDC investments at the start of the modern development epoch in the 1950s. Now, however, it has steadily declined so that this source is barely significant for most LDCs. The limited amount of aid funds is increasingly targeted mainly for humanitarian and emergency purposes. Other politically motivated aid is sometimes mislabeled as economic aid as, for example, United States aid to Israel, Egypt, or Honduras (see Table 7-4). A significant component of aid to really poor LDCs is directed through multilateral channels, such as the International Development Agency (IDA) of the World Bank. (Various European countries and Japan continue to maintain substantial bilateral aid programs.) This kind of aid is offered in the form of long-term loans at concessional terms. But for the most part, the typical LDC in Asia or Latin America must rely on commercial borrowings at market rates. Table 7-4 also presents some evidence about the impact of foreign aid on recipients.

The first column shows that the most destitute of the LDCs can get an extremely significant

Table 7-3   Statistics for various LDG groupings

	All LDCs	**Low income**	**High income**	**LDCs with debt problems**	**LDCs without debt problems**
1976–1981					
Savings	26.9	20.7	27.7	23.0	26.1
Investment	27.4	23.6	27.6	26.9	27.8
Growth rate	4.4	4.3	4.4	3.9	5.2
1983–1988					
Savings	22.5	16.9	22.5	18.0	26.1
Investment	23.4	20.2	22.5	19.1	27.6
Growth rate	3.7	3.6	2.6	2.0	6.5

Source: IMF Survey, 3/19/90.

Table 7-4 Size of recent aid flows

Aid as percent of recipient's GNP		Dollars per capita aid receipts	
Mozambique	66%	Israel	$282
Chad	29	Jordan	109
Malawi	26	Egypt	30
Bangladesh	9	Senegal	79
Kenya	11	Nepal	22
India	.6	Ethiopia	21
China	.6	Bangladesh	15
		India	2.58
		China	1.09

Source: *World Development Report* 1989, Table 20, 21 updated with 1990 data.

portion of their entire GNP as foreign aid. Such large flows are exceptional in that they follow episodes of war and famine (as in Mozambique) or natural disasters (as in Bangladesh). Similar figures are likely for aid flows to Somalia in 1992. The large inflows, however, are almost entirely emergency relief used for immediate consumption rather than investment purposes. It is notable that the percentage of GNP often is largest for the smaller countries. Aid appears to be allocated, at least partly, on a national basis rather than on the per capita income. Thus the largest countries, such as India and China, get just a tiny fraction of their GNP as foreign aid. Still, due to their huge size, this means a very large absolute amount of $1.5 and $2 billion, respectively. Yet this works out to an average of just $1.09 per person in China, as seen in the second column.

As suggested earlier, the foreign sources of capital may not be independent of domestic capital accumulation. Some evidence suggests that increased foreign inflows tend to depress domestic saving. Thus foreign investment may be a substitute rather than a supplement to domestic investment. Further, if these are borrowed funds rather than aid inflows, the build up of foreign indebtedness has other ramifications. This entire issue of international capital flows will be examined in chapter 16 on macroeconomics in the open economy.

The debt crisis of the 1980s had such bitter lessons for both borrowers and lenders that private bank lending to LDCs almost dried up. The prospects for renewed commercial funding have revived only modestly in international loan and bond markets in the 1990s. At the same time, the rich countries are suffering from a sort of **donor fatigue.** Many donor countries feel that they have transferred too much for too long in view of the dubious effectiveness of such funds to improve living standards. Many DCs have now become absorbed in their own financial problems, for example, the chronic United States budget deficit, while the internationalist imperative seems to have waned with the end of the cold war.

As official aid and commercial lending have declined in importance, there has been a recent spurt of **foreign direct investment (FDI).** For the more buoyant NICs, such as Thailand or Malaysia, there appears to be no serious foreign capital constraint. In fact, the internationalization of global manufacturing and finance now seems to be restricted more by opportunities than by the reluctance of investors. A relatively small set of countries, with the confidence to participate in fairly free trade and capital movements, has received an enormous economic boost. Nigel Harris (1986) of the University of London notes the important benefits of such transnational corporate activity. It is difficult, and beside the point, to figure out the source or ownership of foreign funds. In many LDCs, for example, the foreign investors often are none other than domestic investors who have chosen to park their funds abroad to escape domestic regulations and taxation. Thus it is often Peruvians, Mexicans, or Argentines who turn around and invest at home because they have the best knowledge of its markets and opportunities. Yet another set of countries continues to regard foreign investment and Multinational Corporations (MNCs) with suspicion and fear instead of confidence. Such countries remain frozen out of this bountiful flow of private capital and business opportunities. Then they are obliged to face the dried-up stream of development capital that used to flow freely in the past.

Foreign direct investment is a part of total foreign resources that earlier fell into disfavor as the LDCs learned to tap world financial markets directly through bank loans. In recent years FDI again has gained favor in comparison to foreign borrowing. This issue can be viewed as analogous to the equity versus debt issue of corporate finance. Countries that scorned foreign equity in favor of debt have learned the hard way that more debt and less equity is not necessarily good for them. While FDI means giving up some control to foreigners, retaining control also implies retaining all responsibility—including the risk associated with variable interest rates. Even if the investment turns sour, the country is still obligated to repay the debt. By contrast, foreigners with an equity stake would closely monitor the viability of their investment, and failure would oblige them to share the.

Apart from the risk-sharing aspect, FDI also is recognized as an ideal vehicle for the transfer of technology, or capabilities, more broadly defined. All of these countervailing aspects have induced a reappraisal of FDI in the developing world. Formerly exclusionary countries such as Peru, India, and Tanzania now court rather than spurn foreign investment. And as the LDC debt crisis gradually has been resolved, the average annual inflows have soared from $14 billion in the 1980s

to $36 billion in 1992. Obviously the nominal increase is exaggerated due to inflation, but after we remove the effect of inflation, the real investment flows also are seen to increase significantly.

The direction of FDI also changed markedly, as the booming economies of Asia have become the largest recipients. In the 1980s the percent of total FDI flows that went to Asia was 27%, to Latin America 51%. In the early 1990s, 60% of total FDI is directed to Asia and only 28% to Latin America. The numbers in Table 7-6 tell a complex story after the size of annual flows is corrected for inflation. FDI has increased in real terms, but not so much as the nominal numbers indicate. Some flows in the 1970s constituted a special case associated with the expansion of petroleum investments. Much of the foreign funds invested in Nigeria and Indonesia was of this kind. A more general lesson to be learned from the historical data is the strong correlation between FDI and country performance. Thus an openness to global markets and receptivity to multinational corporations seems to be both a cause and effect of FDI flows.

The benefits of FDI are touted by the **International Finance Corporation (IFC),** the arm of the World Bank responsible for promoting private capital flows to LDCs. Yet one must mention an inevitable qualifier: Much of the capital flows to LDCs are highly concentrated. Over 55% of FDI flows in 1985–1991 went to just six countries. This generates a virtuous cycle since countries with good economic performance are rewarded with capital inflows that further reinforce their growth performance. While this seems only fair, it does tend to increase the disparity between developing country haves and have-nots.

Table 7-5   Foreign direct investment into LDCs

(Average annual flows in billions)				
Late 1970s	1980–89	1990	1991	1992
$7	$14	$18	$31	$36

Table 7-6 Largest recipients of FDI (billions $)

1970s		1980s	
Brazil	1.3	Singapore	2.3
Mexico	.6	Mexico	1.9
Egypt	.3	Malaysia	1.1
Malaysia	.3	Brazil	1.8
Nigeria	.3	China	1.7
Singapore	.3	Hong Kong	1.1
Indonesia	.2	Egypt	.9
Hong Kong	.1	Argentina	.7
Iran	.1	Thailand	.7
Uruguay	.1	Taiwan	.5

Source: IMF Survey, 7/92.

The Global Capital Market

For countries integrated into the global economy, the level of interest rates is determined by demand and supply of funds from a global pool. Over the past decade the world (real) interest rate has risen to about 3% for a variety of reasons. (1) Net saving by the industrial world has dipped as it becomes increasingly spendthrift. The persistent budget deficit of the United States exemplifies this tendency. Moreover, with the opening up of Eastern Europe, a smaller part of Western Europe's savings are available for the developing world. A prominent example is Western Germany's redeployment of its foreign assets to rebuild Eastern Germany. (2) The vast pool of surplus funds from the OPEC countries has largely evaporated as oil revenues have receded. Meanwhile, the OPEC countries have learned to increase their own spending. (3) Lastly and importantly, the debt crisis of the 1980s has highlighted the risk of lending to LDCs. Risk-averse lenders therefore add a **risk premium** to the interest rate charged to LDCs. Thus many LDCs must service the already outstanding debt, even as the high rate of interest inhibits investment demands.

When talking of capital accumulation for LDC development, the oil exporting countries constitute a very special case. These countries belong in a separate category that is further bifurcated into (1) capital-surplus countries, such as the Arab Emirates, Libya, and Saudi Arabia, which earn enough oil revenues per capita to essentially buy their way to complete development; and (2) another group whose primary export revenues finance a significant part, but not all, of their development effort. Countries such as Indonesia, Nigeria, and Mexico, which are large and densely-populated, still need a substantial amount of foreign capital to supplement their oil revenues. Thus these countries more closely resemble the average LDC rather than the other OPEC countries.

The capital-surplus primary exporting countries share certain characteristic features. First, export revenue accrues mostly to the government, which becomes the instigator of most developmental investment. At the same time, all sorts of people are attracted to this source of funds through rent-seeking behavior (as explained in chapter 13). Investment activity becomes intermingled with this distributional activity, which invariably gives rise to a variety of abuses. The second problem—if one may call it that—is preparing for the day when such windfalls might run out. Export revenues would drop if either the quantity produced or the terms-of-trade drops, turning the boom into a bust.

Analysis: Individual country in a global capital market

A country's capital market may be analyzed using familiar demand and supply tools, with a minor modification to account for the **global capital market.** Only if a country is entirely insulated will its domestic supply of savings S and investment demand D be the sole determinants. The resulting price and quantity are shown as the autarchy point A in Figure 7-4. In the context of capital markets, price refers to interest rate and quantity to the amount of domestic saving and investment. Next consider the alternative case of a country well-integrated into global capital markets: The world interest rate i_w is now, in effect, the relevant supply curve. Market equilibrium occurs at point F, where domestic investment is obviously larger. The quantity of funds borrowed from abroad is indicated as distance DF, while domestic savings provide the remaining funds at point D. If the world interest rate rises, the quantity demanded for domestic investment contracts, point F, moves up and left. Whereas if investment is cut back, the quantity of domestic savings D expands along the supply curve S.

Often, the international capital market is unwilling to lend a country unlimited supply of funds at the world interest rate. Credit to a particular country is rationed in a fixed amount R. When the country obtains these foreign funds, its supply curve of saving, in effect, shifts right by amount R. Clearly credit rationing is less preferred by the country than the perfectly free market case, but access to even a rationed amount of foreign funds is an improvement over autarchy. Domestic investment increases by the limited amount shown as the highlighted segment of the investment D curve.

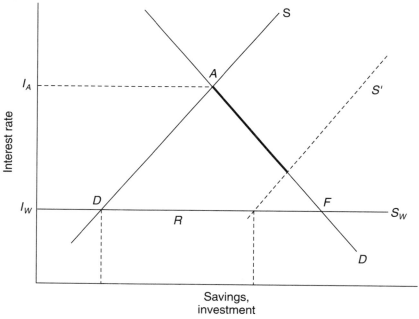

Figure 7-4 *Global capital market*

Modern examples are Chile after the copper boom of the late 1970s and Mexico after the oil price decline of the mid-1980s.

The boom/bust cycle that often follows an export boom is named the **Dutch disease** after the experiences of natural gas discoveries in Holland. The immediate effect of large foreign inflows is to stimulate the economy and raise all prices. The increased supply of foreign funds, however, strengthens the exchange value of the local currency, so that all tradable goods, imports and exports, become relatively cheaper. The net result is that nontraded goods—ranging from haircuts and cab rides to real estate—become expensive, while traded goods become so cheap that domestic producers find it difficult to compete. It is simply cheaper to import them all at world prices. This chokes off most production of import substitutes and exports other than the booming export product.

Ultimately, almost inevitably, the day arrives when such export revenues dry up, either due to a price collapse or depletion of the export good. The country is then left even poorer structurally than if the bonanza had never happened. This problem is exacerbated by the uncertainty of predicting how long the windfall revenues will continue. The country must make an intertemporal decision about an appropriate level of present consumption versus saving and investment to provide for future consumption. This decision depends crucially on forecasts. If the capital inflows will run forever, it would be rational to consume now when we are poor rather than invest for future generations to become even richer. Various countries like Mexico, Venezuela, and Nigeria borrowed for vastly expanded current consumption in the 1970s with such optimistic expectations. The unanticipated decline of oil prices left them with a serious debt burden, as well as a highly uncompetitive productive structure.

Domestic Sources

Domestic sources of capital must remain the most significant quantitative source of investment funds, and the largest domestic contributor to national savings is the private sector. An idea whose time came and passed was for the government to directly raise resources by taxation or via the simple expedient of printing money. Before the current development epoch, **government saving** was never a major element except in stray cases such as Russia's rapid industrialization early in this century. The worldwide experiences of the 1960s and 1970s has taught us that this seemingly promising source has a tendency to degenerate. The revenue raised often is wasted in the government's own consumption and overhead. Public behavior tends to follow Parkinson's Law: Expenditure rises to meet revenue! Expenditures may even run ahead of tax revenues, giving rise to chronic budgetary pressures and financial problems that can doom the entire development process. Chapter 16 entails the distortionary macroeconomic impact of government interventions. Here we only note that taxation tends to be designed more for convenience of collection than to advance overall economic efficiency. Taxation, in general, distorts incentives, which damages the efficiency of resource allocation. Alternatively, governments may seek to raise revenues through money creation rather than the more difficult process of taxation. Either way, the excessive tax or inflationary distortions act to impede growth and may eventually halt it.

Mobilizing resources through money creation soon becomes counterproductive. Creating money at too rapid a rate in effect constitutes a tax on existing money holdings. Just as a tax on any commodity influences its quantity demanded, the imposition of an inflation tax will similarly discourage real money holdings; carried to excess, an increased inflation can reduce rather than increase real tax revenue. Such **inflationary finance** by the government can result in massive dissaving rather than enhancing national savings. The macroeconomic ill effects operate through various channels as detailed in chapter 16.

The effects of inflation on the fiscal budget may be summarized as such: By distorting relative prices in the economy, inflation tends to reduce overall efficiency and thereby depress the rate of output growth. This results in a drop in regular tax collections. While the inflation tax may initially rise, it becomes limited as continued inflation induces people to turn from monetary transactions to barter so as to avoid the tax on money holdings. The worsening government budget deficit tends to worsen the inflation in a vicious cycle. Government expenditures, typically based on current prices, rise faster than tax receipts based on past prices. Attempts to close the budget deficit by more money creation exacerbates this process and culminates in a fiscal crisis. An interesting exercise would be to examine data from the *World Development Report* to confirm that countries with acute inflation suffer sharp drops in their national saving rate.

Even if the government does not directly contribute much to national saving, government policies nevertheless are extremely influential in raising savings indirectly. The amount of direct saving can be determined from the government's fiscal accounts by splitting out the current budget from the capital budget. Often a surplus in the current budget may be directed toward public investment. (This topic is examined in greater detail in chapter 16.) Beyond the direct effects, virtually all economic policy impacts private saving behavior. While this is obvious for banking and financial policies, other policies also influence saving—perhaps in unintended ways. For instance, an income tax that applies to interest earnings will act to discourage saving. Thus the government's contribution to national saving must be evaluated from its overall policy stance.

Determinants of Saving

Finally, we turn to the main source of capital accumulation, the **private saving** effort. Various theories that aim to explain the determinants of private saving are based on the level of income, the growth rate of income, and the distribution of income.

The layperson might casually assume that richer people must have a higher rate of saving than poor people. Surprisingly, there is no sharp relationship between the saving rate and level of per capita GNP. Cross-sectional data from across the world present rather mixed evidence on this. While it is true that middle-income developing countries generally have a higher saving rate than the poorest LDCs, the saving rate declines for the higher income countries. In particular, the United States has a remarkably low saving rate of 15%—even lower than the 22% in Sri Lanka, a country with 1/40th its per capita income. On the other hand, high-income Japan maintains one of the highest saving rates in the world—34% in 1990. See Table 7-6 for examples of other countries' gross saving rates.

Early development economists, such as Ragnar Nurkse around 1950, thought that a low level of income induced a low saving rate. This meant low K accumulation, which in turn restrained the growth rate. This vicious cycle is completed as the low growth rate keeps income from rising and so on . . . . Such an explanation in terms of the level of per capita income is contradicted by an anomalous finding: In traditional societies the response following natural disasters that destroy a substantial part of the capital stock often is an astonishingly high saving rate—even at very low levels of income. Why do people stop accumulating after they have rebuilt back to their previous assets level? Why don't they continue accumulation for unlimited growth?

Empirical observations do not support the theory that the saving rate depends on the level of per capita income. As noted, people get accustomed to the higher level of income and change their consumption behavior. Then the saving rate reverts to a lower level (point C in Figure 7-5). The degree of this adjustment depends on the speed at which income changes. The faster the income growth, the less time there is for changing consumption habits, so the higher is the saving rate. If, instead, expectations leap ahead of a rising income, the saving rate might even drop as

Table 7-6 Gross saving rates for various country groups and sample countries, 1990

	Income level	Saving rate
Low-income countries (excluding China and India)	$320	20%
Malawi		10%
Kenya		18%
Indonesia		37%
Middle income countries	$2,220	23%
Morocco		20%
Colombia		25%
Malaysia		33%
High income countries	$19,590	22%
Britain		17%
Switzerland		30%

Source: *World Development Report* 1992, Table 9.

income grows. This actually occurred in Mexico's boom years of the late 1970s. On the other hand, if the saving rate rises with income growth, the happy result is a virtuous cycle. In this case a high growth rate encourages saving. The added capital accumulation enhances the growth rate of output, which induces more saving and so on.

Yet another theory of saving derives from structuralist ideas such as incorporated in the Lewis model. An economy's saving rate may depend on its income distribution. An unequal distribution of income used to be viewed favorably because it was supposed to induce higher national saving as the (rich) capitalists have a low marginal propensity to consume, while the (poor) workers consume nearly all their subsistence wage. This argument may be understood using the consumption function analysis presented earlier. Suppose everyone starts out with equal incomes and saving rates as given at point A. Now introduce income inequality by moving half the group to a lower income and the other half to a larger income such that aggregate income remains constant. This results in lowering and raising their respective saving rates. The increased saving by the richer group, however, will exceed the reduced saving by the poorer group. The consequence is to raise the aggregate saving rate.

Contrary to the theoretical argument, however, the empirical evidence points out that highly unequal societies (such as Venezuela or Pakistan) do not exhibit exceptionally high saving rates. This might be due to the fact that the rich keep much of their savings abroad instead of domestically. In contrast, some countries, such as Taiwan and Korea, have very high saving rates (induced by a high productivity of investment) even though their distribution of income is rather equal. Another structuralist explanation of saving rates is the age profile of the population. We noted earlier how a rapidly growing population implies more younger people, which necessitates more consumption, not saving.

The arguments so far have examined various ways in which the income variable may shift the savings function.

$s = fn(Y)$ Income level

$s = fn(\hat{Y})$ Income growth rate

$s = fn$ (Distribution of income, age profile)

$s = fn$ (Interest rate, Y variables)

Analysis: Consumption function analysis of saving behavior

The influence of income variables on saving behavior can be analyzed using the **consumption function** construct that is taught as part of introductory macroeconomics. A consumption function shows how consumption and saving increase as the level of income goes up. The level of consumption rises with income, but the increase is less than proportionate as the consumer slides along the consumption function from A to B in Figure 7-5.

Saving is indicated by the vertical distance from the consumption function to the 45o line. Clearly, the saving amount S is larger, but also the saving rate S/Y is larger at B than at A. This constitutes the most simplistic static theory of saving: Richer people save a higher proportion of their income. Yet behavior appears rather more complex. The movement along the consumption function holds only in the short term. As people get used to higher incomes, they learn to spend accordingly. The consumption function itself shifts upward over time as shown on the right in Figure 7-5. In the long run, a richer country might eventually end up with approximately the same saving rate at C as a poorer country at point A. To repeat: While the level of saving S must certainly grow with income Y, this is distinct from the ambiguous behavior of the saving rate, S/Y. The relation of saving rates to income level and growth may be examined through time-series data for a single country, in contrast to the cross-sectional data noted earlier.

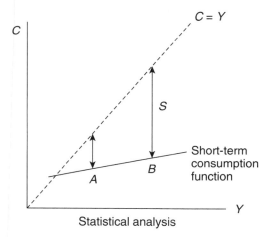
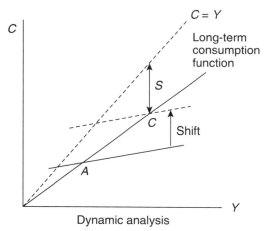

Figure 7-5 *Saving as a function of income*

In contrast to structuralist determinants of saving, the neoclassical approach highlights the effect of prices. The intertemporal price, or interest rate, is crucial for saving, in addition to other variables, such as the level of income or its distribution. Thus the amount saved can be influenced by financial policy that operates through the institutions of financial intermediation. Saving will be induced by increased incentives (higher interest rates), which cause a movement along a given supply curve. Also, easier access to banks, especially in remote rural areas, can cause a rightward shift in the supply of saving. Similar structural shifts may derive from other factors that influence saving. (Recall this neoclassical/structuralist distinction made in the Introduction.) One example is the age structure of the population: A large fraction of school-age children implies large outlays made for their upbringing, at both the private and social level. By contrast, people who are further along in their life cycle tend to have large saving for their impending retirement.

Financial Intermediation

Improving the efficiency of banking institutions also serves to increase saving by raising the interest rate paid on deposits. Ronald McKinnon has urged such **financial deepening.** As intermediation becomes more efficient (lower cost), it narrows the spread between the lending and deposit rates in the organized financial sector. This prompts an increase in quantity of saving supplied as well as an increase in the quantity of funds demanded for investment (seen as movements along the S and D curves rather than shifts of these curves). In terms of the familiar curves in Figure 7-6, this is seen as the supply and demand for funds.

This Figure also can illustrate the corrective policy of **financial liberalization.** This policy urges raising the deposit rates that have been artificially depressed. Sometimes due to deliberate government policy, this often was just an inadvertent consequence of the policy of fixing the nominal interest rate. Fixed-interest rates usually were instituted in times of low inflation. But as inflation soared world wide during the 1970s, the **real interest rate** dropped and often became negative. (Chapter 16 will elaborate the **Fisher equation:** Real interest rate equals the nominal rate minus the rate of inflation. For instance, a nominal interest rate of 8% when inflation is running at 15% implies a real rate of interest of –7%.)

When the real interest rate is low or negative, the demand for investment funds increases while the supply of saving drops. As in all cases of artificially low prices, the banking system is required to do **credit rationing.** Raising the deposit rate induces more saving by a movement along the supply curve, as opposed to the aforementioned shifts in supply. Max Fry is a prominent proponent of financial liberalization, while others, including Rudy Dornbusch of MIT, point out the limits of such policy. Raising the real interest rate is a good thing only so long as it is still below the equilibrium level. Financial liberalization is most appropriate for countries in which the financial sector has been seriously repressed; but within a normal range, do not expect much growth enhancement by pursuing such policy. Also, such policy applies only to the formal financial sector, which generally coexists with an informal financial market with rather different determinants of savings supply and demand. The upcoming case study illustrates the important role played by less formal institutions of finance.

Improvement of financial intermediation does not just involve extending the banking system through financial deepening. Another exceeding important aspect is the treatment of risk, which is inherent in any investment activity. Investment is not simply a matter of putting resources into projects with the highest rate of return. One must also guess correctly their rate of return. Risk-averse firms and individuals thus face

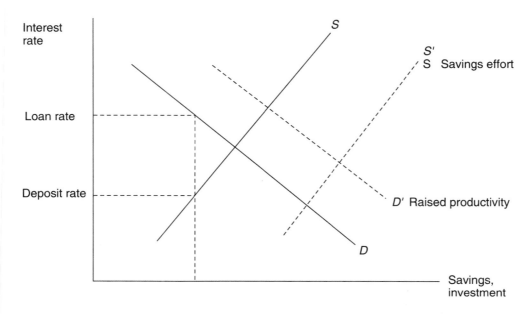

Figure 7-6   *Saving as a function of interest rate*

an unavoidable element of risk. Uncertainty in such choices can mean the difference between a fortune and going bust. Speculation activity is necessary and healthy even in a development context. An appropriate mechanism for making such decisions is a stock market, which forms an integral part of the overall capital markets. Many developing countries are belatedly realizing the importance of such mechanisms for the raising and allocation of risk capital. For this they need to fight a common distaste for speculation.

The focus on intermediation also highlights the fact that saving is crucially influenced by the **productivity of investment.** A higher return on investment is shown in Figure 7-6 as an upward shift of the investment demand schedule. This raises equilibrium saving as well as the quantity of investment, which, in turn, boosts the growth of output. This phenomenon may explain the very high saving rates in fast-growing countries such as Taiwan. Our earlier explanation postulated a high growth rate leading to a rightward shift in the sav-

ing rate. An alternative explanation may be that a high investment curve intersects a normal savings curve, leading to a high saving rate. (From introductory microeconomics, you may recall the distinction between movements along a supply curve versus a shift in a supply curve.)

Financial intermediation plays a crucial role in the mobilization of domestic resources. Perhaps its most important function is **risk pooling,** since risk is a defining feature of all investment. If I build a factory, will its product sell? If I borrow for farming, will the rains fall? In figure 7-6 this may be seen as an uncertain location of the curve depicting the productivity of investment. For example, the demand curve, as drawn, is only some kind of a probabilistic average. If there were no banks to pool risks, each investor would be obliged to bear risk independently. This risk might be so high that no investment would occur. On the other hand, by pooling a number of separate projects, a bank can expect to get the mean return. More investment projects are likely to get funded, and growth is thereby encouraged.

Traditional societies use other methods to pool risks, but borrowing and lending is generally restricted to transactions between family and kin. Modern banking allow a much wider expansion of imper-

sonal transactions among strangers, which enhances economic efficiency. (For a broad review of the role of domestic finance in development see the 1989 *World Development Report*.)

CASE STUDY: BANGLADESH'S GRAMEEN BANK

The development literature has highlighted how underdeveloped financial structures inhibit economic growth. The standard prescription is for modern financial institutions to gather savings and allocate funds to worthy investment projects. Modern generally is understood to mean large formal sector institutions. Thus it is rare to report the success story of a small, self-reliant institution that profits by extending tiny loans to the very poor. The Grameen Bank in Bangladesh has overturned conventional wisdom and has come to serve as a model throughout the Third World.

The Grameen (Rural) Bank was established in 1976 along the lines of cooperative, rotating saving and loan associations that are common in many LDCs. These pool the savings of a small group, then loan the funds to each member in rotation. The Grameen Bank is restricted to the very poor in rural areas. It is especially renowned for granting access to women: As many as 90% of all members are women, accounting for 70% of outstanding loans.

The Grameen Bank organizes five-member groups that must establish a track record of regular saving deposits before becoming eligible to seek loans. Similarly the group must establish a regular pattern of loan repayments on initial loans before it gains access to further credit. Thus loans are based on demonstrated performance and character of the borrower rather than on collateral, which they do not have. These seemingly onerous conditions have three motivations that account for the program's success: (1) The group commitment ensures group responsibility. If one person defaults, the entire group suffers since it will be cut off from further credit. (2) An important com-

ponent is education of backward segments of the populace, who are gradually introduced to alien concepts of finance and financial responsibility. (3) An intimate and ongoing relationship with a bank officer allows for close monitoring.

Inevitably, such close monitoring is costly in terms of resources and staffpower. The bicycle bankers, who have considerable delegated authority, pay repeated visits to each group. Consequently the ratio of expenses to loans has ranged as high as 10–20%, even as loan losses remain extraordinarily low. These expenses add up so that the real interest rate on loans can reach as high as 30%. If this seems high in comparison to bank lending in the DCs, remember these are loans in the informal sector of LDCs to the very poor who previously had no access to credit or only at usurious rates reaching 100% or more.

The Grameen Bank has taught new lessons about the viability of the group finance method. The group lending experience overturned previous doubts about finding renumerative occupations and the likelihood of repayment by the very poor. In fact, such lending has induced entrepreurship in various activities such as lime making, pottery, weaving, garment sewing, and transport services such as rickshaws. As for repayment, the effect of peer pressure as well as rigorous selection of borrowers and projects results in loss rates of less than 3%. The group saving experience is likewise heartening. Even the very poor engage in the token act of saving one taka a week (less than 5 cents). More substantially, they save as much as 25% out of the income generated.

The Grameen Bank's success is reflected in its growth from 15,000 borrowers in 1980 to about a million in the early 1990s. Now over 900 branches nationwide service 21,000 villages. The total saving deposits of about 700 million taka (approximately $23 million) may appear tiny in comparison to typical financial figures in DCs, but, remember, these are for the poorest segments in one of the poorest countries. This success story attracted the attention of international agencies, which have spread this concept across the Third World. The IFAD has used experts from Bangladesh and a minimal amount of seed capital to propagate new institutions, such as the Muzdi Fund in Malawi, and to reorient established rural credit institutions across a range of LDCs. An essential ingredient is self-help rather than aid where the outsider does it all.

Finally, this institution has made an impact on overall national development. The primary contribution is poverty alleviation, particularly for the most destitute segments. Landless labor and marginal landholders have benefitted the most. The average household income for members is 25–50 percent higher in comparison to nonmembers or nontargeted villages. The shift from agricultural wage labor to self-employment has the indirect effect of improving wage and employment conditions for remaining agricultural laborers. This approach fits into the poverty eradication strategy advocated by Amartya Sen (1982): to develop indigenous capabilities and provide entitlements that eliminate the worst manifestations of poverty such as mass starvation.

SUMMARY

The rate of economic growth is the product of the quantitative size of investment times the qualitative efficiency of its use.

Of these two factors the efficiency of investment appears more critical in explaining differences in growth performance across countries. For this reason policy emphasis is now being redirected from merely increasing capital accumulation toward allocating capital to its most efficient uses. More generally, project analysis aims to ensure that funding priority goes to those investment projects with the highest overall productivity—carefully defined according to the precepts of social benefit cost accounting.

The primary focus of the past has now become secondary, but still remains important: Try to raise the quantity of saving and investment. For the main sources of funds we find that, contrary to popular perceptions, only a small fraction of LDCs' total investment comes from abroad. LDCs therefore must rely largely on their own domestic saving effort. An earlier optimism about direct resource mobilization by governments has ultimately proved disappointing so emphasis has shifted to the private saving effort.

The determinants of private saving may be split into two parts: These due to increased price incentives and all other influences on saving. In particular, the effect of increased income is highlighted by a consumption function analysis. Within a standard demand and supply framework, the saving effort acts as an outward shift of the supply curve of savings, while raising the return on investment shifts out the demand for funds.

The neoclassical approach to capital accumulation places the emphasis on a policy of streamlining domestic financial markets. Market forces can operate so that market-determined interest rates can serve to improve efficiency in the market for funds, and thereby to improve its responsiveness in resource allocation.

KEY TERMS

Augmentable factors
Scale economies
Allocation of capital
Capital mobilization
Book value
Market value
Working capital
Shadow costs
Project evaluation
Foreign savings
Foreign aid

Donor fatigue
Foreign direct investment (FDI)
International Finance
    Corporation (IFC)
Risk premium
Global capital markets
Dutch disease
Government savings
Inflationary finance
Private savings
Consumption function

Financial deepening
Financial liberalization
Real interest rate
Fisher equation
Credit rationing
Productivity of investment
Risk pooling
Government expenditure
Public investment
Conditionality

Chapter 8

Human Capital

The next major ingredient that accounts for growth within a production function is human capital. Workers produce not just by using their muscles, but primarily by using the wide variety of skills embodied in the human mind. Unskilled labor is dealt with as the labor input *L,* while human capital represents the skills acquired by education. This chapter examines human capital input in two parts—through the individual and through society. First, the Human Capital model highlights the *individual* decisions that determine demand for **human capital investments,** quantitatively and qualitatively. The second part presents the *social* or institutional aspect, which represents the supply side, as well as the overall planning of the educational sector. We also review issues relating to the social role of knowledge, particularly within the modern global context.

Human capital is notably heterogenous. Knowledge is qualitatively so diverse that it would be misleading to consider human capital as just a quantitative amount. A dollar's worth of human capital investment in the form of electrical engineering is quite different from a dollar's worth of human capital in dentistry skills. Human capital, in turn, must be distinguished from skills such as entrepreneurship. The latter skill probably cannot be cultivated by spending money on education.

Entrepreneurship might be determined by cultural and societal norms (for example, certain ethnic value systems such as the social framework in Japan). Prominent economists, such as Joseph Schumpeter, have argued that this skill may be the most productive of all. However, this chapter concentrates only on that kind of human capital that is amenable to economic analysis.

At the outset you should be warned against the casual presumption that human capital must be a crucial ingredient in growth simply because developed countries seem to possess larger stocks of educated manpower. This correlation between education and level of output may appear because education is an effect, rather than a cause, of development. Moreover, human capital might operate more as a complement than a substitute for other inputs, such as capital or technology, which are ingredients in the production function.

DEMAND SIDE: THE HUMAN CAPITAL MODEL

As suggested by its name, human capital may be viewed as just another form of capital—a durable resource that returns a stream of services (for production or consumption) into the future.

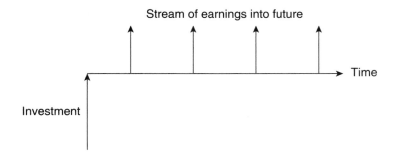

Figure 8-1   *The Human Capital model*

Thus there is a demand for human capital, which, like a machine or building, is durable and similarly subject to depreciation and obsolescence. Let us start the analysis of human capital, highlighting its durability, which provides a flow of services into the future.

Figure 8-1 depicts the essential elements of the capital construct used to evaluate and choose among projects. Let us say one investment of $100 yields $20 per year while a $50 investment yields $12 annually. The second project clearly is better since it provides a larger rate of return (24% compared to 20%). Such an evaluation in effect compares cost and benefits. The benefit is the sum of the **present value (PV)** of the earnings stream, with each future receipt discounted depending on the time of its receipt. The ratio of present value *PV* to investment cost *C* can be compared across projects. Individual investment in human capital is also subject to diminishing marginal productivity, since it works with a fixed factor—the person's innate ability given at birth.

With diminishing marginal productivity, too much expenditure on any project tends to successively lower benefits. Thus investors adjust the investment across projects, so the numerator adjusts over projects *i* and *j* such that.

$$\frac{PV_i}{C_i} = \frac{PV_i}{C_i}$$

As a matter of choice, an educational investment with low returns relative to its cost would not be undertaken. (Note how this condition resembles the one from the context of capital allocation in which the ratio of marginal productivity to price was equalized across all projects.) The Human Capital model can be used to address various questions relating to choice of the educational investment.

Q: Why don't more older people go to school?

A: They have a shorter lifetime remaining in which to reap benefits. Thus their rate of return on a given human capital investment is low or possibly even negative. This is a rational choice derived from the Human Capital model compared to other kinds of explanations that tend to be much fuzzier: Older people have less energy; they are less able to learn; they are inflexible; and so on. The explanation due to the Human Capital model is simpler and more elegant.

Q: Would demand for schooling change if interest rates went up?

A: Yes, there would be fewer students. Recall that present value of future income streams is a sum of the returns A_t in each year *t*. Each return is discounted by a factor that increases with the interest rate *r*, as well as time *t*, which indicates how far in the future the return lies. Thus, as the denominator gets large, the value of the benefits decline.

$$PV = \Sigma \frac{A_t}{(1+r)^t}$$

The Human Capital model is especially useful to analyze expenditure decisions on intangibles such as health or education. Suppose a country has a $10 million budget for social purposes such as health and education; how much should it spend for each? A rule of thumb might be to split it equally between the two, then estimate the present value of returns in each sector so as to compare the benefit/cost ratios to see which is higher.

Suppose the benefit/cost ratio is higher in the health sector; clearly it would be smart to shift some resources from education to health. As the health sector expands, it is subject to diminishing marginal productivity, while the opposite occurs in education. Keep transferring until the ratios become equal. Using this methodology, social expenditures can be treated in much the same way as physical capital projects. While it is notoriously difficult to assign values to the quality of life or extended lifespans, such social decisions no longer need to be considered outside the domain of concrete economic analysis. Before the Human Capital model can be used in practice, one must note various other caveats and refinements to the basic concept.

Refinements to the Human Capital Model

It is necessary to account for financial as well as non-financial costs and benefits. For example, the major cost of education is not necessarily the tuition fees paid; rather, it might be the opportunity cost of time spent at school. Thus a direct cost of $2000 for tuition may seem a very good investment if it returns $500 extra annually. But if you also consider the $3,000 **opportunity cost** of time you are away from work, then the same return does not look so exceptional.

Figure 8-2 allows one to explain various kinds of human capital investment decisions.

Q: What might happen to high school dropout rates if the wages of gas station attendants increased?

A: The dropout rate would increase since the opportunity cost of staying in school rises even if the financial cost of education remains unchanged.

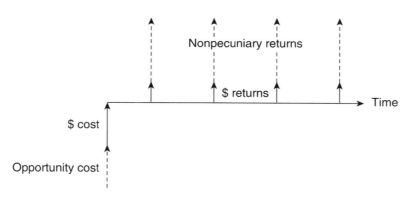

Figure 8-2 *Human capital including nonpecuniary costs and benefits*

Q: Why do some people spend a lot of money on education only to become low-paid professors or judges?

A: Again, **nonpecuniary benefits** must be added to the financial returns to rationalize that decision.

Another refinement to the Human Capital model is to make a careful distinction between those who bear the costs and those who reap the benefits. Often, the public sector bears the cost while private individuals get the benefit. Yet observed educational decisions are the result of individual responses to private costs and benefits. In Figure 8-2, suppose the private cost of education was only $5,000, while the public cost was an additional $10,000. These figures would drastically change the private rate of return, and thus alter the individual incentives for investing in education.

Q: From a societal point of view, who should get more public aid, MBA students or public health students?

A: The latter, obviously, since they will return large benefits to society, while their (private) wages are not so high. Without such subsidies, individual expenditures for public health education would not be forthcoming.

Education can provide benefits to society from positive externalities apart from the private returns that accrue to individuals. (Of course, individual returns also add to total societal benefit since each individual is part of society.) For this reason, most societies generally opt to subsidize education. In postindependence periods, many African nations, in particular, faced a critical shortage of people with higher education. Thus social returns to this factor were high. Governments gladly subsidized college education, even if the individuals worked for high private sector salaries. Yet there can be serious drawbacks to such public subsidies, as we shall see.

In a perfect market (with free competition and no externalities) there is no divergence between public and private benefits since earnings precisely reflect an individual's contribution to society. But as soon as there is a divergence, distortions in resource allocation creep in. For example, in Brazil an excessive number of colleges and universities were established and funded. Why? The public sector pays, while individuals reap the benefits. The beneficiaries then combine as an interest group to exert political pressure on the government. The result? The nation makes a bad social investment. Using this example, the private cost is only $1,000, so the private rate of return is 10%. Since an additional $1,500 cost is borne by the public sector, the social rate of return is only 4%. This overinvestment in projects with low social returns stems from distortions in the price system. By contrast, the upcoming case study indicates high social returns to education in Brazil. But that refers to the general education of the labor force, not particularly to university-level education.

At the start of this development era, higher education generally had a high productivity. Later, the educational sector tended to expand excessively. Ever more graduates with advanced degrees led to diminishing marginal productivity and eventually to the emergence of educated unemployed. The Indian subcontinent, for example, has many unemployed scientists and engineers who generate few private or public benefits. A prime source of distorted incentives are the administered salaries in the public sector that drive a wedge between private and social benefits and costs. Even as late as the 1970s, many governments opted to be the employer of first resort. Facing such incentives, people thronged to college simply to obtain the certification required for government jobs. Public sector salaries are slightly related to productivity; instead, each job classification is assigned some certification level, and a wage scale is attached to match the status of the required degree. The lucky few who manage to obtain these limited government jobs, enjoy a windfall—in a sort of socialism for the middle classes.

The Human Capital model can be used more conveniently by restating benefits and costs in terms of the percent **return on investment (ROI).** (The net present value criterion is distinct from internal rate of return, as we shall examine in a later chapter.) Once all social investments, including those on education, are put on a comparable basis, then the entire investment program may be planned effectively. As shown in Table 8-1 (for various years before 1980), **social benefit–cost analysis** is used to find that the rate of return on

Universal primary > Higher education
education ROI   ROI

The development community began to recognize this around the mid-1970s. Thereafter the support of technical and higher education was gradually phased back in most LDCs. Various research findings, such as those of George Psacharopoulos (1985) of the World Bank, have spread the conventional wisdom that the eradication of illiteracy (for adults or children) provides a higher rate of return than most physical investment projects. Note that the measured low ROI

for higher education does not mean that it is intrinsically unproductive in some sense, but rather that such education typically costs more per student. The implication for current educational policy is to divert scarce resources from higher education to increase school expenditures to at least ensure **universal primary education.**

The pattern of enrollments is shown by an **educational pyramid.** Figure 8-3 illustrates the percent of the population enrolled at each educational level. Enrollments are highest at the lowest, primary, level. Inevitably they decline at higher levels as students drop out at the intermediate and higher education level. Such decisions are based on rational responses to the perceived costs and benefits. The educational pyramid can take diverse shapes as seen for three Asian countries in Figure 8-3. It is instructive to examine the educational sector in three countries, Pakistan, Indonesia, and South Korea, that span the spectrum from among the least to the most advanced of the LDCs.

The three LDCs differ vastly in educational structure as well as in economic performance. (They are classified by the World Bank as lower-, middle-, and upper-income LDCs respectively.) While South Korea's economic success is widely admired, even envied, it must be noted that

Table 8-1 Social returns to education (percent rate of return)

		Primary	**Secondary**	**Higher**
Africa	Ethiopia	20	19	10
	Ghana	18	13	17
	Kenya	22	19	9
Latin America	Brazil	—	24	13
	Chile	24	17	12
Asia	India	29	14	11
	Indonesia	22	16	15
	Pakistan	13	9	8
	Japan	10	9	7

Source: Psacharopoulos 1985.

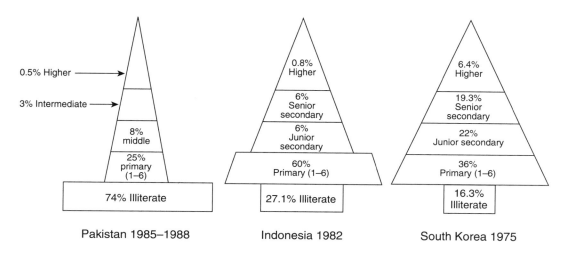

	Pakistan	Indonesia	South Korea
Growth rate of per capita income	2.5	4.5	6.4
Education expenditure as percentage of government expenditure	3	13	18
Income distribution Percentage share of poorest 40% of population	9 (est.)	14	17

Source: McMahon and Boediono 1992.

Figure 8-2 *Educational attainment of the labor force. Pakistan surpassed by Indonesia and South Korea (before it began rapid growth).*

Korea paid its dues through many years of investing heavily on education.

Detailed estimates are available for the **ROIs** in Indonesia's educational sector. The social rates of return for various levels of education are summarized in Table 8-2. The rates are clearly lower at the higher levels, even though they were still a healthy 11% in 1982. As education expanded the marginal productivity of graduates inevitably declined, as seen in lower ROIs at all levels by 1989.

Table 8-2 Social returns to education (Indonesia)

	1982	1989
University	11	5
Academy (3 years)	13	5
Secondary vocational	16	6
Secondary general	22	11
Middle school	17	14

The Human Capital model also can be useful in deciding between different types (as opposed to levels) of training. Let us say marginal productivity, as measured by the wage of doctors, is high compared to the cost C of studying medicine. Then the ratio MP_{med}/C_{med} will be abnormally high, reflecting its scarcity. Many students will crowd into this career path, with the eventual result that the divergence will disappear. The equalizing process works through lowering return and/or raising the cost of such education until the ratio matches those in law or business. Thus, in the long run, the relative returns in the different fields become equalized.

$$\frac{MP_{law}}{C_{law}} = \frac{MP_{med}}{C_{med}} = \frac{MP_{mba}}{C_{mba}}$$

Exercise   Review the tables on human capital in the *World Development Report* for data about literacy and the levels of education across countries. Over recent decades there has been a marked expansion of all levels of education. Poorer countries have achieved primary education for about 60% of their population while the middle income developing countries average more than 90%. Note also the differences between the sexes in educational attainments and observe how this gap has changed over time.

Critique of the Human Capital Model

The Human capital model is criticized on various grounds. An obvious flaw is that it does not distinguish between qualitatively different types of skills. Just as a farmer cannot be a computer programmer, the reverse is also true. Also, the needed skills can change over the course of development. The goal of education cannot, therefore, just be to accumulate quantities of particular high-level skills. Instead of the early emphasis on technical skills, the unembodied skills of flexibility and creativity might be more beneficial to future development. Such broad

skills must, therefore, be cultivated through a liberal education.

Further, the analogy of human capital to physical capital may be carried too far. Human capital may be attached to capabilities rather than to certain skills for example, a runner or swimmer involves a particular form of human capital, unlike athletic training in general. The basic skills that improve general performance resemble disembodied technology, but with a crucial distinction—while technology can be purchased off-the-shelf for a one-time jump in productivity, the human capital needed for ongoing progress simply cannot be purchased. For example, the large windfalls Saudi Arabia and Libya accrued enabled them to buy technology, but not human capital. The development of human capital takes time, frequently generations, for the labor force to be educated enough to significantly affect productivity.

Another criticism applies in common to all intertemporal neoclassical constructs. The implicit assumption of perfect capital markets is particularly invalid for investments in humans. Ever since slavery was abolished, investors cannot bind returns from human capital investments—that would amount to bondage. Corporations have tried to do it, as have whole nations, but no foolproof institutional means have been found for investors—outside of the individual and his or her family—to gain from a human capital investment. For example, the People's Republic of China places stringent obligations on its students who go abroad for higher education. Countries are motivated to do this since educational investments are rife with positive externalities. The nation wants to gain the social benefits that cannot be captured by private individuals—as in the public health example cited earlier. The appropriate policy prescription would appear to be the public provision of education. The institution of compulsory education also may be viewed in this light.

In its own terms, the human capital methodology is criticized for its assumptions that education causes productivity, and productivity causes income. Each of these causal connections is challenged by an alternate view that dispenses with the productivity link. The **screening hypothesis** postulates that the main purpose of the educational system is to separate potentially poor workers from potentially good workers—not to improve their productive ability. The long process of grading and selection by the school system serves to identify those individuals with the highest innate intelligence, persistence, and ability to take directions: all valuable virtues in the working world. The connection between income and productivity is challenged by pointing out various instances of established wage structures that have no relation to productivity.

A **Marxist critique** by Bowles and Gintis (1975) charges that the existing educational system serves mainly as a device for the ruling (capitalist) class to replicate itself. They point to various underprivileged groups, such as minorities and women, that have been educationally deprived and do not earn equal pay for equal work. However, the category of women does not constitute a "social class." While it is certainly true that disadvantaged groups get lower returns for the same human capital, observed wage differentials within any given group stem from educational differences precisely as predicted by human capital theory. Furthermore, if schooling is only a state policy to reproduce the social structure, this should be inimical to a healthy rate of growth. The upcoming case study of Brazil uncovers substantial contributions to economic growth from expanded education of the workforce. In sum, it can be said that educational systems certainly can bear improvement both in qualitative and quantitative terms. But the Marxist critique provides little direct policy guidance besides its usual condemnation of economic power and class structure.

Another critique by sociologists attacks the methodological individualism of the human capital construct: All decisions are individual, and all productivity is defined for the individual, not the group. Thus **social learning** may be neglected in the Human Capital model by assuming that learning is transmitted only one way—from those who know to those who do not. By contrast, social learning is more dynamic and interactive. People learn from each other and tap the vast pool of knowledge inherent in social forms and traditional methods. Such knowledge spans subjects as diverse as personal health and nutrition, livestock husbandry, and local geology and ecology. Using such methods, the learning that occurs is sure to be relevant to local needs. An example of such interactive learning is presented as a case study of technical innovations in chapter 14. (See also Hawkins 1988.)

Despite all the criticisms, the Human Capital paradigm has reigned since the 1960s after education was incorporated in a consistent way with the rest of economics. Historic forerunners of the concept had existed in the literature from Adam Smith to Irving Fisher. T.W. Schultz and Gary Becker of the University of Chicago ushered in the unified theoretical concept by identifying education as an investment that enhances the productivity of humans. Standard economic analysis could now address various issues that formerly had been treated as purely sociocultural disciplines. The next theoretical step, in 1964, was use of the production function concept to determine that a large portion of U.S. productivity growth was not attributable to increases in capital or raw labor. The excess might derive from improvements in the quality of human input. Mincer (1962) split out the part attributable to formal education from on-the-job training. Harbinson and Myers (1964) used a cross-sectional sample of a large number of countries to confirm a significant correlation between higher education and indices of economic development. Their research was careful to warn that correlation does not signify causality; yet policy makers were quick to promote education. We shall examine the expansion of supply of education in the next section.

CASE STUDY: EDUCATION AND GROWTH IN BRAZILIAN STATES

The growth of output in any country can be attributed to the separate contributions of various factors of production. Typically these effects are studied across a sample of countries. In this case, cross-sectional data are available for a number of states within a single country. Lau, et al. (1993) studied the economic growth of Brazilian states over the 1970–1980 period in order to isolate the particular contribution of human capital.

Output growth depends on the growth rate of the principal inputs: capital K, labor L, human capital H, and technology T. Here technological progress is construed broadly as any increase in productivity beyond quantitative increases in the measured factors. The production function is stated in terms of growth rates of output and inputs as follows:

$$\hat{Y} = \varepsilon_K \hat{K} + \varepsilon_L \hat{L} + \varepsilon_H \hat{H} + \varepsilon_T \hat{T}$$

Where ε_K is the elasticity of output growth with respect to capital growth, and so on. For instance, if this elasticity is .1, growth of capital by 20% would lead to output growth of 2%. In a similar way, the contribution of each factor is the product of its effectiveness times its quantitative rate of growth. The individual contributions for Brazil during 1970–1980 are shown in Table 8-3.

To estimate the statistical relationship, output growth from the set of Brazilian states is regressed against the measured growth rates of capital and labor, as well as years of education. In addition, an imputed term for technological progress is estimated. The contributions may be understood as follows:

Labor force grew at an annual rate of 4.68%. This is higher than the overall population growth rate due to new entrants, especially women, in the labor force. This growth varies widely across states due to interstate migrations, as seen in the table 8-5. The elasticity of output with respect to the labor input is estimated to be about .4. Thus its contribution to output growth is 4.68 * .4 = 1.8%.

Capital stock grew at a very rapid rate of 20% per annum. Since there is no easy measure of capital stock, it was proxied by the growth of industrial consumption of electricity. As noted earlier, this accounted for 2% of the overall growth rate of 10.9%. This contribution is on the low side, possibly because capital grew so rapidly that complementary inputs were lacking.

Technological growth is an abstraction that obviously is impossible to measure directly. Instead it must be inferred from the regression as the residual of output growth that is not attributable to the measured factors. This effect is determined statistically by entering time as a regression variable. This trend variable picks up the systematic excess increase in

Table 8-3   Decomposition of Brazil's growth rate

	Physical capital	Labor	Human capital	Technical progress	Total growth
Growth contribution	2.0	1.8	2.6	4.4	10.9
% share	19%	17%	24%	40%	

annual output. An implicit assumption is that technological progress proceeds steadily across time and is the same across all states.

Human capital as measured by years of education of the labor force. From an average level of 3.0 years in 1970, it grew to 4.4 years by 1980. This means that formal schooling grew by an average of .12 years during each year of that decade. While these numbers may not appear impressive, they actually represent a very significant achievement. For the average schooling of an entire labor force to rise by these amounts, a massive expansion of education was required. Given the elasticity of output of about 21%, the rise in average education level of .125 years led to 2.6% output growth. This factor accounts for approximately a quarter of the 10.9% aggregate growth rate.

In a previous cross-sectional study of all LDCs over 1960–1986, Lau and others found generally lower elasticities with respect to education across various regional sub groups as follows:

Sub-Saharan Africa	Mid East	East Asia	Latin America
.03	.10	.13	.17

The estimated impact of education in Brazil (20%) appears so large by comparison that Lau et al. are pressed to seek some special explanation. They postulate a threshold effect in the way education affects economic productivity. Somehow, as the labor force goes from three to four years of average schooling, the contribution to growth becomes exceptionally large. This threshold is depicted in Figure 8-4.

The implication of the threshold effect (if it exists) is that similar productivity increases could not be sustained as Brazil expands education beyond four years of schooling. This provides a good news–bad news lesson for other developing countries. This good news is the existence of increasing returns to education, at least over a given range of years of schooling. The bad news is that the LDCs have a long way to go before their average years of schooling reaches the level where they can benefit from these increasing returns.

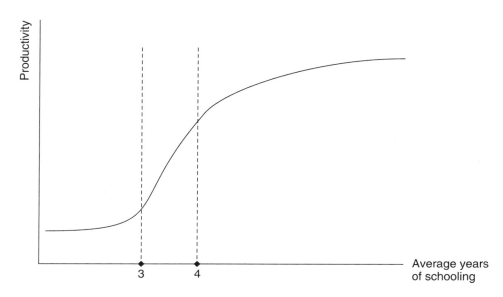

Figure 8-4 *Threshold effect of schooling on productivity*

The idea of increasing returns to education has been advanced in models of endogenous growth by Romer (1992). Expanded education offers positive externalities as people with a minimum level of education can network with each other in a productive way. The implication is that it is not enough to just raise the average level to four years of education, if half the workforce has six years of schooling and the other half has two years.

The decade of the 1970s was one of extraordinarily rapid growth for Brazil. The relevant data for states are shown in Table 8-4 as the national economy grew at an annual average rate of 10%, ranging across the states from 8% to 14%—apart from a few outliers. Note that the labor force of states can grow at rather high rates due to migration between the states within the nation's boundaries.

Table 8-5   Annual % growth rates 1970–1980

State	GDP	Capital	Labor	Years of education in 1980
Rondonia	17.7	52	16.2	3.1
Roraima	12.3	4	8.5	4.0
Amapa	4.9	25	5.3	4.4
Amazonas	14.1	22	5.0	3.7
Para	12.8	27	5.0	3.5
Maranhao	9.7	23	3.0	1.9
Piaui	9.8	23	3.1	2.1
Ceara	10.1	14	3.1	2.6
Rio Grande N.	10.8	21	3.7	2.9
Paraiba	8.6	15	2.2	2.5
Pernambuco	8.1	11	3.0	3.2
Alagoas	9.2	18	2.4	2.2
Sergipe	8.8	13	2.9	2.7
Bahia	10.8	24	2.8	2.6
Minas Gerais	10.6	13	3.1	4.2
Espirito Santo	11.6	23	4.4	4.5
Rio De Janeiro	7.9	11	3.9	6.2
Sao Paulo	9.0	11	4.9	5.5
Parana	10.2	14	2.3	4.2
Santa Catarina	11.2	16	4.3	4.9
Rio Grande S.	8.7	13	3.4	5.2
Mato Grosso	13.8	16	5.9	3.5
Goias	11.4	32	4.1	3.8
Distrito Federal	14.0	41	9.8	6.8
National Average	**10.7%**	**20%**	**4.7%**	**4.4 yrs**

Source: Lau, et al. 1993.

SUPPLY SIDE: INSTITUTIONS OF EDUCATION

The Human Capital model illuminates the demand side based on choices made by individuals. We now turn to the supply side, as represented by the institutional framework for providing education. This aspect also involves practical policy issues of education for development. Policy has been closely tied to evolving theoretical ideas. At the start of this development epoch, education always had a prominent place in practice, but lacked a solid theoretical foundation. From the 1950s, education in the LDCs needed to be expanded at all levels for good historical reasons.

The first obvious need for education was to replace departing expatriates in many former colonies. This broadened to a demand for **modernizing elites** to undertake the task of development—from the president down to judges, university administrators, pilots, and engineers. The lesson drawn from the contemporary international context seemed clear: While capital infusion had been very successful in rebuilding the war-shattered economies of Europe and Japan, that alone would be less useful in building the LDCs due to their lack of complementary human development. Again, this obviously called for an expansion of education. A final rationale for expanding education—if one more was needed—was presented by the example of the Soviet Union, whose impressive growth record was attributed to detailed planning that included manpower requirement computations. The educational sector was planned accordingly with a specific emphasis on scientific and technical training, which was seen to be directly productive in modern sector activities. Technical education was believed to be the cause of increased productivity, not merely something that happened coincidentally in the process of development.

The early empirical analyses of human capital distinguished between technical and nontechnical education. The latter was considered as just another kind of consumption expenditure.

The emphasis on costly technical education (in trade schools, polytechnics, etc.) implied economizing elsewhere. Unfortunately this led to a deemphasis on primary education, which was seen as merely a feeder for the higher levels. At this stage of development thinking, the main thrust of policy was to train an expanded elite. Thus only a technical education at secondary and higher levels was deemed to be productive.

The educational context also highlights the clash between neoclassical and structuralist ideas about development. The Human Capital approach is an integral part of the neoclassical resurgence that challenged the structuralist views that reigned in developing countries during the 1950s. The **manpower planning approach** was part of the earlier school that highlighted structural constraints to development. Like all exercises in economic planning, that approach emphasized physical quantities for resource allocation as opposed to the neoclassical reliance on the price mechanism. (A later chapter elaborates this issue in the context of industrial planning while the so-called Input/Output method is examined in a critique of industrial policy.) The quantitative approach suffers from all the problems intrinsic with any planning scheme.

1. The assumption of fixed relationships between inputs and outputs ignores the vast scope for substitution between inputs. Differently trained labor can very well produce the same output, and the different kinds of training can have very different costs.

2. The assumption of a fixed relationship between inputs and output forces development into rather rigid patterns: If human resources were deployed in the exactly the same combinations as indicated by a developed country's input/output table, this could result in a clone that might be ill-suited for an LDC. (As an example, the use of teachers' aides and nurses' aides is quite prevalent in the mix of the DC labor force.

This stems from the high wage structure for those professions. In the typical LDC, however, such skill categories might be superfluous given that wages are generally so low that no lower paid assistant is needed.) In a similar way the use of historical input/output tables may give rise to an inappropriate skills mix, as it perpetuates the past structure. A trivial example may illustrate this issue. Consider the labor planning for a hospital where, say, ten physicians work with three surgeons, thirty nurses, and two pharmacists. These categories might substitute for each other in some tasks. Such substitutions would be particularly efficient when a surplus/scarcity in some category alters its relative price.

The manpower planning framework underestimates both the flexibility that exists and the flexibility that is desired in a process of development. Psacharapoulos (1979) therefore made a plea for the expansion of liberal education in developing countries, rather than a focus on vocational and technical training. Note, however, that this approach does retain some relevance in the context of small numbers of people and a small number of skills subject to central planning. It can work fairly well within a narrowly defined sector, for example, forecasting teacher requirements within a school system.

The Human Capital model came along about the same time as doubts emerged about the contribution of education to development. By the 1960s it came to be recognized that narrowly construed technical training was rarely as productive as promised. Balogh's calls for wider vocational education at the 1961 educational conference in Addis Ababba, Ethiopia, were criticized as misdirected. In practice, the official enthusiasm for **vocational training** was defeated by private incentives. Trainees with diplomas were more interested in pursuing white-collar employment as rational career choices pushed them inexorably to seek higher university degrees. From the vantage of private sector employers, the demand for such trainees was

only lukewarm. The kind of training imparted tended to be far too capital-intensive for local employers. Other than generic skills, such as drafting or welding, **on-the-job** training continued to be a cheaper substitute.

As technical trainees pursued even more elusive white collar employment, the pressures through the 1960s were all for expanding general university education as far as possible. The new elites wanted it, the **certification syndrome** required it, and the widely prevalent subsidies made it a rational choice for individuals. Governments clearly would have preferred to expand technical and scientific education except for the cost. The inevitable consequence of the educational expansion based on the **social demand** was the emergence of a new phenomenon of the **educated unemployed,** particularly in the Indian subcontinent, where education had expanded at a faster clip than economic development. As we shall see, dualism in the labor market was a prime reason for the divergence between the demand for education and its real productivity. Todaro in 1973 noted that a degree was just one way of improving chances in a lottery for prized formal sector jobs. This challenged casual assumptions about a direct relationship between education and growth of productivity.

One last consequence of the divergence between private and social costs and benefits is the problem of the **brain drain,** which arose with the worldwide expansion of higher education. The **benefit/cost analysis** confirms the intuitive explanation for this phenomenon. The high rate of return to working in the advanced countries attracts individuals to migrate. In the LDCs, the private rate of return can be much lower than the social rate of return. An educated emigrant enjoys a return indicated by the ratio of a rich country's income/poor country's low cost. Policy prescriptions to deal with this issue match the other recommendations: Reduce the large subsidies to higher education in LDCs so that the home cost no longer appears so low. The reduced demand for college education also would ease the unemployment problem as supply more closely matches demand; thus more graduates would stay at home. On the other side, there is an argument that the brain drain is not necessarily harmful. The movements of educated people provide another channel to interchange new ideas and attitudes with the DCs, which can serve to vitalize both the home economy and the host country.

Generally, the issue of brain drain (of human capital) is intertwined with the issue of international migration (of labor), which will be examined in the following chapter. For example, the Ivory Coast benefits from migrants from neighboring West African countries, even as the latter benefit from funds repatriated home. As an earner of foreign exchange, brain and muscle power comprise the largest export of Pakistan, amounting to over half a billion dollars a year.

Let us summarize how development thinking has been influenced by the human capital concept. In the early postcolonial era, a major role for education was the need to produce indigenous modernizing elites. This aim began to fade as democratic and egalitarian ideals spread worldwide. By the 1970s, national elites were becoming less welcome, while the ideal of equity gained ascendance. By the 1980s, most societies had to settle for a less ambitious equality of opportunity rather than actual equality of results. The earlier elitist system of higher education was challenged, and universities were opened to all. Yet social equity suffered as higher education was expanded before universal primary education was achieved. (See Klitgaard 1986.) The equity issue has been further transmuted as employment creation emerges as a primary goal.

The human capital idea, of course, applies mainly to the contribution of education in raising productivity. Quantifying the idea in terms of rates of return, Psacharopoulos' analysis (1973) demonstrated that primary education is usually more productive per dollar spent than university education. The indicated policy is to divert some resources from the university level so as to expand primary education. Thus grade schools are promoted from their role as merely feeders for the higher levels. No longer should it be considered a waste that most students will be educated only up to the secondary level. School curricula must be explicitly designed with the recognition that this level may be a terminal stage of formal education.

The application of **cost/benefit analysis** to the educational sector was initiated by Psacharopoulos and Blaug in the early 1970s. It was used to compute rates of return in various disciplines as an aid in educational resource planning. Later, entire levels of education were compared to derive a new support for primary education. Economic analysis offered other useful insights, such as diminishing returns operating in the higher education sector. When expanded excessively, its rate of return declined. Scale economies also may be relevant in higher education as costs fell with expanded enrollments. Another insight was the possible gap between private and social rates of return. Thus efficiency objectives can be frustrated in cases where the individual incentives are perverse. While theory provides clear-cut prescriptions at both the individual and the aggregate level, the policy problem is to make them match.

The higher educational sector in many developing countries has handled the diverse demands placed on it by the expedient of creating dual institutions. All LDCs have a concrete requirement for a small number of high quality technocrats to run the modern sector. For small LDCs this need is most efficiently met by sending promising students abroad for higher education. The larger LDCs can set up elite institutions for this purpose. The far wider social demand, however, is met separately by a lower quality educational stream at a much lower cost. This constitutes yet another example of dualistic development, which stands in sharp opposition to the goal of equity.

The graduates from the latter stream do enjoy some benefits from their subsidized education. Yet they are often disaffected since they may suffer unemployment or low productivity due to the poor quality of their education. While individual graduates may be unhappy, this large, educated group nevertheless serves a vital function of disseminating social awareness among the populace. While this awareness often extends only to their rights as citizens rather than their duties, it can serve as a powerful tool for forcing social change. But this kind of educational setup inevitably creates contradictions; the poorly educated masses must also be made productive to solve the problems of both growth and employment. Even more critical, perhaps, are the inequities generated by the dual system that present yet another set of problems for the developing society. Recall the introductory warning: To every solution a problem!

Financing Education

An important issue on the supply side of education relates to financing. We must, therefore, elaborate on the costs of providing education and the appropriate pricing policies to determine the overall fiscal impact. We proceed on the assumption that public involvement is appropriate when there are social, as opposed to purely private, benefits. Where the two are mixed, it is desirable to separate out the social element by appropriate design of the pricing policy. Since such a separation often is difficult, the typical expedient is simply to provide public education entirely free of charge. (It may be noted that student loan programs have not been too successful as administrative costs tend to be rather high. As a practical matter, cost recovery is achieved better through discriminatory devices such a need-based scholarships.)

To induce the optimum amount of education Q^*, the appropriate price is P^*. **User fees** provide revenue of P^*Q^* that serve to reinforce the financial soundness of the educational system.

The policy of **cost recovery** is justified on two grounds: (1) Where private and social benefits are mixed, the rationale for government involvement applies just to the social part. There is no reason for the public to bear costs to provide private benefits as highlighted by the previous example of social versus private medicine; and (2) In practice it is important to distinguish financial viability from net social benefits. Even a project with great economic benefits may be rejected due to a lack of stable financing. Thus an administrative rule of thumb is to ensure autonomy and financial viability to the extent possible. This point was emphasized in an earlier reference to project evaluation. Table 8-5 shows how educational user changes are progressively decreased for higher levels of education.

Of course, user charges can also have deleterious side effects. The poverty situation can worsen as the very poor are simply not able to afford charges for textbooks or schooling. Even more vital for human development are expenditures made for basic health services. In the past decade the budgets of many governments have been drastically squeezed as economic conditions deteriorated in Africa. As a consequence many of the poorest LDCs now undertake a form of triage for providing many basic needs.

The "Bomako initiative" of 1987 was a bitter policy reality mooted at a UNICEF sponsored conference in Mali. Many African countries were obligated to recognize their severe financial crisis and to cut back social services and institute user charges. They have drastically slashed public health expenditures with the hope that international humanitarian organizations will take up some of the slack. In Burkina Faso, for example, the outlay for public health fell to about $21 million in 1990. This compared with a total of $200 million of foreign aid. Inevitably the user charges have led to reduced use for such essential services as AIDs tests, immunizations, or pre-natal care for pregnant women. Likewise primary education has suffered. In all sub-Saharan Africa, about one third of children are not even getting a primary schooling.

In the educational context, the social demand and supply analysis can provide other useful policy insights. In the case of excessive

Analysis: Pricing of publicy provided education

The situation of the educational market is analyzed in Figure 8-5. The private demand for education is shown by the familiar demand curve, while the supply curve corresponds to marginal cost (shown constant for the sake of simplicity). Due to the positive externalities that derive from education, the social benefits *SB* are higher than private benefits *PB*. This market would normally settle at equilibrium at point *A*. However, point *B* is most efficient from a social point of view. But when education is provided free of charge, the public demand for education will settle at *C*. This amount of education is excessive from the social point of view since the cost of education exceeds its social benefit. The resulting efficiency loss is indicated by the marked triangle.

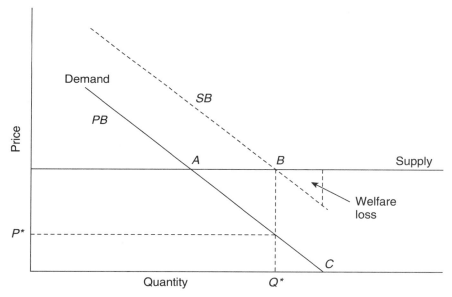

Figure 8-6   *User fees for financing education*

social demand for higher education, the social benefits *SB* are notably lower than private benefits *PB*. Now the optimum price *P** should be set higher than the cost of supply. A final microeconomic insight is that public revenue can be enhanced by price discrimination—charging higher prices to those who benefit the most. This is in fact the logic behind a composite system of fees and scholarships. Those who gain the highest private benefit are required to pay the standard fees set at a high level; at the same time those with the lowest demand price are accommodated by scholarships awarded on a discretionary basis.

Table 8-5   Public education user charges in Asia (as % of operating costs; mid-1980s)

	Primary	Secondary	Higher
Korea	0	34	46
Indonesia	7	27	19
Nepal	0	41	10
Philippines	0	9	15
Thailand	0	18	5
India	0	12	5
Malaysia	4	4	6
Bangladesh	7	4	0
Sri Lanka	3	3	3
China	5	3	0

Source: 1991.

Knowledge in the Global Context

The foregoing analysis is rather conventional in its treatment of knowledge as the demand and supply of just another commodity. Yet, knowledge is so fundamentally different, and the modern context of global knowledge flows so dramatically changed, that such an approach may be too simplistic. Arguably, the acquisition and intelligent use of knowledge may have become the preeminent determinant of economic advance. We already have noted some aspects of knowledge that make it unique. Knowledge has the property of a public good: Use by one does not diminish the amount available for use by another. Another feature has been initiated by the computer revolution, which drastically cut the cost of information acquisition, processing, and transmission. Today, the old complaint about a lack of knowledge can no longer be the main problem in LDCs, whereas the proper absorption of already existing knowledge certainly remains a major constraint. (This is closely tied to the problem of technology transfer that may similarly be construed in terms of software rather than just hardware.)

Every LDC in today's world will have to adapt its own educational structures to plug into the new world context. By analogy to distributed computer networks, each individual station within this network must be able to rapidly access the vast pool of already existing knowledge and adapt it for its own purposes. The creation of new knowledge per se becomes much less important. (See Romer [1992] on using ideas versus producing ideas.) It also must be noted that the ability to digest, adapt, and disseminate knowledge requires much of the same sort of skills as the creation of brand-new ideas. In this new context of a global interchange of knowledge, the exchange of personnel across national boundaries takes on a new importance, so the brain drain no longer looks so bleak and one-sided.

SUMMARY

The human capital ingredient is recognized as a major input in the production function that generates growth. The skills enhanced by education are complementary to the technological input to advance overall productivity.

This issue is examined in two separate parts. First, on the demand side, investment in human capital is seen as a private decision based on costs and benefits faced by the individual. Quantification of these benefits and costs allows a country to determine the appropriate kind of education measured in terms of its social rate of return. The Human Capital model is criticized on various grounds: A causal link between education and productivity may be more apparent than real. Instead, education may serve mainly as a screening function, marking out those individuals with higher innate abilities. Another criticism is directed at this construct's (implicit) reliance on perfect capital markets. Since investors cannot bind the returns from an individual's education, there is likely to be underinvestment in human capital. This is the rationale for government provision of education.

Next, the supply side is studied in terms of the institutional framework for providing education. Mainstream views about educational policy for LDCs have evolved in step with contemporaneous ideas about development in general. The early postcolonial imperatives for indigenous control led to an emphasis on elite education at the higher (university) levels. Also the prevailing fascination with technology—with the attraction of quantitative planning—encouraged narrow technical and vocational training. Later, as policy came to focus more on equity, governments chose to become the major employer in the economy. An unintended consequence was the certification syndrome, which induced a social demand for education solely to obtain those coveted government jobs. By the 1970s misgivings about such a strategy were prompted both by its low social rate of return as well as concerns about equity. Thus modern thinking now favors a broader-based educational system—in particular to ensure universal primary education before anything else. Education also must be qualitatively broader than the narrow specialization of the early years.

On the supply side, practical concerns are arising about the financing of the educational system. By distinguishing between private and social benefits, the government will be able to set an optimum fee structure. To the extent that there are purely private benefits, a case can be made that the beneficiary should pay the costs of education. Instead of providing entirely free public education, such a system would allow at least partial cost recovery to buttress the financial viability of the educational sector.

A recent focus is on the role of knowledge in a global context, as national borders become ever more porous and modern computers and communications spread rapidly. A forward-looking strategy must modify the domestic educational system accordingly. A major new role is to facilitate the absorption within any LDC of new knowledge that is continually generated worldwide.

KEY TERMS

Human capital investment
Present value (PV)
Opportunity cost
Nonpecuniary benefits
Private benefits and costs
Social benefits and costs
Return on investment (ROI)
Universal primary education

Educational pyramid
Screening hypothesis
Marxist critique
Social learning
Modernizing elites
Manpower planning approach
Vocational training
On-the-job training

Certification syndrome
Social demand
Educated unemployed
Brain drain
Benefit/cost analysis
User fees
Cost recovery
Global knowledge network

Chapter 9

Labor and Employment

The developing world has only slowly come to appreciate the crucial role of labor. Just a generation ago most theoretical and policy attention was directed toward the accumulation of physical and human capital (education). The shift in focus was forced by the changing context. As development continued, many LDCs found that labor could no longer be considered as virtually a free resource, as in the Lewis model. One must take explicit account of labor's contribution in the production function. The flip side of this issue is the acute problem that arises when labor is idle. An attitude of benign neglect used to prevail due to the assumption that unemployment would disappear automatically with development. Today, after four decades of concerted efforts, the unemployment problem remains large and persistent. Thus there is a renewed respect for labor's important role, both as an essential productive factor and as a problem. Labor's role in the development process can be summarized as follows:

1. Labor is seen as a productive factor in the production function—its marginal product certainly is not negligible. An increase in employment is bound to increase economic output. This may seem paradoxical since most LDCs are still burdened with large surpluses of labor whose marginal product appears quite low.

2. Unemployment is, of course, devastating to the morale of the individuals affected. And isn't the ultimate goal supposed to be increasing the welfare of humans? At the collective level too, unemployment can foment major social tensions, causing critical political problems for the developing society. Thus the creation of jobs becomes an important intermediate target. The process of development itself creates unemployment by upsetting traditional economic arrangements. This, in turn, may prompt a severe social reaction that upsets the very consensus that allowed development in the first place.

3. Another effect of unemployment, apart from the waste of a productive factor, is in exacerbating income inequality. A major contributor to the problems of income inequality and poverty is the gap between employment earnings and the zero wage of the unemployed.

Defining Under-and Unemployment

Our study of the labor issue begins with some careful definitions. The seemingly familiar notion of **unemployment** turns out to be more complicated, particularly in the context of developing countries. As a first step let us examine this concept in the standard neoclassical framework. In normally operating markets, labor demand must meet supply at a market clearing wage; thus unemployment simply cannot exist in equilibrium. The demand and supply diagram in Figure 9-1 shows that neoclassical unemployment arises only if the wage rate exceeds the equilibrium wage. Only those people who are capable of working and actively seeking a job at the going wage are considered unemployed. (Another kind of unemployment allowed by neoclassical theory is that due to voluntary job-seeking activity. By its very nature such unemployment must be quite transitory.)

At a wage rate W'—somehow held higher than equilibrium—the labor supply curve shows

$U + E$ people want to work, while employers demand only E. The excess labor is U, and the unemployment rate is $U/U + E$. This measure also depends on other factors that influence **labor supply.** For example, if labor demand shifts out in a booming economy, the numbers of unemployed would certainly fall. Yet, the unemployment rate might rise. This is because the heightened optimism may also sharply increase labor supply as previously discouraged workers reenter the labor force to seek jobs. Thus the unemployment rate can rise simultaneously with employment. (Such an effect is also observed as developed economies emerge from recessions.) To avoid the troublesome notion of willingness-to-work, a more robust measure of unemployment is $(L - E)/L$ where L is total labor force.

In LDCs there is a further difficulty in measuring unemployment by asking a yes/no question whether a person is working. Bruton (1981) suggested that it might be better to study how an adult typically spends time (in terms of hours of productive work) so as to distinguish involuntary

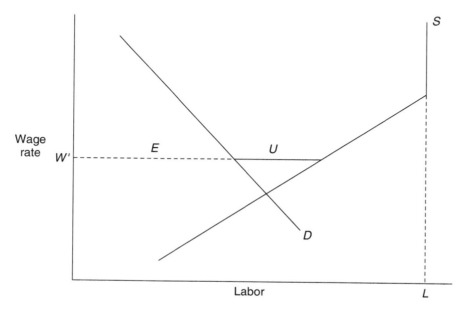

Figure 9-1 *Unemployment in the labor market*

from **voluntary unemployment.** Simply counting heads (the number E above) may be inappropriate in the presence of **underemployment.** People work, but may not accomplish much. This kind of disguised unemployment is better viewed as three people sharing a job rather than workers aren't working very hard. Then each of them gets at least one-third of a full wage in a context where alternative employment is scarce. This is how Lewis characterized household production arrangements in the traditional sector. Such underemployment means that if one worker is removed total product will not fall. Sen (1982) suggests that the quantity of labor performed should be distinguished from the number of laborers to clarify this concept. Various empirical research studies confirm that the **marginal product of labor (MP_L)** in rural areas is generally low, but greater than zero.

$$0 < MP_L < W = AP_L$$

For a profit-maximizing firm it would be strange for wage to exceed MP_L. But this is not unreasonable in the case of households, which are not run on the lines of employer-employee relationships. Rather, a farm family typically opts to share total output so that each family member gets the **average product of labor, AP_L.** Hopefully this is a sufficient amount so that each person at least reaches a subsistence standard of living. The idea of people earning a wage (or income from self-employment) that exceeds marginal product in LDCs has been challenged by neoclassical economists. They aim to show that the marginal product is being measured incorrectly. Various studies find that the MP_L is actually higher; it only seems low because of the marked seasonality of agricultural production. (We shall further examine this issue in chapter 14.)

The idea that average product exceeds marginal product may be visualized as fishermen on a lake. As the number of fishermen increases, output also rises, but at a diminishing rate; thus the marginal product of labor is lower than average product. While each fisherman is equally productive as any other, the average is pulled down by the added fisherman at the margin.

Finally, another feature of labor supply may have relevance for development. In many societies women from rich families do not need to work or may not want to as a mark of their status. They are not part of the labor force L. Similarly, in hospitable climes with easy living, as say on a tropical island, people who voluntarily choose leisure over low paid labor must not be classified as unemployed. This phenomenon results in a **backward-bending supply curve** of labor, which contrasts with standard supply curves that always have a positive slope. The negative slope indicates that as wage rate increases beyond a certain level, workers will cut back their number of work hours.

This phenomenon occurs since individuals derive utility not just from the consumption of goods, but also from **leisure.** More work time implies less leisure time, so the marginal utility of leisure will increase. The utility curve U on the left in Figure 9-2 shows all the combinations of goods and leisure that give equal utility. The consumer would be willing to swap goods for leisure at points along this curve. This is an equivalent substitution of labor for leisure, since labor hours provide the wages to buy the goods. The dotted lines show the applicable budgets at various wage rates. At higher wage rates the budget line has a steeper slope. Then the worker can access a higher combination of leisure and market consumption.

Some economists used to be concerned about a possible decline in work effort as the LDCs become richer. Once earnings begin to exceed a customary (low) level in poor countries, people might opt for more leisure instead of more money income. (This is not exclusively an LDC phenomenon as people in rich countries might also display such behavior.) As an empirical matter, however, a slackening of productive efforts is not much of a concern. These days, the increased integration of the world economy

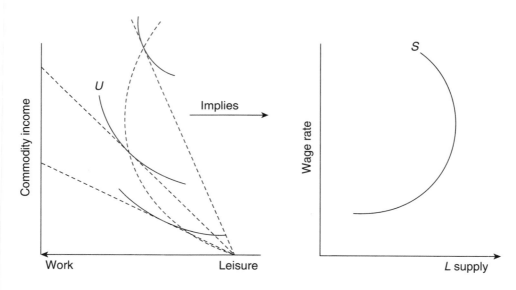

Figure 9-2   *Backward-bending supply curve of labor*

through the media and travel brings an exposure to advanced lifestyles that alter LDC tastes. Almost inevitably, this **demonstration effect** increases the desire for purchased goods and tends to straighten out the labor supply curve.

DUAL LABOR MARKET

So far, we have highlighted the stylized fact that a low rural wage coexists with a higher urban sector wage. This was a prominent feature of the Lewis model presented earlier. While the idea of dualistic markets has been extremely useful, Lewis' construct provided only a static view of wages and employment within a dual economy. A more dynamic view is required to explain empirical observations such as the emergence of open unemployment. Another puzzle was the observed **migration** from areas of low unemployment to urban areas that had high unemployment.

A succession of models aim to explain the prominent stylized fact of migration. Massey et al. (1994) survey the contrasting approaches. First came Lewis' dual sectors with differing wage

rates. Labor migrates from agriculture to industry in response to the wage differential. A later explanation pioneered by Michael Todaro turns from a macro sectoral focus to the microeconomic behavior of individuals. This analysis works out how wages, employment, and unemployment change with the flow of migration. Lately a "new economics of migration" emphasizes household rather than individual decisions. The motivation to diversify household risk is important in the migration decision, and not just the expected income differential.

This section concentrates on the microeconomic perspective. We analyze how employment and unemployment numbers in urban labor markets of the LDCs adjust in response to the fixed urban wage as well as rural wages and underemployment. The numbers in each market segment change endogenously as labor migrates. The **Harris-Todaro model** explains how the migration from rural areas continues despite urban unemployment. The key assumption is that rural migrants are attracted by the **expected value** of city wages as in a lottery. If there's a 20% probability of getting a fancy $20-per-hour job while the alternative is a lowly job in the informal sector with wage W_I = $5, the expected wage will be $20(.2) + 5(.8)$ = $8. The flow of migrants is regulated by p, the probability of winning a high-paid organized sector job with wage W_O. Migrants will continue to add to urban slums so long as the expected wage exceeds the agricultural wage W_A.

$$W_O \cdot p + W_I \cdot (1 - p) \geq W_A$$

If the urban informal sector wage is low, the equilibrium equation may be simplified by assuming wage $W_I = 0$. Further, the probability p may reasonably be assumed to depend on the number of contestants for the fixed number of positions L_O in the organized sector. (For example, if L_O is 1 million and total labor force is 20 million, this probability would be 5%.) p is given by L_O/L, where the total urban labor force is L.

$$W_O \, \frac{L_O}{L} = W_A$$

Notice that this is an equation of a hyperbola. (Recall the general equation is $X \cdot Y$ = constant. In this case $W \cdot L$ = constant.) This hyperbola may be drawn as the equilibrium condition for the urban labor market outside of the formal sector.

The hyperbolic curve in Figure 9-3 shows how the size of the urban labor market is determined from the size of the organized sector and its wage rate. These institutional features determine the parameters: L_O, the number of jobs in the organized sector, and W_O, its fixed high wage. The vast rural sector also provides an elastic wage W_A as a sort of wage floor. All these parameters determine how many migrants will crowd into town and force down the expected wage until it equals the agricultural wage W_A.

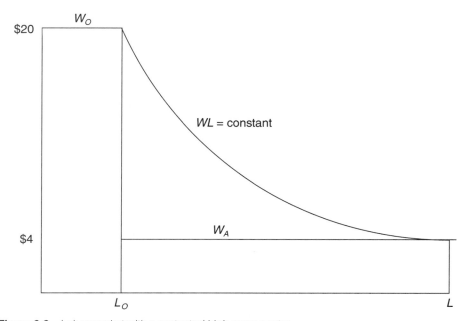

Figure 9-3 *Labor market with a protected high wage sector*

$$\$20 \frac{L_O}{L} + \$5 \left(1 - \frac{L_O}{L}\right) = \$8$$

This equilibrium condition indicates that so long as expected urban wage (on the left in Figure 9-4) exceeds agricultural wage W_A, migrant inflows will swell the urban labor force L. Since organized sector employment L_O is fixed, urban unemployment will be $L - L_O$. But how is labor demand in the organized sector determined? This is found from the MP_L schedule for industry, given its high wage W_O. The hyperbola shows the effective demand for labor from rural areas. Note what happens when industrial employment L_O is increased. When Kenya tried this labor policy in the 1970s, the unfortunate result was to increase urban unemployment! This sharp contrast to standard D and S analysis occurs because many more migrants are attracted, as indicated by a new shifted hyperbola. The complete analysis includes the demand for labor by industry and its supply curve from agriculture as shown in Figure 9-4.

This issue has a close analogy in the United States. The ongoing immigration from Mexico and Central America into the United States also can be understood by the Harris-Todaro model. In this case, the United States corresponds to the advanced sector with its high wage, and the Mexican economy corresponds to the backward agricultural sector. The elastic supply of low wage labor is beneficial to U.S. industry as a high profit rate encourages capital accumulation.

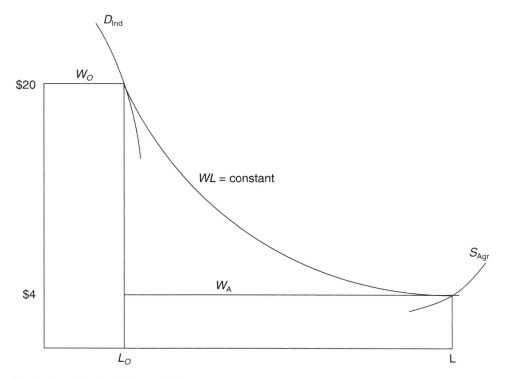

Figure 9-4 *The dual labor market*

Not surprisingly, such immigration is welcomed by capitalists and resisted by organized labor. The high wages that prevail in the organized sector are threatened by the unorganized free labor market that springs up—union construction workers are undercut by street-corner immigrant workers. Only a few of the immigrants will be lucky enough to break into the formal sector, yet the high wage differential will continue to attract migrants according to the Harris-Todaro model. Migration also could be stemmed by raising Mexican productivity and wages. (In Figure 9-4 this would mean raising the schedule of labor supply from agriculture.)

Urban Labor Market Problems

Strictly speaking *dual* means twofold. However, the concept can be generalized to cases where a market is segmented into more than two pieces. In the broader sense, duality means that the labor market is not strictly unified. Lewis' original idea must be modified in view of empirical observations from the urban setting of many LDCs. Two stylized facts are prominent: (1) the existence of another major labor market segment, the **informal sector,** and (2) the emergence of open unemployment in a big way. For instance, note labor market shares in Table 9-1.

Table 9.1 Latin America 1980–1985
Urban labor force distribution

	1980	1985
Formal sector		
Large firms	39.3%	34.2%
Public sector	21.5	22.2
Small firms	5.6	6.6
Informal sector	27.2	29.6
Unemployment	6.4	7.5
	100.0%	100.0%

Source: *ILO World Labour Report* 1987.

While this table presents only one example—Latin America during the economic crisis of the 1980s—it also illustrates the situation in many other countries where policy was biased in favor of a narrow modern sector. The debt-induced crisis had the effect of squeezing organized sector employment. Displaced workers swelled unemployment rolls, which increased by 1% of the labor force, and also entered the informal sector, which picked up almost 2.5% of the labor force in just five years. Such employment trends and wages are intimately related to the macroeconomic crisis, as will be examined in chapter 16.

We examine each of the stylized facts in detail. First, the emergence of true unemployment (not just underemployment) in LDC cities is possible since people can now afford to be unemployed. Even in very poor countries urban political pressures can force the provision of some welfare facilities, such as, subsidized food and housing, directed particularly at the urban poor. Some of the measured unemployment can comprise of youths from middle-income families who are in the process of a **job search** after leaving school or college. Meanwhile, in the rural sector, very few can be truly unemployed without the safety net that is available in urban areas. A stark example of this was provided by the recent crises in Ethiopia and Sudan. Vast numbers of destitute people migrated to the cities to avail of the barest subsistence; staying back in the villages would have meant certain starvation. Table 9-2 indicates unemployment rates for various countries in sub-Saharan Africa in the mid 1980s. The average rate of 18% was up from 10% in the mid 1970s.

The second interesting stylized fact of LDC labor markets is the newly identified segment of an unorganized informal urban sector. This sector is not merely a provider of services; it often has substantial involvement in manufacturing. Earlier we studied the genesis of this sector: Given the fixed low rural wage, rural workers migrate to the cities hoping to land a privileged job in the organized sector. The vast majority, however, do not succeed and must turn to jobs

Table 9-2   Urban unemployment rates in
Africa, mid-1980s

Botswana	31%
Ethiopia	23
Somalia	22
Tanzania	22
Ivory Coast	20
Zambia	19
Zimbabwe	18
Senegal	17
Kenya	16
Nigeria	10

Source: *ILO World Labour Report* 1992.

in the unorganized sector. While this market-determined wage may appear nominally higher than farm incomes, it partly compensates for the higher urban cost of living. The informal sector wage adjusts as migration continues, while urban unemployment remains chronically high.

Despite the measured unemployment, one observes that most people are occupied doing something in the informal urban sector. This so-called **underground economy** engages in business activities that are not officially sanctioned. It also avoids tax payments, regulations, licenses, and so on. To test this, a researcher in Lima, Peru, attempted to set up a small-scale plant through official means (see case study in the policy chapter 13). Soon he had enough paper to fill a truck. If such enterprise thrives, it does so despite, rather than because of, government help. The **International Labor Organization (ILO)** mission to Kenya in 1974 marked a turning point in granting formal recognition to the informal sector. For the first time, the development community voiced its misgivings that the formal sector just was not succeeding at creating employment.

Meanwhile, the masses who remain outside the organized sector have resorted to self-help. The informal sector is increasingly seen as a boon rather than a problem. It advances economic efficiency since it bypasses inefficient regulations,

pays market wages, and uses appropriate labor-intensive technology. This sector also demonstrates a remarkable rate of productivity growth. Hirschman, the noted development economist, noted that progress often comes due to challenges that stimulate a response. The millions who crowd into the cities certainly have been challenged in their lives of desperation and squalor. (This constitutes an urban analog to the Boserup idea that population pressure can prompt technical changes in agriculture.) The informal sector has blossomed, producing not just services, but also many manufactured goods. In some cases this exceeds the output of the organized sector! Therefore, it is imperative that government policy be reoriented to correct both biases that impede overall development.

To summarize the argument so far: The observed duality in LDC labor markets was welcomed by the development economics school for its presumed benefits for industrialization. Yet the resulting **urban bias** had negative side effects in the form of serious social and economic problems stemming from urbanization. The Harris-Todaro model explained why the flow of migrants continues despite growing open unemployment in the cities. Meanwhile, a parallel **organized-sector bias** intended to encourage industrialization, often served to discourage entrepreneurship in the informal sector. Both of these biases—urban versus rural, organized versus informal sector—become entrenched due to vested interests that build up in the political economy. In particular, a political alliance forms between controlling bureaucrats and industrialists and labor in the organized sector.

High Wage in the Organized Sector

Wages in the organized sector of the dual economy shot to a dramatically high level even as unemployment and underemployment continued to be widespread throughout much of the developing world, at least up to the late 1970s. Since then important exceptions to this pattern have emerged, as detailed later. The general pattern has been an ongoing migration into the cities, while a large **wage gap** remained in favor of the formal sector. Neoclassical economics initially found this very difficult to explain. But this gap got so large and so obvious that it could not be ignored any longer. Diverse explanations attribute this to

1. Trade union activity

2. Government wages unrelated to labor market conditions

3. Political clout associated with urban labor

Detailed LDC data reveal that urban areas always have higher wages than smaller towns and villages. (For that matter this is also true in the developed countries.) This feature is especially true for the capital cities where political responsiveness tends to be highest. Another prominent stylized fact is that urban organized wages far exceed the wage in the urban unorganized sectors. Data from India reveal striking differences in wages (up to ten times higher) for the same occupation. Some semiskilled jobs in the organized sectors, for example, chauffeurs, receive wages higher than senior professionals. (In some celebrated cases, they earn even more than the president of the country!) Does the monopoly position of unionized labor explain this large wage differential? Perhaps it does in part; but what is harder to explain is how this monopoly power can be maintained in a situation of continued surplus labor.

Yet another explanation of the higher urban wage attributes it to the higher cost of living in the cities. Many services, such as child care by grandparents, that were free in the village must be paid for in the city. Counterbalancing this are various nonwage benefits available in urban areas: subsidized transport, health care, and entertainment. All these explanations, however, remain inadequate in face of the extremely large wage differentials that can exist. Recent

theoretical advances provide somewhat more satisfactory explanations.

The new labor economics presents the concept of an **efficiency wage.** The productivity of employees does not stem primarily from an application of raw labor. Rather, in the modern work environment, employers must increasingly rely on the efficiency or effectiveness of employees' work. In a complex environment, a worker's effort is difficult to monitor or measure. In such situations the overall productivity depends intrinsically on teamwork, which calls for initiative and creativity from the individual worker. The firm pays a wage premium to elicit such effort. Moreover, the existence of abundant surplus labor (presumably of the same quality) does not eliminate the necessity for the employer to pay these higher wages. If any one of those outsiders was hired, he or she would also have to be paid the higher wage to elicit the special efforts. Note that such ingenious explanations are just an extension of neoclassical theory. Markets still clear, but what is traded is not raw labor but rather effective labor. This theory, due to Deepak Mazumdar and Joseph Stiglitz, may explain why the formal sector wage gap becomes larger as economies become more decentralized and complex.

Another explanation of the high organized sector wage is made by Svejnar (1989). His construct is based on the idea of political bargaining. (The topic of political economy is examined more generally in chapter 13.) The agents in this political economy game are firms, which aim to maximize profits; **labor unions,** which aim to maximize wages; and government, which aims to advance the national interest by maximizing employment. This analysis may be understood by reference to the familiar diagram of the segmented labor market (Figure 9-5). If the unions and government were powerless, firms would expand employment along the demand curve for labor to the profit-maximizing level. At that point, *A,* the area of the profit triangle, *X,* is largest. If unions have the power to enforce a higher wage, they will push firms up the MP_L curve to points such as *B,* which has a higher wage but lower employment in the organized sector. If the government exercises its power, it could force minimum employment goals in addition to the high wage requirement. Such a power game can result in wage/employment points such as *C* (outside the MP_L schedule) in which firms' profits are reduced to area *X – Y.* Even though this position reduces profits for firms, it is just as socially efficient as point *A.* The distribution of income at such points is split differently between labor and firms.

This analysis may become more comprehensible in a real-world application such as the semi-public political game played for the separate goals of wages and employment in Detroit's auto industry. The labor union's private interest is to seek higher wages, while the public interest concentrates mainly on the creation or maintenance of jobs. Clearly there is some overlapping of interests, which the various parties—the auto companies and the unions—try to exploit by enlisting government and political apparatus to further their private aims.

The implication of this analysis is that wages are not necessarily too high if the government also enforces employment requirements on firms. Don't be overly influenced by the chorus of business leaders complaining that wages are too high. Other things equal, they would, of course, prefer lower wages to boost profit margins. Yet, regardless of the wage level, the socially optimum amount of employment is nevertheless attained. Lowering the organized sector wage will not necessarily raise employment; it only serves to tip the income distribution in favor of capitalists. This analysis implies that a policy package of wage and employment requirements can be implemented by the means of public sector enterprises. More than 60% of all organized sector employment in LDCs is, in fact, due to the public sector.

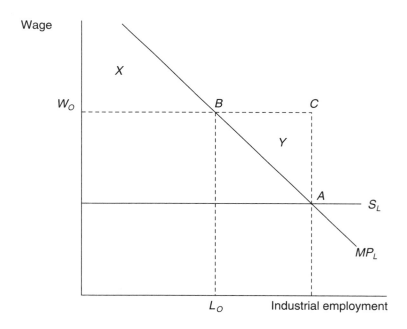

Figure 9-5 *Political economy of employment and wages*

Important exceptions to the stylized fact of high wages in the organized sector arise from three different sources.

Rural-Urban Income Gaps In a few instances (for example, China, Botswana, and Malawi), the elimination of rural-urban income gaps is an explicit policy objective. Such policy also has been pursued elsewhere even when not stated explicitly. A downward trend in real wages of employees outside agriculture can be discerned, especially after the global recession that started in 1979.

Administered Wage The organized sector usually has an administered wage set by administrative fiat. During inflationary times the nominal wage adjustment may lag behind the rate of inflation, so the real wage drops. Meanwhile wages and prices in the market sector adjust roughly in step with inflation. As an illustration, suppose inflation averages 40% annually over five years while the nominal wage is adjusted upward twice in 50% increments. The result is that the real wage, the ratio of wages to prices, will fall drastically by over 58%.

$$\frac{W\,(1+.50)^2}{P\,(1+.40)^5} = \frac{W\,2.25}{P\,5.38}$$

Even if the nominal wage increases were larger, there still would be sharp fluctuations in the real wage. This describes the essential story in much of Africa and Latin America over the past two decades. In many countries, the drop in the real wage has been 30% or more (Ethiopia, Ghana, Kenya, Malawi, Tanzania, Zaire, Zambia, Burma, Bolivia, Dominican Republic, Peru, and Uruguay). The *World Labour Report* (1987) described the specific case of Sudan:

The public sector dominates regular wage employment, providing 500,000 out of 600,000 jobs. Civil service pay scales have been adjusted infrequently even though prices doubled between 1977 and 1980, doubled again between 1980 and 1983, and yet again between 1983 and 1985. By November 1983 civil service pay scales were one-fifth of their real level in 1970. The severe erosion of real pay has had serious adverse effects on morale and productivity.

Another example of the adverse impact is that of Ghana, where the purchasing power of lower level public pay scales in 1984 was only 20% of its value in 1977. For higher grades it dropped as low as 6%! Civil servants were obliged to resort to moonlighting and graft, and public sector efficiency suffered enormously.

Wage Restraint Policy Another effect on wages derives from a wage restraint policy implemented to control a budget deficit. The cut in real wages usually is achieved indirectly—by not raising nominal wages during inflations—rather than by directly cutting nominal wages. The severe macroeconomic disturbances in the 1980s were associated both with inflation and chronic budget deficits. The severity of the economic crisis, mostly in Africa and Latin America, has forced their governments to reconsider their role as employer of last resort. As much of the formal sector is comprised of the public sector, the austerity measure inevitably required cuts in public sector wages and/or employment.

Government Employment

Direct job creation through government actions has other attendant dangers. In becoming the employer of first resort, government may misinterpret its role and create jobs that have no economic justification. Since these jobs can only go to a subset of the population—as the budget is ultimately limited—such programs are manifestly unfair to those who are excluded and subject to manipulation by political-economy forces. The organized sector constitute just a small part of the dual economy. The high wage bill for this

Table 9-3   Some African countries in 1970s with an inverse relation between formal
sector employment and growth

Country	Annual GDP growth rate	Formal employment as % of population	Public employment as % of total employment
Uganda	.7	5.9	42
Ghana	.9	10.1	74
Tanzania	3.6	6.3	66
Zambia	3.8	14.3	72
Malawi	4.0	9.6	39
Kenya	5.6	12.4	42

Source: World Bank study on sub-Saharan Africa, 1981.

kind of employment program can become a major drag on the overall economy, with adverse effects on both equity and efficiency, and is especially harmful to the government's finances. Table 9-3 shows a sample of African countries with a high negative correlation between growth performance and large formal sector employment programs. This historical data illustrate a period when the idea of public employment was ascendant (1970s), while its costs in terms of reduced growth over an extended period (1965–1984) was not sufficiently appreciated.

Many developing countries suffered from a severe fiscal crisis in the 1980s. Government payrolls had to be cut. Part of this was achieved by the wage restraint noted earlier. The other part was achieved by layoffs of public employees. This is seen as virtually the last resort, undertaken under duress in times of severe economic crisis. Such retrenchments may follow the **privatization** of public sector enterprises. Thus the unemployment rate tends to move up sharply in those countries that had the largest proportion of government employment. In short, government employment is seen as a two-edged sword—easily added in times of fiscal laxity, only to be removed very painfully in times of crisis that occur as a consequence of the inefficient policy.

Low Job Creation by Industry

If the organized sector wage is held at a high level for whatever reason, the private sector will respond by employing excessively K-intensive methods that stifle potential job creation. For this reason the early optimism of industry to generate vast amounts of employment has turned out to be a major flop. As noted earlier, this failure of the Lewis model is attributed to industry that did not absorb much surplus labor due to the marked rise in industrial sector wages even before underemployment was eradicated.

Another explanation for weak job creation is based on inappropriate government interventions affecting employment quantities rather than on wage rates. Whereas enforcement can vary widely, a large part of labor legislation is devoted to ensuring job security. In effect, employers are free to hire but not to fire. Fluctuations in the demand for output, as well as technological changes, inevitably alter the demand for labor. Yet labor laws can seriously restrict the flexibility of large industrial firms to which such legislation typically applies. A 1991 study by the World Bank found that the rational response of affected firms is to hire at the minimum from the outset instead of opting for labor-intensive techniques. To get a sense of the magnitude of employment creation by the industrial sector, let us examine Malaysia over the period 1960-1979.

g = Industrial growth = 10%/year

h = Elasticity of employment growth with respect to industrial growth = 0.5 (If industrial output increases by 1%, employment grows by .5%)

s = Share of industrial labor to total labor = 12%

Growth of industrial employment is the product of these items.

$$g \times h \times s = (.10)(.5)(.12) = .6\%$$

Compare this with the annual growth rate of labor force = 2.7% over the same period. Starting with a size of 10 million, in the next year 270,000 more people will enter the labor force. Of these, only 60,000 will get jobs in the industrial sector. Where are the other 210,000 to go? This is a serious question for development policy. Note that this applies for a fairly advantageous case. Malaysia, after all, has had a decent annual industrial growth rate of 10%, while it also managed to keep its industry L-intensive—its labor absorption parameter is fairly good in comparison with other countries. Korea provides a rare counterexample where industrial job creation was successful. The approximate figures are s = .25, h = .6, and g = .14. Growth of the industrial labor force is 2.1% compared to labor force growth of approximately 2%. Thus Korea seems well on its way to solving its unemployment problem.

The policy implications from this simple arithmetic exercise are thus: To decrease unemployment it is desirable to have a large share s for industry. But note that this is an exogenously given parameter in the short run. Increase the rate of industrial expansion g. For decades the policy that attempted to do this was import substitution, but results generally have been poor as we will study in chapter 12. Instead of relying on the inherently limited domestic market, industrial expansion could be based on export promotion, as shown by the Korean example. The other possibility is to use more L-intensive industry (a higher h). Korea also succeeded in this effort by initially concentrating on L-intensive production like textiles and shoes, instead of K-intensive heavy industry. Korea avoided the mistake common in many developing countries of making labor artificially expensive. A separate policy variable is, of course, to reduce the growth of labor force by controlling population growth, but this applies only in the very long run. Finally, developing countries must consider other rural-based activities for their employment creation potential, for example, the new agro-based industries. Also valuable for this aim is the informal sector in urban areas with its small-scale and microenterprises.

Exercise: For some important developing countries, for example, Mexico, Brazil, Nigeria, India, and China, determine the actual g and s from the *World Development Report*. For various postulated values of h see how prospective growth of industrial employment compares to growth of the labor force.

CASE STUDY: THE ROLE OF LABOR IN EAST ASIA'S GROWTH

The exceptional growth performance of the Asian tigers has been much celebrated, while the source of this growth continues to be a matter of debate. A controversial new claim is that increased labor participation has played a substantial role (Young 1994). The growth contribution of this mundane source contradicts the conventional wisdom that technological progress was especially large. The new argument claims instead that East Asia experienced sharp increases in labor participation as an increased fraction of the population entered the labor force. In addition, a dramatic increase in human capital accounted for a substantial part of output growth. (Note, however, that the extended years of schooling reduces the available raw labor input.)

Next, if we account for the remarkable increases in capital accumulation—as emphasized by the old development economics—the remaining contribution of technological advance no longer seems exceptional by comparison with other countries. The ratios of investment to GDP, ranging from about 24% for Taiwan to 40% for Korea, stand among the highest in the world.

This case study focuses on the labor mobilization aspect. As noted earlier, this factor receives little positive attention as a possible contributor to growth—even as it remains the object of negative concerns relating to unemployment.

Table 9-4 tells a revealing story. The extremely high growth rates of output per capita (sustained over a quarter century) are significantly lower when viewed in terms of growth per worker. The data show labor force growing much faster than overall population in all four countries. This fact is summarized by the dramatic increase in participation rates over this twenty-five-year period. These are largely accounted for by women entering the labor force and having fewer children. Meanwhile, the hours of work did not fall appreciably as these countries rapidly become richer—except perhaps in Hong Kong.

An important part of Young's methodology is to carefully measure output and the various inputs. Data for the labor input were obtained by six categories: sex, age, education, income, hours of work, and class of worker (employee, self employed, etc.). For each sub-input, the corre-

Table 9-4 Annual growth rates over 1966–1990

Growth rates	Hong Kong	Singapore	Korea	Taiwan
GDP	7.3	8.5	8.5	8.6
Population	1.6	1.9	1.8	1.8
GDP per capita	5.7	6.6	6.9	6.8
Workers	2.6	4.5	2.8	3.1
GDP per worker	4.7	4.0	5.7	5.5
Nonagricultural Output per worker	N/A	4.0	5.0	4.9
Change in labor	.38	.27	.27	.28
Participation rate	.49	.51	.36	.37

Source: Young 1994.

sponding wage was determined from income data. From the available cross-tabulations the labor input was determined in terms of **full-time–equivalent workers (FTE)**. This concept of effective workers can be illustrated by a trivial example: Two half-time workers count as one FTE. By splitting labor into each subinput, the research determines total FTEs. For example, the age variable may indicate that 40-year old workers are 25% more effective than 30-year olds due to experience gained on the job. In the same way human capital serves to increase the effectiveness (or quality) of the labor input.

The standard sources for such data are annual labor force surveys and more comprehensive census figures. While the former source reports more frequently, it is also far less accurate than the census due to small sample sizes. Also, the scaling factors drawn from the previous census get progressively outdated due to the rapid transformation of these economies. Thus much massaging of the data and interpolations are needed. Such detailed adjustments also create a source of criticism of Young's results.

By contrast, Kim and Lau (1992) use an aggregate measure of hours worked, with no adjustment for the subinputs. In particular, by making no allowance for human capital, they find a much lower growth contribution by labor (about 20%) and a higher contribution by capital (80%). Interestingly, they too find little evidence

of technological progress. These relative contributions are likely to change as the labor force and technological capabilities mature in the Asian NICs. Already in the 1990s, female participation rates have reached a plateau while the labor force is aging and human capital acquisition has accelerated. Thus the effective labor force is bound to increase even as capital growth tapers off.

Finally, a distinction between the productive sectors must be made. Growth has been significantly influenced by the transfer of labor between sectors. For Taiwan and Korea, in particular, labor migration into nonagricultural sectors increases the denominator, and therefore decreases the growth rate of output per worker: Q/L.

The nonagriculture sectors include manufacturing, services, and other industry (for example, mining and utilities). While emphasis usually is placed on export manufacturing, research finds growth of productivity to be highest in agriculture. Moreover, evidence suggests that the output of services may be overstated. This research has interesting policy implications: Both the intersectoral transfers and increased labor input can only provide one-shot boosts to the growth rate. Yet their conventional nature assures us that other developing countries can also hope to match the growth experience of the Asian NICs.

SUMMARY

A study of labor markets in developing countries starts by distinguishing the concepts of unemployment and underemployment. The latter is uniquely an LDC phenomenon, particularly as rural underemployment exists simultaneously with a higher urban wage. As a consequence there has been a massive migration into the cities. An earlier puzzle was why this migration continued in the face of high urban unemployment. The Harris-Todaro model explains that rural workers are attracted by the high expected value of urban wages. In fact, the majority of them do not get highly paid jobs in the formal sector; instead they must settle for a lower pay in the informal sector. The informal sector is expanding despite policy biases against it. The high wage structure in the organized sector adds a labor-market bias on top of an overall urban bias that generally prevails. The artificially high formal sector wage generates the further problem of excessive K-intensity in LDC industry. While job creation by industry remains disappointing, a new problem is the emergence of true unemployment in LDCs. This arises as the skeleton of a welfare state, at least for a privileged urban class.

Another pathology of the dual economy is the very high formal sector wages that coexist with widespread underemployment and low wages in the rest of the economy. Neoclassical economics strives to explain this phenomenon through the concept of an efficiency wage that is deemed a rational response in certain labor market conditions. Alternatively this high wage may be explained in terms of wage bargaining by unions combined with the government's aim to ensure high employment. Such an aim leads directly to the proliferation of public sector enterprises. As a consequence, most LDCs are stuck with overstaffed and inefficient public sectors, while the government overregulates private labor markets.

The severe inflations of the late 1970s through the 1980s created further distortions in the wage structure of many LDCs. As the organized sector wage is largely set by administrative fiat, it can only be changed by explicit decisions. Often nominal wages were not adjusted regularly enough or sufficiently to keep pace with inflation. The sharp fall in real wages added to the poverty problem, especially in urban areas. In effect, this constitutes a drastic reversal of the former pro-urban bias, especially in some African countries.

KEY TERMS

Unemployment
Underemployment
Labor supply
Voluntary unemployment
Marginal product of labor
Average product of labor
Backward-bending supply curve
Leisure
Demonstration effect
Dual labor market

Migration
Harris-Todaro model
Expected wage
Informal sector
Job search
Organized sector or formal
  sector?
Underground economy
International Labor
  Organization (ILO)

Urban bias
Organized-sector bias
Wage gap
Efficiency wage
Labor unions
Administered wage
Government employment
Privatization
Full-time equivalent workers
  (FTE)

Chapter 10

Technology

An important ingredient in economic growth is technology, which can be viewed as just another ingredient in the production function. Among all productive factors, technology is especially interesting since it appears to promise something for nothing; thus it has had great appeal in the LDCs. Technology differs importantly from other factors. Unlike capital accumulation, it does not require the painful act of refraining from consumption. Human capital formation is also a long and expensive process, as every student knows. On the other hand, natural resources are inherently limited, while labor supply grows exogenously. By contrast, the intangible knowledge, once produced, may be costless to acquire. In international fora the idea of technology transfer is also commonly espoused. Moreover, compared to the tangible factors, technology contributes much more to modern economic growth.

...the direct contribution of man-hours and capital accumulation would hardly account for more than a tenth of the growth in per-capita product....The large remainder must be assigned to an increase in the efficiency of the productive resources. (Kuznets 1981)

What precisely is technical change? What are impediments to acquiring and implementing technology? What are its effects? We shall address each of these questions in successive parts of this chapter. We start by characterizing technological progress in a very general way to dispel various misconceptions. First, one must not think of technology, especially in the development context, primarily in terms of "hi tech." The immediate needs are typically far more modest in such low-tech activities as the production of shoes. Second, the concept of technological progress must be construed widely, not applying just to industrial activities. For example, in the service sector, the concept may apply even in mundane tasks, such as transacting more efficiently at a post office window; in the agricultural sector, as the shift from herding to farming. A third important distinction is that technology refers to both **production processes** and products. Whereas new **product innovations** and materials are fairly important in our everyday experience, the concern in LDCs may be more with process improvements that will be the main source of advance.

DEFINING TECHNICAL CHANGE

The layman is often more familiar with product innovations than with process improvements. For the developing countries, which aim to rapidly expand production capabilities, the focus is on the latter. Economic textbooks also seem to place an emphasis on process improvements, perhaps because this aspect fits easier into a theoretical framework. But, of course, both forms of technical progress are important.

Product Innovations

Even if there were no process improvements, innovations in products certainly would enhance well-being. Product innovations economize on the use of all resources, while process improvements save on productive inputs. A simple example would be an improved automobile engine that reduces fuel consumption. Such technical advance reduces fuel usage, in contrast to process improvements that reduce the capital and labor needed to produce engines. (See James and Stewart [1990] on the role of product innovation in developing countries.)

An example of product improvements in LDCs is the common plastic bucket that has supplanted the earlier galvanized steel model. The new product is lighter and more durable, and helps economize on natural resources. It is wrong to equate improved technology for LDCs with hi-tech computers or equipment. Yet certain advanced products have allowed LDCs to leapfrog intermediate steps that other countries were obliged to follow. For example, the use of communications satellites and remote antennas in India and Indonesia allowed social education to be disseminated in a new and efficient manner. There is also great interest in new materials, such as composites and plastics, which offer better performance at much cheaper cost. For example, the introduction of teflon has made obsolete precision metallic bearings, at least in small sizes.

The effect of product innovations show up mainly as increased welfare, which is hard to measure. An improved bicycle, for example, enhances utility as reflected in a higher demand price. It is possible that the demand curve shifts in such a way that the value $P*Q$ that enters aggregate GDP would be unaffected. Yet consumers of that product are enjoying a higher consumer surplus. By contrast, process improvements lower production costs by reducing usage of factors, as shown by a downward shift of the supply curve in Figure 10-1.

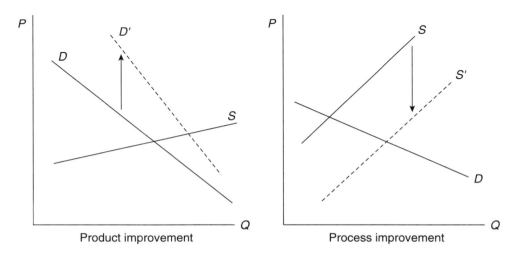

Figure 10-1 *Product versus process innovations*

Production Processes

As noted, technological progress for LDCs is focused largely on improving the efficiency of production processes. Production technology can be represented in alternative ways.

$$\text{Engineering specifications} \rightarrow \text{Production function} \rightarrow \text{Cost function}$$

The economist translates detailed engineering designs and formulations into a production function. The **production function** shows how a given output requires a certain amount of inputs. Thus technological change may be thought as a multiplier, T, to the effectiveness of other tangible inputs.

$$Q = T \ f(\ K, L, HC \ )$$

The production function is depicted by a map of isoquants drawn in factor space. (Figure 10-2 shows only two factors, K and L.)

The curved **isoquant** (iso = equal, $quant$ = quantity) shown in Figure 10-2 indicates the different combinations of K and L that can produce a given amount of output Q. If the same quantity can be produced with improved technology, it is represented by an inward shift of the isoquant curve. Fewer factor inputs are needed to produce a given output. The isoquant representation can illustrate the various properties of technical transformation, each of which we will examine in detail.

• Factor intensity

• Factor substitutability

• Economies of scale

• Total factor productivity

On these curves the particular production combination chosen depends on the relative price of capital and labor. The optimum (lowest cost) combination of factors is the point of tangency with the budget line, which shows the factor

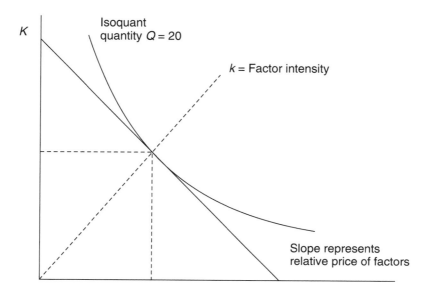

Figure 10-2 *Production isoquants*

combination that can be bought for a given budget. The slope of this straight iso-cost line indicates the relative price of factors. At the point of tangency, the *K/L* proportion chosen is called **factor intensity,** *k*. Picking the economically efficient factor proportions is called **choice of technique.**

The functional form of the isoquant map has been extensively studied by mathematical economists. Different forms have been tested to see if they conform to the empirical reality of technology used in various industries. The three most prominent candidates are the Cobb-Douglas form, the constant elasticity of substitution form or CES, and the Leontief function. All of these differ in their elasticity of substitution as will be defined. (However we choose not to go into the mathematics of the different forms of production functions.) Modern processes typically have little **factor substitutability** between *K* and *L,* whereas traditional technology tends to be quite flexible. As an example, consider a street entrepreneur in Kenya who makes bicycle parts. If labor cost becomes rela-

tively more expensive, he would promptly increase the use of capital and substitute away from labor. (From *A* to *B* in Figure 10-3.)

The curvature of the isoquants indicates the possibility of substitution taking place between *K* and *L* in response to changes in the relative price of these factors. This relative price is represented by the slope of the dashed lines. By contrast to the above smooth curve, modern hi-tech processes tend to have a squarish isoquant, which indicates that even large changes in factor prices will not induce much change in the factor use. The elasticity of factor substitution is defined as the percent change in the *K/L* ratio for each percent change in the relative price of capital and labor, which are the rental rate and wage respectively.

$$\frac{\%\Delta \, K/L}{\%\Delta \, r/w}$$

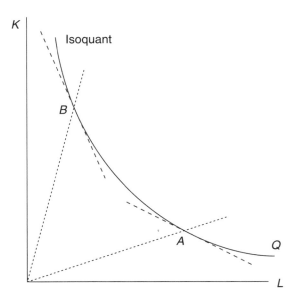

Figure 10-3   *Factor substitutability*

Modern technology tends to move the isoquants leftward toward greater *K*-intensity, while also reducing substitutability. For example, a modern oil refinery typically is very *K*-intensive. But its design is so specific that even at sharply lower wages, it would be difficult to substitute labor for capital along square-shaped production isoquants. These features create **technological dualism** as a counterpart to the labor market dualism noted earlier. A traditional sector may coexist with a modern sector with radically different technological features such as: (1) higher capital intensity, (2) lower factor substitutability, and (3) greater possibilities for scale economies. Technology tends to evolve such that the modern sector becomes increasingly *K*-intensive. If capital is drained away from the traditional sector, the dualism becomes even more pronounced.

The modern sector also is distinguished by its high wage structure. Chapter 9 elaborated the efficiency wage argument that applies to the modern sector. Its high wages may also arise due

to the characteristic of low factor substitutability. Employment will not change much even if wages fall drastically. Such a wage drop is depicted as a flatter tangent to the isoquants in Figure 10-4. Modern sector employment (in a refinery, for example) can be so small that the wage bill is just a small fraction of output. Thus there is a smaller incentive to adjust the employment level as wages change—in sharp contrast to the traditional sector.

The modern sector of LDC industry closely resembles similar industries in the DCs. A resulting advantage is that the LDC factory does not need to continually invent technological improvements on its own. It typically has easy access to the fast-paced progress in modern sector technology. In diagrammatic terms, this constitutes another difference as: Modern sector isoquants tend to move inward much faster than the traditional sector's technology. Such rapid technical advance in refinery design and operation, for example, have now become common worldwide (see Bardhan 1975).

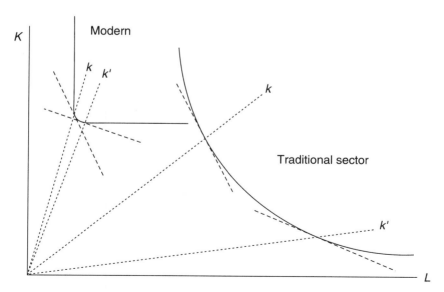

Figure 10-4 *Technological dualism*

Economies of scale is a prominent characteristic that distinguishes production processes. In particular, increasing returns to scale usually apply for modern industrial technology. As the scale of production goes up, the average cost per unit tends to decline. In Figure 10-5, a given increase in factor inputs (say, 50%) is associated with an output isoquant that increases by a larger proportion (say, 70%). Returns to scale can equivalently be depicted in the familiar supply curves shown in the right panel, in which average cost is lower at an expanded level of output. Typically, this long-run *AC* curve is derived from a series of short-run *AC* curves.

(At this point it is useful to reiterate the distinction between returns to scale and marginal productivity. The former relates to change in output as *all* input factors are increased proportionately, while the latter refers to output change due to increasing *one* input alone, say labor, while keeping capital constant.)

Whereas the average cost curve may decline over a given range, it may also reach a minimum point. Beyond this, an expanded scale of production runs into decreasing returns. This point of optimum scale may vary widely for different industries. For example, a typical petrochemicals complex needs to be quite large to attain the cheapest per unit cost. On the other hand, specialized fabrication and assembly is most efficient at small scales. The optimum scale is associated not just with the technology of plants and machinery, but also crucially with the human factor. The range of managerial control is critical, due to the principal-agent problem that arises in any teamwork. As a team gets larger, it becomes progressively harder to monitor individual performance and to maintain the appropriate incentives. We will note this effect particularly in the organization of agricultural production in chapter 14.

The technological feature of scale economies provides another reason why LDCs favored industrialization, which promised large economies of scale. The import substitution strategy aimed to restrict imports so that domestic industry might produce more efficiently at larger scales. However, a country does not necessarily have to be large to reap these benefits. A small country like Hong Kong achieves scale economies by large-scale production for export.

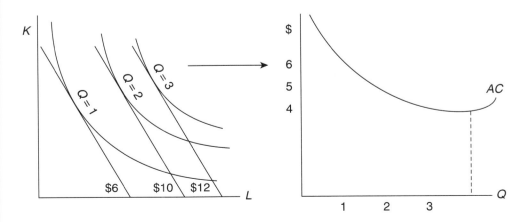

Figure 10-5 *Economies of scale*

Last on the list of technological characteristics is **total factor productivity,** or the overall efficiency of production. Often this feature is confused with the productivity of a single factor such as labor. For example, on hearing that American workers have high labor productivity the student may think that American workers must be working very hard or very smart. But note that output depends on the entire production function.

$$Q = \text{fn } (L \text{ or } K, \text{ etc.})$$

An increase in the quantity of any one of the factors causes output to increase. The productivity of labor, Q/L would then appear to be high. Output per worker rises due to larger amounts of capital used, not necessarily because labor is working harder. A bulldozer operator is bound to generate more output than a worker with a shovel. (Single factor productivity could likewise be stated in terms of any factor whatsoever, for example, as output per acre of land. However, we tend to emphasize labor, since the very purpose of development is to raise the output per person.)

The concept of total factor productivity is relevant when choosing the optimum production technique. Often this choice must deal with a conflicting set of goals. It is not enough to focus just on labor productivity, as is common in the advanced countries. Here progress is defined as simply to raising labor productivity. A similar error is to focus just on capital productivity in the developing countries, using the Harrod-Domar model. (Recall the discussions of capital allocation in chapter 7.) Clearly, a more encompassing goal is to raise total factor productivity.

Technology obtained from advanced countries is often the best in terms of total factor productivity. Even though the K-intensity of such processes tends to be higher, they are factor saving overall and therefore cheaper. Such improved technology is depicted in Figure 10-6 by the isoquant Q_2. Compared to the original Q_1 (which used factors $5K$ and $5L$), the new technology uses less of both factors ($4K$ and $2L$) to produce the same amount of output. However, it is a more capital-intensive technique. Production cost is obviously lower since the new technology uses less of both factors per unit of output. In general, however, the new technology could have slightly higher capital intensity K/Q counterbalanced by a large reduction in labor intensity L/Q. It still may be the better choice since it reduces the use of scarce capital (per unit of output) even as some laborers are laid off, adding to the surplus pool.

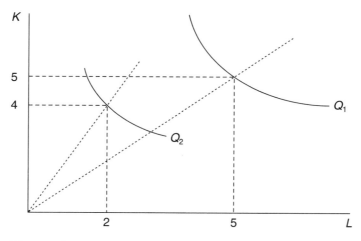

Figure 10-6 *Dilemma of automation*

Technical progress, which involves an inward shift of the isoquant map, can be of various different types. **Neutral technical change** causes isoquants to shift inward in a proportionate way so that the K/L proportions remain unchanged. Continue with the previous example, where 5 units of K and 5 units of L initially are used to produce a certain output. After neutral technical progress, only 3 K and 3 L are required to produce the same quantity of output. Thus the K/L ratio remains the same—provided that factor prices remain unchanged. Such neutral technical change, as defined by Hicks, contrasts with the typical situation of isoquants moving leftward in a manner that is biased either toward laborsaving or capital saving (See Figure 10-7). Again, be sure to compare the technical choice on the old and new isoquants at a constant relative price of factors.

When technical progress is **laborsaving,** there is an obvious conflict with the desire to utilize the abundant labor resources of LDCs. In fact, this situation is an exact analog of concerns from the nineteenth century when Luddites went about smashing new machines that took away their jobs. As history has shown, those concerns were as overblown then as they are now. The process of development inevitably involves a reallocation of labor from lower to higher productivity activities. However we must make certain that the higher K-intensity is indeed better in terms of overall productivity. The danger is that much advanced technology is sought merely for the sake of progress or glamour and is inappropriately K-intensive for the capital-scarce LDCs.

An interesting example of biased technical change is presented by the Green revolution in LDC agriculture. The technological change in this instance was of a land-saving nature rather than laborsaving. This innovation served to enhance the "effective quantity" of land, rather than of labor. The happy implication has been that the Green revolution did not add excessively to unemployment in rural areas. By contrast previous agricultural progress used to be laborsaving. For example, the use of tractors and mechanical harvesters put many peasant laborers out of work.

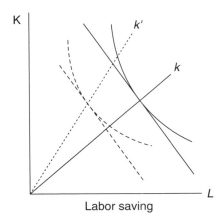

Laborsaving technology uses a more K-intensive ratio, K/L

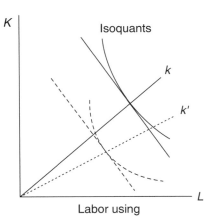

Labor-using technology is less capital intensive.

Figure 10-7 *Biased technical progress*

IMPLEMENTATION OF IMPROVED TECHNOLOGY

For the implementation of improved technology in LDCs, its policy must deal with two separate issues. One is to ensure that (A) as far as possible a country's choice of factor intensity should match its factor endowments. For LDCs this means moving along an isoquant to a lower K/L ratio. The other, possibly more important, issue is (B) to speed up the rate of technical progress. This involves shifting the isoquants inward as fast as possible. Regarding the first issue, the recommendation for the adoption of L-intensive **appropriate technology** is often disregarded in LDCs even though capital is scarce in relation to its relative price. We start by examining various reasons for this, some of which are good while others are misguided.

Choice of Technique

Earlier we presented an example that highlights the dilemma of choosing between a technology with better total factor productivity versus one that has low K-intensity. While automation will certainly raise the K/L ratio, it can also reduce the capital use per unit of output, K/Q. The factors that are rendered surplus due to the automation can be redeployed to expand output, so that the scarce pool of capital is utilized more efficiently even as labor employment does suffer somewhat. In sum, the goal of growth may conflict with the goal of employment. In the long run the labor released may be used to expand output in the same industry or in some other industry. This is part of structural adjustment programs that we will discuss in Chapter 16. However, many countries are so fearful of the immediate impact effect that they resist making the adjustment for long-term growth.

The aim is to show that choice of technique is a more involved decision than simply picking the lowest K/L ratio. This is not just a tough choice between employment and output.

The technique chosen also can affect the balance between present consumption versus savings (that generates future consumption). In turn, each of these choices conflicts with the goal of increasing employment. The conflicts between employment and output and between employment and savings are illustrated for a K/Y versus K/L criterion for choosing techniques.

$$ \frac{Y}{K} = \frac{Y}{L} \cdot \frac{L}{K} $$

Recall that the Harrod-Domar model focuses on optimizing the use of capital by minimizing the capital/output ratio. This is equivalent to maximizing its inverse, capital productivity Y/K, shown on the left side of the equation. This need not be synonymous with maximizing labor intensity. In other words, a lower K/L ratio sought to boost employment, may lead to lower capital productivity Y/K. This would occur if the labor-intensive techniques also happen to have low labor productivity Y/L. Fortunately, this theoretical possibility does not appear to hold empirically for most production in LDCs. Labor-intensive techniques generally are found to furnish a higher Y/K ratio, so no conflict appears between output versus employment.

Unfortunately there is no such happy resolution of the conflict of employment versus savings. Figure 10-8 shows output as a function of labor in a production process operating with a fixed amount of capital. The horizontal axis can be read as either labor use or as labor intensity L/K. Output grows at a diminishing rate as a greater amount of labor works with a fixed capital stock. The payment to labor is depicted by the straight line whose slope is the wage rate.

At an employment level of $L_{\max}$, maximum output is attained at the highest point on the production function. However, maximum profits obtain at a different level L_S, where employers hire labor so that marginal productivity (slope of the dotted tangent line) equals the wage rate. If we make the classical assumption that capitalists are the best savers, then maximum profits also imply maximum savings. In that case picking an output level that maximizes savings is seen to conflict with the objective of employment maximization. The special assumptions of this analysis must be highlighted: All profits are saved, and the wage rate is a given constant. Then the wage cost is the straight line wL, while the point of maximum profit is the highest vertical separation of productivity from wage cost. A society that chooses saving over employment thus may choose production techniques at L_{max} rather than L_S in Figure 10-8. This implies raising the capital intensity K/L and reducing employment.

These various arguments provide theoretical backing for why a K-scarce LDC might nevertheless rationally choose to use K-intensive techniques. We also point out more practical reasons for such a choice.

1. Capital-intensive techniques already have been invented in the developed countries. On the isoquant diagram, this is shown as a point with a high K/L ratio. It may not be possible to slide down to an L-intensive technique since the isoquant might simply not extend that far. In short, the advanced technology is not readily adaptable; LDCs that wish to utilize it must face the dilemma of automation described earlier. One way to get around this is for LDCs to conduct their own **Research and Development (R&D)** for machinery and processes. This would accomplish both aims: advance the isoquants inward, and ensure that these are appropriately capital-saving. Inducing LDCs to develop their own capital goods industries is not easy since most LDC economies are too small to enjoy the needed economies of scale. However, there have been some promising beginnings of such

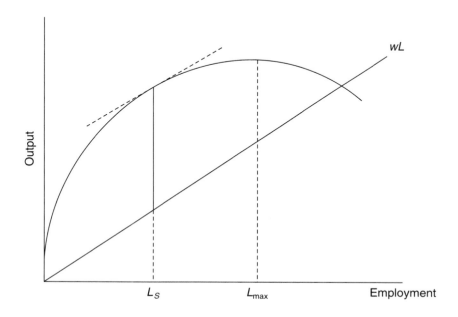

Figure 10-8   *Choice of technique*

technological development in the larger LDCs such as Brazil and India.

2. Foreign investors from K-intensive DCs tend to bring their own technology with them in the form of imported capital goods. The foreign investors often are none other than vendors of various items of capital equipment. Thus, if a K-scarce country wishes to obtain capital through foreign direct investment, it might be obliged to accept the K-intensive technology that comes with it. We have seen that such technology usually is better in terms of its capital/output ratio even if its K/L intensity is worse.

3. Remember that labor is different from human capital. Calls for L-intensive methods may be difficult to implement since they often require more developed skills than for K-intensive techniques. Some of the latest capital-intensive processes are purposely designed to be idiot-proof, even if their repair and maintenance certainly do require special skills.

4. Capital-intensive technologies generally manage to avoid messy labor/political problems. Such problems appear to be endemic in large L-intensive facilities, in which industrial relations tend to become radicalized; prominent cases in point are the textile industry and coal mining. The social and political organization skills needed to manage this problem may also be lacking in the typical developing country.

5. The final reason for excessive K-intensity is least justifiable of all. The bias toward K-intensive technology was reinforced by the proindustrialization policies of LDCs that started out by subsidizing capital. Consequently, the distorted relative price of K to L encouraged private entrepreneurs to adopt K-intensive policies that were not socially optimum.

Despite all the attention focused on the topic of labor-intensity, this is not the sole requirement for "appropriate technology." LDCs must also choose technology that is robust and simple to apply in the rather rough conditions that prevail in the countryside. In addition it should be designed specifically for small scale use, avoiding "lumpiness" in the required capital investment. In short, appropriate technologies have to be specifically designed for the conditions prevailing in developing countries.

Accelerating Technical Advance

The second aspect of technology policy is speeding up the pace of technical progress. In the previous figures this is depicted by an inward shift of the isoquant map as opposed to choosing a particular point on it.

The rate of technical advance may be analyzed within a growth accounting framework. This involves taking the overall growth rate, splitting out the part that can be attributed to growth in the measured factors, and attributing what remains to growth of total factor productivity (TFP). Table 10-1 shows TFP growth across various regions in the developing world in comparison to France and the United States. Also shown are the world average figures, which refer to a sample of sixty-eight countries for which data were easily available.

Table 10-1 is a revealing summary of the sources of growth. The first set of figures show the raw growth rates of input factors. The actual contribution to GDP growth will depend on the share of that factor in the production function. Consider, for example, the concrete case of the United States. Capital's share of output is typically about 25%; thus 3.4% rate of growth of capital stock will contribute about .8% to the overall growth rate. This comprises about 23% of the observed 3.0% growth rate. (The numbers differ because of rounding errors and averages taken over several years.) Among the developing world, East Asia, which has the best growth

Table 10-1 Contributions of inputs and technical advance to GDP growth
Annual % growth rates over 1960–1987
(Figures in parenthesis show the % contribution to overall growth rate.)

Region	GDP	Capital	Labor	TFP
Africa	3.3	6.3 (73%)	2.2 (28%)	0.0 (0%)
East Asia	6.8	10.7 (57%)	2.6 (16%)	1.9 (28%)
South Asia	4.4	7.2 (67%)	2.1 (20%)	0.6 (14%)
Latin America	3.6	5.6 (67%)	2.6 (30%)	0.0 (0%)
France	3.9	4.8 (27%)	−0.2 (−0.5%)	1.7 (78%)
U.S.	3.0	3.4 (23%)	1.8 (27%)	0.5 (50%)
World*	**4.2**	**7.2 (65%)**	**2.3 (23%)**	**0.6 (14%)**

Source: *World Development Report* 1991.

performance, can attribute its success to a healthy growth of TFP combined with a dramatic increase in capital formation. The percentage contribution of capital growth appears high in the other regions simply because their productivity growth was so small.

The speed of **technical advance** can be explained by considerations of incentives and behavior. Just as any policy of change creates winners and losers, so does the implementation of improved technology. Inevitably this involves a redistribution of rewards among the factors of production: capitalists, laborers, landowners, educators, and so on. Political forces tend to arise to obstruct such redistributions. In chapter 13 on political economy, we will note that the group of present losers is usually more powerful than the group of potential future winners. For example, declining industries rationally should be shut down so that resources can be diverted to new expanding industries. But people who have specific human or physical capital tied up

in these "sunset" industries tend to resist. They certainly will suffer in the short run, even though everyone stands to gain in the long run. Resistance to mechanization or computerization also may be seen in this light.

Another impediment to technological advance arises from the fact that know-how, like all knowledge, is a **public good.** Public goods are those for which exclusion of nonpayers is not possible. The consequence is a chronic tendency to undersupply public goods, such as innovations, because the inventor may not be able to fully capture the benefits from the innovation. Thus it is not profitable for an individual or firm to expend resources to acquire the knowledge, since all others will then avail of its benefit for free. The rational individual will rather wait for someone else to do it first so that he or she can freeride on the other's efforts. To deal with this intrinsic problem, society's solution is to grant a temporary monopoly in the form of **patents.** In cases where patents are not feasible there may have to be public provision of such goods. Chapter 8 on Human

Capital, presented one such example in which ownership rights are limited. Since slavery no longer exists, a social problem arises in that firms do not find it in their private interest to invest in improving an employee's skills. The worker can easily quit and start working for a competing firm. Yet the firm cannot legally oblige the employee to remain and continue to provide it an exclusive return for its investment.

This special problem of property rights stems from technical knowledge resembling a public good. (Computer and software firms have a similar problem keeping secure the ownership of ideas that they generate.) A possible solution is to employ researchers in public institutions that are required to disseminate the new knowledge throughout the nation. Unfortunately, government research institutions must contend with other clashing incentives. The salary and status structure are such that the researchers are more prone to pursue **pure science,** which brings them international recognition. This may be more in keeping with their individual interests rather than the mundane applied sciences useful to the developing country. The basic lesson is that incentive problems, in general, have to be addressed in designing policies for **technology transfer** or development. Organizational considerations are relevant, for example, in arranging contacts between government researchers and industry. An innovative arrangement might be to encourage a two-way interchange of personnel, but this typically is very hard to arrange under existing civil service rules and bureaucratic procedures of most countries.

The process of technological improvement does not necessarily imply innovation starting from scratch. There is a preexisting **technological gap** between the already developed countries and the LDCs. Gershenkron saw this gap in a positive light since it allows the LDCs to acquire and adapt already existing technology from the advanced countries. Then learning-by-doing can proceed in stages:

- operation
- maintenance
- adaptation
- imitation
- quality imitation
- innovation

To adopt and inculcate technical advance calls for a certain kind of attitude. Advanced technology must not be viewed as a tangible thing, but rather as an intangible process. Contrary to naive expectations that often prevailed in LDCs, it is not simply a matter of going out and buying the technology even if one could afford it. The capital-rich OPEC countries have learned this lesson in an expensive way: Technological improvement is a process that must occur on an on-going basis. In many cases it may require major changes in existing institutions or culture. Moreover, it is not just foreign processes/products that need to be acquired, but also sophisticated techniques of product differentiation, financial practices, quality control methods, management systems, and so on.

The best source for advanced technology is often the large **Multi National Corporations (MNCs)** of the developed countries. Many LDCs just want to acquire the process or products, however, without the wrappings of an MNC. Where LDCs just bought the unbundled technology separately, outcomes have often been disappointing since the various other capabilities constitute an equally important form of technology embodied in the MNC itself. The relations between LDCs and large MNCs have the troublesome nature of bilateral monopoly. Both LDC buyer and the MNC seller are of comparable size and power. Thus their interaction is far from a competitive model that applies to many, small agents. The solution to such a microeconomics problem depends on which side can muster the greater power and best strategy. Negotiations are further complicated since the parties may lack full information. Usually the LDC finds it difficult to split out the cost of the desired technical component from the total investment package, which combines the costs of royalties, management fees, marketing, and returns to risk capital.

Successful technological adoption and advance is closely tied to the entire setup—institutions, culture, and policy—that shapes incentives. Even random changes in the economic environment can serve as a stimulus for progress. For example, the oil crisis led to development of more energy-efficient products, showing how "necessity is the mother of invention." Such innovations were not attempted earlier in the absence of an urgent necessity, but when fuel prices soared, **induced technological change** occurred spontaneously. Today, even if fuel were to become cheap again, the new technology would not be abandoned. This situation can be illustrated in terms of the isoquant diagrams that depict technology.

Neoclassical economics claims that free markets provide the best incentive to speed technological advance. This goes beyond the static argument that market prices encourage appropriate techniques. The dynamic impetus is provided by the pressure of competition. If a firm succeeds in lowering costs by technological improvements, the resulting drop in price reduces the profits of competitors. Firms throughout the industry are then obliged to upgrade their technology. All the firms would not just act defensively; they would proactively cultivate such progress.

Such technical advance is related to Harvey Liebenstein's concept of *x*-inefficiency—that most of the time firms lie far below the efficient production frontier, so average costs are higher than they need be. All that is lacking is the little motivational impetus to move upward to the frontier. In LDCs in particular, a series of small efficiency improvements can have a major cumulative effect on productivity—attitudes and behavior in labor markets, better allocation of capital and labor, attention to seemingly minor

details in quality, and so on. Harberger (1985) has urged that policy reform be based on this premise. Consider, for example, a situation of production initially taking place about 50% below the efficient frontier, it would then be possible for the country to derive a 2.5% rate of annual growth for 20 years from increased efficiency alone, quite apart from enhanced capital accumulation or exogenous technological advances.

GLOBALIZATION OF TECHNOLOGY

The latest revolutionary aspect of technology is the fact that it has become global. Even though this secular development unfolded steadily over the course of the past few decades, it does appear to have sprung full-blown and dramatically just recently. This turn of events, with profound implications for the LDCs, is a consequence of historic changes in the global environment. They are

1. A marked speeding up of the systematic creation of new technology across a wide range of countries

2. Vastly improved global access to technology in a tangible way, and due to political and institutional openings

Both of these imply a new stance toward technical advance different from what prevailed even a few short decades ago. The technological policy in LDCs must specifically face up to these dynamic features as compared to the rather static assumptions that prevailed earlier. Attention must be refocused from the creation of new technology to its rapid absorption. The new main imperative of technology policy is to facilitate technology transfer and to develop the capability to absorb this new knowledge through technical and institutional reforms. The global system may be characterized in a simplistic way: Each new technical advance immediately gets thrown into a common pool regardless of its original source, be it Switzerland or Thailand. From this pool, all the other countries may take what they can, subject to their own absorptive capacity. In short, access to most knowledge is so cheap as to be practically free. The main constraint is the domestic framework that can absorb and utilize this cornucopia.

Technology transfer can take many forms: (1) incorporated in machines or products, (2) licensed trade secrets for which exclusion is easy, and (3) intellectual property rights for which exclusion is harder. The first two are conventional forms whose acquisition and transfer may be treated in the same way as international commodity trade. The last item is the newest and most unsettling since all the countries have not learned how to deal with it. Examples of this are new medicines or computer software, which are created by a lot of hard work, research, and creativity, but which cannot be hidden once they are revealed. Of course, the producers of brand-name spreadsheet software, for example, do try to capture the rewards of their creative and marketing efforts; but the idea itself, somewhat like the multiplication tables, has become the possession of all humanity.

The LDCs must learn to tackle this new situation in a way that is most advantageous for themselves and to the social good. In the new division of labor, the developed countries undertake the vast bulk of R&D in international laboratories, often with a substantial contribution of engineers and scientists who migrated from the Third World! Typically these are profit-making firms that see the need to maintain the right incentives through the protection of patents and copyrights. Yet the LDCs want to free ride by enjoying the benefits of the inventions without contributing to rewarding the inventors.

The maintenance of **intellectual property rights** has become a contentious international issue, due to the urging of governments in the west. Yet this problem may be somewhat overblown by its ideological antagonists. Often inventors are amply rewarded anyway from their earnings in the advanced countries themselves. Very poor countries cannot be too concerned that Bill Gates, the founder of Microsoft, gets a fuller return from his inventions when his individual net worth exceeds the GDP of entire LDCs. Note the vast chasm between the perceptions of rich and poor countries in this regard. The latter emphasize the social progress of their impoverished masses, while the former aim to uphold the principle of private property rights. This conflict may come to a head when, for example, a drug vital to fighting AIDS might be withheld till the rich inventor extracts a large payment from a poor LDC. The argument becomes further politicized when tied together with other international negotiations, such as trade talks through GATT. The countries that have most at stake due to their large exports (for example, Singapore and China) are the first to concede to the new enforcement of intellectual property in the international context.

CASE STUDY: TECHNOLOGY TRANSFER THROUGH MNCS IN INDIA

India presents an excellent case study that illustrates many issues relating to the process of technology transfer. India is a large diversified economy that can realistically choose from the entire menu of methods. Moreover, its mixed economy has substantial involvement by both public and private sector enterprises. It also had an early start with a domestic R&D effort as well as widespread technical education. Finally, the government explicitly considered the appropriate attitude toward technology and the best means to acquire it from abroad.

The changing policy stance toward technology transfer must deal with each of the following interrelated components.

1.   Import of technology

2.   Import of machinery

3.   Multinational investments

India is notable for persisting in a closed economy strategy long after its failings became manifest. Its socialist inspiration in the early years caused India to view most foreign involvement suspiciously as a form of exploitation or control. Until quite recently, the government remained ambivalent toward direct foreign investment by MNCs. Joint ventures or foreign-controlled firms generally were discouraged, even as capital inflows were desired. A prominent example was the much publicized tiff with IBM that resulted in its withdrawal from the Indian market in the 1970s to much populist acclaim.

The import of capital goods also was resisted in order to promote development of an indigenous capital goods industry. (As a result, India has built up substantial capacity for producing machine tools, heavy electrical equipment, as well as machinery for sugar and paper mills, and so on.) Such protectionism also was based on the infant industry idea of inducing technical advance by learning-by-doing. Restrictions on the first two forms left just one channel relatively open to access foreign expertise through technology imports. Yet the actual amount of technology transfer remained relatively small.

The paucity of foreign technology transfer came on top of poor productivity advances domestically. Technology transfer was small because needed foreign technology often comes as a package along with the foreign machine or corporate involvement. This may be inevitable when the technology is inseparable from the physical machine. In other instances, the **bundling** stems from the desire of foreign firms to maintain proprietary control for business reasons.

The government commissioned a study to examine reasons for the obviously poor performance in the area of technical advance. The Hussain Committee of 1984 noted that restrictiveness on the first two channels was most to blame. Indigenous technical advance also was disappointing as total factor productivity in Indian industry grew very slowly in comparison to the other NICs since local incentives to innovate were lacking.

The preferred channel of technology import operated through **licensing** of products and processes. In India this mode is commonly referred to as collaboration agreements. In each case the government would conduct a detailed screening process that, if successful, would permit a domestic firm to purchase specific technology from a specific foreign vendor. Seen in the context of overall industrial regulation (described in chapter 15), the net effect of such micromanagement was discouragement rather than promotion of technological advance. Singh (1991) notes that: ". . . both the existence of a myriad of regulations and their manner of application, have had a deterrent effect beyond paper intentions." The last clause is notable since the Indian regime professed to be ideologically predisposed toward science in general, and technological progress in particular. Yet the technical and scientific ambitions were defeated due to the neglect of economic motivations and behavior.

The government further regulated both the pecuniary and nonpecuniary aspects of license agreements. Negotiations were conducted on a tripartite basis: The domestic and foreign firms negotiated with the third party, the government, ostensibly representing the national interest. Since the rate of royalty payments were restricted, industry ended up buying low-cost low-tech packages. Some evidence suggests that Indian firms preferred it this way as industry sought profits not mainly by lowering costs in a competitive environment, but rather by monopolistic positions obtained by government favor.

SUMMARY

Technological advance is increasingly seen as the predominant factor contributing to growth in modern times. Thus it merits careful study both in its causes and effects. We begin by distinguishing two forms of technical progress: product and process innovations. While acknowledging the importance of the former type, the chapter's focus turns largely to the latter aspect. Production processes are usefully characterized within a production function framework, in which technology defines how much output may be produced by a given amount of inputs. The function may be represented by a map of isoquants whose relevant features are factor substitutability and economies of scale.

Given the inputs of capital, labor, and human capital, the main issue for technology policy is (a) to ensure that the production possibility frontier advances as fast as possible, and (b) to choose the right technique, or appropriate mix of factors, given a country's overall endowment of factors.

The first of these two issues, rapid advancement of total factor productivity, is taking on far greater importance in the modern world. For many developing countries that aspire to attain newly industrialized status, the previous concerns about small is beautiful and a focus on appropriate technology appear archaic and peripheral to rapid progress. This is especially true in the new global context in which technological advances and transnational flows of knowledge have become very rapid and ubiquitous. The older resistance to direct investments by MNCs is now seen to be counterproductive, since that has been a major channel to bring in technology transfer.

KEY TERMS

Kuznets	Total factor productivity	Technology transfer
Production processes	Neutral technical change	Technological gap
Product innovation	Laborsaving technology	Adaptation
Production function	Appropriate technology	Multi National Corporation
Isoquant	Research and Development	(MNC)
Factor intensity	(R&D)	Induced technical change
Choice of technique	Technical advance	X-efficiency
Factor substitution	Public good	Intellectual property rights
Technological dualism	Patents	Bundling
Economies of scale	Pure science	Licensing

PART IV

TRADE AND DEVELOPMENT

So far, this text has assumed an essentially closed economy framework. While it serves to keep the exposition clear, this assumption is clearly inappropriate in today's world. The global reality of vastly cheaper transport and communications obliges all countries to operate within an **open economy** context. Widespread connections across national boundaries have a profound impact on development. The key question is whether such influences are to be viewed as beneficial or harmful. A given country's stance toward openness is inevitably based on its own historical experience as well as the cross-sectional experience of others. The impact on development, good or bad, stems from various kinds of international flows.

Knowledge. Flows across the world have the effect of homogenizing consumer tastes through the demonstration effect.

Technology. It constitutes a specific subset of the knowledge flows that serve to spread a common body of know-how about production processes and products.

Factors. Movements of capital and labor across countries alter their available productive resources.

Goods. Trade in goods and services as well as raw materials constitute, by far, the largest volume of transnational flows.

This part of the text will focus on the last type of flow, the international trade in goods, which has a profound impact on the development process. Chapter 10 already dealt with technology flows. Other factor flows certainly are important, but are smaller in scope. Labor flows across borders can have a large localized significance in different times and places. For example, there are large flows of labor from countries around the Mediterranean to Western Europe and from neighboring regions into the oil-rich Middle Eastern countries. However, immigration restrictions reduce the overall impact, which remains much smaller than from global trade flows.

Capital flows also have a role. For example, in the 1970s, substantial flows went into Latin America from the developed countries. Such capital inflows and their abrupt reversal can have an enormous impact on trade and development, so the issue of international finance merits separate study. Some idea of the relative magnitude of the various influences may be gained from recent numbers: The size of annual flows of capital to LDCs ($100B) in the 1990s is far exceeded by the volume of trade ($500B). Moreover, the volume of world trade has grown at a much faster rate (5%) over the past decade than the rate of growth of output (about 3%).

Chapter 11

International Trade

Measuring Openness

In talking about individual countries' involvement in trade, note that openness is a matter of degree. The smaller a country's size, the greater is the pure geographical necessity to deal beyond its borders. The level of development is another influence, as an advanced country is obliged to interact with foreign countries to obtain the increased diversity of goods and technology it needs. After all, only the most primitive economies are truly self-sufficient. A simple measure of openness is the exports/GNP ratio. (One may substitute imports for exports in this ratio, But since these are often quite close, it doesn't make much difference.) Using such a measure we can gauge the openness of a country. We may compare the country's measure to the average or characteristic value for a group of countries of approximately equal size and level of development.

Beyond these natural reasons for international trade, the **degree of openness** is a matter of explicit national choice. Countries with a socialist bent tend to consider self-reliance a virtue and try to isolate themselves from international economic influences. The most extreme cases in recent decades have been Albania and North Korea. Yet for many LDCs it was their historical experience, not merely ideology, that turned them away from free trade at the beginning of this development epoch. After all, most LDCs had operated historically within a regime of essentially free trade. Especially in Latin America, economic growth was noted to have been quite poor over the first half of the twentieth century. This disappointing experience with a free trade policy regime led many countries to try out some other strategy for growth.

TRADE THEORY VERSUS DEVELOPMENT THEORY

The fundamental question addressed in this book is: What makes countries grow? In the present context, this question becomes: Does participation in international trade advance or hinder a country's development? In the search for an answer we encounter the recurrent clash between the two dominant paradigms: the structuralist versus the neoclassical schools of economics. Not surprisingly the latter theory highlights the benefits of free trade against the development economics school, which tends to deny them. To evaluate the various arguments we must critically examine the theories in light of empirical facts that evolve over the years. We begin with a brief review of the pure theory of trade, its tests, and its implications. Then a summary of the significant empirical facts of trade and growth follows. After these preliminaries, we are set to evaluate the conflicting arguments to choose an appropriate strategy for trade and development. This has specific implications for micropolicies regarding exports and imports. Thus the following chapter makes the transition from theory to policy. Within a real-world context, various motivations—other than just growth—are seen to influence trade policy. This leads to an examination of the political-economy reasons that make it so hard to reorient trade strategy, despite the obvious benefits that can derive from such reforms.

Clearly trade orientation affects the qualitative nature of development—the type of goods produced as well as the arrangements of production. But what effect does trade have on the quantitative rate of growth? Standard trade theory promises significant gains from trade, but this is challenged by the development school based on a different theory and interpretation of historical facts. (A classic reference is Chenery "Comparative Advantage and Development Theory," 1960.) While neoclassical theory proves that trade provides **static gains** in the level of output, it does not guarantee a sustained higher rate of growth.

Figure 11-1 highlights this difference in terms of the growth paths over time. The left panel shows a one-time increase in the level of output, while the right panel involves a permanent shift to a higher growth rate.

To study how trade might have **dynamic effects** on overall economic growth, we must examine the precise channels (or mechanisms) through which trade may affect growth. The dynamic effects may be analyzed using the familiar production function framework restated in terms of rates of growth. From this equation we note that the rate of output growth must be determined by the growth of inputs (K, L, HC) and/or through technical progress (T).

$$\hat{Y} = \text{weighted avg}\left(\hat{T} + \widehat{\text{inputs}}\right)$$

This growth accounting equation provides a framework to evaluate the different theories relating trade to growth. Each explanation points precisely to alternative channels through which trade may affect the right-hand side determinants in this equation, and thereby influence the overall rate of growth. (A review of the current status of the ongoing debate is provided by Lal & Rajapatirana or Edwards.)

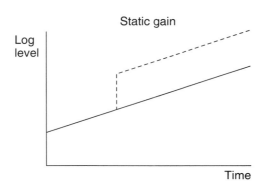

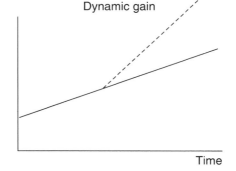

Figure 11-1 *Static versus dynamic gains*

Historical Ideas about Trade and Growth

The early arguments in favor of free trade dating from Ricardo through Marshall to Viner cite the gains from trade based on comparative advantage. Each highlights different channels that operate either through increased factor accumulation or technical progress. An early connection was Adam Smith's idea that trade serves to expand the size of the market. This encourages **specialization,** making it possible to reap economies of scale. Such a rearrangement of productive resources also can be called technical progress in its broadest sense, since it allows increased output from a given amount of inputs. Ricardo pointed out a different channel whereby trade can be beneficial through its impact on income distribution. Export production often is organized in large-scale units run by capitalists; thus a protrade strategy would redistribute income toward this class, which has a high propensity to save (and invest). Consequently a free-trade strategy can promote overall growth through boosted capital accumulation.

A similar focus on the distributional effect is echoed in modern times, as in the Lewis model's assumption that the industrial sector has a higher rate of capital accumulation. However, this very feature has been used as an argument against a reliance on international trade. LDCs traditionally have concentrated on exporting primary products while importing manufactured goods. Primary production often was concentrated in **export enclaves.** A serious concern was that such mining and plantation enclaves were so tightly controlled by foreign or domestic interests that their profits could easily be transferred abroad instead of being used for domestic development. This concern is less relevant today, as most natural resource industries have been brought under national control.

A more relevant critique is that export enclaves may have few economic **linkages** with the rest of the economy. Such export production would induce little technological change to prompt overall economic growth. The copper industry of Chile or Zaire provides a classic example of an export sector that has few externalities apart from generating useful foreign exchange. It provides little business to domestic suppliers, nor does it serve many domestic customers. Domestic benefits only flow to the privileged few who are employed in this segment of the organized sector.

The experience of the oil-exporting countries over the past two decades also presents a similar example of missing linkages. The main benefit bestowed by the oil sector on the domestic economy is its expansion of available capital. (Even that benefit may have a downside, since the capital inflows tend to strengthen the exchange rate and damage the viability of other export industries. This so-called Dutch disease was discussed in chapter 7.) Channeling the capital inflows toward a sustainable form of development turns out to be surprisingly difficult; however, a few positive examples of successful development can be cited. Ivory Coast provides one such example. Its primary producers are small peasants, widely dispersed across the economy, growing coffee and cocoa; thus export production has widespread and direct linkages that lead to a successful pattern of export-led growth. Malaysian rubber exports are another example.

Another mechanism for trade to influence overall growth stems from its stimulus to aggregate demand. Recall that the Keynesian revolution was much in fashion in the 1950s, the same was the time that most LDCs began their major push toward development. The promising new Keynesian idea was that underutilized resources could be utilized to enhance the output of an economy. While this theory specifically sought to explain cyclical unemployment in the industrial countries, it was also considered compatible with the ideas of developmental economics. In the 1940s, Myint noted that trade can mobilize large pools of underemployed labor available in underdeveloped countries. In particular, net exports appeared to be one component of aggregate demand that could be expandable by appropriate policy.

$$Y = C + I + (X - M)$$

Thinking of exports as a component of aggregate demand, in effect views exports as a vent for surplus. Expanded exports X add to output Y and thereby encourage growth. This idea assumes that underutilized resources are available for expanding supply. The Keynesians of Cambridge (England) flipped around this argument to oppose rather than support an expansion of trade. Aggregate demand can be bolstered equally by restricting imports, M, as by increasing exports. The equation shows that, either way, domestic demand is increased. Orthodox Keynesians such as Joan Robinson supported the latter strategy because they shared the common pessimism of the 1950s that growth of primary exports was doomed to stagnate.

Traditional exports were viewed in a negative light due to a pessimism about the possibility of quantitative revenue growth. There was also a disdain for qualitative nature of LDC exports. Traditional export production, such as growing bananas or coconuts, was unlikely to advance technical advance in LDCs. Instead the LDCs wanted to rapidly become competitive in manufacturing. For these reasons many economists argued against specializing production in the traditional sectors of LDC comparative advantage. Instead, they argued that balanced growth across all sectors would enhance productivity growth in the long run. This interventionist view of development economists such as Lewis, Nurkse, Prebisch, and others, led to a strategy of **import substituting industrialization (ISI).** The idea was to protect infant industry from cheap foreign imports, at least for a transitory period. Ultimately the protected industry would become competitive, and the LDC would become industrialized. ISI was expected to provide dynamic growth through various channels: (1) Capital accumulation, which is supposed to be highest from indus-

trial profits according to Kaldor and other pioneers of the development economics school, and (2) technical progress, spurred by learning-by-doing in the protected industries.

The trade strategy, in turn, has important implications for industrial strategy. Not coincidentally, an ISI strategy fitted in with the dominant ethos of the 1950s, which equated development with

Modernization = Industrialization = Protectionism

In those early days most LDCs harbored strong feelings of humiliation from their years of colonial subjugation and subordinate status in the international order. They were loathe to continue exporting primary commodities that kept them in the unglamorous position of hewers of wood and drawers of water. This view had a basic flaw in that comparative advantage need not have an exclusive connection with primary goods. The experience of the past forty years has taught us that an outward-oriented strategy can just as well imply the production and export of labor-intensive manufactured goods. In evaluating comparative advantage as a development strategy, the cases of Malaysia or Thailand can be cited as success stories, not just Zaire or Tanzania as failures.

Back in the 1950s, however, an outward orientation and reliance on markets was defeated by interventionist (structuralist) views. At the start of the modern development epoch, most LDCs came out in favor of protectionist policies. They rejected a strategy based on free trade due to a skepticism about the underlying trade theory.

Structuralists reject the static nature of neoclassical equilibrium. They may even deny the very possibility of equilibrium. Instead the developmental school emphasized how government interventions can provide dynamic advantages by promoting domestic industry. These advantages would derive from economies of scale in domestic production and by inducing technical change through learning-by-doing. Also rejected was the (implicit) idea that comparative advantage is immutable; only the industrialized countries could ever be competitive in manufacturing. The LDCs hoped to increase the quantity and quality of their productive factors during the phase of protected industrial development. Structuralists emphasize that various structural constraints are widespread in developing economies. As noted in the introduction, this view is in sharp contrast with the neoclassical assumption of competitive free markets.

STANDARD TRADE THEORY

Despite all the challenges cited, a robust theoretical proposition is that there are gains from trade based on comparative advantage. More debatable is the actual source of the comparative advantage. The standard theory of trade has gone through a series of modifications as global circumstances changed over time. To evaluate the relevance of trade for development, we first must take a brief diversion to review the pure theory of trade.

The pure theory of trade is founded on the doctrine of **comparative advantage.** Roughly, this implies that each country can maximize its welfare by concentrating on the production of what it does relatively best. Thus it should cut back production of goods that other countries produce cheaper and divert those freed resources to producing more goods in which it has comparative advantage. Exporting the surplus good and importing the other enables the country to attain a larger consumption set than it could under autarchy, or self-sufficiency. Figure 11-2 demonstrates the static gains that derive from international trade using a simplified model with just two goods.

A country's production set is defined by its limited resources and available technology. The maximum combination of both goods are shown by the **production possibility frontier (PPF).** In autarchy the country would choose to produce at point A, which allows it to reach its highest utility according to its tastes. The closed economy's consumption of each good x and y would exactly

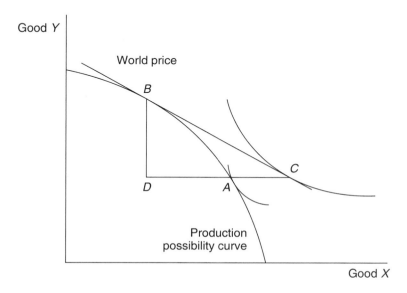

Figure 11-2 *Gains from trade (general equilibrium)*

match its production. At this point the slope of the tangent indicates the relative price of goods P_x/P_y. Now suppose the country is exposed to the world price (indicated by the slope of line BC), which is different from the autarchy price. The country will choose to shift production to point B to produce more y than before. Of this production, amount BD is sold abroad in exchange for imports of amount CD of good x. Consumption

is now possible at point C outside the PPF and on a higher utility curve than before. (Note that no matter which direction world prices differ, the country benefits from trade. Reduction of the high cost production enables resources to be moved to produce goods with lower opportunity cost.) When each country concentrates on what it does relatively best, more can be produced worldwide with the given resources.

Analysis: Gains from Trade (Partial Equilibrium)

Trade theory makes extensive use of the tools of general equilibrium analysis. The beginning economics student is usually more familiar with partial equilibrium, which considers the market for one good at a time. The gains from trade depicted in the general equilibrium analysis in Figure 11-2 can be translated in terms of the familiar supply and demand diagram of partial equilibrium analysis. As an example, consider the market for steel, in which trade moves between two countries in response to international price differences. If the price of steel is low in Belgium (relative to other goods) and high in Morocco, the latter will import steel from Belgium, eventually causing the price to equalize.

Figure 11-3 shows how lower price foreign steel alters the supply of steel in the Moroccan market. The price differential induces trade to flow. This, in turn, forces the good's price to equalize in both countries. Each country moves from autarchy (Z) to the trade position (T), resulting in larger social welfare as indicated by the shaded triangles. In each country the sum of consumer and producers' surplus increases compared to the original position at the autarchy prices P_A and P_B respectively.

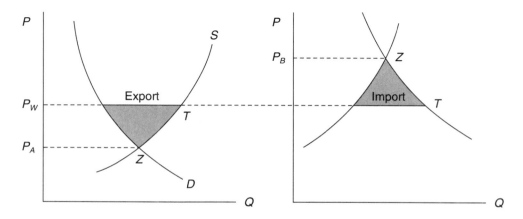

Figure 11-3   *Gains from trade (partial equilibrium)*

This example presents the concept of comparative advantage more concretely in terms of comparative costs. But what enables one country to produce some goods cheaper than another? Standard theory that aims to explain a country's comparative advantage has progressed through three versions over the years.

1. The earliest **Ricardian trade theory** attributed the different costs to differences in natural resources, for example, climate, soil, minerals, or even differences in national temperaments.

2. Neoclassical trade theory developed by **Heckscher and Ohlin** in the 1930s attributes these cost differences to the relative scarcity of factors available in different countries.

3. The most recent progression, modern trade theory, emphasizes that transitory differences in technology can be more crucial for explaining trade flows than differences in endowments.

The relative standing of these theories may be assessed by a tally of trade in different categories of goods. Even without such data, one can get an impressionistic idea of the size of trade flows between countries. Trade among the developed countries (North-North trade) amounts to well over 50% of all world trade. One may assume that much of this trade stems neither from marked differences in natural resources, nor from differences in factor endowments. Thus a large part of trade is likely to be of the type explained by modern trade theory. By contrast LDC exports are comprised largely of the first two types. Yet even the developing countries are increasingly engaging in the third type of trade that is based on small (often transitory) differences in technical capabilities.

Ricardian Trade Theory

The early trade theory was part and parcel of the classical economics paradigm. Based on the labor **theory of value,** it assumes labor is the only factor of production. Labor productivity and the fixed resource endowments determine the maximum combinations of goods a country can produce. Figure 11-4 shows the production possibility frontier for two goods, bread and cars respectively. The slope of the *PPF* indicates the opportunity cost of good C in terms of B. If the world relative price of C is cheaper (slope of the dotted line), the country would export B and import C. The size (position) of the *PPF* indicates the national income of the country.

The gain from trade is shown in an obvious way as the country can now consume at points outside the production limits of the *PPF*. The real income may be measured either in terms of good C or good B (translated at the trade price to point X on the cars axis). The figure shows how a country's income can be further improved by either increased export price (swinging out the dotted line) or increased L productivity (expanding the PPF size). These two elements are components of the index called the factoral **terms of trade.**

$$\frac{A_x \ P_x}{P_y}$$

A_x is an index of productivity in the export goods sector. The numerator indicates export

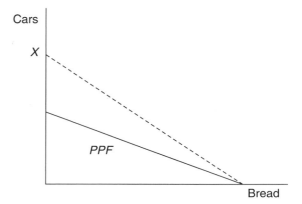

Figure 11-4 *Terms of trade versus productivity increases*

revenue, which is the product of export productivity times export price. Dividing this by import price we get the quantity of import goods that can be purchased. As a concrete example, consider cocoa exports from West Africa. Increased productivity in cocoa has precisely the same impact on export revenues as a higher world price of cocoa. This concept is useful for analyzing various historical episodes of prosperity that stemmed from export price rises. Unfortunately, such price rises usually are temporary, so their reversal leads to a painful crash. The one reliable way to improve income is through productivity growth. However, there is not much scope for improving productivity in the extraction of minerals. A country either has those deposits or does not.

Heckscher-Ohlin Model

When neoclassical economics superceded classical economics, the pure theory of trade was also modified accordingly. Prices are determined both by supply and demand conditions. Trade theory still retains the basic idea of comparative advantage and the resulting gains from trade. The main difference is the source of cost differences across countries. These are postulated to arise primarily from differences in factor endowments across countries. Instead of relying on undefined differences, such as work culture, soils, or climate, the Heckscher-Ohlin theory focuses on measured differences in productive factors, such as K, L and HC. To continue with an earlier example, Belgium is postulated to have a lot of capital relative to labor; therefore, it can produce K-intensive steel relatively cheaply. By contrast, Morocco's abundant labor endowment gives it comparative advantage in producing textiles. Heckscher-Ohlin theory highlights the relative scarcity of productive factors that influence the factor prices P_K/P_L prevailing in the country and the cost of goods. To elaborate further, Heckscher-Ohlin theory makes certain assumptions.

Immobile factors define an economy in terms of its given endowments of capital and labor. This assumption is justified by the observation that factor movements between countries is far smaller than the trade of goods. Even where factor movements do occur, they are not so large as to alter the ranking of relative factor abundance across countries. For example, while Japan is a major exporter of capital, it remains one of the most K-abundant countries, as in its pattern of trade reflects.

The entire world has essentially *similar tastes*. This assumption is made in order to sustain the Heckscher-Ohlin explanation that cost differences arise mainly from differences in resource endowments. Otherwise any pattern of trade whatsoever could be explained away as arising from idiosyncratic tastes. A country could have such unique tastes that despite having an initial advantage in production of a particular good, it may consume all it produces and even have to import more of it.

All countries have access to the *same technology*. (All have access to the same map of isoquants, but each may utilize a different capital intensity K/L depending on the different relative factor prices prevailing across countries.) Of all the assumptions this one is the least plausible. Theoreticians make this assumption just so comparative advantage remains predictably attached to a given country. If the technological lead kept switching around, it would not be possible to identify which country has comparative advantage in which good. Yet much of trade today derives precisely from such transitory technical differences. This idea is elaborated in modern trade theory presented following the Heckscher-Ohlin model.

An important implication of the Heckscher-Ohlin framework is that free trade leads to **factor price equalization** among countries. Samuelson showed that factor prices actually must equalize: This is not merely a tendency. For example, the wages in Somalia, about $300 per annum, eventually would become equal to New York's $18,000! This is a powerful argument in favor of free trade in goods. This prescription also happens to be convenient for the rich countries whose enthusiasm for free trade is not matched by an equal enthusiasm for free movements of labor. If labor could move freely across countries, wages would equalize much more directly and surely. The recent debate on North American Free Trade Agreement (NAFTA) also was couched in these terms: Let's import goods produced by Mexican labor rather than have Mexicans migrate across the border. Either way the Mexican wage will rise.

For proof of the factor price equalization theorem, refer to any text in international trade. For our current purposes it will suffice to give an intuitive feel for the logic behind this theorem. Consider the case of free trade now starting between the United States and Mexico. Right away L-intensive industries in the United States become uncompetitive at the going wage rate. Industries such as textiles and foundries will be forced to retrench. These layoffs will put downward pressure on wage rates nationwide, inducing other industries to expand their employment. The reverse occurs in Mexico as wages rise and L-intensive industries expand. This process will continue until wages equalize in the two countries. (Of course, wages also tend to equalize due to actual migration of the labor factor. Thus trade is a substitute for factor movements.)

A minor footnote is that equalization of wages does not necessarily imply equalization of income. (Recall this point from chapter 3.) Income is comprised of wages plus earnings from capital. Of course, the ownership of capital remains strikingly unequal across countries. Per capita income levels can diverge even further since the ratio of working members to family size is usually smaller in the LDCs.

Further implications of the Heckscher-Ohlin theory The Heckscher-Ohlin theory can be

extended beyond the two-factor two-country two-good framework that is used for simplicity of exposition. (See Leamer for a diagrammatic extension to the case of many factors.) It is also useful for indicating the pattern of trade in many goods between many countries. For example, consider three countries each having a characteristic capital/labor ratio, k, indicating the overall capital abundance of the country.

$$k \, \text{United States} > k \, \text{Korea} > k \, \text{India}$$

Similarly the production techniques of various industries have certain characteristics so that capital intensities of goods may also be ranked.

$$\text{Aircraft} > \text{Steel} > \text{Textiles}$$

According to Heckscher-Ohlin theory, the United States naturally will export the most K-intensive good, jet aircraft, to India and Korea while importing steel and textiles from them. Korea might import textiles from India and export some steel to it. The relative factor endowments K/L are not immutable; they can change as countries grow. In particular, the accumulation of capital and human capital can alter a country's comparative advantage and its trade patterns.

The qualitative effects of growth on trade were worked out by H. Johnson in 1962. When an economy expands it undergoes particular changes in factor endowments that cause its PPF to shift from AB to $A'B'$ as shown in Figure 11-5. The effect on trade would be neutral if imports and exports both increased proportionate to overall growth. (In this example the country exports good B, and imports good A.)

In general the effect of growth on trade is not neutral. As incomes rise, consumption may be biased in the direction of more imported goods. (From chapter 2 recall the Engels' effects, which indicate the relation between income growth and commodity demands.) In the figure, higher indifference curves indicate

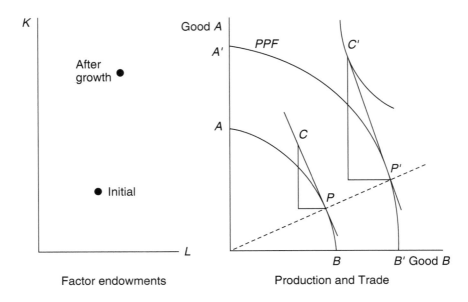

Figure 11-5 *Effect of growth on trade*

how preferences change with growing income. In a similar manner the shape of the enlarged *PPC* also can dictate whether the trade triangle will be larger or smaller (protrade or antitrade bias). The combined production and consumption effects determine the overall bias. How the demand side can generate a protrade bias can be grasped intuitively. For instance, as people get richer, their demand for pineapples and chocolate increases. Also, a specific taste for variety can only be fulfilled by imports. The empirical evidence confirms that trade does, become a larger fraction of GDP as output grows.

A quirky possibility noted by J. Bhagwati is that a country with a large share of a particular product might expand its exports too far and thereby flood the market. This would depress the world price of its export good. In our figure this worsening of the terms of trade would make the sloped line become flatter. If the % price reduction exceeds the % increase in export volume, export revenues decline, resulting in **immiserising growth.** This analysis is only relevant for a handful of exceptional countries that have such a large share of world trade in a particular commodity that they can influence its world price. This explains why Brazil, which supplies a large share of the world's coffee market, would prefer to destroy part of its coffee crop than to sell it in a year of glut.

Empirical verification of the Heckscher-Ohlin model must examine real-world data to verify whether labor-abundant countries actually export *L*-intensive goods while importing *K*-intensive goods. Leontief attempted this exercise using trade data for the United States from the 1950s. He found that the *K*-abundant United States seemed to export *L*-intensive goods and import K-intensive goods. Puzzled researchers reexamined the statistics and research methods to confirm the data procedures were sound. Thus other explanations had to be sought for Leontief's paradox.

1. The assumption of homogenous tastes worldwide might be questioned. It is possible for a K-abundant country to have a particular preference for K-intensive goods. Thus a country might consume all its own output (for example, Brazil—coffee, and France—wine) and need to import more of it. But this hardly seems general enough to explain the paradox.

2. A more plausible explanation is that the United States actually exports human capital–intensive goods, which are mistakenly identified as L-intensive. The accounting of labor income must be revised to separate out returns to human capital. For example, labor incomes account for a large part of the production costs of Boeing aircraft, but many of these are really returns to human capital.

3. A rather theoretical explanation of the Leontief paradox blames it on possible factor intensity reversals. Note that Heckscher-Ohlin assumes a K-intensive good is clearly distinguishable from an L-intensive good. But the production functions could be such that the ranking of factor intensities is unclear. For example, rice produced in Texas is more K-intensive while Thai rice is L-intensive. While each area produces according to its comparative advantage, there is still no basis for trade. Let's say the other good is steel. The isoquants could have such a particular shape that steel is more K-intensive at a high wage/rental ratio while rice is identified as more K-intensive at a lower w/r. Again, this theoretically interesting argument does not provide a general enough resolution of the paradox.

4. Finally, the Heckscher-Ohlin explanation may be erroneously applied to Ricardian exports that are actually based on natural resources. An example is the production and export of oil. Oil production requires large outlays of capital as a complementary input. Thus when Nigeria or Indonesia export oil, this should not be taken to mean that these are K-abundant countries.

Modern Trade Theory

The latest progression in trade theory, developed during the 1980s by Paul Krugman of M.I.T. among others, advances a new source of comparative advantage. While the Ricardian model attributes comparative advantage mainly to differences in natural resource endowments, the Heckscher-Ohlin model is based on differences in factor endowments of capital and labor. However the standard theory is becoming increasingly inadequate to explain a large part of today's trade flows. E. Leamer of UCLA has made detailed efforts to expand the number and definition of factors to provide a better explanation for observed trade flows. Yet there remains the bothersome observation that Fords move from the United States to Japan and Toyotas move in the opposite direction, even though both countries have very similar factor endowments.

The trouble with standard theory is that the postulated source of comparative advantage is changing ever more rapidly. In Ricardo's day, comparative advantage for a given good was attached permanently to a country with its given natural resources endowments. Later, the Heckscher-Ohlin theory emphasised factor endowments, such as K and L, that serve to explain trade in manufactured goods. In both cases the indicated endowments changed only gradually over time. By contrast, in today's world the most important input in most production processes is technology; but possession of this factor changes rapidly across countries.

Modern theory accounts for the changing ownership of technological knowledge in various ways. The **product cycle hypothesis** presents the idea that development of new products and processes requires special kinds of skills. Advanced countries initiate production and export of such human capital–intensive goods using skilled labor. Here comparative advantage derives from a transitory technological advantage, rather than natural resource or factor endowments. Later, as the product matures and becomes standardized, the LDCs can acquire the widely known technology. They produce far more economically using their abundant factor, unskilled labor. A familiar example of this progression is the personal computer that was invented in Silicon Valley. A few years later most production moved to the NICs of Asia. Progressions of the product cycle: innovation to maturity to obsolescence have so accelerated that we observed comparative advantage in shipbuilding moving from Britain to Holland to Sweden to Japan and on to Korea—all in the course of a few decades following World War II.

Another technological feature that upsets standard trade theory is the existence of increasing returns to scale. It is quite plausible that scale economies are particularly applicable for the case of industrial technology. Thus cheap production costs may have nothing to do with either existing natural resources or factor endowments. Instead, whichever producer grabs the largest market share obtains the comparative advantage. Any means—fair or foul—to obtain this lucrative position could be used by contending producers.

A well-known example of such contention for market share arose in the world market for jetliners. Until quite recently, the Boeing Company held a commanding share of the market due to the advantage of economies of scale. It had moved so far down the average cost curve that potential rivals would find it extremely difficult to compete starting from a small output. Observing this, the Europeans realized they would have to heavily subsidize their new entrant, the Airbus, if they were to compete at all. In the long view this introductory strategy has been validated as the Airbus made the transition

to a successful competitor. Yet, such a market intervention is clearly contrary to free market tenets. For similar reasons, many emerging NICs are unwilling to passively accept their existing comparative advantage as preordained; instead, they are ready to make a contest for it.

These new theoretical developments obviously alter the policy implications that favor free trade. If comparative advantage can change so rapidly, why should an LDC patiently accept the existing comparative advantage? Why not step out and aggressively change it through some kind of industrial policy? Such a transitory protectionism has been used with great success by countries such as Korea and Taiwan. By producing and exporting aggressively, they gain an edge by scale economies and learning effects that accrue to large producers. These new considerations modify the very concept of comparative advantage, perhaps beyond recognition. Trade can flow in either direction for any good, contrary to standard trade theory, which claims it must flow only in one direction. When countries can actually construct their own comparative advantage, the older vision of trade policy becomes obsolete. Then trade negotiations between countries take on a special relevence. We will study such **strategic trade policy** in chapter 12.

FACTS OF TRADE AND GROWTH

From theory we move to the empirical facts of trade and growth. Even a casual view of history reveals important insights: England's experience over the period 1700–1815 provides the classic example of dynamic growth spurred by trade. England's industrial revolution was clearly boosted by being the first exporter of manufactured goods. The growth of such exports slowed after 1815 when other European countries also began to industrialize. Among the LDCs, too, there are many examples of economic growth prior to the present development epoch. These are credited mainly to primary exports that derive from the countries' natural resources. For instance, the climate or soil made it possible to grow rubber in Malaysia; coffee in Brazil and Columbia; tea in India and Sri Lanka; beef and wheat in the United States, Argentina and Canada; butter and wool in New Zealand; cocoa in Ghana and Nigeria; and mine copper ore in Chile and Zaire. By contrast, today's successes are the oft-cited examples of LDCs with extremely rapid growth of manufactured exports. Among these countries, whose comparative advantage initially stemmed from their abundant labor, are notably the Gang of Four—Taiwan, Hong Kong, Singapore, and Korea.

Despite these success stories, some influential policy makers in developing countries still resist the idea that trade promotes growth. They cite various failed cases of countries that based their growth strategy on comparative advantage. Examples are the banana exporters of Central America and other primary exporters, such as Peru and Bolivia. In particular for Latin America from the vantage of the 1950s, structuralists Raul Prebisch and Nurske argued persuasively that growth based on primary exports could not be sustained. The concentration on such primary exports left these economies vulnerable to secular declines in their terms of trade. Hence, Prebisch urged a strategy of inducing industrial development within a protected closed economy.

To evaluate these arguments, let's look closer at the empirical evidence. The historical data up to the 1970s pointed to various cases of countries that had growth with no trade, while others had trade with no growth. Kravis presented evidence to challenge past notions that trade was necessarily an **engine for growth.** Instead the correlation of trade with growth may indicate the opposite causality: Economic growth causes increased trade, rather than vice versa. Whatever might have been the past relationship, Arthur Lewis argued in 1979 that mechanism had now become unreliable. He noted that demand for LDC primary exports depends on the rate of

growth of the DCs' economies with an elasticity of .87. (This means that a 2% growth of GDP in the industrial economies would raise LDC exports by .87 * 2% = 1.74%.) Since the developed world was in the grip of recession in the late 1970s, its demand for primary goods was stagnant or dropping.

Lewis recommended that LDC exporters ought to rely more on South–South trade instead of the dominant North–South path. For example, Brazil should attempt to set up more trade channels with Nigeria, Thailand, and so on. This involves unlearning the habits formed under colonialism in which countries in the periphery each traded with its metropolitan patron: India with Britain, Indonesia with Holland, and so on.

Reidel (1984) rebutted Lewis by arguing that it is not mainly demand from the developed countries that propels LDC exports; instead, such exports depend on the LDCs' own capabilities of resolving their supply-side problems. Therefore, it is not justified to blame the DCs for any slackness of LDC export growth. Such pro- and counterarguments about a trade-based strategy suggest that the terms of the controversy need to be reoriented. A finer disaggregation of the facts of exporting may be worthwhile. The data can be split out according to different country groups as well as commodity groups in different eras.

Table 11-1 offers more detail about the striking changes in composition of LDC trade that have occurred over the past few decades. In a short period, manufactured goods rose from a mere 11% share of nonfuel exports to more than 45%. The early developmental economists, such as Nurske and Prebisch, were pessimistic about the market prospects of primary exports. This prompted their gloomy prediction that the LDC terms of trade would continue to fall. But already by the 1970s, this focus on primary goods was no longer very relevant, certainly for the aggregate of all LDCs. The LDCs as a group now export a large percentage of manufactured

Table 11-1   Composition of LDC exports

Export type	1955		1978	
Fuels	25%	excluding fuel	53%	excluding fuel
Food and agriculture	57%	76%	21%	45%
Minerals	10%	13%	5%	10%
Manufactures	8%	11%	25%	45%

goods, rather than just simple consumption goods or raw materials.

Reidel further disaggregates these data to highlight the performance of various country groups to explain which groups have been largely responsible for the dramatic transformation of trade. Most of the change is found to be attributable to the first two of the following groups.

1.   The oil exporting countries that formed the OPEC cartel managed to raise oil prices through the exercise of their monopoly power. The increase in their export volume has been much more modest.

2.   The Gang of Four (Korea, Taiwan, Hong Kong, and Singapore) are responsible for much of the increase in manufactured exports that initially were based on the aggressive use of labor-intensive methods that utilized their cheap labor. More recently, as their wage rates have risen, they have turned to exports that are intensive in human capital and skills. Thus their exports are more likely to be electronics and cars, rather than just textiles and steel.

3.   Other diversified exporters are the other NICs that include Brazil, Mexico, India, Pakistan, Egypt, and Thailand. Their exports and growth performance is somewhat less dramatic, while they continue to have a substantial share of primary commodities in their export bundle.

4.   Other primary goods exporters include the Philippines and Argentina. These countries protected their domestic industry until very recently. This sector has very high costs that destroy their competitiveness in world markets. Over the last decade, Chile has deliberately altered its policy to escape from this group, while Mexico is in the process of doing so.

5.   The African primary exporters includes most of non-oil–producing Africa. This group is highlighted in a separate category in Table 11-2 because, unique among all the LDCs, this group seems stuck in the old pattern. Both groups 4 and 5 still depend on primary products for over 80% of their exports, so the old trade pessimism may still be applicable in certain parts of the developing world. The export performance of the latter three types of exporters is summarized in Table 11-2.

The structure of an LDC's exports appears closely related to its growth performance. The trade composition of the worst performing region, Africa, has hardly changed over time. Most African countries continue to rely on a few primary exports, while the share of manufactured goods has barely grown. Another curious observation is that countries well-endowed with natural riches often perform worse than those with few resources. By analogy, individuals who are born with a silver spoon in their mouth have

Table 11-2 Export performance

	African primary exporters		Other primary exporters		Diversified exporters	
	1960	**1978**	**1960**	**1978**	**1960**	**1978**
Primary goods	28%	31%	28%	32%	30%	29%
Manufactured goods	4	7	4	16	15	39
Three largest exports combined	69	62	69	52	55	32

no pressing need to work or study hard. In the end they may be left with just a tarnished spoon; whereas those born poor, must hustle and work hard, and eventually can become successful. Taiwan and Korea can be cited as examples of countries "blessed" with few natural resources.

SUMMARY

A country's openness is the degree to which it engages in international trade. This depends to some extent on its intrinsic circumstances, but is also largely influenced by its policy stance. Clearly, the latter depends on whether trade will aid or hinder overall development. A country's views about this are shaped by the relevant theory and lessons of experience.

Standard trade theory is criticized for its exclusive focus on static efficiency: What ensures that the most efficient necessarily guarantees the fastest rate of growth? By contrast, growth theory attributes growth to either increased inputs or technological growth. In particular, the latter item is highlighted by competing development strategies. Proponents of ISI argue that the fastest technical progress can be attained by a protectionist policy, which promotes domestic industry.

Trade theory is based on the principle of comparative advantage: It is most efficient for a country to export those goods that it is relatively best at producing and to import the others. This source of comparative advantage has evolved over three versions. The earliest Ricardian version attributed this to a country's natural resource endowments or special talents. By contrast, Heckscher-Ohlin theory bases comparative advantage on the given endowments of factors, such as capital and labor. Thus it would be most efficient for labor-abundant LDCs to concentrate on production and export of L-intensive goods. The latest modern trade theory argues instead that comparative advantage is not immutable; it can be changed by learning-by-doing gained by competition in world markets. Thus the East Asian exporters have prospered by producing and exporting goods that are based on production efficiencies rather than cheap labor.

Finally, we examine the facts of trade and growth for representative groups of LDCs. The stylized facts of recent experience are fairly clear. Countries that concentrated largely on Ricardian-type exports have shown the worst growth performance. The ISI strategy, once considered a promising alternative, has not performed too well, either. By far, the best performance has been for those countries that achieved the fastest technical progress by pursuing manufactured exports in competitive world markets.

KEY TERMS

Open economy	Import substituting industrialization (ISI)	Labor theory of value
Degree of openness		Terms of trade (t.o.t.)
Static gains	Comparative advantage	factor price equalization
Dynamic gains	Production possibility frontier (PPF)	Immiserising growth
Specialization		Product cycle hypothesis
Export enclaves	Ricardian trade theory	Strategic trade policy
Linkages	Heckscher-Ohlin theory	Engine for growth

Chapter 12

Trade Strategy

The preceding chapter provided the basic theory that applies to trade and growth as well as the stylized facts of experience in this regard. Those preliminaries enable us to evaluate the appropriate strategy for a given country. This chapter examines trade policy in two constituent segments: imports and exports. Traditionally the focus has been on the first of these two. This importance stems from the protectionist stance that was so fashionable in the early years of this development epoch. The analysis of import policy involves a straightforward application of microeconomic tools. Import tariffs and export taxes are both interesting due to their relevance for public finance.

The analysis of export-led growth has a much less established theoretical foundation that even now is in the process of modification and reappraisal. This strategy burst into prominence due to the success of the East Asian NICs; thus it is based on relatively recent empirical studies of trade and growth, rather than on the established pure theory of trade.

This chapter analyzes in seperate sections the details of import and export promotion policy. It then summarizes all the arguments in terms of the case for and against a reliance on trade for speeding up the pace of economic development.

IMPORT POLICY

A major arm of trade policy is a country's stance toward imports. For most developing countries in the 1990s, both theoretical arguments and historical evidence suggest that growth performance is likely to be enhanced by a general reduction of import restrictions. But this policy prescription is easier said than done. In practice the restrictions on imports derive from a variety of motives other than specifically for a trade and growth strategy. In order to reform trade policy, it is imperative that these other matters be taken into account. The original motivation for tariff policy was often a well-intentioned pursuit of various objectives; only later did their damaging effects become apparent. The various goals of tariffs are

- Generating revenue for the government
- Conserving scarce foreign exchange
- Protection of domestic industry

Historically, the oldest motive for tariffs has been to collect **government revenue.** An old reality of public finance is that certain taxes are imposed simply because they are easy to collect! For countries with relatively few ports of entry, import taxes can easily be imposed on the concentrated commodity flows at these points. Hence tariffs often are applied just because they are convenient for the government, and not for reasons of economic efficiency. A side effect is the impact of tariffs on income distribution. Like most indirect taxes that are prevalent in LDCs, import duties also are typically regressive. Perhaps this was less true in the past when most imports were "luxury" goods, but today, imports can just as well be capital goods, intermediate goods, or even items of ordinary consumption.

A policy of raising tariffs to bolster the balance of payments (BoP) by reducing imports is less rational than it may seem. As an alternative: Why not have a **depreciation** of the exchange rate to inhibit imports and boost exports? An obvious difference is that while both policies raise import prices, a depreciation does not generate revenue for the government. Another important difference is that tariff policy is far more discriminating between products, whereas exchange rate changes apply to all products alike.

A depreciation has important efficiency advantages over a policy of raising tariffs. (Harberger [1987] addresses the relationship between exchange rate policy and tariff policy.) For a given size of desired BoP improvement, the rise in import prices need to be smaller since **devaluations** cause reductions in imports as well as expansion of exports. Second, a devaluation causes less distortions in relative prices. Tariffs insert a wedge between price and the marginal cost of production, whereas a devaluation ensures that the consumer's price remains equal to the world marginal cost; thus a misallocation of resources is avoided. Only for rare cases of completely inelastic export production do the two policies have an equivalent impact on prices. Despite this strong brief in favor of depreciation, tariffs often are used instead. In effect, the fiscal motive for government tax revenues overrides other motives such as BoP improvement. Meanwhile exporters suffer, as does the overall economy, due to the distortion of relative prices.

The third motive for tariffs is to protect certain industries from foreign competition. Such a strategy increases profits to domestic producers of import substitutes, while the government's revenue motive is subordinate as the tariff is not set expressly to maximize tariff revenues. An equivalent savings in the BoP may be achieved by a devaluation of the exchange rate. But a policy of devaluation cuts the protection to the favored producers since it benefits all traded goods—exports as well as import substitutes. In its effect, the protectionist strategy encourages a balanced structure across a wide range of domestic industries. Such production cannot be competitive in world markets, at least for an initial period. This strategy has further side effects.

1. **Infant industries** tend to never grow up. Why should they? They enjoy the luxury of high domestic price sustained by the high tariffs. The resulting excess profits are shared with organized labor and politicians whose support, in effect, is bought in return for retaining the tariffs. Of course, the consumers lose and the nation loses overall. Yet the political-economy mechanism works in such a way that the impetus for reform is ineffective. Argentina's decades-long stagnation may be explained this way.

2. To further benefit domestic industry, imports of intermediate goods and raw materials are allowed at a low tariff rate. As domestic industry expands, this kind of necessary imports tend to rise dramatically. While exports remain stagnant, the import bill jumps, so improvement anticipated in the BoP turns out to be less than expected. Experience has shown that the very strategy intended to alleviate the BoP crunch has, in fact, tended to put the BoP into a chronic deficit.

3. Protection tends to distort the entire system of relative prices. For example, low tariffs on machinery that aim to encourage domestic

Analysis: Effects of a Tariff

The analysis of a tariff is a standard exercise that extends the use of demand and supply analysis to the international context. Figure 12-1 shows the familiar domestic D and S curves for a particular importable good. The prevailing world price is drawn at a level below the equilibrium price in autarchy. If free trade is allowed, consumption will extend down the demand curve till it hits the world price. Domestic production will contract along the supply curve below the level of production in autarchy. Meanwhile, imports cover the gap between demand and supply at the world price. The foreign exchange outlay is the rectangle whose area is import quantity times world price.

When a tariff is imposed on imports, the tariff price P_T is higher than the world price P_W by the amount of the tariff. Consumption decreases while domestic production increases. Domestic producers earn higher profits due to the higher price P_T now prevailing in the market. Their gain due to protection is depicted as the area between the domestic price and world price above the supply curve. Imports are now smaller than under free trade, and the corresponding foreign exchange outlay is reduced. Meanwhile the government earns tariff revenues indicated by the rectangle whose area is the per unit tariff times imports. In summary, this simple analysis highlights the three motives for imposing a tariff: tariff revenue, reduced foreign exchange outlays, and protection of domestic industry.

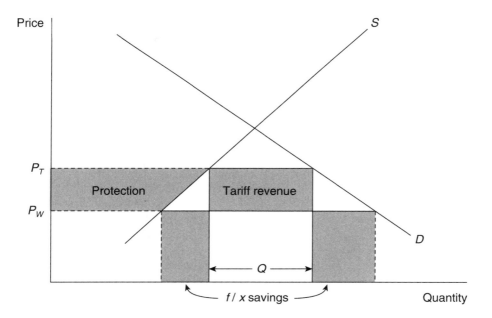

Figure 12-1 *Analysis of tariffs*

industry and high tariffs on luxury goods have the perverse effect of encouraging the manufacture of the latter type of goods of supposedly low social value while discouraging capital goods production. Most countries have such a **cascaded tariff structure:** Highest tariffs for light manufactures, lowest on raw materials. This distortion operates through the mechanism of effective protection as detailed on page 222. Such perverse effects are analogous to the LDCs' other mistake of subsidizing capital to encourage investment, which ends up creating *K*-intensive sectors in capital-poor countries.

4.   Foreign MNCs sometimes manage to get under the umbrella of protection designed to aid domestic industries. Hence they also can earn high monopoly rents. For example, in the protected Argentine automobile market until the 1990s, Ford was able to earn the same level of monopoly rents allowed to all domestic producers. Not surprisingly, this multinational corporation had no desire to export nor could it realistically do so, given the high cost structure prevailing in that protected market.

Trade Policy Instruments

Once a country decides to make policy interventions in markets for traded goods, there are a variety of instruments it might use. Each has its own advantages and drawbacks. Three prominent instruments are tariffs, **quotas,** and subsidies. The choice of tariffs versus quotas can be quite revealing because both instruments initially appear so similar in their effects. Both raise domestic price of imports, and encourage import-competing industries. Limiting imports either by tariffs or by quotas has an equivalent impact on prices and the balance of payments. Yet tariffs and quotas differ importantly in that the government gets the tariff revenue, indicated by the shaded area in Figure 12-1, and importers who are allocated the quotas get that revenue.

Despite the apparent similarities, quotas are much more distortionary than tariffs for several reasons:

(A) Quotas insulate domestic demand almost completely from the price mechanism. Any variation in the world price below P_T would not alter the import quantity. In Figure 12-1, the size of the quota is measured as the horizontal distance by which demand exceeds supply at the given domestic price. That unchanging price is inefficient because domestic production and consumption do not respond to changes in the world market.

(B) The distribution of quotas to importers is often an arbitrary process. Licenses may be allocated on the basis of first-come-first-served, actual users, or some other noneconomic criteria. This prompts **rent-seeking behavior** aimed to influence the license granter—a polite way of saying corruption. Due to such activities the revenue may go neither to the government nor to importers, but rather is appropriated by the bureaucracy or entirely wasted. (See the section on rent seeking in chapter 13.)

Attempts to construct a fair system of allocating import quotas raise other problems. Licenses granted to actual users have the effect of raising barriers to entry by potential newcomers. If import licenses are granted on the basis of existing capacity, they distort incentives by encouraging license seekers to expand useless capacity and so on. Bhagwati and Krueger (1974) did a detailed study of many countries where quantitative controls degenerated in these ways.

(C) The protective effect of a quota regime can remain uncertain since it is difficult to determine the **tariff equivalent** of a given quota. (Figure 12.2) Suppose an import quota is set at a given amount. Is this equivalent to a nominal tariff rate of $Y\%$ or $Z\%$ to the domestic industry? This question can only be answered later by observing the percent rise in the commodity price. A special case is that of an absolute prohibition (zero quota), which is equivalent to a **prohibitive tariff.** If that tariff level was declared openly, it might be viewed as shockingly high. The regulators may not actually intend to grant that industry such a high level of protection. In reality the tariff equivalent of prohibitive quotas often exceeds 200%. Yet many countries often have imposed a total import prohibition the moment indigenous production begins.

There are other less distorting ways of limiting the import bill in critical times of foreign exchange shortage. If import quotas are allowed to be tradable, the degree of protection would be clearly visible in the size of the market premium placed on them. (If domestic markets are monopolistic rather than competitive, a quota has no tariff equivalent, and welfare losses are far worse.) A better method yet is to auction quotas to the highest bidder. This way government obtains the revenue rather than the quota holders. The use of quotas allows the government to plan the foreign exchange outlay for imports. Under this system the quantities of imports, though not their prices, are known with certainty.

If instead of foreign exchange concerns, the focus is to assist certain industries, alternative arrangement can be devised. An efficient method is to distribute import quotas to favored industries, but allow the recipients to trade them in a secondary market. The quota rents accrue to the favored industry, but the government does not make any budgetary outlay. Such an arrangement ensures that the size of the quota premium (or protective subsidy) is visible to all. Then political forces granting the benefit would be subject to greater discipline. The rents handed out via monopoly import licenses can be very large. These rents have been estimated for Indonesia in the mid-1980s where 30% of total imports were subject to such restrictions. An assumed 20% markup on the $2.7 billion import bill amounts to 1.2% of GNP, and these rents accrue annually! (The capitalized value of such rents for example their present value, amounts to over 10% of GNP and 20% of foreign debt.)

Domestic industry can be protected by a less distortionary method than tariffs; it's certainly much less distortionary than the equivalent quota. In figure 12-3, **production subsidy** per unit

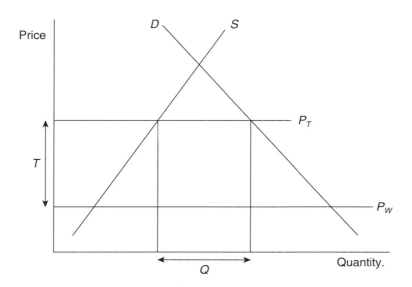

Figure 12-2 *Tariff equivalent of a quota*

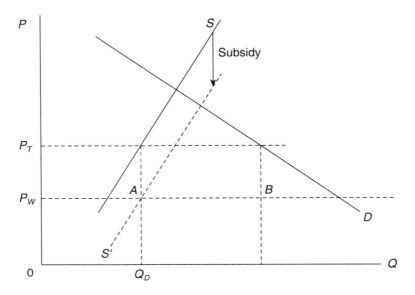

Figure 12-3   *Production subsidies versus tariffs*

paid directly to domestic producers, in effect shifts the domestic supply price downward to S'. Then domestic production expands to Q_D, the same as for the tariff case. However an essential difference is that domestic price remains at the world price P_W level. Consumer surplus remains at the maximum possible—the area between the demand curve and price P_W. Compared to the previous cases in which the efficiency loss was given by the areas A and B, it is now only area A.

The most efficient method of protection through production subsidies is not widely used. An obvious reason is, unlike tariffs in which the government gains revenue, or quotas where revenue is zero, the government in this case must actually spend from its budget. This is difficult to do in the chronically stringent fiscal situation that typically prevails in LDCs. More important, the discrimination in favor of certain producers is plainly visible to all in the polity. It is clear that industry X got $\$Y$, so counterarguments or political forces may be marshaled to enforce accountability. The concerned parties find it far more convenient to keep the protection benefit hidden by means of a quota, which involves no obvious money being handed to the favored ones. A well-known example from the 1980s highlighted how some influential Indonesians benefited by this hidden means of quotas.

Low tariffs are desirable to reduce distortions in the economy. It also is important that tariff rates be fairly uniform across products. This implication arises from the concept of **effective protection.** The typical tariff structure allows intermediate goods imports at a lower tariff rate than final goods. While this seems like a reasonable policy for protecting domestic industry, it is not. Such well-meaning policy can have unintended consequences that are extremely distortionary. Differential tariff rates for intermediate versus final goods result in very different levels of protection to different import-competing industries. Typically these vary widely in their tariff rates as well as their proportions of import content. Even within a given industry, the effective rates of protection can differ for different firms. For example, if one firm makes a product with 80% import content, while another has 60% import content, the effective profit rate is much larger for the former even though the latter achieves more of the desired domestic production. Figure 12-4 explains how import-competing industries can earn much larger profits than indicated by the nominal tariff rates since they also benefit from lower tariffs on their intermediate imports.

The degree of effective protection is indicated by the ratio of profit to domestic value-added. The size of these areas can be seen directly in Figure 12-4. As domestic value-added increases, this ratio tends to drop. Conversely, the effective rate of protection is an increasing function of the import component. An extreme hypothetical example can illuminate this concept. Consider a local car manufacturer that imports large subassemblies at a low tariff rate. Suppose these **intermediate imports** comprise virtually a whole car. The manufacturer simply slaps on a decal (the domestic value-added) and sells within the protected market. Such producers stand to make large profits on a very small base of domestic value-added. It is natural for the

local association of manufacturers to lobby for this kind of tariff structure, which awards them such valuable benefits. They mislead fellow citizens by pointing to the fairly low nominal tariff rates, whereas the rate of effective protection is, in fact, much higher. A useful way to view effective protection is that such policies aim to protect certain activities, rather than goods.

A real-world example of effective protection is provided by the pharmaceuticals industry in Colombia. This industry relies on imports of bulk formulations. Domestic value-added consists mainly of repackaging these in retail form. The tariff structure is cascaded as usual, with high tariff rates for the finished product and low tariff rates for the intermediate goods. Once again, the consequence is an effective protection rate that far exceeds the observed nominal rates. The undue distortion can be removed either by lowering nominal protection on the finished product or raising the tariff rate on intermediate imports. A third possibility, decreasing the import content, is not a parameter that can be controlled by administrative fiat. As part of an industrial strategy, however, the indigenous content can be progressively increased.

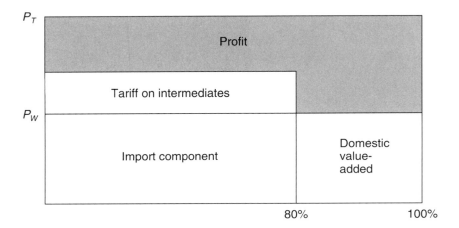

Figure 12-4 *Effective protection*

Trade Liberalization

The above arguments for free trade, based on considerations of static efficiency, urge policy makers to

- Abolish most trade restrictions.

- Implement necessary trade restrictions through tariffs rather than by quotas.

- Make tariff levels low.

- Unify tariff rates to the extent possible across commodities. Notice that an all-round reduction of tariff levels in itself helps to reduce the dispersion of tariffs. For example, if 100% and 20% tariffs are cut to 50% and 10%, respectively, this reduces the absolute spread across the tariff structure. Then, the effective rate of protection would also be reduced.

These normative recommendations come up against the reality of political economy as noted. There is also a fear of the immediate BoP consequences of substantial tariff reductions. The transition away from a protectionist regime may be difficult since the liberalization may prompt an immediate flood of imports, while a hoped-for growth of exports follows only after some delay. Most LDCs do not have the reserves to finance even a transitory dip in foreign exchange earnings.

The transitional problems of changing the trade regime are serious and should not be belittled. A host of other considerations are also relevant to tariff design. Tariff policy is a powerful instrument that can advance a variety of economic objectives ranging from macroeconomics and public finance to influencing income distribution and growth. Accordingly, a program of tariff reform must also take account of the following subsidiary issues:

1. Speed of adjustment

2. Revenue-maximization/consumption tax

3. Control of monopolies

4. Inflation control

5. International repercussions

Adjustment   The powerful effect of tariffs suggests that tariff policy must not be altered too casually or too often, say, not more often than every five years. The vast and unpredictable effects of a general policy of tariff reduction/rationalization would seem to call for a gradual adjustment process rather than shock treatment. The inevitable realignment of profitability across sectors, and therefore of income distribution, would unleash powerful political forces to oppose such proposals. These major changes usually are accompanied by uncertainty whether the policy reform will be sustained. In addition, there is considerable uncertainty about the effects of any given policy. In such an environment, producers cannot plan confidently so they tend to postpone investments. At the same time, other producers may be facing bankruptcy as a result of their sudden exposure to the harsh competition of world markets.

Examples of such transitions abound. All the East European countries have had to undertake this kind of perilous transition following the breakup of the Communist system. They follow the experience of various Latin American countries, such as Mexico and Chile, that undertook the same sort of trade liberalization exercise in the mid-1980s. The severe dislocations associated with implementing tariff reforms suggest that an alternative method might be to announce the entire projected reform up-front, but to implement it gradually according to a preannounced schedule.

Consumption tax   The three main motives for tariffs, protection, tax revenue, and BoP control, often come into conflict with each other. A properly designed tariff structure must make trade-offs between them—a point that is often neglected by policy makers. For example, tariffs can constitute a very effective form of consumption tax, especially on certain luxury imports. Such a tax could be quite progressive, and thus help to improve the income distribution. Yet there may be such a focus on protection or the BoP motive that all luxury imports are summarily banned. This quantitative restriction amounts to a quota = 0, or, equivalently, a prohibitive tariff. Instead of giving up all potential government revenues, many such tariffs could be adjusted towards the **revenue maximizing point.** In Figure 12-5 a reduction of the tariff rate from t_p down to t_m would maximize tax revenue. Of course, finding this precise point may not be easy. This exercise implicitly recognizes the trade-off between fiscal and BoP motives. After balancing these independent motives, the tariff rate might well include a certain degree of protection. In addition, **quantitative prohibitions** may be appropriate for social objectives such as control of pornography or drugs.

Inflation Another motive for altering tariffs is inflation control by selective import liberalization: Allowing cheap imports to rein in the soaring prices of commodities such as cement, vegetable oils, or steel. Strictly speaking, this policy affects the price level, not its rate of change; yet a single sharp reduction can have a salutary effect on the momentum of price increases. Occasionally governments have targeted selected

commodities with precisely timed tariff changes. Such one-shot tariff reductions can be used more generally to counter cost-push pressures that originate in protected industries. Their monopolistic power can be controlled by tariff rates to lower the domestic price of import substituting goods. Such policy imposes a discipline on those favored industries that have come to view their privilege as virtually an entitlement.

Monopolies Haberler, a prominent trade theorist earlier in this century, noted that: "Free trade is possibly the best anti-trust policy of all." Yet this important side-effect of trade liberalization seems to not be properly appreciated. Tariff reductions are powerful tools to suppress the high prices charged by domestic monopolies. In fact, with free trade a country may not even need separate antimonopoly regulations. Import policy can be finely calibrated to discipline domestic producers by means of foreign competition. A country can continue to have large producers that retain economies of scale while at the same time their monopoly power remains under control. India, for example, has not learned this valuable lesson. It continues to have a highly restrictive and onerous monopolies commission while retaining the high tariffs that allow the monopoly profits in the first place. The recent moves toward liberalization are curious half-measures that encourage

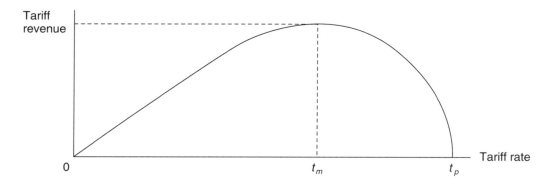

Figure 12-5 *Revenue maximizing tariff*

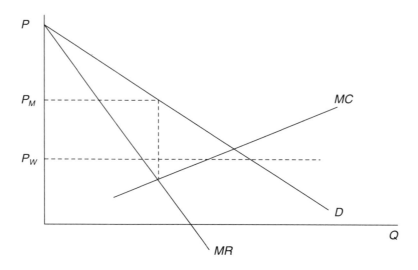

Figure 12-6   *Tariffs and domestic monopoly*

more internal competition (which detracts from scale economies in production) while tariffs remain relatively high.

Figure 12-6 starts as a familiar analysis of monopoly. A monopolist would choose an output level so as to equate $MR = MC$. That output is sold at a high monopoly price P_M. By contrast, with free trade an elastic supply is available at the world price P_W. The domestic producer simply cannot charge above this price. Even a single producer loses all monopoly power as the demand he faces, in effect, becomes flat at the world price.

Repercussions   As a policy which has powerful effects, tariff reforms must also take into account the possible international repercussions as we shall examine later. The following chapter on political economy elaborates some of the domestic political repercussions. Turning to the purely economic effects, we note that a program of tariff reform must also take into account the theory of the second best. This theoretical concept is elaborated in chapter 13. The crucial insight is that in a situation of widespread distortions, as is typical in many developing countries, it is generally not efficient to remove just one distortion, or one tariff. This is a startling implication within neoclassical analysis: *removing one of many distortions may not increase efficiency!* Given that other distortions cannot be removed, the aim is to seek out second-best policy in the design of tariff reform. The following example illustrates this issue.

Consider the situation of a country where a tariff on steel has been set and cannot be removed. If, for example, political realities rule out the first best policy of removing the preexisting distortion, then the reduction of other distortions does not necessarily lead to the highest possible welfare. We must instead work out the second best policy. Let's say the other intervention is a tariff on imported trucks. Normally one might think that reducing any or all tariffs ought to reduce welfare loss; yet it may be even worse to lower the tariff on trucks, which utilize steel in their production. Reducing the tariff on trucks in face of a preexisting distortion (the tariff on steel), may actually worsens overall welfare loss. (This point is expanded further in chapter 13 on policy analysis.)

EXPORT PROMOTION POLICY

The argument about appropriate trade policy for growth has progressed beyond the two simple choices: Free trade based on natural resources versus protectionism to promote domestic industry. An outward orientation is no longer considered synonymous with zero government intervention, nor is LDC exporting supposed to be in opposition to an industrial expansion. There is also an increased recognition that trade-based growth need not rely on just the existing comparative advantage. Instead, governments can intervene to promote L-intensive manufactured exports. The magnitude and composition of such trade is quite different from what it would be under laissez-faire. Success of an export promoting strategy depends on the possibility of increasing export revenues and the extent to which export growth might enhance the growth rate of the overall economy.

$$\text{Overall Growth Rate} = \text{Growth of exports} \times \text{Impact of export growth on overall growth}$$

Expanding Export Revenues

An export-based strategy must begin by examining the degree to which export revenues can be expanded—the first item in the equation. This is largely a practical business matter somewhat removed from economic theory. The country must look on international trade as a corporatist venture following the successful example of, say, Korea or Japan. As in any business venture, the program to expand exports must utilize tools taught in business schools, such as market research, marketing, and promotion. The planning of such efforts must begin by an analysis that splits export revenues into its constituent parts.

$$\text{Export Revenues} = \text{Price} \times \text{Quantity}$$

The **export pessimism** of the past mainly focused on price declines, while assuming that world demand remained inelastic. Nurkse in the 1950s warned that an individual LDC's export revenues would stagnate if all countries attempted simultaneously to increase their volume of exports. Lewis arrived at a similar pessimistic conclusion, but from a different perspective. He focused on falling export quantities instead of prices. A fixed supply price is consistent with his assumption that production cost remain fixed due to an elastic supply of labor in LDCs. Thus the supply price would remain constant even if export demands did increase. Export revenue would then be proportionate to sales, but Lewis remained pessimistic about sustained developed country demand for LDC primary exports.

One well-known example of increased export prices is the relative success (until recently) of the cartel operated by OPEC. An important question is: Why can't OPEC-style cartels boost prices of other primary exports? Over the years other producers have, in fact, tried to form **commodity cartels,** but failed. The latest collapse was the tin cartel in the 1980s, which was coordinated by Malaysia. Some intrinsic reasons for these failures are: (1) It is hard to form and maintain cartels if the number of producers is large simply due to the costs of negotiating and monitoring the agreement. (2) Demands for most primary products are more elastic than for oil since there seem to be many substitutes for the other commodities—which is unfortunate for their producers.

Design of a successful export promotion strategy must account for a variety of factors that vary by product and by country. The traditional explanations of export growth have focused on the demand side as export quantities are supposed to depend on (blame) the developed country buyers. Another set of explanations highlights the country's own role in fostering exports. This focus on the supply side is a relatively new emphasis. The different factors that influence LDC exports are summarized.

Demand elasticity.   Demand elasticity depends on the availability of substitutes, for example, as artificial rubber was substituted for natural rubber, the demand for natural rubber dropped. Likewise there is a long history of synthetic textiles supplanting natural fibers. These movements can also reverse due to fluctuations in the market for the substitute good. For example, as the price of oil used for synthetic rubber rose in the 1970s, natural rubber made a comeback. Such a shift may also be prompted by technical reasons as in the case of newly-invented radial tires, which work better with natural rubber than with synthetic rubber.

Income elasticity of demand.   Primary goods were thought to be mainly necessities. It was feared that demand for such goods would suffer from low growth as world income rose. But this seems to hold true only for basic foodstuffs. Other demands for tropical luxury foods like pineapples or chocolate might rise. Note also that the category of primary goods also includes various industrial raw materials for which income elasticity could be high. (The higher these elasticities are, the greater is the share of LDC exports in DC consumption.) Through this channel, LDC export revenues vary in response to economic fluctuations in the DCs.

Protectionism.   The DCs often are blamed for blocking LDC exports because they wish to protect employment in their own industrial sectors. The labor-intensive manufactures such as shoes, textiles, and apparel, which are usually most affected are precisely those goods for which LDC exporters have comparative advantage. Also, the agricultural sector often gets exceptional protection for political reasons. Examples include sugar producers in the United States, and citrus and rice producers in Japan. There is a fear that such protectionism may increase as LDCs increasingly turn to exporting. Yet the GATT talks, concluded in

1993, succeeded in generally reducing trade barriers, as did the NAFTA agreement for the specific case of Mexico. In recent years, though, non-tariff barriers have tended to increase even as tariff levels have fallen. On the other hand, certain LDC groups have benefited from a preferential market access granted by the DCs. Only recently have these LDCs grudgingly reciprocated by reducing their own barriers to trade.

Supply elasticity of LDC production.   Increasingly recognized as perhaps the most crucial determinant of export growth. Unlike the previous business considerations, the supply elasticities involve policy at the macroeconomic level. Sound policies for economic management and trade are significant for boosting exports of either primary or manufactured goods. Misguided policies, such as the old bias against agriculture, or protection of high priced local industry, reduced competitiveness and the incentive to export. The accompanying policy of overvalued exchange rate similarly made domestic goods relatively more expensive. As seen, an ISI strategy virtually guarantees to harm export growth. Recognizing this at last, many countries are reorienting their policy in favor of an export orientation.

Growth Stimulus from Exporting

Having discussed the possibilities of expanding exports, we now examine the second aspect of an export-led growth strategy: Through what channels does export growth enhance the overall growth rate and by how much? This is both a theoretical and empirical question. How do expanded exports enhance the productive efficiency of the entire economy? One important channel may be linkages that connect the exporting sector with other sectors. The perceived failure of the old primary exporters may stem from the lack of forward and backward linkages between export enclaves and the rest of the economy. A highly centralized mine producing solely for export can earn a lot of foreign exchange, but remains isolated from the domestic economy. Benefits from such operations typically flow to a small group of domestic citizens and do not spread all over the economy. On the other hand, export manufacturing is far more likely to have widespread linkages, while also being more L-intensive.

The **diversification of exports** to nontraditional items should enhance linkages by dispersing the export production effects throughout the economy. If production of traditional export items is geographically dispersed, there can be similar linkage effects. One example is provided by the small-holder rubber producers of Malaysia. They comprise a large number of rural families, each of whom owns a small number of rubber trees. The benefits from rubber exports are therefore spread widely throughout the economy. Export diversification also means exporting a wide variety of commodities to a wide range of customer countries. This reduces the overall riskiness associated with fluctuations in world demand or prices compared to putting all your eggs in one basket.

The domestic linkages emanating from export production comprise of the direct value-added and indirect multiplier effects that spread beyond that export industry. (We will elaborate the concept of linkages more fully in chapter 15.) Domestic value- added depends on the extent to which domestic inputs are used in the production process as well as the nationality of owners. Obviously the higher the domestic component, the greater the stimulus will be to the overall economy. Table 12-1 illustrates the possible categories of linkages for a hypothetical export project.

An easy way to garner many of the benefits of domestic linkages is to set up export industries in **export processing zones (EPZ).** These specially-designated geographical zones within a country have special rules intended to bypass all the distortions that bedevil efficient domestic production. So many interventions exist, and for so many different reasons, that their removal would entail a major effort that may be postponed indefinitely due to political and logistical obstacles. The appeal of the EPZ idea is to begin reaping incremental benefits of export industry without waiting to resolve all the policy debates and internal battles that can drag on interminably.

The most obvious domestic linkage from EPZs is the employment generated. Also, the foreign exchange earned can benefit the whole economy. Through such a strategy a country, in effect, aims to get itself a "Singapore" appended within its boundaries—hopefully with similarly spectacular performance. Among the 100 or more EPZs set up worldwide, perhaps the most successful example is the entire province of Gwangdong (around Canton in China) that has enjoyed explosive growth. It operates almost as if it were a separate entity insulated from the rigid controls that inhibit the rest of communist China. By contrast, a rather unsuccessful example is the EPZ near Bombay, where the regular Indian bureaucracy has managed to infiltrate its rules and controls, and stifle an independent node of growth.

Table 12-1 Linkages from export production

		Domestic	Foreign	
Purchased inputs	40	35	5	Imported inputs
Labor	30	25	5	Expatriates
Capital	20	5	15	Foreign borrowing
Profit	10	5	5	Foreign equity
	—	—	—	
Total cost	100	70	30	

CASE STUDY: EXPORT PROCESSING ZONE IN MAURITIUS

The small island in Mauritius of the Indian Ocean provides a successful application of the EPZ idea. Set up early in the 1960s, its aim was to move away from the sugar-based economic structure. Its implementation involved a learning process that altered targets and policy in an evolving situation. Initial policy aimed for import-substituting (light) industry in keeping with the spirit of the times. This was promoted by tax exemptions and subsidized long-term loans.

Investment   The Mauritius EPZ was unusual in that much of the investment originated locally. The small component of foreign investment came largely from Hong Kong and a small part from France, the former colonial power.

Exports   Initially the EPZ had a 100% export requirement. In other words, production for the local market was prohibited. The principal customer is the European Community, which grants preferential access to African countries under the Lome Convention. Exports are concentrated in apparel (80–90%), with small amounts of other labor-intensive manufactures such as footwear, jewelry, and, recently, electronic goods. Lately much of the exports derive from Hong Kong entrepreneurs who, having filled their garment export quotas, set up shop in nearby countries that have not.

Employment   Given the small size of the country, the EPZ makes a significant impact on the local labor market. Unemployment in Mauritius, which was as high as 14% till 1985, plummeted to 3% by 1989. Meanwhile wages have stayed low—only 25% of the level in Singapore. Labor policies such as hiring, firing, and overtime are flexible in the EPZ. The government also has provided vocational training facilities as part of the supportive infrastructure.

Infrastructure   The Mauritius EPZ is unusual because it is not locationally segregated. Rather,

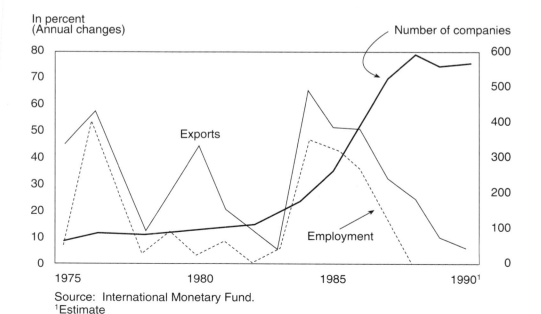

Source: International Monetary Fund.
[1]Estimate

it is spread across the island. Participating firms are only required to designate their EPZ production, imports, and exports. One advantage is that the EPZ does not require extra investment. Firms can go to the workers, rather than the other way around. In fact, most EPZ firms rented ready-made facilities in industrial estates where they enjoy subsidized rents and utilities. While the much increased volume of exports required an expansion of shipping and airport facilities, these benefits are shared by the economy at large.

Achievements.　The achievements of over thirty years of experience with the Mauritius EPZ may be summarized.

1. Clearly, employment creation has been its biggest success.

2. The measurable effect on output growth seems relatively small. Yet a significant indirect stimulus might be uncovered by a detailed study. Like the connection between trade and growth, the issue is more readily resolved by comparison with other similar economies—Mauritius has enjoyed over 6% growth rate of GDP over the past decade.

3. The foreign exchange contribution was smaller than expected due to imports of plant and machinery. The net export coefficient (ratio of net to gross foreign exchange receipts) has gradually risen from just 10% to about 40% in recent years. The potential exists for future large increments.

4. Diversification away from a heavy dependence on sugar certainly has occurred. The new concentration on apparel exports should not, however, cause too much concern since light manufacturing skills may easily be transferred to other products.

Future challenges also present new opportunities. The EPZ firms must continually seek out new products and markets. A natural progression is to begin exporting services such as offshore banking and data entry. Following the lead of Singapore, this will entail upgrading skills to move into higher value-added activities. The policy package must also be refined in various ways in light of the experience gained. The tax structure can be better harmonized across the domestic sector and the EPZ.

General Lessons.　In an IMF study, Alter (1991) draws out some lessons from the Mauritius EPZ that would apply to others. First and foremost, there is no substitute for a general liberalization. Recall that the original rationale for EPZs was to set them up only in situations where bureaucratic and other distortions cannot be removed. If an EPZ is so successful, why not expand it to cover the entire economy? In the same vein, linkages with the rest of the economy will be reinforced if the 100% export requirement is relaxed. As a practical matter, this requirement is often imposed just as an administrative convenience to keep tax-exempt EPZ goods segregated from domestic market goods. However, if such administrative hurdles can be overcome, then economic efficiency considerations can prevail.

The second general lesson is that EPZs have a high budgetary cost. These include actual outlays such as subsidies, infrastructure costs, "tax expenditures" as the government forgoes many revenue sources such as income taxes and import duties. Fortunately the private benefits far exceed the public costs, giving a net national gain. Yet the distinction between financial and economic rationality is crucial for maintaining a viable program (as discussed in the next chapter on social benefit/cost analysis.) A natural solution is to internalize all benefits and costs within one entity, which suggests that EPZs may perhaps be operated on a commercial basis.

Finally, the export effort must not rely too heavily on preferential market arrangements. While Mauritius has benefited from such access in the past, these very arrangements could become a limiting factor in the future. For example, Hong Kong investors were attracted because Mauritius' apparel export quota was underutilized. But what will happen when this quota is used up, or when the entire Multi Fibre Agreement is phased out as agreed by the latest round of GATT talks? Instead of relying on such political deals, it would be better to streamline internal policy to keep Mauritius attractive to foreign investors. Global competition is likely to get even stronger as more countries begin to emulate the Asian tigers and as the East European countries become more competitive.

TO TRADE OR NOT TO TRADE

Arguments against a reliance on free trade or comparative advantage are based on alleged failures of the neoclassical assumptions: Technical capabilities can change significantly, or factor endowments change by participation in trade. If a country's savings rate depends on industrial profits, then a simple free trade strategy may not necessarily be most desirable. In this case, trade restrictions may serve to enhance capital accumulation by increasing profits to domestic industry, as per the Lewis model. If technical efficiency can be enhanced by learning-by-doing, then again it's possible that protected industrialization might turn out to be a better growth strategy. The key issue here is whether a country should follow its current comparative advantage or anticipate or force future changes.

As mentioned before, many LDCs were quite averse to the pattern of production implied by comparative advantage. They felt they would forever be relegated to being "hewers of wood and drawers of water." Instead, these LDCs aimed to emulate the glamorous industrial production of the DCs through a more balanced economic structure instead of the specialization implied by comparative advantage. This can be initiated by protecting the domestic infant industry from the harsh competition of the world market. For a transitory period (about two or three decades) the country must limit imports to allow productivity to improve through learning-by-doing. The protective barriers result in raising the domestic price. For example, if Bolivia imposes a 100% duty on bicycles, domestic producers can sell at up to twice the world price. Such infant industry protection is familiar even in the United States, as the auto industry urged the government to install quantitative import restrictions that boosted car prices above world prices during the 1980s. (To call this industry an infant is ridiculous, perhaps it is better called a "sick" industry that needed a period of recuperation.)

Terms of Trade

Another argument against a reliance on comparative advantage stems from a fear of a **secular decline in the terms of trade** of primary exporters. Two pioneers of the development economics school, Raul Prebisch and Hans Singer, used this to make a strong argument against a trade oriented development strategy. The terms of trade is defined as the ratio of export prices/import prices. LDCs that mainly export primary goods in exchange for manufactured imports fear that their export prices will continue to decline. We first examine the empirical evidence for this presumption before elaborating the theoretical model.

After the earlier work in the 1950s, a major reevaluation of this research was done by Grilli and Yang (1988). They constructed a new series of primary goods prices from 1900 to 1986. These data have formed the basis of much similar research, culminating in Bleaney and Greenaway's work that extends the series to 1991. Their data are presented in Figure 12-7.

The research uses sophisticated statistical techniques to extract a trend line from this graph. Note that we can find any trend at all by choosing arbitrary end points. For instance, from the depths of depression in the 1930s to the commodity price boom of the 1970s the trend in primary goods

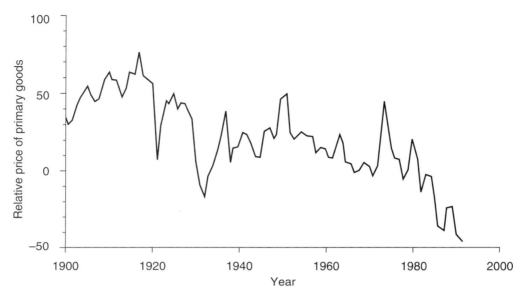

Figure 12-7 *Trends in the relative price of primary goods*

prices was definitely upward. (Analogously, Prebisch's data for the period 1870 to 1930 did indicate a downward trend.) Another statistical challenge is to determine whether the data show a trend or a series of jumps (or structural breaks). While this may seem esoteric to the student, it is relevant because random jumps can go up or down in an unpredictable way, whereas a trend implies some mechanism driving prices inexorably downward. All research does agree on a downward trend of between .6% and .9% per annum so far this century.

One more cautionary note is that these data refer to aggregate indices of commodity prices. One cannot derive broad policy prescription for all developing countries from this aggregate data. Moreover, a decline in primary goods prices must be distinguished from changes in LDC terms of trade. After all, many LDCs export manufactured goods, while DCs such as the U.S., Canada, and Australia export primary commodities.

A proper approach is for each country to decide its trade orientation based on the specific commodity it exports. Some countries have indeed

suffered a long-term decline in export prices and export revenues, relative to the price of manufactured goods they import. Typically hard hit are primary exports for which new substitutes are found. Examples are Bangladesh's exports of jute; Cuba and the Philippines, sugar; and Jamaica, bauxite. On the other hand, the price of oil went up dramatically and has recently drifted back down again. As a counterexample, the price of natural rubber was thought to be in terminal decline, but bounced back with the invention of radial tires.

The evolution of the terms of trade for various primary commodity groups can be charted over a turbulent 25-year period in recent times. Table 12-2 shows the relative price of various nonfuel commodities from 1957 to 1982.

This table also appears to indicate that prices of primary commodities have declined relative to manufactured goods prices. But a closer look reveals an important qualifier. The prices used are unit value indices for manufactured goods, which do not account for possible improvements in their quality. Suppose a hundred tons of wheat could be exchanged for two

Table 12-2   Ratio of commodity prices to manufactured export prices

	Foods	Beverages	Agricultural raw materials	Metals
1957	100	100	100	100
1960	92	78	97	92
1965	91	67	61	114
1970	91	75	63	111
1975	111	58	61	76
1980	96	82	67	82
1982	73	73	55	72

Source: IMF Base index for unit value indices 1957 = 100

motor scooters in 1965, but only a single scooter in 1985. Must we conclude that the terms of trade for wheat have dropped? Not necessarily. The motor scooter is likely to have evolved to an improved model, while wheat remains the same old commodity, wheat. After allowing for quality improvements, the apparent relative price movement in favor of manufactured goods no longer appears marked. Again, if different starting and ending dates are picked, the secular trend in the terms of trade may well remain steady over long periods of time. (Recall the case study in the introduction, which shows how a trend growth rate may be estimated from numerical data.)

One unambiguous observation (from both the aggregate and disaggregated data) is that commodity prices can fluctuate quite dramatically. The best known example is, of course, the price of oil, which has fluctuated sharply over the past few decades. Similar fluctuations occur in the price of wheat, coffee, bauxite, and most other primary commodities. The resulting **instability of export revenues** makes some export economies acutely vulnerable on their foreign trade side. Table 11-2 showed how many primary exporting countries in Africa and Latin America have a particular concentration of a few export commodities. Note, for example, the role of copper in the economies of Chile or Zaire. On the other hand, India and China are large countries that rely relatively little on world trade. Thus they

remained largely unaffected by the 1981–1983 world recession. As export quantities and prices declined sharply worldwide, most trade-dependent economies were plunged into recession.

The unavoidable instability that stems from primary exporting is a disadvantage that must be juxtaposed against any benefits. This risk-return trade-off decision is based on a country's attitude toward risk. For example, would the country prefer an average growth rate of 7% with a range of ± 5%, or an average growth rate of 4% ± 1%? Evidently Brazil has chosen the former high risk strategy, while India opts for a more conservative growth path. A strategy based on comparative advantage generally promises a higher growth path, which also comes with trade instability. These two examples, Brazil (high growth, low stability), and India (low growth, higher stability), represent real choices made by their governments.

Prebisch and Singer argued that the terms of trade must turn against primary goods in the long run. Their theoretical explanation is based largely on Engel's law: As incomes rise worldwide, the proportion of that income spent on foodstuffs and simple necessities declines. More precisely, the income elasticity of primary goods is less than unity, whereas it exceeds unity for manufactured goods. But the primary goods category includes raw materials, and wouldn't the demand for raw materials rise as the world industry develops?

Another cautionary note is to remember that price is determined by demand and supply. Thus we must also examine the supply conditions when considering price developments. The manufacturing sector is notable in that supply can expand explosively, which must surely put downward pressure on the price of manufactured goods. Figure 12-8 demonstrates how the supply cost of manufactures can fall further than any price decreases for primary products due to sluggish demand. Thus the price of manufactures may fall in relation to primary goods. In sum, there is no conclusive argument that the terms of trade for primary products is bound to fall over time.

Aside from the terms of trade prospects, other arguments against a trade orientation stem from the rejection of neoclassical assumptions. Factor markets are often far from perfectly competitive, while the level of technological knowledge differs widely between nations or even between different sectors of a dualistic economy. Furthermore, there are widespread possibilities for learning-by-doing, economies of scale, and so on. Such deviations from free market assumptions can justify appropriate government interventions to improve dynamic growth possibilities. In practice, however, the ISI strategy often was marred by interventions that persisted far too long. A different kind of intervention is to focus on export promotion, as in Korea and Taiwan. This strategy also promises dynamic improvements, but through the channels of scale economies and induced technical change. The export promotion strategy is also preferable to ISI since it can be pursued beyond the limits imposed by the size of the domestic market. Further, this intervention provides all the benefits while avoiding a hazard endemic to an ISI strategy: Monopolistic tendencies that are reinforced within the protectionist framework.

Arguments in favor of trade-based growth have been based mainly on empirical results, whereas theoretical explanations only followed later to rationalize the observations. As we have seen, neoclassical trade theory promises the potential for factor price equalization, hopefully within a few generations. Such benefits did occur historically in the nineteenth century as the United States, Canada, Australia, and Argentina in the New World developed through trade with Europe, each relying on its particular comparative advantage. (The prevailing high transport costs certainly afforded a natural protection to those countries' budding industries.) A modern example of wage

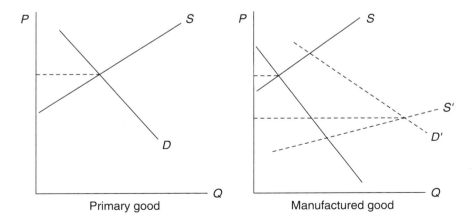

Figure 12-8 *How the terms of trade may change*

equalization is Korea, which moved from its starting position as one of the poorest countries in the world in the 1950s. A mere four decades later it has boosted its income from under $200 to over $2000 per capita by utilizing a trade-based growth strategy. A few decades from now its level could well approach DC standards.

Heckscher-Ohlin theory suggests that L-intensive production is an appropriate policy for labor surplus LDCs. Earlier comparative advantage placed an emphasis on natural resource based primary exports, but we now know that L-intensive manufacturing (for example, textiles, and shoes) also can be successful. An especially hopeful implication is factor-price equalization, in which free trade will (rapidly?) equalize wages across countries. Furthermore, the existing comparative advantage itself changes as factor endowments change due to capital accumulation. For example, if K accumulates at the rate of 10% and L grows at 2%, the K/L ratio would increase annually by approximately 8%. This allows changes in production techniques as well as changes in the qualitative pattern of development.

Import Substituting Industrialization

Perhaps the strongest case in favor of trade-based growth is made by the demonstrated failure of ISI strategy in recent times. This experience has been well documented for a number of countries, notably by the Bhagwati and Kreuger study for the National Bureau of Economic Research in the 1970s. The anatomy of decay of the ISI regime has certain common elements.

1. ISI tends to progressively worsen the balance of payments crisis in LDCs. This came as a surprise since ISI originally was intended to cut imports, and thereby to improve the trade balance. In fact, machinery and raw materials imports needed for domestic industry expanded dramatically at the same time as exports stagnated. Such an autarchic industrial strategy becomes an all-or-nothing proposition. The country must have a fully integrated industrial structure that produces every single item since there is no assurance of being able to import intermediate goods. (This possible foreign exchange shortage was one of the constraints built into the 2-gap model examined earlier.)

2. The ISI regime usually involves extensive quantitative restrictions that form distortions that reduce the overall efficiency of the economy. The following chapter will examine the precise nature and effects of such distortions. Export interventions, by contrast, tend to be less distortionary.

3. Even as growth and exports stagnate under ISI, a political economy effect obstructs moves toward reform. The protected industries earn high rents, which they use to reinforce and maintain the protective regime. In effect, the infant industry does not grow up because it does not need to. By the same token, ISI limits incentives to innovate and improve quality in the monopolistic protected market. By contrast, a highly competitive export sector encourages and forces learning-by-doing.

4. ISI proponents use the observed stagnation of exports to validate their export pessimism. They fail to acknowledge that the ISI regime itself acts to inhibit export growth. Protectionism creates a bias against exports by turning the terms of trade in favor of domestic industry, inducing resources to flow away from the exports sector. Figure 12-9 shows how a tariff on imports raises the (relative) price of importables, thereby expanding importables production. Given the economy's resources, total output is limited as shown by the production possibility curve (PPC). Thus export production must be cut. In short, the high price of domestic and imported inputs makes an adverse impact on export volume and price competitiveness.

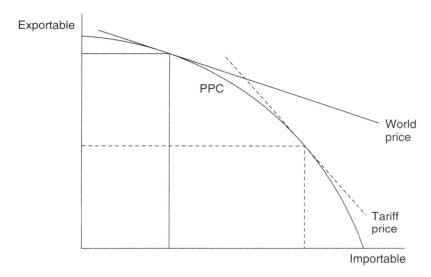

Figure 12-9 *Import protection harms exports*

All this does not mean that an ISI strategy is worthless. In fact, virtually all the export success stories had initiated industry by judicious use of ISI. Their policy aim was to gradually lower tariffs (or other trade barriers) after an appropriate time during which learning occurred so that domestic producers eventually became competitive in the world market. The former "importables" sector may then turn to exporting. Japan based its export drive on a domestic industrial base created by ISI, as did Korea a generation later (see Amsden 1991).

Note that a large domestic market is not a necessary prerequisite for building up technical capabilities. Scale economies in production need not be limited by the size of the domestic economy since exports can provide a virtually limitless market to any country, although the largest exporters, Taiwan and Korea, are now running into protectionism by their biggest customers among the OECD countries. An export promotion strategy can go further than just removing the tariffs that keep industrial prices high. Instead, direct subsidies to exporters actually tilt relative returns in favor of exports, which enables a country to garner dynamic benefits not solely derived from ISI production.

Trade and Growth: Empirical Studies

Since economics aspires to be a science, its theories must be tested against real-world empirical data. One example of this is the large set of empirical studies that attempt to establish whether a broader participation in trade leads to overall economic growth. Recent research uses more sophisticated econometric techniques than an earlier vintage of casual studies that addressed the question: Is trade the "engine" for growth? The empirical studies all seem rather atheoretical. Whereas the standard trade theory (chapter 11) is logically tight, it does not explain well the facts of actual growth. By contrast, a theory relating growth to trade is loose even though the relation is strong enough to qualify as stylized facts. Thus it still remains a task for theoreticians to provide a robust theory that explains the empirical facts of trade and growth.

Participation in trade appears to have significantly boosted overall rates of growth, especially since the 1960s. There are, of course, stray exceptions and residual doubts about statistical inferences; yet the evidence as a whole is compelling. A long string of empirical studies since the 1970s is surveyed by Lal and Rajpatirana (1987), and Edwards (1989). Empirical studies of trade and growth typically use cross-sectional data for 25-100 LDCs to uncover statistical relations that aim to explain country growth rates. (This econometric technique is well-known as regression analysis.) A production function framework is used for a growth accounting exercise to identify the usual determinants of growth—input factors such as K and L—and export growth is included as a separate explanatory variable.

$$\hat{Y} = fn\left(\hat{K}, \quad \hat{L}, \quad \text{etc.,} \quad \hat{X} \right)$$

Invariably the exports variable is found to be highly significant and to have a positive sign. A correlation definitely exists between the growth rate of exports and the rate of overall growth, but does this signify causation? Much recent research aims to answer this question. These studies explore the different channels through which exports might affect overall growth. Subtle econometrics is required to obtain robust conclusions from the data in face of all sorts of spurious correlations. For instance, many successful exporters are also countries with good economic management. Thus a successful export performance and rapid growth may both be consequences of sound economic policies at the macro and micro levels. Then export growth per se cannot get the credit for a beneficial impact on growth. In short, the remarkable growth performance of countries such as Taiwan and Korea must not be attributed exclusively to export led growth, but also to sound economic management of the overall economy.

The Global Trading Environment

Last, but certainly not least in importance, is a different aspect of trade policy. The individual LDC cannot be considered as just a powerless entity facing a monolithic rest-of-the-world. Few LDCs are so tiny as to have no influence at all on the trading environment. Each has some degree of choice in designing its trade policy subject to the **international repercussions** that may flow from it. The LDC's protectionist policy directed against foreign goods is bound to be viewed with disfavor by the affected foreign countries. They might retaliate against their imports from that LDC. (Note that most of the LDCs' imports come from the developed countries.) The relevant theory comes from basic microeconomics of competitive markets, which applies to a large number of atomistic agents. In contrast, when the number of agents is small, the applicable tool is game theory in which issues of power and negotiations take central place.

LDCs may affect their trading environment through three distinct methods: (1) Multilateral negotiations, (2) bilateral bargaining, and (3) regional trading blocks.

Multilateral negotiations   All countries participate in a series of multilateral trade negotiations that aim to liberalize trade in general. These negotiations are conducted under the aegis of the **General Agreement on Tariffs and Trade (GATT),** an international organization based in Geneva. The big players in these talks are the industrialized countries that usually have major issues to be resolved among themselves. A secondary emphasis is their combined stance vis-a-vis the developing world. These negotiations often interact in a complex way with other North-South political issues such as aid, international monetary reforms, and, most recently, global environmental concerns examined at the Earth Summit at Rio in 1992.

The DCs have granted a special exception to LDCs in the form of preferential access or

The Uruguay Round of GATT Talks

This monster round of multilateral trade negotiations was successfully concluded in December 1993. It was dubbed the Uruguay Round because it started in Uruguay seven years earlier. The arduous negotiations sometimes seemed to reach an impasse, but in the end, major trade issues were addressed and resolved, however imperfectly. The talks succeeded, in effect, simply because the world community saw collective benefits for continued world economic growth, while the consequences of failure were too grim to imagine.

The GATT talks are mainly of interest to influential players such as the United States, European Economic Community, and Japan. For the first time, however, the developing countries became involved in a big way, realizing that their interests also would be affected for good or bad.

Industry   Textiles and apparel constitute about one-fourth of all LDC industrial exports. The LDCs must be thankful for such exports that have sparked much of their industrialization. Yet the import limitations by the DCs are becoming more evident. The complex system of quotas set by the old **Multi Fiber Agreement (MFA)** is becoming more binding. These quotas will be phased out over the next decade, while tariffs are also cut. In return, the LDCs must concede reciprocal access to textiles from DCs.

The strictures against dumping have been stiffened. While this has mainly been a DC weapon, the LDCs are also now becoming aware of it. Dumping occurs when a country export price is lower that its domestic price or the cost of production. The savvy traveler knows that the most expensive place to buy a Japanese camera is in Japan. In that case, other camera producers can bring a dumping complaint against Japan. Steel is another commodity in which charges of dumping are exchanged in fierce international competition.

The generalized tariff reduction also will help LDC industry, even though the remaining DC tariffs are relatively low. The coverage of tariff-free goods will more than double to about 40% of all goods. As an example, the U.S. tariff duty of 12% on toys will be eliminated.

Agriculture   The most notable success was in attacking the thicket of protectionist measures in agriculture, which so far had seemed immune to liberalization. The DCs—especially the European community—had maintained heavy agricultural subsidies, keeping out LDC (and each other's) agricultural exports. The new agreement scales back these subsidies and relaxes outright import bans (such as of rice in Japan) and quotas. LDC exports of commodities such as rice, sugar, oilseeds, and peanuts are bound to rise considerably. For instance, Brazil will be able to expand its exports of soybean and poultry.

Services   Restrictions against imported services will be relaxed. The most likely gainers will be the developed countries with their long established service companies. The LDCs, even though reluctant, also may benefit from the increased efficiency that the foreign service companies will introduce to their economies. The agreement allows legal and accounting firms to imports, but does not extend to banking and securities firms.

continued

The DCs also gained some measure of protection for intellectual property rights. As the main producers of copyrights and patents, the DCs will be able to prevent outright copying in many LDCs. The LDCs have argued against such a sanctity for property rights. This opposition takes on a moral tone particularly in the case of pharmaceuticals since the very life and health of their citizens is involved. The moral argument is less valid for software that is developed at great expense by R&D, then knocked off virtually cost-free by pirates in some remote land.

In sum, the new GATT agreement has winners and losers across countries and for different sectors within countries. Yet overall, the LDCs have to consider themselves as net winners from the more open global environment.

lower tariff rates to their exports. This **generalized system of preference (GSP)** is an established feature of the world's trading system. The GSP only covers a limited range of products—less than 20% of LDC exports to DCs. Moreover, as the overall level of tariff rates has continued to decline, the importance of this concession has also fallen.

As previous rounds of GATT talks succeeded in reducing the average level of tariffs worldwide, another aspect of trade policy has come to the fore. Trade negotiators have come to realize that any (domestic) policy resembles trade policy in effect! Though this may sound paradoxical, on reflection you will begin to see how it works. Consider, for example, a country that wants to protect some economic sector for some reason. Why antagonize other countries by raising tariffs or other explicit trade barriers? It causes much less friction to simply help the favored industry in some other way. Granting tax rebates, subsidized utility rates, or other infrastructure services may be passed off as purely domestic policies. Yet these have just the same effect of limiting imports or promoting exports as any policy normally considered trade policy.

This is the reason why trade negotiations soon begin to trespass into the other country's jealously guarded sovereignty over internal matters. A logical consequence is the common market approach, which aims to form free trade areas that also harmonize domestic policies. A recent example, familiar to Americans, is the campaign to force Mexico to adopt the same environmental, occupational, and safety standards as the United States. This is only fair, otherwise Mexico would have an undue advantage in production costs.

Bilateral bargaining   The second form of international bargaining about trade is growing rapidly in importance. It impinges much more directly on the prospects of LDC exports as various conditions are imposed bilaterally on the larger LDC exporters. This obliges such LDCs to consider reciprocity when designing their own trade and industrial policies. For the most part, the industrial world does not bother much about the tariff stance of small LDCs—small is defined in terms of the magnitude of their trade. Whether or not such countries import freely, they hardly make a dent in the overall volume of DC trade. By contrast the more successful NICs manage to pile up enormous trade surpluses. From countries such as Korea, Taiwan, China, and Brazil, the industrial countries are now demanding much more reciprocity in trade concessions. The developing countries have to temper domestic policy considerations (discussed earlier) when they are simultaneously engaged in a strategic game of reciprocal concessions, threats, and punishments with their trading partners. This new kind of trade policy analysis is developed under the rubric of strategic trade policy. To gain some degree of power in this context, many countries are considering forming associations so as to negotiate as a group rather than alone.

Regional trading blocks The trend toward forging closer interconnections is spreading rapidly across the globe. Trade barriers have dropped faster within defined geographical regions, rather than in general, as various trade blocs spring up following the successful pattern of the EEC. A recent example is the formation of NAFTA among the United States, Mexico, and Canada. Various regions in the Third World have had a long history of forming **free trade areas,** but their performance so far has been rather poor. Table 12-3 highlights the contrast between regional trade arrangements in the DCs and the LDCs in this respect.

Table 12-3 shows the EEC to be particularly successful in promoting trade among its members, while expanding its share of world trade at the same time. Among the LDC groups, the ASEAN formed by Southeast Asian countries only recently has moved toward freer trade among its members. Also quite recently, Brazil and Argentina altered their aloof policy stance to breathe new life into a long established Latin American trade bloc. Their

previous attempts were half-hearted and failed to promote either trade or development.

The difference in performance of the LDC free trade areas versus the DC groups raises the obvious question: Why? One common explanation is that neighboring countries have similar comparative advantage, so they have little to gain by trading with each other. But this does not justify barriers to imports from neighbors. Also, North-North trade flourishes among the developed countries because they rely much less on old-fashioned comparative advantage. Instead they have much more intraindustry trade in differentiated products. (Recall the modern trade theory presented earlier.) The newly reactivated regional trading blocs in the Western Hemisphere bring together countries of disparate size and level of development to form larger, more viable units.

The design of free trade areas involves an extensive exercise in harmonizing tariff and tax structures among member countries. The same way tariffs have to be equalized across different

Table 12-3 Export shares of regional trade groups

	1960	1970	1980	1990
DCs				
EEC	35[1]	51	54	60
(Europe)	25[2]	39	35	41
Canada-U.S.	27	33	27	34
(North America)	22	21	15	16
ANZCERTA	6	6	6	7
(Australia-New Zealand)	2.4	2.1	1.4	1.5
LDCs				
ASEAN	4	21	17	19
(Southeast Asia)	2.6	2.1	3.7	4.3
ANDEAN	1	2	4	5
(South America)	2.9	1.6	1.6	.9
ECOWAS	—	3	4	6
(West Africa)	—	1.0	1.7	.6

[1] % share of intraregional exports to total exports
[2] % share of the region's exports in total world trade

Source: IMF Finance and Development, 1992

Table 12-4   Size of trading blocs in Western Hemisphere
(GNP in billion $; population in millions)

	GNP	Pop		GNP	Pop		GNP	Pop
United States	6400	260	Colombia	64	34	Brazil	423	157
Mexico	371	91	Venezuela	95	21	Argentina	186	33
Canada	567	28	Ecuador	18	11	Paraguay	9	5
			Bolivia	8	8	Uruguay	12	3
NAFTA	7338	379	Andean bloc	185	74	Mercosur	630	198

Source: IMF Finance and Development, 1992.

industries to avoid distortions, countries that aim to link their economies must also try to equalize their tariff structures, as well as their regime of taxes and subsidies. Otherwise resources and goods will flow wastefully across borders merely to take advantage of arbitrary differences in tax rates.

SUMMARY

The design of trade strategy is critical to a country's growth performance. The decision to trade or not to trade depends on whether a reliance on comparative advantage is deemed beneficial. While a trade (and production) structure based on comparative advantage clearly will be most efficient in a static sense, the question remains whether it will ensure the dynamic fastest rate of growth.

Two questions are relevant for an export-led growth strategy: (1) Can LDCs realistically expand their exports given their comparative advantage and the world trading environment?; and (2) Would expanded exports indeed speed up the overall growth rate of the economy? We examined some of the channels through which the second element may operate. These explanations remain diffuse, especially in comparison to the tight constructs of the pure theory of trade. Yet, the existence of the effect itself is an empirical question that can be directly studied. Lal and Rajapatirana (1987) provide a useful survey of recent results. Most of these are cross-sectional studies using sets of developing countries that differ in various ways including their chosen trade strategy. The econometric studies control for differences in all the other variables and thereby isolate a definite contribution to growth contribution by an export promotion strategy.

The study of import policy is more standard. The microeconomics of import tariffs is similar to the analysis of incidence of any other tax in its effects on equity, efficiency, tax revenue, and relative prices. The clear implication is that tariffs are less distortive than quantitative restrictions. Further, the rates of effective protection can diverge considerably to worsen distortions in the economy. Thus tariff policy should strive to both lower and equalize tariff rates. In spite of the demonstrated efficiency losses, many LDCs have chosen a protectionist development strategy by setting up various trade barriers. Somewhat less obvious is the motivation for allowing quantitative restrictions to flourish. This is explained by the new political economy, which stresses the redistributive aspects and their interaction with political power.

KEY TERMS

Government revenue	Effective protection	Instability of export revenues
Foreign exchange savings	Revenue maximizing tariff	Trade liberalization
Devaluation; depreciation	Intermediate imports	International retaliation
Infant industry	Quantitative restrictions	Free trade areas
Cascaded tariff structure	Export pessimism	Generalized system of preferences (GSP)
Quotas	Commodity cartels	
Rent-seeking behavior	Diversification of exports	General Agreement on Tariffs and Trade (GATT)
Tariff equivalent	Export processing zones (EPZ)	Multi Fiber Agreement (MFA)
Prohibitive tariff	Secular decline of terms of trade	
Production subsidy		

PART V

POLICY ISSUES

Chapter 13

Theory of Policy

The book now switches its focus from theory to policy—from a positive study of how the economy works to a prescriptive analysis of what should be done. This chapter introduces the idea that policy choice in itself can be the subject of study, a "theory of policy," if you will. Two succeeding chapters turn to policy making in the specific sectors of agriculture and industry. The final chapter discusses macroeconomic policy.

The study of economic policy as a concept may be neatly split in two distinct parts as seen in the familiar demand and supply diagram in Figure 13-1. Any policy choice by the government whatsoever will affect both efficiency and income distribution. As an example, consider a price ceiling set at P_c which is lower than the free market price. Then triangle A measures the efficiency loss addressed by the neoclassical tools of **applied-welfare analysis.** Rectangle B shows the corresponding redistribution, which is the domain of the new political economy. The relative importance of these two aspects may be gauged by the size of the two areas. Further, a struggle over the redistributed portion may result in an additional social loss.

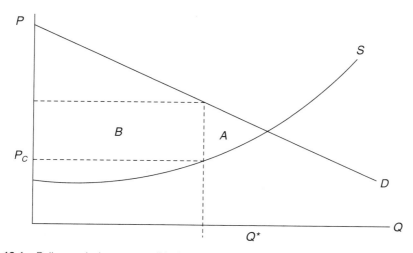

Figure 13-1   *Policy analysis versus political economy*

Both types of policy analysis have a role in policy design as summarized below (adapted from Stern 1989). The standard tools of applied welfare analysis have a role when market failures make it necessary for a rational government to design appropriate interventions. Meanwhile, when the interventions themselves become harmful distortions, the strictures of political economy apply.

Note an important distinction between these two types of policy analysis: While standard neoclassical tools have an obvious role in policy formulation, political economy theory appears subversive to normative analysis. The latter gives deterministic reasons why certain policies will be accepted or not, as group interests tend to prevail over the national interest. But then, why bother to figure out how the world works, except perhaps as an intellectual curiosity, if we are unable to do anything about it anyway? (This would be analogous to studying science in a world where it is unrelated to technology.) To challenge this kind of determinism it is imperative for would-be policy advisors to study the new political economy. To provide advice in a real-world context they must be thoroughly conversant with such theory of policy. Otherwise, the construction of policies based purely on positive theory, as in the preceding chapters, would be pointless if not misleading.

APPLIED-WELFARE ANALYSIS

Applied welfare analysis uses standard neoclassical tools in the real-world context of detailed policy choices. In the tool kit of standard economics there is a useful tool called **second-best** analysis. This tool is especially appropriate in the developing countries since their markets have many deviations from what would constitute perfectly undistorted free markets. Second-best analysis applies precisely where first best is infeasible. To understand this concept let's remind ourselves what constitutes "first best."

Neoclassical theory proves that an undistorted free market gives rise to the most efficient

---

Market Failures

Monopoly
Externalities—positive and negative
Increasing returns to scale
Missing markets—particularly for insurance and futures
Slow adjustment to imperfect information
Taxation that is unavoidable

Government Failures

Government has less information about consumers tastes
Administrative inflexibility
Individual incentives hard to replicate in centralized system
Rent seeking behavior such as corruption
Lobbying of government by interest groups
Government bureaucracy itself forms an interest group

---

allocation as depicted in the familiar demand and supply diagram. The sum of consumer surplus and producer surplus is maximum at the equilibrium price P^* and output Q^*. (This is the area between the demand and supply curve up to the quantity produced. Check for yourself that any other P or Q results in a lower total welfare.)

Economic welfare is maximized in an unconstrained free market equilibrium. If there are deviations from a free market that cannot be removed, the best attainable alternative is called second-best policy. Examples of such deviations are price ceilings or floors, monopoly, and externalities. In Figure 13-1, we consider the example of a ceiling price P_c which is pejoratively termed a **distortion,** since it reduces total welfare. (Those who favor government involvement prefer the less incendiary term, intervention.)

The magnitude of any distortion is measured by reference to the benchmark first best. In Figure 13-1 a distortion in the form of a price ceiling causes the quantity produced to be less than optimum Q^*. The welfare decrease is measured by the area of triangle A, while rectangle B indicates the amount of redistribution. Consumers get a larger consumer surplus, while the producers' profit is reduced. What kind of policy intervention might salvage some (or all) of the welfare loss? It might appear that neoclassical policy must oppose any and all deviations from a free market; one should reduce as many distortions as possible to move closer to the first best. But this is not true. The remarkable implication of second-best theory is: Given an existing distortion(s) that cannot be removed, one may have to add another distortion to improve welfare! This insight gave a new twist to economic policy analysis. Policy makers now must design appropriate intervention(s) that will enable us to reach the favorable second-best position.

Applied-welfare analysis is developed fully in the framework of social **benefit–cost analysis.** As an illustration we apply this apparatus to the case of pollution in which a (negative) externality

prevents the economy from reaching the first best that would prevail if markets were perfect. The aim is to design a suitable intervention that will take the economy to second best. A pollution tax may provide the best possible welfare gain. This cannot, of course, match the efficiency of no distortion at all, which would be first best, but it does improve the existing welfare situation. Social benefit–cost analysis provides a step-by-step procedure for selecting among proposed projects in the presence of such unavoidable distortions.

Benefit–Cost Analysis

As a concrete illustration of project evaluation let's continue with the pollution example. Say an existing steel mill creates this negative **externality,** which cannot (or will not) be removed. Now let's analyze a proposal for a factory that will be a customer for the steel. Suppose the project appears profitable based on an accounting that uses the market price of steel, P_M. As seen in Figure 13-2, the low-cost steel will allow the proposed factory to be quite profitable. This conclusion changes when the full social cost (SC) of pollution is included in the supply curve, not just the private cost (PC). Then output will be cut from point A to B. At the original point A, the shadow cost of steel P_S could be so high relative to benefits in the steel-using industry that the proposal should not be undertaken. (Note that benefits to the downstream industry are indicated by the demand curve on the right.) In sum, this exercise shows that the project is socially unprofitable even though it appears profitable according to a private accounting of costs and benefits.

Social benefit–cost analysis was briefly mentioned in the context of project evaluation techniques to allocate scarce capital optimally from a social point of view. (It was also illustrated in chapter 8 design the socially optimal system of education.) This procedure is used extensively in practice and is supported by a vast literature. Its essential features may be summarized as follows:

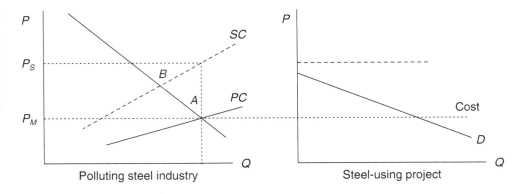

Figure 13-2 *Social benefit–cost analysis*

1. In the presence of distortions or imperfect markets, the market does not automatically reach the most efficient outcome—where social cost equals social benefit. Yet the existing externality or distortion cannot be removed for some reason.

2. The design of a project or program seeks to attain the second-best result. The technique of benefit–cost analysis begins with the set of prices prevailing in the markets; it then makes needed adjustments to one or more of these prices.

3. The key problem is determining what the appropriate corrections to prevailing prices should be. Private costs and benefits must be corrected so as to reflect the true social values, which are termed **shadow costs.** Thus a private accounting of profit is replaced by the criterion of net social profit for accepting or rejecting a project.

4. Important prices that typically need correction are the exchange rate and factor prices of labor and capital, the wage and interest rate, respectively. Note that the latter is an intertemporal price—the relative price of present goods to future goods. Another important price that may need correction is the exchange rate, which is the relative price of tradable to not tradable goods.

5. There is considerable debate about what price corrections best reflect the true social values. A basic difficulty is that society has no single aim, but rather a range of independent, often conflicting, objectives such as growth, distribution, and employment. Earlier we noted one such conflict in the choice of technique. One technology choice maximized employment while the other maximized saving that raises future output and consumption.

Let us detail one of the most critical corrections made to market prices. Investment projects invariably involve intertemporal decisions as a project promises a stream of returns that stretch over many future years. But an apple tomorrow is valued less than an apple today in terms of current utility. Thus all future dollar amounts must be discounted back to a single present value—even if the inflation rate is zero. The discount factor is related to the interest rate, which indicates how society values present versus future consumption.

Project accounting must have a set procedure for translating the dollar amounts in various time periods into a single measure. Two alternative methods allow a comparison between competing projects. These closely related methods, the **net present value (NPV)** and **internal rate of return (IRR),** are contrasted in an analytical box on page 249.

The rate of discount used to evaluate future amounts will have an obvious affect on project choice. In general the social discount rate differs from the market interest rate. Proponents of capital-intensive, or long-lived, projects argue for a low rate of discount that raises present value of the benefits stream. The U.S. Army Corps of Engineers, for example, uses a discount rate on its projects that is lower than the market interest rate. They argue that the private sector is not looking out for future generations since a high rate of discount reflects short-term thinking, which underinvests for long-term growth. The social rate therefore must be set low so that public policy might counter private myopia. This issue is debated as part of a broad ranging critique that is summarized below.

Critique

Criticisms of the benefit-cost construct range from skepticism about its very foundations to more practical concerns. The basic critique of welfarism is whether it is people or commodities that is the ultimate goal (see the review by Sudgen). Are people to be the subjects or objects of development? Huge proposed dam projects in India and China threaten to displace large numbers of poor people and to disrupt forever an entire way of life. While these projects purport to represent "progress" as measured by their projected benefits, the affected people do not necessarily agree. In response, the benefit-cost practitioners claim they are merely technicians who provide the most efficient means for socially decided ends. Their main concern is with the following more mundane practical difficulties.

Financial versus Economic Criterion The goal of benefit–cost analysis is to move toward the highest attainable economic welfare for the overall economy. This tool is specifically designed to choose between projects whose economic profitability is not truly reflected in its financial profitability using prevailing prices. (The public need not worry about projects that offer a financial profit, since private enterprise will likely proceed with those on its own initiative.) Unfortunately, projects that offer low financial returns are also the hardest to sustain in the real world. For example, a primary health program may offer high social returns but zero direct financial returns. Its financing from the public budget is typically subject to all sorts of political strains. By contrast, projects that directly earn revenues retain greater control over their own destiny. No wonder national oil companies worldwide seem so autonomous. On the other hand, projects that provide large positive externalities, such as those relating to the environment, tend to receive lower priority because they are users rather than suppliers of public funds.

Project versus Program The benefit-cost tool is best suited to the analysis of concrete projects. Yet the more narrowly it is construed—say, as applied to one particular power plant—the narrower its overall economic impact. However if it is used for an entire program—say, for designing the entire health sector—the analysis tends to become more tenuous and therefore less credible.

Fudging the Numbers The student may be somewhat surprised by this possibility. Isn't all analysis supposed to be entirely honest and disinterested? Alas, it is not always the case in the real world. In practice benefit-cost exercises tend to be so complex and technical that a skilled analyst can make the numbers come any way described. Thus comparison of project proposals prepared by different analysts (employed by interested agencies) requires another level of technically proficient proctors. An aprochryphal story highlights the extent of such fudging. Once upon a time, a minister of development raised the threshold rate of return on projects to 15% from the previous level of 10%. All pending proposals were withdrawn for one day. Presto, the reworked proposals all came back showing that they earned the required 15%! One wonders if that also happens if the rate is raised to 20%. The moral of this story is to be wary about making important choices based on small differences in computed returns.

Is the benefit-cost exercise justified even if doesn't furnish definitive results? Protagonists argue that it is still worth doing for the insight it provides. This sounds suspiciously like other fancy techniques that were oversold in the past. The analyst certainly can learn by playing with the numbers about the most crucial variables or interactions, but such knowledge is less useful if the decision maker or "line" manager is functionally separate from the "staff" analyst. Meanwhile the separation grows as technical analysis becomes more sophisticated.

Our introduction to the topic of applied welfare economics remains rather abstract. Chapter 14 will present specific applications of second-best policy designed for the agricultural sector. Before

that, we turn to study the new political economy, another important aspect of economic policy that has received new attention in recent years. As noted, these two aspects are not unrelated: Applied welfare analysis must be used in the presence of unremovable distortions. Such distortions often are prompted by an overriding social concern about distributional issues. The resulting social loss has been depicted as the inefficiency triangle in Figure 13-3. This kind of loss tends to be small in comparison to the size of the rectangle that measures the redistribution, so efficiency concerns can be safely ignored. However, this original rationale tends to become compromised as interest groups and rent seekers both in and out of government press for ever increasing amounts of redistribution, and the efficiency loss continues to rise. Inevitably this ends in a crisis, usually a fiscal crisis in which the polity is obliged to reassert the primacy of economic efficiency. This leads to various structural adjustment or liberalization policies, as discussed in chapter 16 on macro policy.

Analysis: Net Present Value or Internal Rate of Return?

Since project evaluation invariably involves comparisons of dollar values across time, both the cost and benefit streams must be appropriately discounted. The method used for this translation may give different answers. The IRR criterion might indicate that project A is more desirable than project B, while the NPV criterion indicates the opposite ordering.

Future dollars are translated into current dollars by discounting using the rate of discount i, which is related to the interest rate. Thus the net present value of a stream of payments A_t received at time t in the future is

$$NPV = \Sigma \frac{A_t}{(1+i)^t}$$

Two competing criteria for picking among alternative projects are

1. Determine the value of i that makes the $NPV = 0$. This value is the IRR. It would seem reasonable to accept all projects whose IRR exceeds the market rate of interest.

2. Pick a minimum threshold value for the discount rate, say $i = 15\%$. Accept all projects that have a positive NPV using this threshold discount rate.

continued

Both of these methods intuitively seem reasonable, so it may come as a surprise that they can indicate conflicting choices. But note that conflicting results can arise whenever the alternative criteria are not identical. (For example, in picking big players for a sports team, it is quite possible to get a different roster if the choice criterion is height as opposed to weight.)

To comprehend the precise reason for the difference, let us trace out the *NPV* using various discount rates, *i*. Plotted against each other, let's say the alternative projects *A* and *B* have the pattern as indicated in Figure 13-3.

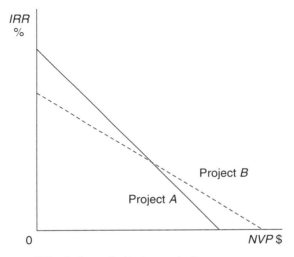

Figure 13-3   *NPV versus IRR criteria applied to two projects*

Project *B* has a higher net present value than project *A* at lower interest rates, and vice versa. So which one are we to pick? We must first distinguish what is meant by "alternative" projects. Projects *A* and *B* are fiscal alternatives if they compete for the same funds. The choice of one uses up the available budget and thereby precludes building the other. In this case the IRR is clearly the appropriate criterion since we aim to get the biggest bang for our buck from our limited budget. Projects *A* and *B* might be physical alternatives for one another. For example, at a given river location, you may either build one type of dam or another, but you physically cannot do both. Now the appropriate criterion is to choose the project with largest *NPV*. A common hurdle rate of discount is used to evaluate all candidate projects. Say, this society's opportunity cost of funds is 15%. Whichever project gives the largest *NPV* is clearly best, since it provides the largest increment of net benefits.

Various complications arise in the choice of an appropriate **social discount rate.** There is also the possibility of not being able to compute a unique IRR in certain situations. Even in the example of choosing dams, conceptual problems can arise when project sizes are unequal. Finally, when there are other constraining factors, other criteria become appropriate along the lines of linear programming.

POLITICAL ECONOMY

Standard economic theory may be considered fairly successful in explaining the effects of a given policy. This kind of applied economics includes the foregoing second-best analysis. But what determines the actual choice of policy is much harder to explain. It is naive to imagine that policy choice follows automatically from an analysis of effects: All one does is study the effects of alternative policies and choose the one which best advances "the public interest." Instead, in the real world, the policy chosen is most likely to be that which best serves the interest of some powerful subgroup(s) of society. Such influence by so-called **special interests** results from the nexus of economic interests and political power as played out in the political arena. This process of policy choice can itself be explained by a branch of economic theory called **political economy.**

An earlier view of policy went something like this: Technocratic economists work on a value-free analysis called positive economics, which scientifically predicts that policy X will have effect $Y,$ and so on. Separately, a political patron supplies particular objective(s) as, for example, a desired pattern of income distribution. The economist then figures out which policy package would be best suited to achieve that desired objective. As an extra bit of service, the economist may complete this normative analysis by highlighting the most efficient solution as a sort of benchmark. The purpose of providing the latter is to indicate the sacrifice that is being made in order to reach the politician's favored objective rather than the most efficient one. In any event, the analyst's positive analysis would indicate the best (most efficient) policy design to reach the desired objective.

Traditional policy analysts still tend to operate with this naive policy framework in mind. A classic example arises in the context of trade policy. Economists have long recommended policy derived from the theoretical proposition that free trade is most efficient. When this clear-cut policy

advice is widely disregarded throughout the world, the naive observer is left perplexed.

The political-economy perspective assures us that political decision makers are neither fools nor knaves. The puzzles about their behavior disappear when it is understood that it is all but impossible to find a **benevolent dictator** as a patron for policy analysis. There is no single entity that is all powerful, all knowing, and whose sole aim is to advance the public good. On the contrary each of these attributes is notable for its absence in the real world. We cannot make such heroic assumptions about the capabilities and motives of decision makers. Realistically the government has very limited knowledge about agents' tastes and constraints. Also, government is not necessarily benevolent. Typically it operates at the behest, or under the threat, of one or the other political group/coalition.

Political economy is based on the philosophical notion that interests are the main determinant of everyone's behavior, including people in government. This argument due to Burke was a major tenet of classical economics. Analysts from Adam Smith to John Stuart Mill have argued that economic policy is dictated by class interests. Later the Marxists went on to explain most economic developments by the interplay of class interests. They claim that the state is just a tool for the capitalist class, until the inevitable revolution when workers will capture the state and turn it into a tool serving their interests.

Modern political economy analysis is likewise based on interests, but the modern concept uses a broader definition of interest groups. Unlike Marxist doctrine, the groups have no necessary relation to classes with a definite hierarchical order. Instead, groups may comprise of different production sectors, or even coalitions of diverse interests formed by political parties. For example, the bureaucrats who implement government policy can constitute a separate interest group, quite apart from their diverse class affiliations. Thus a lowly blue-collar government worker may share an overriding interest with high-ranking bureaucrats who come from the aristocratic class. Both share a common interest in expanding the scope and power of government.

The new political economy is consistent with the Chicago tradition, which is suspicious of government's motives and capabilities. This school emphasizes that all economic agents strive to further their own self-interest; why should bureaucrats be exempt from this fundamental law of economics? In a study of regulatory behavior in the United States, Stigler and Peltzman found that the formulation and administration of regulations was quite removed from the public interest. Not surprisingly, regulators pursue their self-interest just like any homo economicus. Yet the **bureaucracy** manages to disguise these motives by constant reference to "the public interest," thereby fooling at least some of the public. In practice, over time the interests of regulators come to coincide with those of the regulated and not the public at large: The medical board with doctors they oversee; the Public Utilities Commission with utility companies; and so on. This phenomenon is termed **regulatory capture.**

Another issue addressed by political-economy theory is: What determines the formation and cohesion of interest groups? Olson's classic work, *The Logic of Collective Action,* indicates how agents with a variety of interests might come together. Certain interest groups find it easier to coalesce than others. For example, a million individual agents who stand to lose $10 each from a certain policy are less likely to combine in their common interest than ten agents who stand to lose $1 million each. In the larger group, the transactions and information costs for getting together are so formidable that they might never combine to effectively exert collective influence. A specific difficulty is the **free rider problem:** Individual beneficiaries find it rational to free ride on the collective efforts that others are making on their behalf. (An example from our daily lives is the struggle over bounced check charges by banks, which many people perceive as unfair. Yet a small

number of banks can organize a far more effective interest group to influence government regulations in their favor.)

In developing countries, too, well-organized groups such as protected industries usually represent the interests of a tiny minority of the population, yet manage to exert a decisive impact on policy. Another example is that of well-to-do farmers who prospered with the Green revolution and began to exert a collective influence far out of proportion to their numbers. In some countries this group manages to garner a large share of subsidies out of the government budget at the expense of everybody else. The possibility of organizing also depends on logistical factors. For example, in earlier times poor farmers would be fragmented and dispersed across the countryside, unable to exert effective pressure. Lately their political clout has been facilitated by an increase in their incomes and easier communications. This framework may provide an alternative explanation for the urban bias prevailing in the dual economy. Instead of springing from (misguided) ideas, the root cause may have been the power of urban/industrial interests, which dominated a fragmented and politically weak peasantry.

Political-economy theory has been developed further in recent years. James Buchanan's Nobel prize winning work extends beyond the Chicago school's realm of economic regulation to the fundamentals of political decision making and the design/choice of institutions in general. Other scholars relax the stylized assumption that agents are constantly aware of their self-interest. In fact, some groups coalesce and begin effective action almost by accident as they uncover their interests in a gradual and haphazard process of learning. Anne Kreuger's study of the sugar lobby in the United States notes that controls may be imposed by politicians who are initially naive about their ramifications. Later, diverse groups of people begin to realize some commonality of interest in aspects of the regulation—only then do they begin to organize for political action. There can even be mistakes as groups take policy stances that later turn out to have been against their self-interest.

Defining the State

For a realistic political economy analysis one must start by defining what is meant by **government.** (Even though used interchangeably here, **the state** is a wider concept than the concrete set of institutions that comprise the government.) The Liberal economic tradition considers government to be an abstract "rule maker" apart from other agents in the society, the "rule takers." A parallel assumption is that individual agents are atomistic price takers in competitive markets; they are influenced by prices, but have no power in setting them. The polar opposite approach views government to be constituted of the group of politicians and bureaucrats that maximizes its self-interest in setting the rules that affect everyone else's decisions. A deeper question emerges: How did those in government acquire this enviable position?

A radically different view of the state divorces it from any public interest whatsoever. Instead, the state is seen as an entity whose main purpose is the extraction of rents from an economy. The term *rents* in economics describes any income deriving from a special position or talent. The ability to appropriate rents in a given economy defines the political economy of its state. In turn, the state's chosen policy influences development performance. The best contemporary example is the oil revenue that flows into the OPEC countries. This basic economic fact is highly significant in explaining the political nature of those states, their economic policies, as well as the resulting development performance.

The origin of the state is explained theoretically by economic historians in the form of a parable of "Publicans and Thieves." This stylized sketch of history posits that sedentary peasants raise crops in the plains while mobile marauders swoop down from the hills to steal the produce. The plunder becomes so routine that it comes to

be seen as annual taxation to support the "King." In exchange, the gang of thieves in power keeps away other gangs. In time, this is seen as "national defense." This kind of a **minimal state** constitutes a contract—exactations by the powerful state in return for protection for the powerless. This is distinct from a **social compact,** which justifies a redistributive state that directs benefits to the poor.

In the limit the revenue-maximizing state turns into a **predatory state.** It places particular emphasis on those rents that are easiest to appropriate. Hence its main economic focus is to develop natural resource sectors (for example, mining for minerals), while the government's primary goal is unabashedly redistributive toward the ruler and his or her clan or oligarchy. Consider the case of Haiti under the Duvalier regime. Such states exist even today when colonies are defunct and democracy is ascendant. All the characteristic features may be discerned in such a state, including cultural attitudes derived from the old predatory model. (Such attitudes include glorification of the military, scorn for savings and investment, and so on. We leave such conjectures at this cursory level, since here we are trespassing into the domain of sociology and anthropology.)

The political-economy model has economic implications across a wide variety of existing economic structures. These range from entirely rent-based economies to the opposite extreme. Different types of LDCs may be ranked by this criterion. At the top are the OPEC countries, followed by other natural resource extraction economies (such as Zaire), then plantation economies (most of Central America), and agricultural economies based on cash crops. At the other extreme might be economies dominated by subsistence agriculture (as in much of sub-Saharan Africa), where few rents are available to redistribute. Elements of the predatory state are arrayed in much the same order. In the most established rent-based economies we find entrenched bureaucracies whose main purpose appears to be to extract and distribute rents.

The political-economy discipline leaves the uncomfortable impression that economic and social outcomes are rather deterministic. However, some room for affecting outcomes arises through the operation of **politics.** There is a role for political activism operating through the institutional framework. Thus the design of a country's political and social institutions can play a determining role in its development. The categories of dictatorship or democracy become relevant as in the old debate on whether authoritarianism is more conducive to economic growth than democracy. (This aspect was mentioned in the introduction, but it will take us too far afield to probe this question further.) Theories of democracy highlight the effect of institutional features, such as parties that vie for power in elections, multi-party versus two-party systems, and the rules of deciding—winner-take-all, plurality, simple or large majority voting schemes, and so on.

In short, (political) institutions matter for (economic) outcomes. In the democratic case, **politicians** may be defined as "political entrepreneurs" who seek to represent interest groups. They attach themselves to some preexisting group—or even form them from scratch—then ask for this group's votes to gain power. From this position they can advance their constituents' interests as well as their own. A complete model of rational politicians recognizes that their aim is to maximize some combination of money plus power. In sum, they don't just aim for an ultimate material objective, they also value power, the intermediate instrument, for its own sake.

Another major theoretical distinction arises once we move away from the liberal model of political economy. Instead of a large number of powerless atomistic agents, a small number of interest groups have measurable power to influence the rules. Their interactions are better modeled by **game theory** instead of standard theory, which assumes that a single agent's action cannot have any affect on the rule makers. Interactions between a small number of actors are termed strategic since each person picks a strategy (or course of action) that takes into account the expected response of the others'. A well-known implication of this theory is the possibility of a "Prisoner's dilemma." In certain games everybody acts rationally (and with full information), yet the outcomes chosen can be suboptimal for the society as a whole. In such a political-economy framework, the government, viewed as just another player, must contend with strategic responses to its own moves from the public which it governs.

In chapter 12 we saw an example of game theory applied to interactions between a small number of nations engaged in trade negotiations. Another example was a model of employment policy in which three domestic groups with appreciable power (business employers, labor unions, and the government) participate in a strategic game in which each aims for a different objective. In the present context, we note the emergence of different interest groups, that are not necessarily defined according to class. Since the number of such groups is tiny—certainly far fewer than the number of individual agents—their interactions take the form of a strategic game to determine the choice of policy and, therefore, of economic performance.

The political economy idea has rather mixed implication for policy formulation. One can no longer simply presume that economists offer advice for "the good of the country." By contrast, in the Liberal model, the main problem is that the authorities misunderstand facts or theories: Economists need only work out the "correct" efficient policy, and this policy will be implemented to universal acclaim. In reality, the authorities are likely well-aware of what they are doing in their attempts to advance the interests of their favored group(s). Even a neoclassical recommendation of free markets is bound to advance some groups at the expense of others. What can the policy analyst do in a framework in which policies and outcomes appear so deterministic based on group interests? What should be the role of the professional (and supposedly well-intentioned) policy analyst?

Rent Seeking

The notion that government itself constitutes an interest group, and that policy is determined in a "political market," radically alters our view of economic policy and performance. On one side there is competition for power and a price for offices that goes hand-in-hand with policy designed to extract rents from the private sector. On the other side, the private sector finds it more profitable to influence policy through bribes and lobbying than to seek profits through hard work and business skills. The former set of activities are labeled **rent seeking** or directly unproductive activities (DUP). The new theory provides great explanatory power. It explains, for instance, why countries blessed with abundant natural resources often display the worst growth performance. In the United Arab Emirates, for example, it would not be rational for an economic agent to try to succeed by economic competition, hard work, or technical innovation. Instead, it makes far more sense to compete politically for the grant of favors from the authorities who control the rents derived from oil exports.

Note how far such notions are from the previous liberal idea of a monolithic government that designs policy to advance the public interest. We now see that phenomena such as corruption are not just aberrations; they are a necessary adjunct of the political economy of the institutions of governance. Since self-interest is an inevitable and basic facet of human behavior, we must redesign the entire policy regime allowing for this from the start. Even sound policies must be reviewed in light of the likely political-economy response. For example, a purely technical analysis may suggest a particular policy to further some social objective, yet the likely response, including fraud and corruption, by self-serving private agents and bureaucrats may negate that objective, or achieve it at too high a cost. We may

even be obliged to (reluctantly) give up the desired objective.

The difficulty of designing workable policy may be illustrated by an example from our daily lives: The objective of aiding the handicapped prompted the policy of assigning them special parking. What starts out as a laudable social objective is enthusiastically taken up by interested parties. Then bureaucracy tends to proliferate detailed regulations in the form of multiple categories, rate schedules, and so on; all these methods allow the bureaucracy room to apply more discretion and thereby to extract more rents. A drastic simplification of detailed policy would eliminate all the rent-seeking inefficiencies in one stroke: What T.N. Srinivasan of Yale has called a "bonfire of regulations."

The above mentioned skepticism about motives constitutes one major difficulty. Another quite different problem is the inability to compute the effects of a complex of interacting policies. This difficulty applies even if policy makers were entirely pure in their motives. Yet earlier proponents of planning used to blithely assume it was possible to shape all the policy instruments to achieve the desired policy goals. Gradually it has become evident that this is not possible technically. Even well trained economists, with the best of good intentions and the fastest computers, may find it impossible to design a complex of internally consistent regulations. What's hardest in such planning exercises is to ensure the consistency of incentives across all those involved—including the rule makers with rule followers as economic actors. It is easier to ensure the consistency of goals and instruments. This is a purely mathematical problem worked out by Tinbergen—and given prominent coverage in older textbooks on development planning—matches goals with the most appropriate instrument, and urges that the number of instruments must not exceed the number of goals.

CASE STUDY: THE STATE VERSUS INFORMAL SECTOR IN PERU

The case of the Peruvian state offers a sharp repudiation of the precepts of neoclassical political economy. Until quite recently, the primary aim of the state seemed far from maximizing the creation of new wealth. Instead it focused on redistribution of existing wealth to favored groups. In response, a vast informal sector developed in defiance of the laws and enforcement efforts of the state. Hernando De Soto has studied this phenomenon at the Institute of Liberty and Democracy (ILD) in Lima. His revolutionary book *The Other Path* has been very influential in a similar context throughout Latin America. The title of his work pointedly offers an alternative to the extreme Left-wing "Shining Path" movement and to the traditional Right-wing regimes that long dominated Peru's polity.

The normal discourse presents a false dichotomy: Since Peru is not socialist, it must be capitalist. Political battles in Latin America and elsewhere often have been fought on these faulty grounds. In fact, the rightist political regimes generally are far removed from free market capitalist economics. Instead, their political economy resembles the Mercantilist states of medieval Europe. Even when the Left has come to power in this context, it has just meant that organized labor gained power relative to other corporatist groups, while the basic structure remained essentially unchanged.

Neither of the polar paradigms offers the possibility of individual liberty or true democracy. Rights are conferred or taken away by the state. Moreover, these rights are granted not to individuals, but rather to groups that can exert the requisite political power. The majority of the population does not belong to any such group, so it is left powerless. The legal structure and bureaucratic procedures make it very difficult and costly to acquire any legal rights. This is the true genesis of the informal sector.

The enormous size of the informal sector has been documented by ILD surveys. 48% of Peru's labor force and 61% of its work hours occur in such activities that produce 39% of the country's GDP. In the capital city of Lima, 50% of the population live in illegal homes, while 95% utilize urban transportation that is unsanctioned. Ponder the significance of these numbers: A staggering share of Peru's economy and essential services is technically illegal. The problem is that most economic activities must be sanctioned by the state. If a Peruvian citizen wants to provide goods or services to earn a living—and incidentally to benefit society—that activity is automatically considered illegal. Yet the costs for obtaining all the legal permits is, in practice, beyond the means of the common citizen. In turn, the illegal activities add extra costs for society either for avoiding authority or bribery to allow the illegal activities to continue. All of this adds up to huge costs that hinder overall economic growth.

The costs of bureaucracy have been studied in detail by the ILD. In 1993 ILD researchers conducted a simulation exercise to chart and measure the costs of access to industry. They set out to establish a small garment factory that was ostensibly a proprietorship, which would produce garments with a small number of knitting and sewing machines. This was designed as a fairly representative production unit that required most of the commonly needed permits and procedures. Then the researcher went about in very deliberate fashion to fulfill all the bureaucratic requirements legitimately. The chart on page 260 shows the minimum elapsed time that it took without recourse to bribery or political influence.

The chart tells a vivid story of how the legal and institutional structure is severely biased against economic enterprise. The ILD has similarly detailed the costs of initiating various economic activities such as setting up housing, transportation, retail services, and the like. Attempting to start business legally would be an arduous, even foolhardy, undertaking in Peru. Each law and bureaucratic requirement, taken by itself, may seem sensible enough for the orderly direction and control of society. But their overall economic impact is devastating. It is hard to imagine why any country would so hobble itself—unless one invokes the political-economy explanation.

Peru's continued stagnation is rooted in the vested corporate interests that benefit from the existing dispensation even if overall growth suffers. Breaking the stronghold of the parochial interest groups typically involves fairly drastic social and political upheavals. In fact, the Peruvian story did reach some kind of social and political crisis in the early 1990s. The microeconomic inefficiencies detailed here combined with macroeconomic disequilibrium (detailed in chapter 12). President Fujimori staged a coup by dissolving parliament and declaring a state of emergency. Since then he has moved to liberalize the economy. The results appear to be encouraging. Yet it remains an open question whether political reforms will be adequate to allow the economic gains to become permanent.

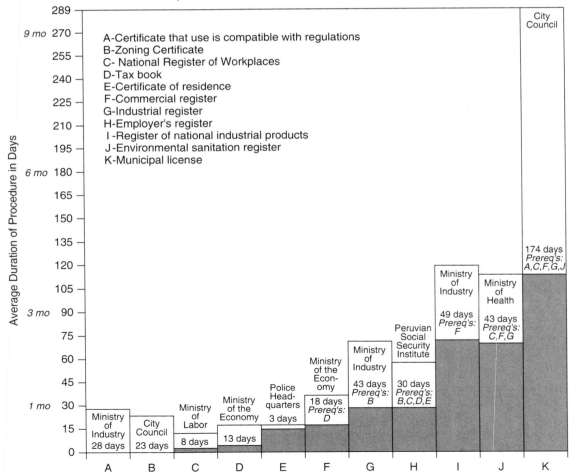

Graph 1. Procedures to Set up a Formal Industry

A-Certificate that use is compatible with regulations
B-Zoning Certificate
C- National Register of Workplaces
D-Tax book
E-Certificate of residence
F-Commercial register
G-Industrial register
H-Employer's register
I -Register of national industrial products
J-Environmental sanitation register
K-Municipal license

Average Duration of Procedure in Days

Procedure	Authority	Days
A	Ministry of Industry	28 days
B	City Council	23 days
C	Ministry of Labor	8 days
D	Ministry of the Economy	13 days
E	Police Headquarters	3 days
F	Ministry of the Economy	18 days *Prereq's: D*
G	Ministry of Industry	43 days *Prereq's: B*
H	Ministry of Industry	30 days *Prereq's: B,C,D,E*
I	Peruvian Social Security Institute	49 days *Prereq's: F*
J	Ministry of Health	43 days *Prereq's: C,F,G*
K	City Council	174 days *Prereq's: A,C,F,G,J*

SUMMARY

This chapter examines economic policy in itself rather than any particular area of application. The theory of policy may be neatly bifurcated into: (1) The neoclassical focus on reducing welfare losses due to market failure or inappropriate government interventions; and (2) The redistributive effects that invariably follow from any policy action. This subdiscipline falls under the rubric of the new political economy.

The first kind of analysis aims to design normative policy recommendations that minimize efficiency loss, absent a free market equilibrium. Such second-best analysis is codified in project evaluation procedures that correct prevailing prices for various external effects so as to reflect true social benefits and costs. The choices made using these shadow costs instead of market prices are more likely to attain socially optimum projects or policies. Yet the application of social benefit–cost analysis is criticized on various grounds. An analysis box explores the technical issue about which is the most appropriate criterion to evaluate intertemporal projects.

The new political economy is positive rather than normative analysis. It examines which public choices will be made, rather than which should be made. The interests of various actors (and their given political power) determine which policies actually will be chosen—whether or not these are most efficient from a social point of view. The welfare loss due to activities such as rent seeking can be highlighted against the benchmark case of maximum efficiency under perfect markets. Political-economy theory also differs from Liberal economic theory, which presumes a monolithic government facing a large number of atomistic agents. Instead, as special interest groups that have appreciable power, the relevant analytical tools come from game theory, where a small number of actors interact with each other in a strategic way. Thus it becomes essential to pay attention to the institutions of public choice.

KEY TERMS

Applied-welfare analysis	Internal rate of return (IRR)	The state
Second-best	Special interests	Minimal state
Market failure	Political economy	Social compact
Government failure	Social rate of discount	Predatory state
Distortions	Benevolent dictator	Politics
Benefit–cost analysis	Bureaucracy	Politicians
Externality	Regulatory capture	Game theory
Shadow cost	Free rider problem	Rent seeking
Net present value (NPV)	Government	Rents

Chapter 14

Agriculture

The following chapters revert to standard policy analysis which contrasts with political economy considerations that often lead to precisely the opposite choices. For example, standard economic analysis points to inefficiencies from market distortions; yet farm taxes/subsidies are widespread in the real world due to political-economy reasons. We make another transition in turning to analyze sectors instead of productive inputs as important in explaining growth. In particular we will study the agriculture and industry sectors.

To begin, we must address a possible challenge: Why sectoral analysis? Aggregate output may be split in any number of equally valid ways. For instance, macroeconomics splits GDP into the familiar components of expenditure: $Y = C + I + G$; strategical analysis disaggregates output by its military and civilian components; feminists compare the contribution of females versus males; and so on. The analyst chooses a particular split based on the questions that are to be addressed by that analysis.

The next consideration is whether the components can be directly influenced by policy. The growth accounting presented earlier highlights various factors as important objects of study. By contrast, these chapters view the productive sectors as structurally distinct. Given the growth rates of two economic sectors, agriculture A and industry D, overall growth is just a weighted average of the separate growth rates. The weights represent the respective **sector shares** of total output Y.

$$\hat{Y} = \left(\frac{A}{Y} \right) \hat{A} + \left(\frac{D}{Y} \right) \hat{D}$$

The Importance of Agriculture

The agricultural sector plays a particularly important role in development performance, affecting both economic growth and equity, simply due to its sheer size. In fact, it is the predominant sector at the outset. Another reason it is so crucial is its direct relation to food production, since **nutrition** is surely one of the basic tasks of development. Finally, the agricultural sector can serve as a source of various resources that can be transferred to other, faster growing, sectors in the economy.

At the start of development, the agricultural sector typically constitutes the largest segment of economic activity in an LDC. Its share of employment is even larger than its share of output. Thus agricultural performance determines the well-being of a large fraction of the population. While agriculture usually grows at a slower rate than industry, its contribution is crucial to overall growth since this sector constitutes a high share of total output. The poorest countries, which generate more than half of GDP in the agricultural sector, are therefore obliged to place the greatest importance on it.

The basic stylized facts can be illustrated by data from annual issues of the *World Development Report.* (The 1986 issue specifically focused on the agricultural sector.) For the set of low-income developing countries, annual growth rates in agriculture and industry were 3.7% and 7.5%, respectively, over the 1980–1991 period. For some of the poorest countries in this set, the highest shares of GDP derived from agriculture in 1991 were Mozambique (64%), Tanzania (61%), and Nepal (59%).

This chapter will analyze LDC agriculture in four major sections. (1) The first section follows the early development economics school in viewing agriculture as just an adjunct to the industrial sector expected to be the main source of growth. The agriculture-industry interactions are elaborated in terms of agriculture's contribution of resources such as capital and labor; foreign exchange generated by the export of agricultural goods; as a source of demand for industrial output; and as a producer of food. (2) A major change in development thinking was to regard agricultural growth as important in its own right. The section on microeconomic perspectives examines the supply response of farmers in a neoclassical framework that stresses price responsiveness and in an institutional perspective that stresses nonprice determinants, such as the arrangements of land ownership, the impact of risk and credit, and so on. (3) The next section examines the role of technology in agriculture. This topic is examined into two parts: the choice of technique and the determinants of technological advance. (4) The final section turns from production to issues of distribution, discussing the

role of agriculture in overall poverty and, in particular, the reasons for famines.

INDUSTRY-AGRICULTURE INTERACTIONS

The previous equation of sectoral growth may give the erroneous impression that industrial and agricultural growth rates are independent of each other. Empirical evidence indicates a strong correlation between the two. Note, however, that correlation does not imply causation. Various alternate causal mechanisms (shown by the arrows) might generate the observed correlation.

$$D \rightarrow A \qquad A \rightarrow D \qquad X \Big\langle {}^{D}_{A}$$

Various theories stress different kinds of mechanisms. While the first two are straightforward, the third mechanism indicates that some other variable X actually prompts the growth of both agriculture and industry. For instance, it has been suggested that X represents sound economic management that encourages growth of both agriculture and industry. Such a sound policy regime seeks to maintain relative prices without distortions, such as real exchange rate fluctuations and high inflations (these aspects will be discussed in chapter 16). The empirical evidence of a strong correlation between industrial and agricultural growth is presented for a sample of developing countries in Table 14-1.

Agriculture as a Source of Resources

Agriculture's large share in the economy causes it to be viewed as a source of resources to be used in development. Both the capital and labor employed in agriculture may be tapped for diversion to a leading sector. The Lewis growth model (presented earlier) was based on surplus rural labor being redeployed for industrial

Table 14-1 Growth in agricluture and industry in LDCs, 1973-1984 (Annual percent)

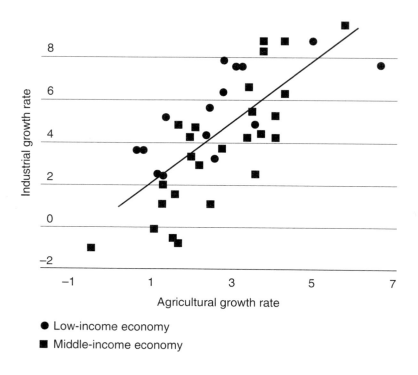

Source: *World Development Report* 1986

development. Capital may also be extracted from this sector by a deliberate policy of depressing agricultural returns. The student must realize that this is not just some dry theoretical issue. A very real debate raged over the appropriate role for agriculture following the Russian revolution. Lenin's colleagues Bukharin and Preabrazhensky were the chief protagonists for the two styles of development. Instead of focusing on agricultural development, the squeeze-the-peasants idea won in the end. The tragic consequence was Stalin's brutal campaign of the 1930s that wiped out 3 million peasants. Only much later, during the Khrushchev regime, did the Soviets acknowledge that continued agricul-

tural vitality is a crucial prerequisite for the advance of any other sector.

For the least developed among the LDCs, the agricultural sector is generally also the main source of foreign exchange earnings. These countries export mainly primary commodities—those produced from their natural resource endowments. While this category also includes minerals, such deposits are rather unevenly distributed across the globe. Thus, for many of the poorest LDCs, primary exports come mainly from agricultural production of food and non-food commodities. In effect, agriculture produces imports: "Want to produce a jet plane? Grow more pineapples!"

The export of agricultural commodities also has a downside. Many LDCs concentrate on a small number of export products. This makes them extremely vulnerable to market conditions in a single commodity. For instance, a recent scare about the health effects of palm oil had a major adverse impact on Malaysia, where palm oil constitutes a large fraction of total exports. Furthermore, if export farming is done by small-holders, market fluctuations can have a severe impact on poverty. Table 14-2 shows various LDCs that have an extreme dependence on a single farm commodity as a share of their total exports.

The agricultural sector also typically plays an important role as a customer for the industrial sector's output. For example, the Indian development plans of the 1950s focused mainly on the stimulation of industry. Later it was found that stagnant agriculture acted as a major constraint by not generating much demand for industrial output. There has been a recent spurt of interest in "agricultural-demand-led-industrialization" spurred by Irma Adelman (1984).

The agricultural sector is, of course, primarily associated with the supply of food. In the least developed of the LDCs it takes the form of **subsistence agriculture.** In such countries markets are poorly developed, so there is little specialization and exchange. Instead, much of the population is engaged in the most basic and essential economic activity—producing food to feed itself.

To the peasant family it is of secondary importance to generate surplus foodstuffs for sale or to cultivate nonfood cash crops. After development begins, however, the focus shifts as this sector is called to provide a surplus to be deployed elsewhere.

The overriding importance placed on **food production** implies that most economies must be largely self-sufficient in food production. Even in open economies with much foreign trade, food is of such strategic importance that a country cannot rely on importing it under all possible future contingencies. Only countries that have no choice live with this risk. City-states like Bahrain, Hong-Kong, and Singapore are perpetually dependent on other countries for their food supply. Others go to extraordinary lengths to gain self-sufficiency in food even if they are quite unsuited for agriculture. A prime example is Saudi Arabia, which uses its oil wealth to create and promote farming and farmers where none existed before. For very large countries like India and China, a goal of self-sufficiency is not just a matter of reducing risk. As a practical matter it would be infeasible for them to rely on food imports. The entire rest of the world could not possibly compensate for a shortfall of just 15% in China's own food supply.

These rationalizations are somewhat condescending toward the agricultural sector. At best this sector is good for being exploited for benefits elsewhere in the economy. Worse than

Table 14-2 Single commodity share in total exports

Coffee:	Uganda	97%	Burundi	89%	Angola	88%
	El Salvador	85%	Ethiopia	71%	Colombia	70%
	Haiti	70%				
Sugar:	Cuba	90%	Mauritius	90%	Guyana	60%
	Swaziland	48%	Jamaica	44%		
Cotton:	Burkina Faso	80%	Benin	73%	Mali	55%
	Togo	48%	Pakistan	46%		
Cocoa:	Ghana	75%	Nigeria	74%	Ivory Coast	39%
Tea:	Sri Lanka	58%	Kenya	31%		

Source: FAO Country Tables, cited in IFAD, 1992.

this attitude of benign neglect was an adverse view that prevailed in the past. It used to be argued that agriculture would remain a hopeless drag on development. As reflected in the terms used, "peasants" were derided as resistant to scientific attitudes and rational behavior, as opposed to "farmers", who were progressive and open to new methods. Peasants had to be taught what to do by outsiders (urban or foreign "experts"). An opposing paradigm violently opposes such views. Cultivators are deemed to know precisely what is good for them. Thus government's role must be to facilitate the agricultural sector's own efforts at improvement. It must develop infrastructure such as rural roads, irrigation, and credit institutions, while also striving to further equality of opportunity. The sluggishness of agriculture is seen to be rooted in institutional constraints rather than in individual failures as such. Thus suitable institutional reforms of inequitable power relations and land tenure arrangements may help transform agriculture into a separate node for economic growth. Agriculture need not remain merely a handmaiden to growth emanating from the industrial sector.

MICROECONOMIC PERSPECTIVES

Agriculture's importance to overall growth is clear. It is either a constraint (negative) or a source of stimulus (positive). This defines the central issue of this chapter: Is the battle for economic growth to be won or lost on the farm? Agriculture is obviously important because of its effect on the overall growth rate. From the macroscopic view associated with the developmental school we turn to a microeconomic focus revived at the University of Chicago. T. Schultz's classic work *Transforming Traditional Agriculture* (1964) was very influential in establishing the new approach and won him the Nobel prize. This work reoriented theoretical views about agricultural development in LDCs. Special sectoral distinctions are downplayed, while the

standard economic principles are supposed to apply the same way in every sector. In fact, since farming is largely private, the issues of incentives and individual choice are particularly crucial. Choices about crops and production techniques, as well as consumption and leisure, are a rational response to variables such as the (relative) prices of inputs and outputs, risk, credit availability, and so on. We shall study each of these components from a microeconomic viewpoint. It is also possible to work out the impact of government policies on changing productivity and the distribution of income.

The Agricultural Price System

The management of prices in the agricultural sector (for both inputs and outputs) has very visible and direct microeconomic effects. As noted before, this sector serves an ideal context for the application of second-best analysis since LDC agriculture is particularly prone to distortions that distance it from a free-market situation. There are two main reasons for this.

1. In LDCs a large proportion of the population lives close to subsistence. Since the major requirement for survival is food, most of the very poorest people must engage in subsistence farming for their own food consumption rather than produce **cash crops** to sell on the market. A basic aim of development is to help raise the incomes of this segment of the population. One method is to lower the price of farm inputs—an effect equivalent to raising the price of farm output. However, such policies tend to move us away from the free market rather than toward it. The prototype farm intervention is a price support program that raises food grain prices above the free-market level.

2. A large segment of absolute poverty in LDCs is concentrated among urban dwellers, who are none other than the rural poor who migrated to the city because their

prospects on the farm seemed so bleak. Their poverty makes it hard for them to purchase the food that is essential for survival. Thus LDC governments are prone to lower the price of food grains through a subsidized **food distribution system.** The conflict between a high price for farmers and a low price for consumers strains the government budget. Recall the example of the general food subsidy in Egypt. In turn, the budgetary strains cause macroeconomic disequilibria that exacerbate other distortions in the system.

Returning to the production side, the overall impact of policy—export taxes, input and output prices, and exchange rates—is generally to lower the price received by the agricultural producer as compared to an undistorted free-market price. This may be seen in Table 14-3 for a representative sample of developing countries.

For a wide range of countries and commodities the table shows that agricultural policies generally (but not always) bias downward the producers' price as compared to the world price. Alternative

motivations are (a) taxing export commodities mainly to raise government revenue, and (b) lowering food prices for consumers. In either case this has an adverse impact on producers' incentives. Many LDCs began to recognize the error of such a policy only recently. They have now started to adjust producer prices upward in most, though not all, cases. It is also striking how low domestic price was as a percentage of the world price. Egypt's price of cotton was less than 50% of the comparable world price during the 1970s. The gap may be attributed to taxation in a variety of forms, not all of which are explicitly defined.

These policies derive from a structuralist view of agriculture as exemplified by the Lewis model. Resources are extracted from agriculture to support industry by manipulating the terms of trade between these two sectors. By contrast, the neoclassical view initiated by Schultz warns to leave relative prices alone while working to remove the various market failures at their source. Further, any budget outlays in the agricultural sector should be directed toward infrastructure investment to raise yields, or agricultural

Table 14-3 Agricultural pricing policy

		Percent local price/border price			
	1970s	1980s		1970s	1980s
Cotton			**Maize**		
Egypt	45%	57%	Zimbabwe	33%	169%
India	78%	78%			
Mexico	89%	67%	**Cocoa**		
Pakistan	46%	87%	Costa Rica	97%	91%
Sudan	96%	104%	Ivory Coast	50%	58%
Zimbabwe	38%	35%	Ecuador	81%	97%
Tea			**Groundnuts**		
India	48%	44%	Egypt	66%	67%
Kenya	92%	86%	India	107%	97%
			Senegal	30%	50%
Rice					
Pakistan	65%	67%	**Tobacco**		
Thailand	113%	94%	Tanzania	43%	33%

Source: IFAD, 1992.

Analysis: Interventions in Food Grains Market

The twin interventions of a price floor for procurement and a price ceiling for distribution (implemented through a rationing system) can add up to a substantial outlay for the farmer/food subsidy as shown in Figure 14-1.

First consider the affect of each intervention separately. A high **procurement price** increases quantity supplied beyond the amount in a free market, while Low **ration price** increases the quantity demanded. Note that there's no reason for these two quantities to match since the two intervention prices are picked separately. Thus the government's food trading agency must constantly juggle these prices depending on changes in warehouse stocks. More importantly, the agency must set the price gap (the subsidy) in keeping with budgetary constraints. If the outlay gets too large, it must lower the procurement price and/or raise the sale price.

Unlike this stylized example, more often than not the procurement price is set below the free-market price. Then there's an incentive for sales to circumvent the official procurement agency. As a black market springs up, the government must resort to stringent enforcement efforts. Also prevalent is a composite public and private food marketing system. Farmers are required to cede part of their output at the procurement price, while the rest may be sold in the free market. Similarly, the government's ration shops provide only part of overall demand through the rationing system, while consumers may buy any excess demands in the free market. Needless to say, this gets to be a very complex system, with all sorts of distortions and possibilities for corruption and dishonesty.

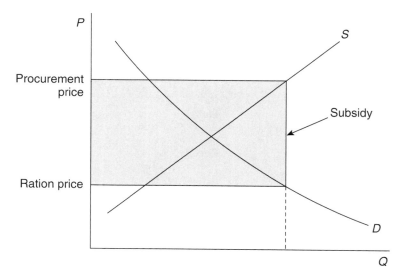

Figure 14-1   *Food grains pricing policy*

productivity, in general. These two distinct factors are summarized in the following equation, in which the given price ratio defines agriculture's terms of trade.

$$\frac{\text{Return}}{\text{per acre}} = \frac{\text{Price of output}}{\text{Price of input}} \times \frac{\text{Yield}}{\text{per acre}}$$

The Farm Household Model

Neoclassical economics emphasizes that the incentive structure will determine the supply response. For this reason we turn to study the microeconomics of the farm household, which is analogous to the theory of the firm. The **Farm Household model** differs in that decisions about production, consumption, and leisure are made in an integrated framework. Since this kind of arrangement is ubiquitous across the world, it needs just as much theoretical attention as is devoted to other institutional features such as sharecropping. Another special issue in the con-

text of agriculture is the impact of risk and the institutional arrangements designed to deal with it. We shall discuss each of these issues in turn.

Subsistence agriculture is of critical importance in the very poorest LDCs. Such production typically occurs in the context of farm households that make a combined production/consumption decision. By contrast, the standard economic problem is the typical agent making one decision of how much labor to sell—the labor/leisure tradeoff noted earlier as the labor supply decision—then separately deciding on consumption purchases.

Figure 14-2 shows how the farmer's resources—including land, labor time, and capital (farm equipment and livestock)—may be transformed into consumption goods according to the production possibility curve (PPC). The farmer may also be able to exchange some labor time for wages in a market for labor. This transformation falls along the straight line *PC,* whose slope indicates the wage rate. Obviously, the farmer will choose a tangency to the PPC so as to achieve the highest possible consumption. Also

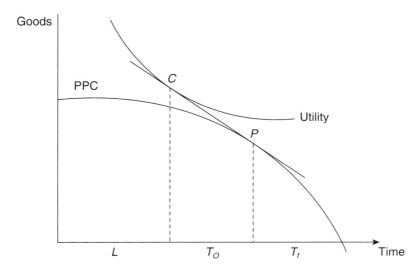

Figure 14-2 *The Farm Household model*

shown in this figure is the utility derived from consumption of goods and leisure. The highest possible utility curve, which is drawn, indicates the highest happiness attained.

The labor decision differs from the standard labor supply derivation (presented in chapter 9) since it is possible to be self-employed on one's own farm in addition to working for others as wage labor. The available time T (say, 16 waking hours daily) is split between work and leisure L. The work time is further split between farm labor T_f and off-farm labor T_O.

$$T = T_f + T_O + L$$

Figure 14-2 indicates how the level of outside wages relative to farm productivity will determine the time spent in the outside labor market as opposed to the farm. Suppose, for example, that industrial productivity and its wages rise. This will prompt an outflow of labor from the agricultural sector. It was widely assumed (as by Kuznets) that the productivity differential between sectors would persist and even increase, but this assumption has been challenged by recent empirical research.

Extension: Household Production of Goods
The basic model may be modified to account for the fact that households often produce goods and services that are not marketed. This kind of production is most important in the least developed countries, particularly in the rural agricultural context. The very poorest do not have the monetary resources to purchase market goods. Thus they are likely to bake their own bread, cut their own hair, and do their own carpentry. We mentioned earlier that GDP accounts may be biased downward due to the omission of such nonmarketed goods and services. A possible consequence also may be underestimation of farm productivity, which is the basis of the Lewis model.

The mode of household production seems somewhat more prevalent in the farm sector than in urban manufacturing, which is typically organized as firms. While this stylized fact is not established definitively, we do offer some plausible reasons.

1. Agricultural economics necessarily involves *spatial* considerations since farms and farm producers are spread out across the countryside. Thus the density of demand for many goods tends to be low. Then specialized firms cannot attain economies of scale to become viable in the face of the large transport costs involved. For example, one would not want to travel 20 miles to get to a barber shop; it is simpler to just do the haircut at home.

2. For similar spatial reasons, activities such as child rearing are necessarily less concentrated than child care facilities in the city. Thus, the women engaged in farm production must play a dual role to produce their own household services.

3. Another feature specific to the farm context is a marked **seasonality.** After the concentrated effort of planting and harvest time come long periods of idleness. Yet the dispersed geography of farm households may limit possibilities for entering the wage labor market. During such periods, when their opportunity cost is zero, family members can be busy producing goods and services. Despite their low productivity as nonspecialists, they knit and sew, make preserves, and build and repair their own homes.

Further Modification: Transactions Costs   An economic rationale for the family as an institution is given by Nobel laureate Gary Becker of the University of Chicago. His explanation relies importantly on the existence of scale economies. Consider that it takes about as much effort to cook for one as it does for two. However, countervailing **transactions costs** can arise in contracting between people: Who does what? What efforts can be monitored? What tasks can be "shirked". . . and so on. In situations where such problems loom large, the institutional arrangement that can minimize transactions costs is the family, be it the nuclear family or the "extended family" that is prevalent in different cultural settings.

The Household Production model provides a microeconomic explanation for the family farm. It is an economically superior institutional arrangement given the cost of supervising a number of workers working as a team. This analysis can also explain the transitions that take place between rural labor markets and subsistence agriculture in contemporary Africa. In East Asia it helps explain the transition of labor between agricultural and industrial activities. A proper accounting of productive household work corrects the underestimation of agricultural productivity in the context of farm households.

Risk and Credit

Next, we examine another microeconomic factor that can have an important impact on productivity growth. A special characteristic of agriculture is that it is especially subject to risk through the vagaries of weather. This causes an obvious variation in the output of individual farms. Further, aggregate variations may affect entire regions simultaneously. As a consequence, the market prices can vary in step with output. This inevitable element of risk in agriculture provides the rationale for institutions set up to mitigate such risk. Traditional arrangements, in a multitude of different forms, are studied by anthropologists in many different settings across the world. The institutions of serfdom, landlords, and share tenancy contracts are all examples of such arrangements.

A new institutional economics explains various facets of underdevelopment using the concept of **risk aversion** in situations of risk. (This concept may even be somewhat overused by enthusiastic theoreticians.) This analysis suggests that technical progress in agriculture might be accelerated by replacing the traditional institutional forms by a new set of incentives. In fact,

various government schemes have been set up just to mitigate the effects of farm price variability, for example, price support systems and buffer stocks. Note, however, that the primary problem is variability of farm income ($P * Q$) not price variability per se.

The behavioral response to risk depends on the variance of income multiplied by the subjective attitude towards risk. Such responses have important consequences for agricultural policy. For example, the Green Revolution was found to have benefited large farmers far more than small farmers. This boon for agricultural growth turned out to be unhelpful for reducing inequality or alleviating poverty. The differential impact may partly be explained by different attitudes toward risk. The transition to modern techniques inevitably carries some degree of risk. Even though the quantitative variance of output is about equal for rich and poor farmers alike, the latter are less prepared to face possibly adverse outcomes. The poor have a higher degree of risk aversion since they live much closer to the margin of subsistence; a failed experiment could put their very survival at stake. One policy implication is for government to provide insurance so as to encourage risk-taking, which is beneficial, not merely to reduce the variability of outcomes.

Of special relevance to agriculture is the supply of **credit** which is necessary for farming. Each planting season the farmer must borrow money for seeds and other inputs, and this advance can only be paid back after the harvest is marketed. A variety of traditions and institutions evolved historically to serve this function. Examples are feudal landlords, moneylenders, and the extended family itself. In reality, the functional relationships are even more complex since they must serve a whole set of different aims. Credit (which involves trades across time) is intertwined with the insurance function (trades across different states of nature). Since the traditional institutions cannot diversify risk as effectively as a modern banking system, the risk premiums charged seem inordinately high by modern standards. Traditional institutions operate in a more personal way— individual moneylender or landlord directly facing the peasant. An asymmetry of power often operates against the individual peasant. Thus traditional arrangements can be detrimental to the reduction of income disparities. To alleviate such undesirable side effects on equity, institutional reforms aim to provide rural credit through a broadened financial system.

The institutions of land use also seek to harness possible economies of scale. Potential scale economies in production are crucial in deciding whether to break up large landholdings. Land reforms that achieve a wider distribution of land might possibly affect efficiency adversely even as it improves equity and employment in the rural areas. This age-old question continues to be a matter for debate. On the one extreme it is widely recognized that the large-scale collectivization attempts in the former Soviet Union and China were grievous disasters, and those countries have acknowledged as much by their return to smaller family farms. On the other hand, there must be a certain minimum size for an efficient farm. The densely populated countries of Bangladesh and Indonesia have learned about the ill effects of the fragmentation of landholdings as the land tilled by an individual farmer became untenably small.

Institutional Arrangements

The **institutional economics** of agriculture is crucial in determining its performance. This aspect tends to be slighted in standard economic analysis, which too casually assumes a similar individualistic basis as in the Western countries. Institutions may be defined as the legal/administrative framework and behavioral codes derived from cultural values that legitimize and constrain behavior. As the economy and environment change institutions and laws adapt accordingly, but cultural norms tend to change very slowly. For instance, while the law may formally allow land transfers, such transfers to another clan or ethnic group may be frowned on culturally. Thus as technology changes in agriculture may require free markets for efficiency, cultural inhibitions may operate to keep it inefficient. Similarly, while the legal code may provide for individual property rights, the administrative machinery for registration and enforcement may be lacking.

Standard economic analysis is based on tastes, technology, and resources. The implicit element is the institutional framework, which specifies the nature of **property rights.** The beginning student tends to think of property as "things" that are owned, not mainly as a "bundle of rights" that have value. Property rights are characterized by the extent that they are exclusive, inheritable, transferable, and enforceable. These rights can exist in various combinations and thus can be defined in quite complex ways: For example, in some places rights to the crop are private, while rights to the stubble after harvesting are communal. In many parts of sub-Saharan Africa, land tenure is separate from tree tenure. Further, property rights may be so defined as to restrict the conditions of transfer. In Thailand, for instance, squatters have been permitted to use government land but cannot sell it, and lacking formal titles, they cannot put up that land as collateral for obtaining credit.

The four basic categories of property rights in land are open access, communal ownership, private property, and state ownership. The prevailing mode of rights has evolved to suit ecological conditions as well as cultural and political structures. As development alters these economic relations and power structures, the institutional arrangements also must change accordingly. While institutional change tends to occur erratically, its general direction is clear. We see a general progression toward more explicit definition of private property rights on land. There's a clear historical justification: With population growth the situation turned from one of land abundance to land scarcity, so land could no longer remain a "free good." The intensification of agriculture is prompted by technical change in agriculture, the earlier-mentioned population pressure that improves the agricultural terms of trade, and an increased commercialization of agriculture. These forces serve to increase the marginal product of land, shifting up its demand curve.

The traditional land rights system often is argued to be a major constraint on development of rural Africa. Agriculture's poor performance is blamed on the widely prevalent system of communal property rights. Communal control might discourage long-term investment in land improvements as farmers are unable to claim the full return on their investment. This lack of incentives similarly inhibit conservation efforts, leading to land degradation through erosion and overuse. Further, since land is an integral part of the social system, its transactions are constrained by social and ethnic considerations, not by the principles of contractual law and economic efficiency as in a market system. In sum, it is quite plausible that the traditional mode of property rights may constrain agricultural development.

We now turn from issues of land ownership to the labor arrangements for working that land. In much of the world—developed as well as developing—yeoman farmers are the exception rather than the rule. Instead of farmers working exclusively on land that they own, a wide range of arrangements are generally observed, such as

· Sharecropping

· Land rent

· Wage labor

Sharecropping is a widespread institutional arrangement in which the landlord contracts with tenants to give a fixed share (often 50%) of the output in exchange for the right to farm on the land. On the face of it, this arrangement appears quite inefficient. Often, laborers have the possibility to offer their labor at a market wage that equals marginal product. Given this opportunity wage, sharecroppers will scale back their work effort to the point where 50% of marginal product equals the going wage rate. In Figure 14-3 hired labor would produce at A, while sharecroppers would produce at B. (Half the marginal product at this point is shown by the dotted line, which has the same slope as the wage rate.)

It appears that from the landlords' point of view it would never be worthwhile to contract with sharecroppers. However this puzzle is resolved if it's possible for the landlord to contractually oblige tenants to provide a certain amount of work effort on a given amount of land. Earlier the intellectual puzzle used to be: Why sharecrop if it is so much less efficient than hired labor? The present puzzle is: Why is sharecropping ubiquitous if it is just as efficient as hired labor? In a word, the answer is uncertainty.

A recent prominent example of fixed land rentals was the "household responsibility system" instituted in China in the late 1970s. Twenty years earlier the Great Leap Forward had forced farmers into large collectives in line with Communist dogma. The result had been a disastrous crash in

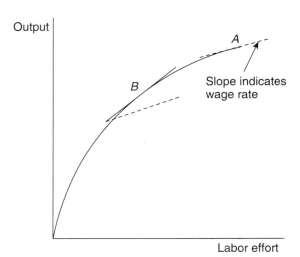

Figure 14-3 *Sharecropping versus wage labor*

Analysis: Fixed Land Rent or Share Cropping?

The institutional arrangements for risk sharing form a crucial feature of tenancy contracts, determining both the security of tenure and the output share. As with the communal arrangement previously noted, a tenant farmer on just a five-year lease would be hesitant to make investments or land improvements that raise productivity. Similarly, too large a percentage share going to the landlord would adversely impact the tenant's level of effort. The rent payment works like a tax to alter the labor supply schedule. This is an important consideration in the design of tenancy arrangements—whether the land is owned by a private landlord or a corporatist entity such as the state.

What is the better scheme for charging rent? (A) A fixed level of **land rent** regardless of fluctuations in output, or (B) a proportionate share of output as in sharecropping? Figure 14-4 depicts both of these schemes, which are calibrated to be comparable at a level of effort *E,* where the output of 100 is distributed as 25 to the landlord and 75 to the farmer.

Given a quick choice between the two options, one might be tempted to pick method B since it seems fair that risk be shared between the farmer and landlord. In years when the farmer's output is unfortunately low, a smaller rent is required. By contrast, method A seems heartless. The landlord extracts a fixed cut regardless of the vagaries of the weather. But observe what these two alternatives do to incentives. Method B acutely distorts the farmer's incentive while method A constitutes a lump-sum tax that leaves incentives undisturbed. Note the marginal return to one extra hour of the farmer's effort (say at the level *E*). In scheme A, by working one more hour, the farmer nets the entire additional productivity; in scheme B, a similar one hour incremental effort provides a smaller return net of the proportionate rent. No wonder neoclassical economists, starting from Marshall, have always been in favor of the fixed rent scheme.

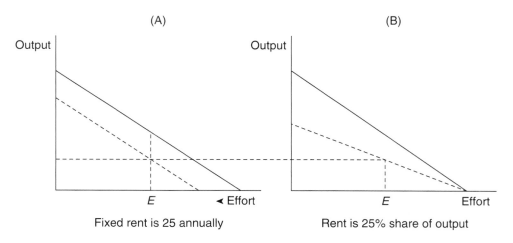

Figure 14-4   *Different incentive effects of tenancy contracts*

agricultural productivity, followed by continued stagnation. The market-oriented reforms initiated by Deng Xiaoping permitted farm households to set up individual contracts with the state to provide a certain fixed amount of crop from plots of land allotted to the farmer. In return the collective provides certain facilities such as irrigation systems and common farm inputs. The crucial element of this arrangement is that the farmer can sell the surplus over his contractual obligation in the market. Moreover the lease on the land implied a return to private land "ownership," even as the fiction of Socialism was maintained. Subsequently the lease periods have been extended, sometimes for indefinite periods.

All these arrangements are, in effect, nothing but a return to free market principles. The long land leases may be seen as private property, and the (in kind) rental obligations as just a form of property tax. The positive incentives in such a system worked predictably as peasant incomes more than tripled in a decade. In fact, the remarkable industrial growth of China in the past fifteen years can be attributed to just these market reforms.

The above analysis also illuminates the issue of agricultural taxation. Should there be a **land tax** or a tax on output (say, in the form of an export tax)? The land tax seems most efficient since it applies to unearned rent; hence it cannot damage incentives. Despite this convenient feature, land taxes are rarely observed in the real world. The standard explanation is that the reduced risk from output taxes outweighs the welfare advantages of the land tax. Jonathan Skinner argues instead that land taxes may not be used simply because they are costly to implement. Land assessments require trained surveyors, must be adjusted for inflation, and are subject to chronic disputation in the courts. It's not just a matter of measuring land area, but rather of assessing the productive capacity of a given plot. The owner will naturally try to misrepresent this potential. Thus total administrative costs of such a tax system can become prohibitively high. As much as 50% of the gross revenue was used for such an effort in Bangladesh in the 1980s. This is a particular instance of a more general lesson in public finance: Instead of a narrow analysis of "optimal taxes", it is necessary to take a broader view of "optimal tax systems."

Theoretical ideas about optimal taxes are quite removed from the real world of public finance, which is replete with political pressures, underdeveloped tax systems, and so on. An old reality is that tax collectors have always preferred the tax that is the easiest to collect, i.e. one that is hardest to evade. Earlier, in chapter 12, we note the widespread prevalence of export taxes, which are easy to collect. Similarly, agricultural export taxes have been the traditional method of extracting resources from the agricultural sector. A prominent and tragic example of this is provided by West Africa, which produces much of the world's cocoa. For decades governments there bought cocoa at low prices through monopolies called **marketing boards** then exported it at the higher world price. Ironically, one rationale had been to provide a higher price to farmers by exercising the market power of a national cartel, otherwise these farmers would be dispersed and individually powerless. However, these boards were "captured" by bureaucrats and the power elites as a machine for extracting rents for themselves. In Ghana the rate of tax extracted in this manner was repeatedly ratcheted upwards, almost killing the goose that laid the golden eggs. In sum, the tax route to extracting resources from agriculture has been much used, and too often abused.

AGRICULTURAL PRODUCTIVITY

As noted, technological advances that raise agricultural yields are just as important as altering the terms of trade. But the early developmental economists were pessimistic about a strong supply response. For instance, a major concern in the Lewis model was that agriculture's terms of trade must not rise lest it choke off industrial expansion. Fortunately, that stance has been reversed in recent years as Schultz' work persuaded policy makers that overall development is retarded by a policy bias against agriculture. As agriculturalists gained political power in some countries, they succeeded in turning things around so much that LDC agriculture receives a net subsidy rather than being taxed. An alternative form of support to agriculture might be public investments that improve productivity, rather than handouts in the form of direct subsidies.

We now direct our attention to policies that aim to advance technological capabilities of agricultural producers. You may recall that the chapter on technology studied this issue in two parts: (i) acceleration of technical change, and (ii) choice of technique. We shall study these aspects of technology as applied to agricultural production in the Third World.

Efforts to advance LDC agricultural capabilities are most visible at the level of specialized multinational institutions. The **Food and Agriculture Organization (FAO),** based in Rome, is the hub of a large network of institutions that seek to advance agricultural technology at both the national and international level. For instance, the International Rice Research Institute in the Philippines is famous for developing dwarf varieties of rice that facilitated the Green Revolution. Such institutions have provided a valuable service over the years, yet they are subject to the same generic criticisms that apply to all international bureaucratic organizations. Typically they are riddled with politics and

bureaucratic machinations. Their very size keeps them distant from the ground level contact that is essential for effective and sustained progress. Their functionaries are paid international salaries, in sharp contrast to the poverty of the clientele they are supposed to serve.

Technical change does not have to be done on a grand scale utilizing highly paid experts from distant lands. Nor must it be based on path-breaking new research. Much smaller scale efforts by **nongovernmental organizations (NGOs)** such as CARE and Oxfam have proved quite effective. An evaluation of their performance may be found in the Human Development Report (1993). Such organizations (both foreign and domestic) play a different role, which is applauded by some as "progressive" in contrast to the "oppressive" top-down approach of official development organizations such as the World Bank. Fortunately the realization has dawned that both types are complementary, so they have begun to cooperate with each other.

In a division of labor, the official agencies focus more on "hardware" projects that involve large scale capital investments in infrastructure, while NGOs deal more with "software" that makes an impact on people's behavior and lives through persuasion and involvement. Consider the analogy of child development in a family context. Both parents bring different complementary skills to the long, arduous task of bringing up a child. An example of such sustained and detailed grass-roots efforts to improve agricultural productivity is illustrated by the case study below.

CASE STUDY: IMPROVING AGRICULTURAL TECHNOLOGY IN AFRICA

Burkina Faso (formerly Upper Volta) is one of the most remote and underdeveloped of the LDCs. It is a landlocked country on the fringes of the Sahara desert, about 300 miles from the fabled town of Timbuktu. This country ranks close to the bottom of international rankings, both in terms of

per capita income and human development, as the poverty syndrome prevails in all its aspects. Burkina Faso's economic mainstay is the agricultural sector, which employs 87% of its labor force and provides 32% of GDP. While food production has risen in recent years, it supplies less than the minimum required caloric supply, so dependence on food imports and aid continues.

Burkina Faso is something of a test case for the development community. Various missions and programs by official agencies have come and gone with little to show for their efforts. By contrast, the NGOs have made modest achievements that provide some signs of hope. Their's is a dramatically different approach based on local participation and self-reliance. The technology used is so "lo-tech" that it can barely be called technology. Consider one successful example reported by the *Economist* (3/13/93).

A major problem in Burkina Faso, as in much of the Sahel, is soil erosion. The growing population and overgrazing has led to a process of desertification. To combat this requires the planting of trees. Some Oxfam aid workers searched for a method to keep the seedlings moist. They laid stones in rows to form minidikes that trapped organic matter around sapling roots. Unless these stones are laid along contour lines, water just flows in a channel along them and carries the soil away. But how to determine the contour line? The ingenious and cheap solution was a length of clear plastic hose filled with water. Held in a bow just above the ground, this provides a simple level to establish an accurate contour. With this simple method the villagers quickly set to work planting along contours across their fields.

Notice how simple this solution is: It requires no fancy surveying equipment or imported materials. However, other problems continue to tax the ingenuity and persistence of reformers. For example, the Oxfam workers next faced the problem of keeping foraging goats from eating the new saplings, yet villagers resist the suggestion to tether their goats. The problem is that if the goats did not forage for themselves, the already over-burdened village women face the additional task of gathering fodder. Note how mundane and interconnected these problems are. Successful solutions only occur by meshing individual motives and social organization. The noted success fulfills a local need rather than imposing requirements from outside. The villagers are self-reliant and eager participants once they are shown a new method that works.

Such success stories stand in contrast to inappropriate new technologies that were rejected by small farmers elsewhere in West Africa. The International Fund for Agricultural Development (IFAD) notes its experience with the Maradi Project in neighboring Niger. The technological package, which required intensive use of costly inputs, had a high risk of failure. An incomplete understanding of the incentives facing the local cultivator undermined the willing absorption of technology. There were similar shortcomings in the Smallholder Rehabilitation and Development Programme in Ghana. Extention workers pushed a standard package of maize/fertilizer credit to all farmers irrespective of their particular situation. The profitability of this program collapsed when fertilizer subsidies had to be eliminated as part of macroeconomic reforms.

Now the government in Burkina Faso also recognizes that development efforts cannot be centrally controlled and directed from above. It has instituted a new plan called *Gestion des terroirs* in which villagers draw up their own plans and allocate tasks among themselves. The government, aided by the World Bank, provides a minimal superstructure of technical help and cash. This is a move in the right direction since it puts initiatives and control back at the grass roots. Yet the existence of distant powerful partners introduces those very elements that have led to failure in the past. There will be heavy administrative costs and the associated problems of patronage, oversight, and evaluation.

Another self-help initiative revives the idea of traditional work groups called the *Groupements Naam*. Its basic aim is to accumulate a surplus from communal projects to be invested in community development. Along with usual agricultural activities and other production in the off-season, these groups also engage in water management and forestry programs. By 1989 there were more than 160,000 members in some 2,800 groups.

Choice of Technique

The second aspect of technology policy is to determine the appropriate choice of technique in the agricultural context. This issue can be illuminated by a simple model that has three variables: land, labor, and output. (To simplify the exposition we omit a fourth variable, capital, even though it has become an important agricultural input in recent times for individual farms in the form of machinery and working capital, and in the aggregate as large public works such as dams and irrigation canals.) Since it's hard to draw 3-dimensional diagrams, we must further simplify the three variables into two ratios that can be depicted in two dimensions. The land/labor ratio and output/labor ratio serve as proxies for resources and income per capita, respectively.

Technical change in agriculture can be either land-saving or labor saving. Earlier technical advances, such as use of tractors, used to be laborsaving that resulted in worsening the rural unemployment even as it increased output. The recent Green Revolution, which uses improved seeds with fertilizers and pesticides is instead a land-saving technical change.

The interrelation of population growth with technological change has been mentioned at various points before in the chapters on structural change, population, and the Lewis model. Two sharply contrasting views of this connection over the long sweep of time are

Malthus

Technical ⟶ population
progress   growth

Boserup

Population ⟶ technical
growth   progress

Malthus developed his ideas for a time and place (England up to the eighteenth century) where land was turning into the limiting factor while rapid population growth was turning labor into a surplus. In such a situation, landowners aimed to maximize yield/per acre. (Historically this was manifested as the enclosure movement that fenced the open fields so as to raise yields.)

By contrast, a modern economist, Esther Boserup, emphasizes those situations where land is freely available. Where, for example, it is possible to slash and burn the jungle or extend into wasteland for additional crop lands. In this case land is a "free good," whereas labor is the scarce resource; thus the aim is to maximize yield/per labor. Traditional methods become increasingly unviable as population density rises. Cultivators are impelled to seek newer ways as necessity is the mother of invention. In effect, it is the challenge that elicits a response. Note, however, that the Boserup mechanism may not work under all conditions. If an already densely populated country—for example Bangladesh—were to have an acceleration of its population growth rate, there's no guarantee of a similar beneficial response in agricultural technology.

A story may be told about what happens as population grows in regions where land was formerly plentiful. Agriculture transforms from using labor-scarce to land-scarce techniques. Political institutions and technological choice also change accordingly (see Lal 1988). As land stops being a free good, it becomes property with defined ownership rights. (Note that ownership itself means little if these rights cannot be sold or transferred subject to certain conditions.) A corollary of property rights is that some members of the community are left without rights or lose them to form a new landless class. This is another illustration of how technical change can alter income distribution for better or worse. The institution of land ownership typically enhances efficiency since it allows individuals to make investments that improve the productivity of land. Such technological changes tend to be land-saving and capital-intensive as noted previously. In this situation of intensive growth, the yield/per acre begins to rise.

A striking empirical relation does, in fact, exist between farm size and the yield per acre. From recent history we may note that the reforms that prompted China's burst of growth started with the break-up of its large collective farms. In a similar way agricultural productivity also is improved in the erstwhile Soviet Union by breaking up its massive state and collective farms and distributing these lands to the peasants. This observation also is verified in a different context. A Japanese researcher conducted a study of farm output in various parts of Asia. He considered regions in which all other factors were fairly similar (except farm size), then measured the yield versus farm size, plotting it as the so-called **Ishikawa Curve.**

Note that this curve merely indicates an empirical regularity, not a causal relationship. How farm size might influence yield per acre needs to be explained. Various theories have, in fact, been proposed. For instance, there might be a rise in K-intensity as postulated here. The price of labor may differ on small versus large farms. The former are likely to be family farms in which the opportunity cost of labor typically is lower than of hired labor to the larger farms.

An alternative explanation is also based on the different ownership structure. The observed increase in yield per acre may be attributed to a greater intensity of effort as the land/labor ratio drops. Farm production is notable in that it

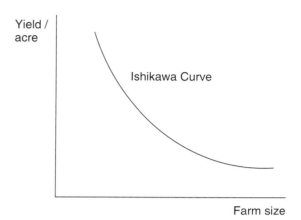

Figure 14-5 *The Ishikawa Curve of agricultural productivity*

involves teamwork, but unlike other situations involving team production, the individual contribution in farming may be particularly difficult to measure. (Communitarian organizations have been prevalent in agriculture throughout history.) In such situations there's always great potential for shirking among members of the team. This suggests another structural reason why smaller family run farms are generally found to be more efficient.

Table 14-4 Agricultural productivity in 1975

	Bilateral comparisons with the United States (index value of 100)			
	Value added per farmer	**Value added per capita**	**Value added per hectare**	**Relative price of agricultural goods**
Argentina	45	163	50	38
Brazil	10	80	82	92
Mexico	7	46	56	108
China	2.3	48	217	N/A
India	1.9	31	211	89
Indonesia	2.4	33	274	72
Korea	3.5	33	1013	141
France	44	115	374	100
Japan	9	31	519	88
United States	100	100	100	100

Source: Maddison and van Ark 1993.

The potential for agricultural advance can also be illuminated by a cross-section from a sample of developing and developed economies. Table 14-4 illustrates the extremely wide range of production conditions that exists in the farm sectors across the world. These include obvious differences in labor productivity, the intensity of land use, as well as policy-determined biases (positive or negative) as reflected in relative price of agricultural versus other goods.

Labor productivity—output per worker—in the first column must not be confused with total factor productivity. The United States looks to be far ahead of all others, whereas Japan performs very poorly in agriculture in contrast to its industrial achievement. The second column makes allowance for the fraction of total population involved in agriculture. Since this fraction is much larger for Asian LDCs than in the United States, their per capita agricultural productivity appears more respectable. The third column, indicating productivity per unit of land, shows most countries doing more land-intensive agriculture than the United States. This is particularly so in densely populated East Asia. On the other hand, Argentina has the same pattern of extensive agriculture on the wide-open Pampas as does Australia or North America. Brazil and

Mexico are statistical anomalies since a vast part of their land area is tropical jungle and desert, respectively. The last column shows the bias in relative price of agricultural goods—again in relation to the United States. As noted earlier, the East Asian countries have developed on the basis of a profitable agricultural sector. In Japan this has persisted even past its development takeoff, so its farmers may be considered especially privileged.

POVERTY ISSUES

Finally we turn from issues of production to issues of distribution. The agricultural sector plays a pivotal role in a country's effort to reduce poverty or achieve an equitable distribution of income. As seen in Table 14-5, the issue of poverty in developing countries is largely a rural problem.

In every case shown, the proportion of a country's total poor living in rural areas exceeds the proportion of population living there. This disparity remains after the massive migrations that have occurred from the rural areas to the cities. Larger samples also confirm that a major part of poverty is accounted for by the rural sector. While urban poverty is rather more visible and politically potent, the problem is quantitatively far more important in rural areas. Tackling rural poverty in Kenya and

Table 14-5   Rural dimension of LDC poverty

		Rural population as % of total population	Rural poor as % of total poor
Africa	Ivory Coast	57	86
	Ghana	65	80
	Kenya	80	96
Asia	India	77	79
	Indonesia	73	91
	Philippines	60	67
Latin America	Guatemala	59	66
	Panama	50	59
	Venezuela	15	20

Source: *World Development Report* 1990.

Indonesia, for example, would eliminate over 90% of their poverty problem. Further, controlling rural poverty would also help to abate the out-migration that adds to urban ills. The chain of reasoning leads from the poverty problem to the rural sector and so to agriculture. Thus the proper design of overall policy—in the choice of agricultural technology—will determine the degree to which landless labor or rural destitution is curbed.

Agriculture's role for food production has an even deeper significance aside from its strategic role. After all, the most basic goal of development is to improve the welfare of the population. What could be more basic that eating enough to survive? Beyond bare survival there must be adequate nutrition for all the populace to participate effectively in the various tasks of development. This problem comes in two parts: achieving enough production in the aggregate and ensuring a minimum distribution to all. What good is it for a country to produce a surplus of food if much of the population is too poor to purchase any? For countries where extreme poverty persists, this requires specific attention toward promoting social justice and welfare in the context of agricultural development.

Famine

A particular manifestation of the distributional problem is the recurrence of **famine.** Despite decades of concerted development efforts, the specter of famine still raises its ugly head in many parts of the developing world even at the end of the twentieth century. Only in the last few decades has it been vanquished in China and most of the Indian subcontinent, but even so, we are not entirely sure that this victory is permanent. On the African continent, however, the problem of mass starvation continues to place a special onus on agriculture. This stylized fact was noted in the introduction, as we generalized about the principal problems faced by each continent. We also noted that famine, or undernutrition in general, seriously exacerbates the problem of poverty and inequity.

For almost all LDCs the agricultural sector plays a special role for providing food. In purely quantitative terms, expanded food production might be expected to reduce the hazard of famine. Lower food prices also make it more affordable. However, a focus on aggregate quantities diverts attention from the importance of income distribution in determining affordability for the very poor. Amaryta Sen (1993) advances this argument through the concept of **entitlements.** If minimum life-sustaining entitlements are guaranteed to all, the poorest will be able to eat even when food output does turn out to be low. Food availability almost always exceeded per capita requirements in historical episodes of famine. Thus famines are primarily a problem of maldistribution. Sometimes this may arise due to purely logistical imbalances, but usually this results from an unequal distribution of income and assets, or, more generally, of social rights or entitlements.

Sen presents striking empirical evidence to support his argument. During the mid-1980s a drought in sub-Saharan Africa resulted in a prolonged drop in food availability. While some countries experienced severe famines, others actually managed to lower mortality rates during this difficult period! Remarkably, the countries with the smallest drop in food output, Ethiopia and Sudan, suffered the most severe famine. Clearly this reflects an unequal distribution of the available food. Efforts to alleviate starvation also appear to be hampered by undemocratic regimes. In democratic Botswana and Zimbabwe, authorities were obliged to act decisively, while the ruling elites in Ethiopia and Sudan responded slowly since they were not personally affected.

Likewise, Sen also contrasts the political systems that allowed the tragic famine in China during 1958-1961 versus India's success in avoiding such disasters. During China's tragic experiment of the "Great Leap Forward," an estimated 16 to 29 million people perished due to starvation. While India has avoided large-scale famine since democracy forces some public accountability, it does however continue to suffer from a disastrous level of chronic undernourishment. Its persistently higher morality rates may in the long run outweigh the more dramatic episode in China. The contrast has turned particularly unfavorable in recent decades as China purposefully made public actions to provide the basic needs for nutrition, health and education. Notably is such progress took place before the spate of economic growth in the 1980s. Again, the lesson is that progress with basic needs and food security are not dependent on increases in production. This is illustrated for the case of Africa below (Table 14-6).

The lack of correlation between food output and famine is also striking for the Bangladesh famine in 1974. (This episode became widely known in the West through George Harrison's music album *Bangladesh*.) The remarkable fact is that per capita food supply in 1974 was the highest in any year between 1971 and 1976. The preceding year, 1973, marked the second best level of food availability. Clearly, factors other than food supply caused the famine. Floods until August 1974 disrupted critical farming activities such as the transplantation of rice seedlings. In

turn, this caused unemployment among landless laborers who typically live a hand-to-mouth existence from day wages.

The looming fear of starvation created a panic in rice markets even though the crop was not to be harvested until December. Anticipation of a shortage led to precautionary buying by consumers and speculative hoarding by traders. The price of rice and other food grains shot up sharply, just at a time when income of the poor landless labor was down. Thus the death toll peaked in October at the same time as food prices. Meanwhile relief efforts were delayed due to a minor political disagreement with the main aid donor, the United States. Once relief began, market prices quickly adjusted to realistic levels in anticipation of the winter harvest. By the end of November most relief centers were closed, and the famine was over by the time the harvest came in. The basic lesson from this disastrous episode is that figures about aggregate food supply can be irrelevant, even dangerous, for ensuring against famines. A much wider perspective is needed for ensuring basic needs for the very poor.

Table 14-6   Famine and food availability in Africa, 1983–1984

Compared to normal years 1979–1981
Sudan (severe famine) ————————————————————> 89%
Ethiopia (severe famine) ——————————————————> 87%
Botswana (no famine) ————————————————> 82%
Zimbabwe (no famine, mortality drops) ——————> 62%
Cape Verde (no famine, mortality drops) ——> 61%

Source: Sen 1993.

SUMMARY

The agricultural sector is important for various obvious reasons. First, the development process is comprised of dramatic structural changes that are both the cause and effect of economic growth. While the agricultural sector figures in this sequence of qualitative transformations, the early structuralist school was pessimistic about agriculture's contribution to the overall growth rate. The Lewis model, for instance, viewed this sector as a passive source of resources, to be extracted and redeployed to the favored leading sector, industry.

The bitter lessons of experience have demonstrated the fundamental errors in that view. Now agricultural development is itself seen as a necessary precondition for sustained overall growth. In the modern view agriculture is viewed more positively as an independent source of growth. Schultz initiated this reappraisal by arguing that the main obstacle had been inappropriate incentives. Thus microeconomic reforms would spur agricultural progress as supposedly traditional peasants respond to the right incentives. All kinds of distortions must be removed, many of them inappropriate government interventions based on the earlier paradigm. There's also hope for continued technical progress, as in the Green Revolution that so successfully raised agricultural productivity. Thus agriculture can contribute to overall growth, though at a rate lower than industrial growth. Meanwhile the share of agriculture in total output inevitably will decline. Eventually, as food output safely exceeds population growth, this sector will cease to have a critical role.

The new institutional economics provides a different explanation for the sluggishness of traditional agriculture. The focus is on property rights rather than on price policies as important determinants of the structure of incentives and behavior. The structure of institutions and arrangements change slowly in comparison to technological and ecological changes in modern times. Thus an important role for government is to push forward institutional reform.

Finally, the agricultural sector is seen to play a crucial role in equity. In fact, much of measured poverty in LDCs occurs in the rural areas. Thus policies for poverty reduction must specifically target the agricultural sector. In turning from production to distribution, the latter problem is attributed to a lack of minimum entitlements for all. Thus famines can persist even when more than enough food is being produced.

KEY TERMS

Sector shares
Nutrition
Subsistence agriculture
Food production
Food distribution system
Procurement price
Ration price
Farm Household model
Cash crops

Seasonal production
Transactions cost
Risk aversion
Farm credit
Institutional economics
Property rights
Sharecropping
Tenancy contracts
Land rent

Land tax
Marketing boards
Food and Agriculture
    Organization (FAO)
Nongovernmental organizations (NGOs)
Ishikawa curve
Famine
Entitlements

Chapter 15

Industry

Our study of sectoral policy now turns to the special role played by industrialization. One common observation is that the industrial sector typically grows at a faster pace than agriculture. Its high growth rate makes this sector important to developing countries despite its small share in the economy. Industry's contribution to the overall growth rate can be seen from the weighted average.

$$\hat{Y} = \left(\frac{Ag}{Y} \right) \hat{Ag} + \left(\frac{In}{Y} \right) \hat{In}$$

Unlike the agricultural sector, industry in developing countries starts from a rather small share of GDP. Thus its contribution to the overall growth rate is also correspondingly small. But no matter how small the initial share, the power of compound growth guarantees that industry will eventually become the predominant sector due to its higher growth rate. And, as its share of total output rises over time, so does its contribution to the overall growth rate.

But why does the industrial sector have a faster rate of growth in the first place? As we've learned from growth accounting, any growth is attributable to either an accumulation of factor input(s) or increases in productivity. We must accordingly rephrase our question: Why is productivity growth inherently higher in industry than in agriculture? We must search for explanations for the observation that technical progress tends to proceed faster in the industrial sector. One plausible hypothesis springs from the fact that manufacturing involves putting together a large number of resources and inputs. The arrangements of production constitute a massive combinatorial problem that cannot be solved exactly. Thus there's greater potential for invention and discovery of efficient methods that previously were unknown. By contrast, in agriculture the basic interactions among a smaller number of variables supposedly have been known for millennia and enshrined in traditional methods and customs.

An alternative explanation for the rapid increase in industrial output is that just measured value is increasing. This rather strained argument is that the relative price of manufactures rises faster in times of income growth. In effect, it is the price rather than industrial output that is increasing.

An earlier generation of development economists had little doubt that industrialization was special. This mere instrument of development was elevated to a status approaching an ultimate goal. (Even today we tend to use "industrial development" for "development," as if these terms are almost synonymous.) The focus was mainly on how to get industrial development started in a backward economy. For instance, in the early postwar years, Nurkse and Rosenstein-Rodan were concerned that the LDCs were stuck in a "trap" that made it difficult to initiate an industrial sector. This problem is supposed to arise from the fact that the industrial sector is characterized by complex linkages that interconnect different segments of industry. A lack of such linkages was seen as the main problem in initiating industrial development.

The concept of linkages can be illustrated by a simple example. One part of the industrial sector, say, an automotive industry, would be hard to initiate if a steel industry did not already exist to supply it with required raw materials. Yet at the same time, it would be difficult to initiate a steel industry lacking a preexisting demand from customers such as an automotive industry, and so on. . . . Multiply this many times over to represent the complex of linkages in a modern industrial economy, and you'll grasp the significance of this problem. For this reason some development economists urged a strategy of a "big push" across a broad front of industries that was to be instigated by government planning and intervention.

At a local level the idea of linkages can be promoted by "industrial estates," in which each firm benefits from the positive externalities generated by others. This locational advantage makes it profitable to set up various subsidiary service activities. For example, a machine shop could do contract work for all the local factories, whereas each would not find it worthwhile to establish one for its exclusive use. Such positive externalities outside of a firm are the counterpart of increasing returns to scale within the firm. Such cases bolster the argument against the perfect competition paradigm, lending support to the idea of industrial policy as explored further.

Industrial Policy

The urge for industrialization—both for its own sake and for its promised boost to overall productivity—induced massive interventions by the state. The "development economics" school perceived the existence of a market failure which provided them the needed theoretical justification. The previously-mentioned linkages, which are external to the firm (unless it is vertically integrated), constitute positive externalities. Likewise, extensive economies of scale also appear to be a characteristic of industrial technology. To benefit from such desirable market failures, some calculated interventions to promote industrialization certainly are justified. However, the industrialization plans of many countries often have involved a wholesale rejection of the discipline of free markets. As neoclassical economists point out, the results were predictably doomed to fail. The set of micropolicies adopted included some or all of the following elements (see *World Development Report* 1991):

Industrial licensing

Barriers to **entry**

Barriers to **exit**

Price controls

Exclusivity granted to specific firms

Allocation of key raw materials

Barriers to exit were set up primarily with the aim to continue employment in industries that have become obsolete or uneconomic. But such an approach is gravely flawed. Like human beings, businesses must die just as surely as they are born. Any business also has a natural life cycle, at the end of which its resources (including capital and labor) can usefully be redeployed in other **"sunrise" industries.** The inevitable unemployment in the transition is painful, but cannot be removed by regulatory fiat. Yet, in an effort to avoid facing the pain, good money is thrown after the bad, as losses mount year after year. These very resources could be invested to generate alternative opportunities for the labor that becomes redundant. Such a policy based on efficiency arguments is reinforced by considerations about fairness. The protection and concern conferred on the favored industrial sector is not real socialism: It can be described as socialism for the privileged classes. The fortunate few in the organized sector normally get a wage two to four times higher than those in the informal sector. Even after their social productivity disappears, they continue to get special benefits while vast numbers of the very poor get nothing. For all of these reasons, an equitable and efficient exit policy must allow firms to fail, while providing a social safety net and job retraining for displaced workers to alleviate their hardship.

The detailed industrial policies have a profound, often incalculable, impact on incentives and therefore on outcomes. Computation of the overall impact becomes even more complex due to the interaction effect of many policies. Among the entire set, particularly egregious was **industrial licensing** policy whereby government issued permits to produce. In effect this government regulation actually prevents some production! This is bizarre considering that the main problem of underdeveloped countries is insufficient production. To be sure, such policy did have a certain rationale when it was initiated in the 1950s. The planning process would forecast demand for each product, and this quantity would be divided among a certain number of firms as exclusive licenses to produce. The justification was to avoid wasting scarce resources for superfluous industrial capacity. Fortunately, by the 1990s, almost all countries have abolished comprehensive industrial licensing that was the Indian pattern until quite recently. Nevertheless, many still reserve the right to sanction large industrial projects, particularly those that involve foreign participation. This kind of industrial policy has been practiced with great success by Korea (Amsden 1989).

The perverse effects of industrial licensing are manifold. For unlicensed firms, attempts to initiate or expand production are actually considered illegal. Implicitly this planning approach assumes that there's no virtue at all in competitive processes: But when competition is eliminated, the specter of monopoly naturally raises its ugly head. Not to worry, say the planners. Monopolistic tendencies will be suppressed by instituting price controls. The other side of this coin is shortage; this, in turn, calls for a regulatory apparatus for rationing. . . . Note how this policy leads us down the garden path as both quantities and prices are controlled in the end. Decentralized firms and consumers are shorn of their role as economic decision makers, while entire control is vested in the bureaucracy. Soon enough, the party with the money (big business) seeks out the party with the power (the regulators). The result is "regulatory capture" as the organized sector finds itself having a commonality of interest with the latter. The result is industrial stagnation within a rent-seeking economy, as outlined in the preceding chapter on political economy.

This picture of an industrial sector strangulated by detailed direct controls aptly describes the South Asian experience. Starting from the early 1950s, this vision also influenced other emerging LDCs such as Indonesia until the mid-1960s, and Egypt until the mid-1970s. Mercifully, the flaws of this strategy soon became apparent, and for other reasons as well, many LDCs opted for other models of industrial development. The dominant alternative model is export-led growth based on labor-intensive manufacturing as adopted by the Far Eastern countries. In all cases the design of industrial strategy must deal specifically with the relationship of technical progress to industrial structure.

Technical Progress in Industry

The standard treatment of technological advance gives a stylized impression of industrial progress as a smooth outward shifting of the technical production function. A more realistic picture would be a sequence of **exit** of outmoded plants (or firms) and the **entry** of new, more efficient, plants. In fact, any industrial subsector typically comprises a bunch of firms of diverse size and efficiency. Technical progress often, though not always, comes through expansion of the market, as reflected by lowered price and larger output in Figure 15-1.

A falling product price P puts pressure on the profits of each firm in the industry. As it drops, the price falls below the average cost (AC) of the least efficient firms. These are successively forced out of business, and thus exit the industry. The new firms that enter make use of more advanced technology (which means cheaper) and typically enjoy larger economies of scale. Thus, overall progress of this subsector is intimately tied to the number and size of its constituent firms. Over time, costs for the whole industry follow along the **long-run average cost** curve. In a sense, this may also be thought of as a sort of **learning curve.**

This model of industrial progress highlights how contention between firms determines the dynamics of any industrial subsector. The same idea can be generalized for all the industries that comprise the overall industrial sector. Industrial policy involves picking winners and losers from among the various subsectors. Governments feel a strong inclination to actively promote the projected winners, not just leaving it to the vagaries of the free market.

Exit policy   On the flip side of promoting potential winners is the issue of industries that seem like losers. Familiar examples of mature industries past their heyday are the so-called Rust Belt industries in the U.S. Midwest. At a more terminal stage are **"sunset industries,"** such as the typewriter industry in the age of word processing personal computers. In an absolutely free market, such producers would simply go bankrupt—as they should. Yet this issue often becomes a matter of social concern as it may involve large numbers of workers becoming unemployed. More insidious forces, however, may invite government intervention as

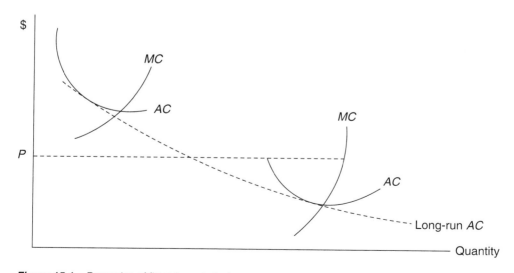

Figure 15-1   *Dynamics of firms in an industry*

entrenched vested interests force society to continue subsidizing such uncompetitive industries indefinitely. In China, for example, many industrial dinosaurs are kept alive for ideological and social reasons. Similarly, in India, industrial progress is impeded by the political clout of certain labor unions that channels public subsidies to many "sick units." Such scarce resources instead could be invested more profitably in sunrise industries. This is why a comprehensive industrial policy should be designed to allow for exit—not just to promote expansion of industrial capacity.

Analysis: Exit decision by a firm

The rationale for the right time and manner to go out of business calls for a review of the theory of the firm from microeconomics. For some time before the end, while profits decline, firms in such industries continue operating using their antiquated equipment and aging labor force. Their shutdown is postponed as long as they continue to meet variable costs. Except for ongoing maintenance, no new investment is warranted, and no large-scale firings are necessary as attrition and retirements reduce the number of employees.

Figure 15-2 depicts the cost curves of a firm. As the market price of the product declines, we can trace how production declines along segment *AB* of the marginal cost curve (*MC*). The price still remains high enough to cover average variable costs (*AVC*), but below the average total cost (*ATC*), which would be needed to induce new firms to enter this industry. However, firms already in the industry can continue to produce as price covers their marginal costs.

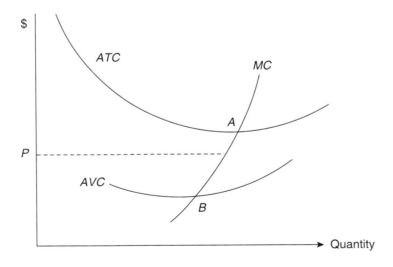

Figure 15-2   *Contraction of a firm in a declining industry*

At what point would it be smart to shut down a declining industry, and what government intervention is appropriate? It is relevant to ask whether the price decline is temporary or permanent as the market price drops below *AVC*. Clearly, if the condition is irreversible, it would be rational to quit sooner rather than later. Yet there's the serious problem of transitional dislocation to the displaced workers while hopes persist for a miraculous revival. This mixture of disappointment and hope combines with the political clout built over many preceding years of prosperity. Management and labor together persuade the government to subsidize the operational losses. The industry continues to operate as good money is thrown after bad. While the subsidy can grow to scandalous proportions, the drain on the public finances stifles other more deserving projects. Ultimately, there's a showdown when the privileged minority is forced to accept the reality that the sun has set on their industry. The polity realizes that huge sums are being spent per job saved in this intrinsically unviable industry. A forceful counterargument becomes "Why not pay each worker half a million dollars to retire in luxury. The economy would still come out ahead by eliminating the wasteful expenditures."

INPUT-OUTPUT ANALYSIS

The impetus in favor of industrialization required quantitative planning to sketch out the specific development of this sector. This technocratic planning exercise uses a methodology invented by Leontief called **input-output analysis.** As suggested by its name, this technique specifies all the inputs needed to generate the planned outputs. Say, for example, the output of industry 1 must fulfill the final demand for that product plus the intermediate demands by other productive sectors.

$$x_1 = a_{11}x_1 + a_{12}x_2 + a_{13}x_3 + a_{14}x_4 + y_1$$

Each coefficient a_{ij} indicates the amount of good i needed as an input to produce one unit of good j. For example, a value $a_{12} = .4$ means that you need .4 units of good 1 to produce a single unit of good 2. Multiply this coefficient by x_2, the actual output of good 2, and sum together with all other needs for good 1.

The technical (engineering) relationships of inputs to outputs are encapsuled in a table of input/output coefficients a_{ij}. The complete set of equations of this form can be stacked in a compact matrix notation as shown. A stylized example illustrates this construct for a small number of goods produced using available inputs for both intermediate uses and final demands.

Outputs	Intermediate uses	Final demands

$$\begin{pmatrix} x_1 \\ x_2 \\ x_3 \\ x_4 \end{pmatrix} = \begin{pmatrix} a_{11} & a_{12} & a_{13} & a_{14} \\ a_{21} & a_{22} & a_{23} & a_{24} \\ a_{31} & a_{32} & a_{33} & a_{34} \\ a_{41} & a_{42} & a_{43} & a_{44} \end{pmatrix} \begin{pmatrix} x_1 \\ x_2 \\ x_3 \\ x_4 \end{pmatrix} + \begin{pmatrix} y_1 \\ y_2 \\ y_3 \\ y_4 \end{pmatrix}$$

y is the vector of final demands for each good.
x is the vector of production quantities.

This notation signifies that output of each good must be the sum of final demand plus intermediate demands for making goods 1 through 4. The above set of equations can be summarized in even more compactly so that matrix A represents all the input/output (I/O) coefficients a_{ij}, while X represents the vector of $(x_1 \ x_2 \ x_3 \ x_4)$.

$$X = A X + Y$$

This matrix equation indicates that the outputs X are a function of final demands Y plus intermediate needs reflected in the *I/O* coefficients A. Matrix algebra helps solve this system of equations to obtain the required production of each good. You may not care to go into the mathematics of matrix inversion, which translates the equation into the following form to determine precisely how much of each x must be produced given the final demands *y*. The matrix on the right, called the Leontief Inverse Matrix, can be of direct use as we shall see.

$$X = \left[I - A \right]^{-1} Y$$

While this apparatus may seem complex, its usefulness becomes clear for a typical economy that comprises a very large number of goods. Even for just 100 distinct industries, the number of technical coefficients in the *A* matrix could be as many as 100 * 100 (or 10,000). Inverting this matrix is a huge exercise in number crunching, which is why I/O analysis only became a realistic tool with the advent of computers after the 1950s.

Once computation is no longer a major constraint, the depth of this analysis depends on the available amount of detailed data by industry. The different industries are distinguished in standard industrial and trade classification **(SITC) code** that is accepted by most countries. The first digit of this code classifies the major industry groups: chemicals, nonferrous metals, and so on. The second digit of the chemical sector indicates further differentiation as, for example, rubber-based or petrochemical-based, and so on. Even at a deeper 3rd or 4th digit level of the SITC code, the technological coefficients tend to be a nonsensical aggregate of quite different industries. Another problem is that the SITC code rapidly becomes obsolete with the introduction of new products. As computers and various electronic devices have become widespread, they comprise an ever larger share of industrial output. Yet they are all lumped into a single code at the five-digit level under "electrical machinery." Such aggregation errors makes the entire exercise somewhat suspect.

A rudimentary application of I/O analysis is presented earlier in chapter 8 in the context of manpower planning. Here we attempt to make the underlying theory somewhat more concrete. The I/O tool can be utilized for a variety of uses within the context of industrial planning.

1. The most obvious use is for determining the size of capacities needed in various input industries so as to provide a given amount of final outputs. In particular, this apparatus makes it possible to identify those subsectors that are considered key to overall industrial growth.

2. If imported goods (both producer and consumer goods) are split out in separate categories, then the total import requirement can be forecast. An obvious application of this tool is for planning in the oil sector. Petroleum is a critical intermediate good imported by most LDCs to keep their industrial sector running. If the availability of foreign exchange is constrained, it would be useful for economic managers to learn this beforehand so that national alternatives can be explored.

3. The I/O apparatus can be used to analyze the requirements of standard factor inputs, such as labor and capital investments needed for industrial expansion. Various types of labor and capital are specified as input goods in the I/O matrix and dealt with in the same way as any other intermediate good.

4. The I/O setup can help illuminate how the industrial structure changes qualitatively with development. The I/O matrix can be rearranged so that it looks largely triangular. Instead of much circularity between subsectors, industry is then seen to have a largely hierarchical structure. The base of the triangle is comprised of many **light industries** that serve final consumer demands. These are provided inputs by intermediate goods industries, which in turn get their inputs from a small number of **heavy industries.**

Linkages

As seen earlier, a significant by-product of the I/O apparatus is determination of the degree of linkage between different industrial segments. Such ideas were initiated by Albert Hirschman (1958) who was a very influential figure in the early years of this development epoch. A concrete example will help illustrate this concept. Suppose a particular industry (say, a manufacturer of motor vehicles) is found to be highly interconnected with other industries both as a customer and as a supplier. The promotion of this particular segment thus might be vital for overall industrial growth in contrast to another industrial segment that has few linkages. A given industry's connections with various customers downstream are labeled **forward linkages,** while those with its suppliers are **backward linkages.**

Hirschman argued that backward linkages are more beneficial for spurring continued growth than forward linkages. This is precisely what is missing in LDCs at the start of their development process. Primary production, by definition, needs few inputs other than labor and natural resource endowments. Its weak linkages are exemplified by the minimal value added in production of semimanufactures, such as refined sugar out of sugar cane or cotton ginning of raw cotton. The implication is: If you wish to set up an industrial sector from scratch, it's best to start with production that requires intermediate goods of various sorts, so other industries will be encouraged to fulfill this need. The reverse stimulus is weaker. Setting up a producer goods industry—say, a steel industry—in itself provides little stimulus for customer industries to spring up. Thus an obvious strategy is to start an industrial sector with simple light industry that merely assembles imported components. Eventually such imports can be replaced by a progressive indigenization of components manufacturing. The upcoming case study illustrates a successful example of such an ISI strategy actually used by the NICs of East and Southeast Asia.

The strength of linkages may be quantifiable within the I/O framework. Recall that the jth column of the Leontief inverse matrix represents the inputs used by the jth industry. Thus the sum of all the coefficients in that column gives the backward linkages while the row coefficients indicate forward linkages. The two together indicate the total linkages deriving from this particular industry. Thus it's possible to pick out the industry with the highest linkages and specifically target it for promotion. Industrial planners did precisely this kind of analysis to pinpoint key industries such as steel, transport, and electrical equipment.

Once key industries are determined, planners can fashion a detailed policy package utilizing many more microinstruments such as public investment, subsidies, and other incentives for these industries. This kind of industrial policy package is deemed to have been quite successful in boosting the industrial development of South Korea. By contrast, the efforts in India and Egypt were failures as they bred vast white elephant industrial edifices with chronically low efficiency. This stark difference in performance might be attributed to the type of intervention. South Korea used instruments that relied on market prices, while the others adopted quantitative restrictions that denied a role for markets and prices.

The qualitative nature of the industrial structure is closely related to level of development and the degree of outward orientation. The former relates output to demands as indicated by Engels curves. Structural change occurs within the industrial sector in a deterministic way. For instance, industrial services, such as utilities, grow at about the same rate as the overall industrial sector: They are not a leading sector. As for the relation to openness, note that the outward orientation of countries such as Korea, Taiwan, and Israel allowed them to progress rapidly with an initial focus on light consumer goods industry. They simply imported whatever primary inputs that were needed. Only gradually, as their industrial sector matured, did they venture into basic heavy industry. On the other hand, closed economies, such as Turkey, Egypt, Argentina, India, and Pakistan, chose to start all levels of industry simultaneously.

The seminal work in this area is by Syrquin and Chenery *Three Decades of Industrialization* (1989). Table 15-1, adapted from their work, summarizes the experience of various countries to show how overall industrial growth may be attributed to various different stimuli for industry.

Table 15-1   Economic structure changes as income rises

	Percent shares of GDP		
	Income per capita (1980 dollars)		
	300	**1000**	**4000**
Agriculture	39%	23%	10%
Services	32	38	45
Industry	28	40	46
Manufacturing	12	18	24

(Percent may not add to 10% due to roundings:
Industry includes mining, construction and utilities in addition to manufacturing.)

Source: Syrquin and Chenery (1989).

CASE STUDY: INDUSTRIAL LINKAGES VERSUS EXTERNALITIES IN ASEAN

The Association of Southeast Asian Nations (ASEAN) is comprised of the Philippines, Malaysia, Indonesia, Thailand, and Singapore, one of the Asian tigers that enjoyed spectacular growth. Later, the rest of this group emulated East Asia's successful strategy of export-led industrialization based on cheap labor. For Indonesia and the Philippines, in particular, this meant a complete reversal of former policy. Their performance and achievements vary in accordance with their backgrounds as well as how late each country switched to the more beneficial strategy. In any case, all have done well in comparison to other developing country groups.

The ASEAN experience illustrates how export manufacturing can spark overall industrial growth. A specific issue is whether export industry offers merely shallow linkages or more profound externalities. Ariff and Hill (1985) summarize the research on this aspect of industrial development. An obvious measure of backward linkages is the share of domestic procurement in manufacturing output. As seen in Table 15-2, this ranges from a high of 57% for a large, closed economy, Indonesia, to a low of 16% for small, open Singapore. Subsequent to these data from 1975, these economies have become even more open, while their industrial

sectors have evolved much further.

Note that domestic value-added gives a limited interpretation of linkages. Much broader externalities may derive from export-oriented industrialization.

Knowledge and contacts with international markets

Internal diffusion of imported technology

Demonstration and competitive effects

Interfirm movement of technical and managerial personnel

Development of subcontracting networks

More detail on linkages is provided in Table 15-3, which splits manufacturing into three subsectors: Natural resource–based industry, a segment oriented mainly toward the domestic market, and one mainly oriented toward exports. For each industry type linkages can be defined in an alternate way.

Dispersion of production into other sectors

$$\frac{\text{Net } f/x}{\text{earnings ratio}} = \frac{\text{net } f/x \text{ earning from export}}{\text{gross export earnings}}$$

Table 15-2 Input structure of ASEAN manufacturing: 1975

Country	Domestic purchased inputs	Imported inputs	Value added
Indonesia	.57	.12	.31
Thailand	.52	.17	.33
Philippines	.49	.15	.36
Malaysia	.49	.15	.34
Singapore	.16	.59	.25

Source: Ariff & Hill, 1985. Percentages may not add to 100% due to rounding.

Table 15-3   ASEAN: Strength of linkages in industrial subsectors

Country	Natural resource–based	Domestic market oriented	Manufactured exports	Total manufacturing production
Indonesia	1.21	1.14	1.09	1.20
	.92	.70	.66	.84
Thailand	1.17	1.02	1.09	1.14
	.92	.64	.75	.80
Philippines	1.15	1.09	1.15	1.14
	.93	.76	.72	.81
Malaysia	1.16	1.12	1.03	1.09
	.86	.64	.62	.77
Singapore	.83	N.A.	.92	.92
	.19		.47	.34

Source: Ariff & Hill, 1985.

The ratio of net foreign exchange earnings is highest from natural resource–based exports. For example, Indonesian oil exports require few imported inputs; thus for each $1.00 of such gross export revenue, net f/x earnings are $.92. By contrast, Singapore acts as an "entrepot." It gladly imports intermediate goods, adds value in domestic production, and then exports. Its net f/x earning ratio is low, even as absolute f/x earnings are high.

Another conventional measure of linkage is based on the spread effects of production computed from I/O analysis. This is large if industry has domestic suppliers and subcontractors, who in turn have suppliers, and so on. This number is expressed as a ratio of average spread effects for the whole economy. The value for manufacturing invariably exceeds unity since other sectors such as primary production, including agriculture and mining, tend to have shallow backward linkages.

Table 15-3 highlights certain regularities: Spread effects generally are lower in natural resource–based export industry than in manufactured production as a whole. Another observation is that ASEAN's primary exporting sector is unusual in having a high degree of backward linkages. From such analysis we may conclude that the concept of linkage does offer some insights; yet it does not illuminate the precise channels whereby export-oriented production might boost overall growth.

A closer view of linkages is provided for the specific case of the automobile industry in Malaysia (Horii 1991). While Malaysia started its industrialization later than the four Asian tigers,

Table 15-4   Malaysian car sales 1984–90 (in thousands)

	1984	1985	1986	1987	1988	1989	1990
PROTON	0	7	22	23	39	48	65
Japanese	72	48	21	9	12	21	31
Other foreign	15	8	4	3	3	5	10
Total	87	64	47	35	54	74	106

Source: Torii, 1991.

its growth performance has been quite good. It also managed to eradicate poverty and achieve equity for the majority of its people. In particular, Malaysia established a competitive automobile industry by means of a deliberate step-by-step strategy pursued by the government.

The World Bank's *Report on the Economic Development of Malaya* gave the initial impetus for industrial development in the mid-1950s. Through various legislative acts the government encouraged investment in industry, particularly by the Malay majority, which lagged economically. The Free Trade Zone Act of 1971 also promoted foreign investment. The United States and Japan have been especially involved in industrial progress with export-oriented manufacturing since the 1970s.

The New Economic Policy (NEP) was based on redistribution-with-growth. This strategy aimed to induce ethnic Malays, or Bumiputera (sons of the soil), into industrial ventures away from their traditional concentration in agriculture. Particular goals were equity ownership, corporate management and entreprenuership, as well as employment for the Bumiputera.

In 1980 the government of Prime Minister Mahathir set up the Heavy Industries Corporation of Malaysia (HICOM) as the institution for implementing the strategy. HICOM established steel mills, cement factories, motorcycle manufacturing, and, most notably, the PROTON automobile production program. (This industry has a special importance since car ownership in Malaysia is generally higher compared to other LDCs at the same level of income.) PROTON took on the Mitsubishi Corporation as

a joint venture partner in 1982, and production of indigenous cars began in 1985. Output expanded rapidly to take away market share from foreign cars (either imported or assembled locally by foreign controlled manufacturers) as shown in Table 15-4.

The car assemblers have various forms of corporate links with foreign corporations. (The importance of industrial organization will be elaborated.) One type of link is a local assembler producing under contract for a local sales company that holds the franchise of a foreign manufacturer. Another more stable type is when the foreign corporation and local sales company jointly invest in the assembly plant. The government acts to influence both the type of control and its ethnic composition. HICOM invested Bumiputera capital for 70% of equity in PROTON, the manufacturing company, as well as a major stake in EON, the local car sales company.

The automobile industry started with an import-substitution strategy. Car imports were subject to high tariffs, while completely knocked-down (CKD) kits of components enjoyed lower duty rates. The resulting high rate of effective protection encouraged local car assembly. Gradually the manufacture of parts began locally. Beginning with general replacement parts, then original equipment manufacturer (OEM) parts, and, finally, key components, such as engines and transmissions. Since 1980 domestic content has been progressively increased by means of a Mandatory Deletion Program, which specifies the components whose import becomes prohibited when domestic manufacture starts. See Figure 15-3.

Figure 15-3   Indigenization of automobile components manufacturing in Malaysia

Pre-1980	Tires, batteries, paints, air conditioners
1980	Safety glass, exhaust equipment
1981	Carpets, seatpads, side moldings
1982	Wiring
1984	Electrical equipment, air filters
1985	Windshields, wiper motors, shock absorbers, fuel tanks, radiators, coil springs
1986	Car seats, fuel and brake tubes, hoses, fuel and air filters, dashboard instruments

The components chosen for domestic production followed obvious criteria: First came products that had large scale general markets, were labor-intensive, or required relatively low technical inputs. This strategy relied on backward linkages for building up a components manufacturing sector. The effort received a big boost as the PROTON project came on stream. PROTON received extra protection by way of exemption from the 40% import duty on CKDs and a 50% discount on excise duties. An important feature of this ISI program was that infant industry protection was lowered as local firms became more competitive. This experience stands in contrast to similar efforts in the Philippines and Latin America, which floundered because effective protection continued at a high level (see Takacs 1994).

Industrial Organization

The structure of linkages is reflected in the organizational structure of industry. The topic of **industrial organization** forms a subdiscipline of microeconomics that explains how technology interact with the market structure to determine how industry is organized into separate firms. The linkages between segments can vary in strength, ranging from strong one-on-one relationships to no discernible relation at all. For example, the manufacture of auto chasses and suspensions are so closely related that they might as well be **vertically integrated** into a single firm. Production by separate units would create a bothersome monopoly-monopsony relationship between the two firms. One would be the sole supplier for the other, which in turn is its only customer. Each one of them could "hold up" the other in chronically unstable negotiations. Instead, if operated under a unified command, profits from both activities would be combined, thus eliminating negotiation and transactions costs. On the other hand, tire manufacturing may well be handled by an independent firm since tires are a commodity that can be sold to other customers as well. Moreover, if a tire industry is organized competitively with production split among many firms, the problem of monopoly would be eliminated.

Industrial structure is importantly influenced by the degree of openness to international trade. In a very open economy the industrial sector only engages in manufacturing activities that match the country's comparative advantage. Other intermediate products are imported. In cases where there must be a close customer-supplier relationship, the appropriate form is a transnational enterprise. Otherwise there may be distributed manufacturing that crosses national boundaries. A country that has comparative advantage in making tires could have many competitive producers, all of whom sell to auto manufacturers located in other countries.

Another pattern of industrial organization is a horizontal **conglomerate,** which brings under one corporate umbrella a bunch of different firms involved in product lines as diverse as beer, pipeline valves, motorcycles, construction, and plastic footwear. The logic behind this structure is obviously not the supplier-customer technical relations already noted, but rather the benefits of sharing common functions such as finance, accounting, and management capabilities. The big business houses of Korea, such as Hyundai and Samsung (called Chaebol), which have now become world famous, have shown the utility of this industrial form. However, this example from that particular context cannot be taken to suggest a simple formula to be replicated for success in other national environments. A direct counterexample is presented by Taiwan's successful industrial development based on a myriad of small to medium-sized family firms. These are imbedded in a complex network of subcontracting relationships facilitated by an appropriate legal and business environment. Large firms have an inherent danger deriving from sheer economic size, however, as such businesses acquire enormous clout with the potential for abuse in the fragile political processes of young nations.

SUMMARY

In the early days of this development epoch, industry was assigned a preeminent role as the leading sector for overall growth and employment creation. Even as these aspirations often were disappointed, the impetus for industrial progress remains the focus for most of the developing world. This is because many successful examples of the NICs have demonstrated the high growth potential of industry as compared to agriculture. A revamped strategy for industry still might rectify the mistakes that have hindered progress in the past. The previous bias against agriculture in order to aid industry is seen to be dysfunctional; excessive capital intensity also must be avoided; the entry and exit of firms must be determined by market viability, not by government hopes and interventions; and, finally, there's no need for lingering protectionism that served more to hobble than to aid domestic industry by curbing technological advance and possible benefits of scale economies.

Next we examine the reason why productivity growth in industry can be so high. Reasons for this are intimately linked to learning-by-doing and to the external economies that accrue within an interlinked industrial sector. The idea of linkages is quantified using Leontieff's input/output framework that specifies the interconnections that are a defining feature of an industrial sector.

Finally, we examine institutional aspects of the industrial sector, which is comprised of different firms. The corporate and legal relationships with regard to ownership and control are a crucial determinant of industrial structure and its performance. The recent vast expansion of transnational manufacturing activities casts a new light on multinational corporations in general. These must no longer be seen as agents of imperialist powers, but rather as autonomous instruments in a shared global enterprise. Individual LDCs may opt out of such participation only to their own cost.

KEY TERMS

Leading sector	Long-run average cost	Forward linkages
Industrial policy	Learning curve	Backward linkages
Sunrise, sunset industries	Input-output analysis	Industrial organization
Industrial licensing	SITC code	Vertical integration
Exit	Light industry	Conglomerates
Entry	Heavy industry	Industrial concentration

Chapter 16

Macroeconomics

This book so far has talked exclusively about the real determinants of a country's growth. A distinct focus on output fluctuations falls under the rubric of macroeconomics. Such a compartmentalization of the economics discipline used to be even more marked in previous decades than it is now. Most developing countries took macroeconomic stability for granted while concentrating on the real economics of expanding roads and factories through capital investment, education, and technological advance. (Conversely, it might be said, the developed countries focused on macroeconomics to avoid fluctuations, while growth theory was considered as a mere esoteric sideline.)

All this has changed within the past generation, so the gap between DC and LDC economics is now much narrower in this regard. Theory has evolved so that the study of fluctuations has become integrated with growth. From a policy perspective, too, the LDCs have learned the enormous cost of neglecting sound macroeconomic practices. The debt crisis of the 1980s resulted in a lost decade for many LDCs as economic growth remained stagnant—or even regressed—while the affected countries, particularly in Latin America, were obliged to focus on stabilization. Thus **open-economy macroeconomics** is now an essential subject taught in much the same way

across the world. The basic lesson is that budget constraints cannot be violated for long without serious consequences. This universal lesson has local variations depending on the specific configuration of the economy.

Macroeconomics has a rather different vocabulary from microeconomics. The former uses general equilibrium analysis, with money included in an essential way to determine the price level, interest rates, level of output and employment, and so on. By contrast, microeconomics theory largely uses partial equilibrium tools that highlight the importance of relative prices. The corresponding distinctions in policy are more familiar to the layperson. These highlight the essence of macroeconomics, which focuses on economywide disturbances. Once the system achieves some consistency, structural adjustment policy can be implemented to improve long-term growth by a more efficient allocation of resources. Such microeconomic reforms particularly apply in economies that had chronically low growth due to highly distorted structures. On the other hand, stabilization programs are responses to short-term macroeconomic crises in which inflation and balance of payments deficits are out of control. To help with such problems, a corresponding functional division exists among international institutions. The World Bank concerns itself with long-term growth and structural change, while the **International Monetary Fund (IMF)** helps countries deal with short-term macroeconomic disequilibria.

While earlier chapters dealt with the World Bank's domain, this chapter turns to the IMF's concern with macroeconomic problems. We will study the various pathological symptoms of macro disequilibria and some suggested remedies. The problems arise from diverse causes such as inconsistent expectations, maladjusted policy, or external shocks. The typical pattern consists of a crisis generated by an unsustainable level of spending. This usually is manifested as a government budget deficit with a counterpart in the form of a trade deficit. Initially this may be financed by short-term capital inflows from abroad. Ultimately, however, the disequilibrium must be corrected. If postponed, the required adjustment involves even more drastic changes. The country is obliged to reduce its level of expenditures and switch from imports to exports. The latter requires an appropriate change in their relative price, for example, a depreciation of the real exchange rate. To summarize, this chapter will study macroeconomic issues in terms of four variables that are symptoms of disequilibrium.

- Budget deficit
- Inflation
- Current account
- Exchange rate

OPEN-ECONOMY MACRO THEORY

Open-economy macroeconomics extends the familiar framework of introductory macro theory to account for international flows. The national income identity must be expanded to include foreign components. Aggregate output Y equals consumption C, investment I, government expenditures G, as well as net exports comprised of exports X and imports M.

$$Y = C + I + G + X - M$$

Separating out taxes T, and rearranging

$$(Y - C - T) + (T - G) + (M - X) = I$$

The bracketed terms are interpreted respectively as net savings by households, government, and the foreign sector. This is the total amount of savings available to fund investment. We see that a budget deficit, where G exceeds T, causes the total amount of savings available for investment to be accordingly reduced. To obtain further insights we may manipulate the above equation to read

$$I - S + (G - T) = (M - X)$$

This important identity indicates that a country's excess of investment over private savings plus the government's budget deficit must be financed from abroad. Thus a trade balance deficit (imports exceed exports) is normal and healthy for an LDC making large investments for rapid growth. Alternatively it may indicate an unhealthy paucity of domestic savings. Thus the trade deficit signals that either investment is high or saving is too low. The connection between the trade and budget deficits, or **twin deficits,** presents a new perspective on the source of disequilibrium in an open economy. A common belief is that trade deficits derive just from international factors such as competitiveness or trade policy per se. Instead the problem may simply be that the country is spending too much or, in other words, saving too little. Typical numbers for a sample of LDCs are presented in a later section on the government budget.

In addition to these goods market flows, the macroeconomics of an open economy also includes financial and monetary elements. The three different kinds of international flows—goods, capital, and money—are summarized in the **balance of payments** accounts.

Balance of Payments

> Exports
> − Imports
> ──────────
>   Trade balance
> ± Transfers + interest on debt
> ──────────
>   Current account (C/A)
> + Capital account
> ──────────
>   Balance of payments

Each item in the balance of payments (BoP) is connected via different channels to important variables in the overall economy. The trade balance depends on competitiveness of domestically produced goods versus foreign goods. This price is reflected in the exchange rate e and domestic price level P. The next item includes mainly foreign interest payments (or receipts). The size of these payments depends on how much outstanding debt has built up through past deficits. The trade balance plus the other expenditure flows add up to the **current account (C/A).** In case the debt is small, and transfers such as aid or remittances are minor, the current account is approximately equal to the trade balance.

The capital account is the next major component of the BoP. It partly consists of long-term capital flows, direct foreign investment (DFI), or development loans, which have significance for growth as noted in chapter 7. Such inflows have the advantage that the country does not worry about repaying principal in the near future. By contrast, short-term capital flows have a critical impact on macroeconomic fluctuations. The amount and direction of such flows can be highly variable depending on the interest rate i and expected changes in the exchange rate e.

The bottom line, the overall balance of payments, is the sum of the current account and capital account. The current account, or net flow of goods, must have a financial counterpart. Part of the C/A is financed by capital inflows; the remaining part must be paid in cash. In the good old days, gold was physically transferred between countries to settle the BoP. In modern times a country's reserve holdings typically comprise strong international currencies rather than gold. A country with a BoP deficit pays out of the foreign reserve R holdings of the central bank. The outflow of reserves directly reduces the "backing" of a nation's currency, or base money. This base can be visualized concretely as the number of banknotes issued as liabilities of the central bank. Part of the monetary base is used by the country's banking system to expand deposits, and, therefore, the money supply, as will be explained. Thus the balance of payments has an intimate connection with monetary changes.

A balance of payments deficit (or surplus) may be settled either by reserve transfers or by changing the exchange rate. Let's examine each of these in turn. Up to the mid-1970s, a system of fixed exchange rates prevailed throughout the world. Any country with a BoP deficit was obliged to pay it out of its cushion of foreign reserves. If the deficit was too large, however, the stock of foreign reserves could be driven down to zero. In such cases the imbalance could not be settled by reserve flows alone; the exchange rate would then be altered in a one-time **devaluation** to regain equilibrium. Say, for example, the foreign exchange rate is originally fixed at 20 pesos per \$. A devaluation that resets it at 30 P/\$ may sufficiently discourage imports and encourage exports to eliminate the C/A deficit.

This example indicates how a BoP deficit can be corrected by devaluation instead of by reserve transfers. If the underlying causes of the disequilibrium persist, say as inflation continues to erode international competitiveness, the exchange rate would need to be repeatedly adjusted. In fact, since the mid-1970s, the prevailing floating exchange rate system accomplishes just such an adjustment. Countries no longer have a BoP that is settled by reserve flows.

Instead, the exchange rate adjusts continually and automatically so as to always keep payments in balance. Devaluations within a fixed exchange rate system have a counterpart as **depreciations** within a floating exchange rate system.

Anatomy of the Crisis

The open-economy macroeconomics crisis takes such a familiar form that the IMF prescribes a standard off-the-shelf cure with only minor modifications. By now the international community has accumulated experience from a distressingly large number of countries that got into similar kind of trouble over the years.

The nature of a typical crisis, as well as the standard IMF prescription, are summarized in a chart on page 312. The macroeconomic disequilibrium may be triggered by different proximate causes, but the generic problem is simply that the country is spending beyond its means. These common problems can be illuminated by the concept of national savings in an open economy, as made explicit in the earlier equation. We noted that the C/A deficit just reflects the fact that investment exceeds national savings. There can be a variety of reasons for this excessive domestic expenditure. Often, the government is directly to blame for generating a budget deficit that is unsustainable (examined more fully in an upcoming section). On other occasions a private spending binge may be financed by credit expansion by the banking sector. You may even observe a similar tendency among individuals: If access to credit is too easy, they may end up spending more than they would rationally want to.

A case of spending "too much" may also occur when a situation unexpectedly turns bad. Consider a country whose spending is initially at a prudent level, then an unexpected adverse shock makes that level unsustainable. Unfortunately countries, like individuals, tend to become habituated to old spending patterns; thus they resist immediate cutbacks. But as adjustment is delayed, the consequences worsen in a predictable series of

steps that lead up to the crisis. Typical examples of this sort were some oil-exporting countries in the late 1970s and early 1980s. Countries such as Mexico and Nigeria set up large expenditure programs based on the anticipation that oil prices would remain high or even rise further (the level then was over $20 a barrel). However, when the terms of trade collapsed, they seemed unable or unwilling to reduce their expenditure promptly.

Access to foreign borrowing modifies this picture somewhat. So long as foreign lenders accommodate a country by lending it funds, its currency remains strong even as money supply expands (see Figure 16-1). Such an accommodation often only serves to delay the onset of crisis. When the country must eventually adjust its spending patterns, the crisis may turn out even worse due to the external debt accumulated in the meantime. Many Latin American countries faced this painful reality as their debt service ballooned at the same time as they were forced to adjust. **Debt service** includes both the interest on debt, which is part of the current account, and principal repayment, which shows up in the capital account. In fact, in the depths of the crisis many LDCs suffered net outflows on the capital account, rather than inflows that could have cushioned their adjustment. There were three reasons for the outflows: repayments of principal and interest on previously accumulated debt; inflows of long-term development funds fell due to political and business uncertainties associated with the tough adjustment; and large outflows of private capital, for example, capital flight.

Even without foreign borrowing it's possible to finance a budget deficit from domestic capital markets. However the financial sector of LDCs is often rather underdeveloped. Only a few exceptional LDCs have an established market for long-term bonds. Thus in most LDCs the last remaining option to finance excess government expenditures is through money creation. The mechanics of this process is simple. The treasury asks the central bank to hand over domestic currency in exchange for bonds issued by the government. As custodian of the nation's money, the central bank might be expected to put up some resistance, but in most LDCs it has little independence from the government. In this way money supply expansion becomes subject to political whims. For politicians, the short-term incentive to continue deficit spending financed by money creation usually overwhelms their sense of long-term financial responsibility.

Expansion of the money supply in excess of normal growth of money demand will determine the rate of inflation. This forms a basic tenet of the **Monetary Approach,** which is a modern version of the old Quantity Theory of money. In an open economy context another important tenet is **purchasing power parity (PPP).** The idea of PPP is that the same good will have roughly the same price in all countries over the long term. This is shown in the equation as the domestic price level *P*, world price level *P**, and exchange rate *e*.

$$P = e\, P^{*}$$

As a concrete example, consider a standard good; say, a can of soda. Its price of about \$.50, not counting local taxes, must be approximately the same in all countries. If a country's exchange rate is 20 peso/\$ the soda can should cost around 10 pesos. If inflation occurs, the country's currency must depreciate proportionally so that international prices remain in parity. The PPP equation can be restated in terms of rates of growth (assuming that the world inflation rate is zero).

$$\hat{P} = \hat{e}$$

Continuing our story of macro disequilibrium, we observe that the extent of exchange rate devaluation often is delayed or incomplete relative to the ongoing rate of inflation. Then the deferred adjustment precipitates a crisis. The currency becomes **overvalued** as this country's prices translated at the existing exchange rate makes its goods uncompetitive in world markets. Exports will decrease while imports increase. This problem should not arise in a floating exchange rates system as the current account deficit should adjust automatically. However, the rate of currency depreciation rarely counterbalances the inflation rate precisely. Thus the macroeconomic disequilibria in the open economy has two defining features: (1) a real exchange rate that becomes over- or undervalued, and (2) a persistent inflation. We shall examine each of these in turn.

Real Exchange Rate

The **real exchange rate** is a key variable in the macroeconomic disequilibrium and its resolution. This concept can be easily understood in terms of the PPP equation. If inflation is 10% and the currency depreciates only 6%, then the real exchange rate has appreciated by 4%. The real exchange rate is observed to vary enormously over time in certain countries. The exchange rate represents a crucial relative price of domestic goods to foreign goods. Swings in this relative price can be especially destabilizing in open economies. An undervalued currency makes it profitable to produce domestic goods, both as import substitutes or for exports, while an overvaluation makes it simply cheaper to import. In response to these relative price shifts, resources must be moved from one industry to another. Thus exchange rate movements can be very disruptive to the conduct of regular business activities or for making long-term investment decisions.

This apparently microeconomic issue—shifts in response to relative price movements—tends to transform into a macroeconomic problem. As the relative profitability of industries changes, some industries start laying off workers while other industries are expanding. Invariably this causes some transitional unemployment. The macroeconomic instability is exacerbated when capital flows are relatively free to move across borders. As an

Analysis: Money Supply expansion by the Central Bank

Figure 16-1 shows how the central bank extends credit to the government. The balance sheet of the central bank is depicted by the box on the left. Central bank assets should consist largely of gold and foreign exchange holdings. Using this as backing, the central bank issues currency, which constitute its liabilities. (As suggested by the term balance sheet, the size of assets must balance the size of liabilities.) When the government borrows funds from the central bank, the latter simply issues more currency in exchange for government bonds. The central bank stores these bonds along with the gold and foreign reserves, which form part of its assets, in its vaults.

The extra currency issued is just an expansion of base money, as more currency is now flowing around in the economy. A part of this extra currency finds its way into the **reserves** of commercial banks. (The righthand box shows the balance sheet of the commercial banking system.) The additional reserves with the banks allows them to expand credit to the private sector. This results in expansion of total money supply: The sum of currency in the hands of the public plus demand deposits. The balance sheet of the central bank can be consolidated with the banking sector to show the total expansion of domestic credit to government plus the private sector. Excessive expansion of domestic credit is often a major proximate cause of macroeconomic crises.

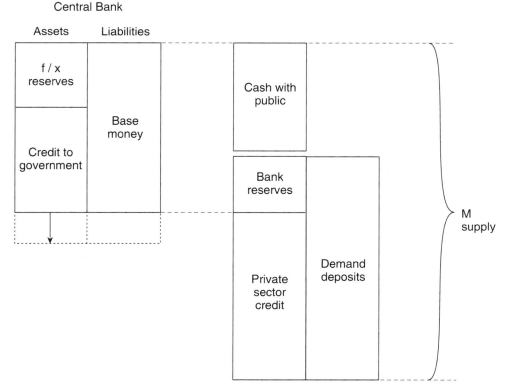

Figure 16-1 *Extension of credit to government by the banking system*

example, consider the experience of the southern cone countries of Argentina or Chile. During the late 1970s and early 1980s, so much short-term capital flowed into these countries (rightward shift of F/X supply in Figure 16-2) that their exchange rates got extremely overvalued.

At times the overvaluation became so extreme that even middle-class Argentines could afford to fly to Miami or Paris to go shopping. Meanwhile domestic industry could barely compete against artificially cheap foreign goods and went bankrupt all around, or relied on large public subsidies to maintain employment. Since many Argentines felt so wealthy (in terms of foreign currency) their expenditures spurred on imports, as noted, but not on domestically produced import substitutes. Domestic expenditures were concentrated on nontraded goods, which especially led to a construction boom. But, of course, the wealth was only borrowed. When the

time came to pay back foreign debts, imports had to be cut and exports increased. However the existing productive capacity for tradable goods was found to be entirely inadequate, both in quantitative terms and competitiveness. A drastic restructuring became necessary, even as the economy was left with many half-built buildings while property values crashed.

Capital flows, which can move almost instantaneously, have a much more immediate affect on the exchange rate than do goods trade. Thus the interest parity condition is more relevant than PPP in determining exchange rates. When capital can flow swiftly across countries, it forces interest parity so that total return on financial assets is equalized in all locations. Total return consists of interest return less the percent depreciation of the currency. Any divergence in interest rates across countries must be counterbalanced by the expected rate of depreciation.

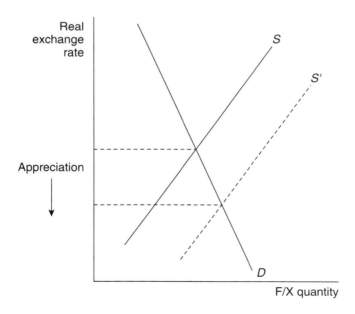

Figure 16-2 *Foreign exchange market*

For instance, if Mexico has a 15% interest rate versus 5% in the United States, one may reasonably expect that the peso will depreciate by about 10% against the $. In short, interest parity is a more direct determinant of exchange rates than PPP since arbitrage occurs much faster in financial markets than in goods markets.

Real exchange rate analysis applies equally to floating rates as for a fixed exchange rate system. The interest parity condition is modified simply in that the interest rate differential equals the expected devaluation. Here ongoing depreciations are replaced by devaluation, a discrete change of the **nominal exchange rate** in an otherwise fixed rate. Central bank or finance ministry officials have a problem figuring out how much to devalue. Deciding the appropriate correction in the exchange rate is difficult because there is no observable measure of the degree of existing misalignment. In the absence of free markets, there's no single exchange rate. Rather, a family of exchange rates prevails in the market. One possible indicator of misalignment is the foreign exchange premium in the **black market.** Say, for instance, the official rate stands at 200 pesos/$, while the black market offers 300 pesos/$. This does not mean, however, that a

devaluation to the latter rate will necessarily reach an equilibrium level.

The enormous range of variation of real exchange rate is shown in Table 16-1. Each year *The Economist* magazine compiles a playful index of PPP based on the price of a Big Mac© in different countries of the world. While it's easy to find flaws in this casual method, it does demonstrate quite concretely the misalignments of various currencies. In fact the price of this rather standard product provides a good comparison, since it should cost approximately the same everywhere. The 1993 figures are shown in Table 16-1.

This table shows how local currencies may be overvalued or undervalued in relation to the U.S. $. Consider, for instance, the price of Big Macs in Hong Kong. The local price of HK$ 9.00 translates to U.S. $1.16 at the going exchange rate. This is 49% below the U.S. price. Thus, according to the Big Mac index, the H.K.$ is undervalued in terms of PPP. The table shows that exchange rate misalignments range from −49% to +58% among a set of representative developing countries. Figures for Switzerland are provided to show that PPP divergences are by no means solely a developing country phenomenon.

Table 16-1 Measuring currency values by Big Mac prices

	Local price	$Price	Exchange rate	Implied PPP	Over-/or undervalue
United States	**$2.28**	**2.28**	—	—	**0%**
Argentina	Peso 3.60	3.60	1.00	1.58	+58
Brazil	Cr 77000	2.80	27521	33772	+23
China	Yuan 8.50	1.50	5.68	3.73	−34
Hong Kong	HK$ 9.00	1.16	7.73	3.95	−49
Malaysia	Ring 3.35	1.30	2.58	1.47	−43
Mexico	Peso 7.09	2.29	3.10	3.11	0
Korea	Won 2300	2.89	796	1009	+27
Thailand	Baht 48	1.91	25.16	21.05	−16
Switzerland	**SFr 5.70**	**3.94**	**1.45**	**2.50**	**+72**

Source: *The Economist* 4/17/93.

An overvalued exchange rate can have a variety of causes and effects. As noted earlier, the **capital account** component of the balance of payments plays a crucial causal role in the anatomy of the crisis. In particular, short-term capital flows are known to be notoriously volatile. Just as easily as they flow in, they can also surge out in a moment's panic. While officials tend to revile such antisocial speculation, it would be wrong to fault investors for their loss avoidance strategy. Their actions are more a symptom than a cause of the disease.

The direction of short-term capital flows depends less on current changes in the exchange rate than on expected future devaluations. This highlights the important role of **expectations.** Typically, in the weeks leading up to the crisis, the finance minister engages in a game of wits with jittery investors. Up to the last minute the minister stoutly declares that the currency is not going to be devalued. But using publicly known information, investors make their own calculations about the viability of current trends to decide where to keep their funds. Risky investors are enticed by high domestic interest rates that are way above world levels. Everyone expects a large percentage devaluation, even though people remain uncertain about its timing. The trick is to stay invested as long as possible to earn the high return, but to bail out before the exchange rate crashes. The effect of such speculative activity on the economy is destabilizing. When funds are pouring in, the real exchange rate remains overvalued, postponing adjustment. When funds are pouring out, the movements tend to cause panic in financial markets, prompting a larger exchange rate change than really necessary. Thus the exchange rate overshoots its appropriate equilibrium value.

The current account and capital account add up to the balance of payments. As both of these items tend to be in deficit in the weeks leading up to the crisis, the overall balance of payments is in deficit, which is the same as saying that the central bank continuously loses foreign reserves. As this foreign exchange cushion is seen to be depleted, private capital outflows accelerate and the crisis comes to a head. At that point the only recourse is for the country to turn to the IMF for assistance.

Inflation

The other defining feature of macroeconomic disequilibrium is a high rate of **inflation.** This pathological situation occurs as the economy lurches into chaos. High inflation generally is accompanied by large fluctuations in the level of inflation and in relative prices; these are reflected noticeably in wide movements in the real exchange rate. Inflation rates also are observed to vary widely, both across countries as well as over time. Some countries, particularly in Latin America, became habituated to living with a high rate of inflation—somewhat like becoming used to living with a disease. Their monthly inflation rates reached as high as the average annual inflation rate in low-inflation countries, many of which are in Asia. Table 16-2 indicates a representative sample of LDCs after the worldwide spurt of inflation following the sharp rise in commodity prices in the mid-1970s. The late 1970s and early 1980s was also a boom period in which the surpluses of the oil exporting countries were recycled throughout the world, thereby increasing global liquidity. Then excessive spending, both by the public and private sectors, caused a spurt in inflation. Later, in the mid and late 1980s, as many LDCs were plunged into recession, many governments tried to resist the necessary restructuring and retrenchment. They persisted in expanding the money supply, which led to even more inflation and economic chaos (see the case study of the Peruvian experience on page 315).

Note the huge variations in inflation rates even for 5-year averages. Undoubtedly the variation in annual rates will be far greater. As noted earlier, the worst bouts of inflation have occurred in Latin America. The Bolivian figures depict the progression over a complete cycle, in which the

Table 16-2 Annual inflation in various developing countries

	1975–1980	1980–1985	1986–1990
Argentina	193	323	588
Bolivia	17	611	15
Brazil	51	149	610
Mexico	21	61	81
Nicaragua	19	54	3130
Latin America	**45**	**99**	**262**
Algeria	12	9	10
Botswana	12	11	10
Cameroon	10	11	8
Sudan	23	32	64
Zaire	66	45	81
Africa	**13**	**18**	**18**
Indonesia	13	10	7
Korea	18	7	5
Malaysia	5	4	2
Pakistan	9	7	7
Asia	**8**	**7**	**8**

Source: I.M.F. International Financial Statistics.

macroeconomic crisis surged out of control, and then was followed by a stabilization program that succeeded. These figures also demonstrate the extremely high levels of inflation that can be reached. Nicaragua's annual rate of 3000+ % is equivalent to a 30% inflation rate per month. At the other end of the scale, the low-inflation countries, mostly in Asia, also reached double-digit levels occasionally, but these countries get so perturbed that they quickly adopt remedial actions to curb the inflations. This sound policy response has ensured macroeconomic stability and facilitated microeconomic efficiency.

The simplest explanation of inflation is monetarist theory, which argues that inflation arises when the supply of money exceeds its demand. Then the price level must rise so that real money demand again equals its supply. A general rise in the price level simply means that all prices— including wages and nominal interest rates—rise by the same percentage. This is an idealized case of money neutrality. As an example, imagine that

all prices rose by a multiple of ten—then you simply append a zero to every price. Since relative prices remain unchanged, there is no reallocation of real resources. But this is a highly theoretical possibility. In reality the prices of different goods rarely change by the same percent. Typical inflation has different prices changing at different times in a jagged manner. Such "noise" distorts the information carried in price signals, leading to the wrong economic decisions and inefficiency.

It is possible to avoid some ill effects of inflation by a system of **indexation,** in which each price is tied to some price index. In particular, the price of labor is changed by a cost of living adjustment (COLA) as measured by the consumer price index (CPI). Nominal prices rise in step so that real wages do not drop during an inflation. There are two basic counterarguments to this arrangement: (1) Indexation is not really feasible; and (2) Even if it were, it is not desirable anyway. Note that indexation cannot be contemporaneous, as every conceivable adjustment clause must be backward-looking. Also, full index-ation would leave little incentive for anyone to fight inflation. The very indexation, in itself, diminishes the discipline for price restraint.

Brazil is the preeminent example of a country with a long history of inflation. Learning from this experience it has set up a sophisticated system of indexation that aims to remove the most egregious redistributions that an inflation might cause. Compared to other countries, adjustments in various prices are made fairly rapidly and completely. Still, the poor tend to bear a greater burden since they do not have access to indexed financial instruments. Also, despite the indexation of wages, there can be sharp variations in the real wages of workers as nominal wage increases lead or lag increases in prices, as seen in Figure 16-3.

No matter how perfect a system of **indexation,** it inevitably remains incomplete. Not all commodities can be indexed: Notably, money cannot be indexed. Consequently domestic money loses real value as the price level rises. In effect, this constitutes a **tax on money** holdings. LDC governments tend to rely more than DCs on this kind of financing due to the limited nature of their bond markets and fiscal structure, as noted elsewhere in this chapter. Since the tax on money prompts people to reduce real money holdings, it thereby diminishes the advantages of a monetary system. Theoretically people might forego money entirely, reverting to barter with all its associated inefficiency. In practice, people tend to stop exchanges since they are confused about what appropriate prices should be. A telling sign in shop-windows is "Closed Due to a Lack of Prices!" Thus inflation caused by macroeconomic disequi-libria has the further effect of generating micro-economic inefficiency. This gives rise to yet another form of vicious cycle in addition to those noted in the introduction. As excessive money creation causes inflation, the result is to reduce the demand for real money balances; the excess of money supply becomes even larger, so there's a narrower base on which the inflation tax may be levied; to extract a certain amount of real taxes, the government must impose an even higher inflation rate, and so on . . . .

In extreme inflations there's a "flight from money" as people seek other means to make transactions. A typical response is **dollarization** of the economy, as strong foreign currencies are substituted for the domestic currency. This is no panacea either since the real exchange rate also tends to fluctuate at the same time. Certain types of transactions (say, haircuts or groceries) con-tinue to be conducted in local currency, while others (say, property transactions) take place using dollars. The daily variations in the real exchange rate implies corresponding fluctua-tions in the relative price of these two types of goods. A car worth 5,000 haircuts may trade for 30,000 haircuts a short while later. The resulting microeconomic inefficiency continues unless all transactions are carried out exclusively using one currency. Panama is a rare example of a country that uses the U.S. dollar rather than its own cur-rency. Unfortunately, this arrangement implies that the poor country must give up seignorage to the money creator in an already rich country. Wouldn't it be better to have the self-discipline to create a stable currency that keeps the rewards of money creation at home?

Turning now from effects to the causes of inflation, a deeper explanation is provided by political-economy analysis. Recall from chapter 13 how interest groups form and begin to strug-gle over society's resources. For example, let's say in an economy with 100 apples, two groups stake claims to 55 and 60 each. Clearly these claims cannot be satisfied since they add up to more than the total. Yet 115 claims might be printed and distributed. The real value of these nominal claims (i.e., money) falls. While the dis-tribution conflict remains unresolved, inflation surges ahead. By the same token, stabilization attempts tend to inflame the politics even more since the distributional conflict must be resolved. (Consider the well-known contemporary exam-ple of Russia.)

Real Minimum Wage (index, January 1978 = 100)

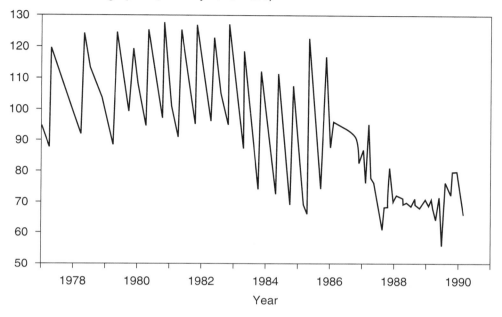

Figure 16-3 *Brazil: Variations in real Minimum Wage, 1977–1990*
Source: Dornbusch and others 1990.

The government is obviously a critical player in the distributional game, and the excess claims are reflected in its budget deficit. Strong governments are able to cut subsidies and raise taxes. In functioning democracies the conflicting claims are worked out, while authoritarian regimes obtain consistency in the distributional game by repressing claims of disfavored groups. For example, Chile's dictatorship in the 1970s sharply reduced real wages as part of its macroeconomic stabilization program. Once the deficit is controlled, there need be no recourse to inflationary finance. It is just when governments are weak, in times of social or political crises, that inflation gets out of hand.

An essential political economy lesson is that inflation must be ameliorated by political remedies, not just by an economic fix. One suggested institutional reform recognizes the reality that political contention is neverending. Instead of waiting forever for a final resolution, it would be smarter to insulate the central bank from political influences and government control. Such **central bank independence** will ensure the soundness of the monetary system while the reconciliation of total demands continues to be fought out in the political arena. Finally, it is important to note that this is not just a zero-sum game. Prolonged inflation tends to reflect a negative sum game. The winners from inflation are gaining less than the losers are losing. Thus eliminating inflation will increase the size of the total pie. This is seen in the case study about Peru, as well as in the general correlation of high inflation with low or negative economic growth. If suitable side payments can be arranged in the political game, all parties could become better-off by removing the chaos and inefficiency that characterize high inflations.

The Debt Crisis

Above we discussed the causes and effects of macro disequilibria for a single country. Often this has been a systemic problem whose proximate cause was too easy an access to foreign borrowing. The start of the debt crisis that affected much of the developing world in the 1980s can be precisely dated to a single event: In August 1982 Mexico's finance minister Silva Herzog announced publicly that Mexico would not honor its debt commitments. From that point on the world of commercial bank lending to LDCs was thrown into turmoil. The financial, economic, and political repercussions would take a decade to play themselves out.

Genesis   The seeds for the debt crisis were sown in the mid-1970s with the sharp increase in oil revenues, mostly to OPEC countries in the Middle East. Initially unable to absorb this huge influx, these countries sought to "park" the surplus funds abroad. They opted mostly for financial investment placed in the World's financial capitals of London and New York. Thus the task of petrodollar recycling fell on multinational banks. They turned around and lent this money to capital-scarce LDCs. Corresponding to the banks' desires to lend was an equally strong inducement for LDCs to borrow, as real interest rates were quite low or negative in those inflationary times.

The nature of bank lending was changed fundamentally during this historical episode. Banks made loans to developing countries with little regard for the financial soundness of the individual borrower. A country's government was, implicitly or explicitly, considered the guarantor of all loans made within a given country. At the same time in the lending countries, private banking institutions pushed the risk onto the shoulders of their own governments. In the U.S., for example, banks passed much of the risk on to the FDIC (Federal Deposit Insurance Corp.). They also relied on the belief that the Federal Reserve would bail out banks that were "too big

to fail." In the end, loans from a private bank in New York to a private company in Caracas became, in effect, a loan from the U.S. government to the Venezuelan government.

Effects   The signal in 1982 about payment difficulties prompted the commercial banks to essentially end voluntary lending to LDCs for the rest of the 1980s. Protracted negotiations ensued between the borrowers and lenders—analogous to bankruptcy proceedings for corporations. The banks sought to reschedule loans so that technically there would be no default. Any new advances simply paid the old interest and principal. Meanwhile the inflows of foreign capital of about $36B in 1981 turned to a net outflow of $30B in 1989 with drastic economic consequences.

1. Reduced investment resulted in slow growth.

2. Economic restructuring to fix the external imbalance required both expenditure switching and expenditure reduction policies.

3. Restructuring almost invariably generates macroeconomic instability, for at least a transitory period.

The macro instability caused by the restructuring (3) served to further depress output growth due to low investment (1). Ultimately the countries were obliged to carry out macroeconomic stabilization simultaneously with the longer term program of structural adjustment (2).

Responses   At the outset the seriousness of the problem was underestimated. All actors thought they could somehow "muddle through" without making any basic changes. The banks insisted that the borrowing countries must simply repay, just as in any standard commercial transaction. On the other side, borrowers maintained that they could not pay back. That raised the tricky question of whether the borrowers were unable or just unwilling to service the debt they had accrued. This distinction becomes important in the case of country lending since, unlike bankrupt corporations, countries cannot be "liquidated." Those economies will–and must–continue to produce and consume, and hopefully to grow. Thus the question of how much repayment and on what terms becomes a matter for negotiation.

The ability to repay may be gauged by considering the fact that the debt/GDP ratio reached 100% for many LDCs, and sometimes exceeded it. If such a country must repay its debt in four years, it would have to allocate 25% of its GDP for debt repayment–or 10% annually if done over 10 years. These magnitudes seem quite implausible, especially if it is a very poor country that is being obliged to cut back. Meanwhile the lending banks were concerned only with their own continued viability, while the main concern of creditor governments was to ensure the overall health of their banking systems.

While a handful of borrowing countries managed to make adequate reforms to deal with their own situation, the majority had to wait for a systemic resolution. Along with other creditor countries, the U.S. government became a major player that actively sought a solution that would be financially viable and politically acceptable. Various approaches to resolve the debt crisis were suggested by successive Republican administrations. Two prominent frameworks, named after the incumbent Treasury secretaries, had the following characteristics:

Baker Plan, 1985
> Debt rescheduling;
> inducements for commercial banks to resume lending

Brady Plan, 1989
> Debt reduction;
> Official flows to borrowers in return for policy reform
> Banks suffer some losses

The first of these two plans was still-born, while the second has had a substantial degree of success. The crisis of the early 1980s continued to worsen as commodity prices crashed in the mid-1980s. In particular, oil exporting borrowers such as Nigeria, Mexico, and Venezuela faced sharply lower terms of trade even as the real interest rate rose. The cumulative burden and passage of time caused all parties to grudgingly acknowledge the realities of the situation: The international banks realized that they would have to take some losses, while the creditor countries conceded that repayment was only possible if the heavily indebted countries could resume growth. In turn, the heavily indebted countries came to realize that there was really no alternative but to undertake the harsh structural adjustment steps that were essential for resumed economic growth in any case.

As noted, the Baker Plan failed because expectations of all actors were initially out of line. Another more basic flaw was that incentives were not properly designed. In particular, the heavily indebted LDCs wondered what was in it for them? The plan seemed to imply that if these countries resumed growth, they would be obliged to turn over all the gains to creditors. (You can observe analogous disincentives in moving people away from welfare and into the job market.) Thus a key element of the Brady Plan was a component of debt reduction. In return for the resumption of partial repayment, the banks agreed to write-down outstanding balances by significant fractions. The countries could then begin with a clean slate. Also, the developed countries stepped in with official lending while the banks remained unable to lend new funds. Such lending has been mainly channeled through the World Bank and IMF to individual countries depending on their progress towards restructuring their economies.

A more disaggregated view presents a range of responses to the crisis. In general, the earlier a country came to grips with the problem, the earlier it returned to the path of renewed growth. For instance, many may no longer even recall that Korea was one of the highly indebted countries. However, in the early 1980s it took rigorous measures to restructure its economy, enabling it to service its debt and return to a high growth plan. Turkey is a similar case, with reforms undertaken by an authoritarian regime. Colombia, which was never so heavily indebted, was able to maintain macro stability aided by substantial foreign exchange earnings from the drug trade. Other early liberalizers were Mexico and Chile; they bore a heavy social cost in the mid-1980s. Yet other countries remained unaffected by the crisis since they had taken on little commercial borrowing

due to an ideological aversion. (See "Is India Overborrowed," Kasliwal, 1989.)

Africa constitutes an entire bloc that has strenuously resisted the rationale for structural adjustment–aside from modest successes achieved by Ghana. The creditor countries allocated official funds that have gone mainly for the purpose of debt forgiveness. But without a plan for economic resurgence, there has been virtually no inflow of private capital as in Asia or parts of Latin America. Meanwhile elites in the African countries resist the IMF discipline as an imperialistic imposition. From this aggregate perspective, let us move to examine the details of an IMF program for macroeconomic stabilization.

Anatomy of a Macroeconomic Crisis

1. Excessive government spending leads to a **budget deficit**
2. Financed by domestic borrowing or money creation
   Borrowing $\longrightarrow$ high interest rates
   Excessive creation $\longrightarrow$ inflation
3. Raised domestic prices worsen the trade balance
4. Given PPP, inflation causes the exchange rate to be overvalued
5. Fears of a currency devaluation prompts capital outflows
6. The two deficits together cause a balance of payments deficit:
   BoP = current account + capital account
7. The BoP deficit means reserve losses from the central bank

The standard IMF stabilization package

1. A currency devaluation
   stems capital outflows as the devaluation threat is past
   improves the trade balance, perhaps after a lag
2. Generally cut trade restrictions to improve economic efficiency
3. Reduces money supply growth, which lowers the inflation rate
   As a bonus, real money demand may increase
4. Cut government expenditures to control the budget deficit
5. Reforms that enhance the **credibility** of policy

THE IMF ROLE

As noted earlier the IMF's function is to help alleviate (and hopefully avoid) short-term macro crises. The IMF has been designed as a sort of "central bank for central banks" (see the survey article in the *Economist* 1991). The IMF lends financial resources from its common pool in a variety of ways. First, each member country is entitled to a share, or tranche, proportional to the subscription it paid as part of its membership dues. When a country does not eliminate the root cause of the external deficit, it may return again and again to seek IMF assistance. When it does access successively higher "upper **credit tranches,**" the country is subject to ever more stringent scrutiny. The IMF has expanded the menu of new facilities for countries in trouble. These facilities differ based on the purpose of borrowing, as well as the conditions attached to them. The list includes stand-bys, a sort of line of credit, as well as compensatory and buffer-stock facilities in case a country suffers a sharp drop in export earnings. A particular example of foreign exchange crisis that was not the fault of the country arose during the oil crisis of the mid-1970s. The IMF set up a special oil facility to finance the sharply higher foreign exchange needs of the oil-importing countries.

In normal times the IMF has little say in a country's autonomy over its conduct of financial affairs. Often, however, a country's own policies prompt a macroeconomic crisis that causes an adverse turn in its BoP. To deal with this unsustainable situation, the country may seek loans ever more frequently, or for larger amounts, from the IMF. In such situations the IMF begins to demand stricter adherence to a prudent conduct of monetary and financial policy. In cases of financial/macroeconomic crisis the standard IMF program can be quite detailed and intrusive as it is designed to deal with each link in the chain of interlinked policies.

Trade policy:	Import restraints
	Tariffs
	Import/Export finance
	Export incentives
	Exchange rate
Fiscal policy:	Taxes
	Public spending
	Public-enterprise reform
	Subsidies and prices
Financial sector:	Monetary policy
	Interest rates
	Capital controls

An important lesson is that the stabilization program is not just a monetary solution to a purely monetary problem. While an IMF loan will alleviate the immediate problem of low foreign reserves, such relief may only be temporary. Unless the root cause—for example, excessive domestic spending, usually as an expanding budget deficit—is addressed, the same problem will crop up again. To avoid a repetition of the same problems, such as trade restrictions, devaluation, and soon, the IMF bases its assistance on a promise that the country will adhere to conditions about sound macroeconomic policy. Of course, such conditions cause discomfort in the form of retrenchment of public employees, higher taxes, tighter credit, and so on. Naturally, a variety of vested interests come out in opposition to the IMF program.

Criticism of IMF Policy

IMF involvement has been severely criticized from various points of view. Many countries resist **conditionality,** calling it an unacceptable interference with a country's sovereignty. This criticism is easily countered since countries voluntarily seek IMF assistance. Consider the analogy of private individuals who normally possess the usual freedoms. Once an individual asks for a loan, the bank delves into all sorts of personal matters to verify that the loan can and will be repaid. It would be disingenuous for the individual to complain about reduced autonomy.

In the country context, complaints about the IMF's political motives may be better understood by stepping from the national level to subgroups within an economy. Just as for any policy action, there inevitably will be winners and losers from stabilization policy. There's continued suspicion about whose interests the IMF is taking care of. Opposition parties find it easy to mobilize those segments that will suffer most from the austerity measures. The IMF program gets kicked around as a sort of political football, even if country managers fully recognize that there is no real alternative to the tough and responsible measures for the nation as a whole. There have been many instances in which embattled governments simply gave up power; Whereupon the opposition, in turn, was obliged to accede to the very same IMF conditions.

A more trenchant criticism of the IMF's "tough" measures is that they may be unnecessary, or worse, counterproductive. The standard prescription of devaluation by itself does nothing to solve the problem of inflation, if deficits and money creation continue unchecked. Meanwhile the prescribed austerity lowers aggregate demand and thereby exacerbates the recession according to **Keynesians.** Structuralists are the strongest critics of a policy of devaluation/austerity. Recall that this school is skeptical about the effectiveness of relative price changes. In the present context this refers to exchange rate changes. A devaluation (which lowers the international price of this country's goods) may be largely ineffective in raising exports or cutting imports.

Two types of policy to fix the external deficit are called **expenditure switching** and **expenditure reduction,** respectively. While the latter policy may be too painful, it is feared that the former might be too ineffective. An expenditure reduction policy, by inducing a recession, is a harsh but effective method of slashing imports. On the other hand expenditure switching works slowly since exports cannot grow immediately even if a devaluation increases the incentive to export. As noted in chapter 12, exports depend not just on price, but also crucially on other factors such as quality, reliability, and marketing. Critics instead recommend heterodox policy that will hopefully get the gain of cutting the trade deficit, while avoiding the pain of recession (see Kiguel and Liviatan 1992). Components of a heterodox stabilization policy package include steps such as trade restrictions and controls on foreign capital flows, which are supposed to keep the country growing while solving the external deficit in the longer run.

In response to such criticism the IMF has lengthened the period of its loans and now tries to coordinate its short-term intervention with the long-term growth/restructuring concerns of the World Bank. But just as the IMF harshness was criticized by liberals, the newer permissiveness is criticized by conservatives. This debate highlights the critical issue: *What is an appropriate role of the IMF?* Is it supposed to be a last-resort corrective/disciplinary institution, or a helpful aide to unfortunate countries that get into trouble for no fault of their own? The focus on culpability, in turn, is tied to the issue of incentives. Will countries make the necessary hard decisions in the future if the IMF is too lenient now? Such considerations make explicit the connection between the short-term and long-term. If the IMF views its role as strictly short-term, as was originally intended, then the problems are solved momentarily, only to recur frequently as the underlying problems remain unresolved. For instance, the IMF's role in Africa has been seriously questioned. Despite an intensive involvement spanning decades, did it do any good whatsoever? In hindsight, it seems inappropriate to deal with the symptoms of financial stringency as just a liquidity problem, when the real problem was one of solvency.

The many zigs and zags of policy, both at the national and international level, give rise to a certain cynicism. After the nth pronouncement of a "new economic policy" or IMF stabilization package, there's little faith this one will succeed where so many have failed or faded away in the past. The public tends to stop believing policy pronouncements leading to **policy ineffectiveness.** The role of agents' forward-looking expectations becomes a separate issue of policy reform. Policy actions "cannot fool all of the people all of the time." Eventually, as private economic agents learn to anticipate the government's policy imperatives, all stabilization policy becomes ineffective—as highlighted by the **rational expectations** school. For effective reforms the government is urged to stick with a policy "regime" so as to rebuild its **credibility.** The temptation to deviate for temporary gain is strong since such policy tends to be quite painful, while pressures for relief are unrelenting.

The lack of credibility can be very costly. A typical example of this is disinflation policy based on orthodox monetarist theory in which the rate of monetary growth must be cut sharply. If the public is not convinced that this discipline will persist, it will keep setting prices and wages ever higher. The consequent shortage of liquidity in relation to the constricted money supply leads to recession. Thus disinflation attempts are typically associated with severe recession. Further, the pain of recession in itself increases pressures for abandoning the disinflation process. A vicious cycle indeed! The experience of Argentina, particularly in the 1970s and 1980s, provides a sharp illustration of this phenomenon. Too many broken promises led to complete cynicism among the public, which in turn, sabotaged even well-designed policy.

A stable and credible policy promises long-term gains by reducing overall economic uncertainty. By analogy with human diseases, the IMF reforms are touted as "no pain no gain," with the prescribed program likened to "bitter medicine." Critics worry, however, that the cure may be worse than the disease. Let's examine a Latin American case study that offers valuable lessons in this regard. After that, we will study in greater detail a root cause of the disease: Chronic budget deficits, which must be cut in order to affect a long-term cure.

CASE STUDY: HETERODOX STABILIZATION FAILS IN PERU

The past decade saw many countries get into macroeconomic difficulties. Each sought a path to recovery and an eventual return to normal growth. While the symptoms of disequilibrium were clearly serious, heated debate continued about the best remedy. The case of Peru in the 1980s provides an example of a stabilization program that failed. Like much of Latin America, Peru fell into a macroeconomic crisis after the debt crisis in 1982. The populist government of Alan Garcia rejected the orthodox IMF approach of budgetary and monetary restraint. For a while the government reaped popularity by resisting the harsh measures pushed by foreigners.

Peru's government opted instead for a heterodox approach based on an incomes policy. It hoped to stabilize the economy, but without much of the pain that the orthodoxy deems unavoidable. By instituting wage and price controls, the government sought to combat inflation without suffering a loss of output and employment. Far from adopting a restrictive stance, the government bolstered aggregate demand in a Keynesian prescription that increased the budget deficit.

This policy stance in the mid-1980s resulted in a drastic plunge in the economy. The macroeconomic deterioration is evident in all parameters in the period 1985–1990. Table 16-3 chooses 1980 as the base year with an index set at 100.

More detailed data reveal that the heterodox program did enjoy some degree of success

Table 16-3 Peru: Economic Indicators

	1980	1985	1990
Real GDP per capita	100	87	70
Real minimum wage	100	54	21
C.P.I.	100	3000	40 million
$ Export revenue	100	76	83
Foreign reserves	100	89	−13

initially, but declined precipitously after 1987. This strategy of growth before adjustment utilized existing excess capacity to expand output and lower unemployment. The program had a fatal flaw: The budgetary measures were unsustainable, and this fact was well-understood by the financial markets. Domestic and foreign investors and currency speculators foresaw that the deficit would continue to mount in an unsustainable way. Much to the government's displeasure, they bet against the currency and pulled funds out of the country. The net outflow of private capital during 1984–1985 came on the heels of a real BoP crisis. Export receipts had dropped 24% in the 1980–1985 period. Foreign lenders stopped lending, and the IMF refused to provide emergency aid unless a drastic restructuring was started.

A bigger failure, judging by the program's own aims, was the drastic deterioration of the poverty situation. A detailed survey of living standards in the Lima metropolitan area over the 5 year period from 1985 to 1990 shows the decline (see Table 16-4).

The macroeconomic decline was rapid and severe—extraordinary outside of war or natural disasters. The fact that the poorer segments were particularly hard hit is confirmed by the tabulation of consumption decline by educational level in Table 16-5.

These data truly reveal a lost decade of development. While the stagnation in the first half of the decade was probably caused by external factors, the later slide was decidedly man-made. Ironically the very same orthodox policies, brusquely rejected in 1985, were adopted in 1990 after a change in government. The new president, Fujimori then set out to remedy deeply-rooted micro inefficiencies after macro stabilization was achieved.

Table 16-4 Declining living standards in Lima, 1985–1990

Population group	Decline in real consumption
Poorest decile	−63%
Second poorest decile	−58%
Remaining richer deciles	−54%

Source: Glewee & Hall 1992.

Table 16-5 Declining consumption by educational level, 1985–1990

Primary or less	−59%
Secondary	−51%
University	−48%

FISCAL POLICY

The rise of macroeconomic crises in developing countries seems to have followed a vastly expanded role of government. Note that I avoid saying the latter "caused" the former, yet a strong correlation is evident. Three or four decades ago, the spirit of the times was to endorse activist governments in many societies. such a concensus prevailed in developed as well as developing societies. We soon learned that government promises and expenditure commitments tended to grow at a faster pace than tax collections. The inevitable result was growing budget deficits with all their consequent problems. The issue of government finance may be analyzed in terms of its constituent parts.

$$\frac{\text{Budget}}{\text{deficit}} = \frac{\text{Government}}{\text{expenditures}} - \frac{\text{Tax}}{\text{revenue}}$$

Each of these items of public finance has a separate set of causes and effects. The budget deficit takes on particular importance due to its macroeconomic consequences. Thus the deficit issue must be distinguished from the separate issue of the size of government. Even if government expenditures are quite large (as a percent of GNP), but matched by tax revenues, there would be no deficit and therefore no macroeconomic impact. But other economic consequences could still arise. A large government share in the economy can typically have harmful microeconomic effects. Also, as shown by the earlier national income accounting, a budget deficit lowers the level of national savings. Such an adverse effect on investment and long-term growth is, again, distinct from macroeconomic effects. Table 16-6 shows the contribution of government savings (or dissavings) into the stream of national savings deriving for a sample of LDCs in recent years.

This table should be interpreted with care. The sectoral surpluses may not sum to zero in cases where figures are derived from independent sources. Note also that this table only indicates surpluses that go through the financial sector. It does not include self-financing when retained earnings are reinvested in a firm's own business, or when households finance one another without going through capital markets. The columns indicate the various sources and uses of funds. Negative savings by the business sector are a good thing, since this sector uses savings for the purpose of productive investment. Large positive numbers in the household column are similarly considered a healthy sign. The deficits in the government column are worrisome to the extent that they represent a "waste" of national savings rather than spending for investment that will cause growth.

Table 16-6 Sectoral surpluses flowing into financial sector (% of GNP)

	Government	Foreign	Households	Business
Tunisia	2.5	9.1	2.1	−13.7
Ivory Coast	1.3	4.4	1.5	−7.7
South Korea	1.1	5.2	7.0	−13.4
China	0.3	0.8	7.0	−8.1
Colombia	−0.2	1.3	3.5	−4.6
Turkey	−0.9	3.2	7.7	−11.0
Ecuador	−2.5	5.0	5.1	−6.8
Philippines	−3.6	2.9	9.1	−7.0
India	−5.5	1.1	5.5	−1.2

Source: article on World Bank in the *Economist*, 9/23/89.

The macroeconomic effects of a budget deficit are also considered harmful in the monetary approach in an open economy. By contrast, the Keynesian tradition looks more benignly at any increase in aggregate demand. Higher expenditure is expected to increase output (with a multiplier) in times of unutilized productive capacity. However, when there's no excess capacity, the consequence is either inflation or higher interest rates that tend to crowd out private investment. In effect, the increased government expenditure simply reduces private investment by almost the same amount. However, accommodating monetary policy can avoid crowding out by keeping interest rates low.

The main critique of such thinking is that stimulation of aggregate demand tends to be excessive, thereby generating inflation. Only rarely do LDCs face a situation of truly inadequate aggregate demand, so the deficits are usually damaging. The basic problem is deficient supply, not deficient demand, and budget deficits do nothing to help the former. Further, in an open economy the budget deficit is matched by a current account deficit that is associated with a depreciation of the exchange rate.

Government Expenditure

Once the budget deficit is singled out as a major cause of problems, we turn to study its determinants. Specifically, does the budget deficit stem from expenditure being "too high" or taxes being "too low"? We can judge this in relation to other countries at a similar level of development. To begin, let's examine the expenditure side. Typically, there are chronic pressures to increase government expenditures stemming from reasons of political economy. At its worst, this phenomenon is manifested as **populism,** where politicians attempt to "buy" support by spending money from the public till. They choose public expenditures that advance their self interest—be it getting reelected or gaining money and influence by controlling the disbursement of funds.

Public expenditures fall into various major categories:

Public employee payrolls

Public sector enterprises

Subsidies

Defense

Our examination of public expenditures starts with a brief look at their causes or motivation before analyzing their effects. It would be wrong to presuppose that public spending is always cynical or self-serving. Expenditure programs often are started for entirely idealistic reasons or seemingly rational policy. Only later are these decisions seen to be misguided, or the possibility of mischief presents itself. As a concrete example, consider the serious and justified concern about unemployment in much of the developing world. This pressing concern often led governments to create employment directly through expanding public payrolls.

A major disadvantage of direct public job creation is that such policy is inequitable as it benefits only a small segment of the population. Further, pressure groups organize to preserve this special benefit. These interest groups make side payments to politicians. As this symbiotic relationship develops, the benefits tend to increase even more, and the budget deficit progressively worsens, leading to the macro crisis that harms overall growth. A similarly excusable—if not laudable—motivation for beginning consumption subsidies derived from equity considerations independent of efficiency. These programs eventually grow into a problem as expanding benefits are directed not to the very poorest, but to those groups who wield the most political power. The heavy toll on public finances is not rectified earlier because such expenditures often take somewhat hidden and indirect forms. Particular examples are the low prices set for publicly provided goods such as electricity, fuel, and transportation.

Direct government employment also seemed justified by entirely respectable macro-economic theory. The **Keynesian paradigm,** quite fashionable a few decades ago, urged that government increase aggregate demand so as to increase output and employment. The suggestion was that any public expenditure would prime the pump for this purpose. There was no mention about waste or the productivity of such expenditures. The affect on aggregate demand was deemed beneficial quite apart from any supply-side benefits. In other words, even if the government threw away money at random, the extra spending in itself would generate macroeconomic benefits. The flaw in this argument is that the Keynesian prescription only works in a depression where there's generalized excess capacity. The LDC situation, on the other hand, is usually a lack of productive capacity. Thus government's role must be to build capacity by focusing its very limited funds for the most productive projects.

Even with a supply side view, public expenditures have tended to have harmful effects. The early enthusiasm for public sector expansion was predicated on a naive faith in government capabilities. Only gradually has it been realized that the bureaucracy had neither the appropriate incentives, nor indeed the information, for efficient operation. Thus the optimistic expectations of earnings from government enterprises often turned into a stream of chronic losses subsidized by the public.

Eventually the time comes to resolve the crisis. By then, however, the people have gotten accustomed to a certain lifestyle, so the forced austerity seems especially harsh. The **costs of adjustment** (both actual and psychological) take various forms with an uneven impact across the economy. Former beneficiaries of government expenditures are obviously hit most directly by the cutbacks as are those segments hit by higher taxes. Usually the first cuts in direct expenditures are aimed at poverty programs, whereas bureaucracy and administrative overhead is largely spared. Eventually, expenditure cuts must affect government employees in the form of pay and/or employment cuts. But cuts (or freezes) in pay scales rarely make a significant enough dent in the budget problem. Thus selective lay-offs of government employees become inevitable.

A new concern faces the international development community in the spate of adjustment crises that have occurred since the 1980s. Equality and poverty conditions are feared to deteriorate sharply as a result of adjustment programs (as noted in chapter 3 on equity). Just as growth efforts suffered a serious setback, particularly in Latin America and Africa, so did attempts to improve equity and ameliorate poverty. This adverse impact occurred in two ways: Direct, perhaps unavoidable, cuts in welfare and poverty programs occurred at the same time as inequality and poverty worsened due to increased unemployment. This overall impact on equity has become a matter of much debate since it is a complex of various offsetting effects.

The adjustment programs appear to have had a worse impact on urban poverty than on the rural poor. The necessary exchange rate devaluations generally tend to increase farm prices in relation to domestic manufactures. (This reversed the previous overvaluation, which had tipped the terms of trade in favor of urban areas away from exportable primary products.) Further, the trade policy measures that aim to improve the current account tend to tip the terms of trade in favor of exports and away from import substitution industry. Again, this hits employment and income in the urban sector, which is the location of much of the formerly protected industrial sector. An unfortunate feature of this adjustment is that just as uncompetitive industry is retrenching and laying off excess workers, outlays for welfare and unemployment must simultaneously be cut.

The last major item of public expenditure is for the armed forces. Often, the proponents of such expenditures deem them to be essential and beyond an economic calculus. After all, isn't the most basic rationale for government the provision of national defense from outsiders? They claim it is especially difficult to optimize the amount of defense in the sense that the marginal social benefit of the last dollar spent on defense equals the benefit of that dollar spent elsewhere in the country. Yet the vast, seemingly uncontrolled expansion of such expenditures since the late 1970s has led to a questioning of how much defense is enough, especially in view of other primary goals, such as economic progress. Moreover, there's mounting empirical evidence that LDCs that spend more on armed forces tend to show a worse economic performance in the long run.

Turning to the effect of government expenditures, it is useful to split out the aggregate number into analytical categories.

$$\text{Government expenditures} = \text{Consumption} + \text{Investment items}$$

Actual financial accounts rarely present such a clear-cut accounting of the government's expenditures. This economic distinction highlights the idea that investment expenditures provide future returns that can service any debt incurred, while consumption expenditures obviously cannot. However, it is often difficult to specify whether a particular item of expenditure has an investment component or is purely consumption. Some examples are social expenditures in health and education. Even if these are indeed investment expenditure, there can be a problem if the future benefits do not come in a financial form that can be used for servicing debt.

Another kind of measurement problem is that of accurately aggregating public expenditures or the fiscal deficit. This difficulty arises since it's often unclear whether a given entity is part of government or not. In decreasing order of clarity this classification includes

Central government (and local government)

Public sector enterprises

Subsidies through financial institutions

While the first two items are well-known, the quantitative significance of the last item is rarely appreciated. In particular, this item became extremely important in the depths of the financial crisis that hit Latin America in the 1980s. In the boom years leading up to the crisis, the banking sector had strong incentives to expand domestic credit, often to ventures of dubious economic value. When the financial crash came, however, governments could not let these unsound institutions go bankrupt for fear of further ripple effects throughout the economy. Thus they were forced to subsidize the losses of financial institutions despite the fact that the latters' problems were of their own making.

Notable examples of such quasi-fiscal expenditures occurred in Argentina and Chile in 1982–1985 when the total fiscal deficit shot up to 25% and 10% of GDP, respectively (see Easterly and Schmidt 1993). In other countries, too, the banking sector is often explicitly or implicitly under public control. It can be pressured to expand credit for political or social purposes that are at odds with economic criteria. For instance, populist governments sometimes have generously granted debt forgiveness to select groups. While this reaped short-term popularity, the long-term consequences typically have been crippling, both in its effect on solvency of financial institutions and as a precedent that set up unsound expectations for the future.

Tax Revenues

Tax revenues form the other part of the budget equation. As expenditure tends to rise inexorably, governments are obliged to raise tax revenues. An unfortunate reality of modern times is that all easy sources of taxes have already been used up. The fiscal problem is that the easiest revenue sources usually are the most distortionary, while the theoretically best ones are hardest to implement in the real world. Among the most accessible taxable bases of economic activity are trade flows. These can be taxed at their most concentrated point, for example, at ports for overseas imports or exports, or at bridges for internal trade. Unfortunately, the easiest taxes also tend to be the most distortionary from the point of view of efficiency. The tax effort progressively moves on to other emergent economic activity in continuing efforts to broaden the tax base.

$$\text{Tax revenue} = \text{Tax base} \times \text{Tax rate}$$

The equation shows that another obvious way to raise tax revenue is to raise the tax rate. Unfortunately this effort also runs into an obvious constraint of the Laffer Curve mentioned earlier. As the tax rate reaches high levels, the incentive for economic activity diminishes so tax revenues begin to dry up. In an early phase of a fiscal crisis, tax rates were ratcheted upward, almost in desperation. In later reforms, governments are sometimes pleasantly surprised to find that lowering tax rates has increased tax revenue.

These issues relating to the distortionary effect of taxes are essentially microeconomic issues. Another causal effect in the macroeconomic sphere is the effect of inflation on tax revenues. Real tax revenues tend to fall when inflation rises. This so-called **Tanzi effect** arises from the fact of lags in tax collections that become critical when the pace of inflation is rapid. The nominal tax bill usually is computed after income and profits are determined for an annual or quarterly period. The taxpayer is further allowed some time to pay. If there's zero inflation, a dollar's worth of tax receipts would remain worth one dollar in real terms at year end. During inflation, on the other hand, that nominal dollar will have a much lower real value at the end of the year. (In the United States the tax deadline is April 15th of the following year. Imagine if inflation was 50% per annum, the value of tax receipts would be about 15% lower in real terms due to the $3\frac{1}{2}$ month lag.)

A similar lagged effect applies to the pricing of public services, such as utilities and public transport. Hence, public enterprise revenue also declines during inflations, as seen in the example of Peru shown in Table 16-7. It shows a drastic fall in public revenues (as a percent of GDP) during the sharply escalating inflation of the late 1980s. Correspondingly, the budget deficit registered a sharp increase. Clearly a stabilization program that cuts the inflation would also serve to reverse the decline in the public finances. Thus macroeconomic stability provides extra benefits by operating as a virtuous cycle.

Table 16-7   Peru: Public finances as % of GDP

	1985	1986	1987	1988	1989
Tax collection	13	11	9	7	4
Public enterprise revenue	26	18	14	12	10
Budget deficit	6	10	12	14	11
Annual inflation rate %	78	86	712	3500	7600

Source: Dornbusch and others 1990.

SUMMARY

Macroeconomic instability is increasingly recognized as a major obstacle to sustained development, particularly as LDCs become more open. The disequilibrium stems from unsustainable levels of domestic expenditures, manifested by a budget deficit. The counterpart to the excessive spending is a trade deficit financed by capital inflows from abroad. This leads to an accumulation of external debt and a consequent appreciation of the exchange rate. The budget deficit may alternatively be financed by money creation, which leads to inflation. Again, the real exchange rate can become overvalued if currency devaluation does not keep pace with the inflation rate. In both cases the characteristic symptoms leading up to the crisis are (i) accelerating inflation and (ii) a deterioration in the external accounts as the current account swings further into deficit.

As the private sector realizes that the situation is unsustainable, it tends to precipitate the crisis by its actions. Foreign lenders, fearing default, stop further lending and demand repayment. Other private investors fear losses from an inevitable currency devaluation and so trigger capital flight. The country then has no recourse but to seek assistance from the IMF. Such assistance aims to remain only temporary, not accommodate a fundamental disequilibrium. Thus the IMF impos-

es conditionality, which is often denounced as unacceptable infringement of the country's sovereignty. The IMF stabilization package typically includes a devaluation to restore external competitiveness and a cut in the money growth to curb inflation. But such short-term measures will not resolve the underlying problem if the country does not undertake long-term fiscal reforms. Moreover, these steps will not be effective even in the short term if they are not credible.

Finally, we study the public sector budget, which is the root cause of much of the macroeconomic problem, in addition to possible adverse microeconomic effects. The tendency for growing budget deficits is seen as a systemic problem aggravated by the operation of political economy. The political incentives are all for gaining support by expanding public expenditure while tax revenues lag. The fiscal crisis itself is subject to a vicious cycle. As the budget deficit is financed by money creation, inflation worsens, which worsens tax collections, and so on. Necessary reforms include cuts in subsidies, which often take the form of low prices of public utilities. In more serious adjustment efforts, the pay and employment of public-sector employees must also be cut. Such deep reforms are part of a thorough structural adjustment program that includes liberalization and privatization.

KEY TERMS

Open-economy macroeconomics	Overvaluation	Budget deficit
International Monetary Fund (IMF)	Real exchange rate	Credibility
	Nominal exchange rate	Credit tranches
Twin deficits	Black market	Conditionality
Balance of payments	Capital account	Keynesian
Current account (C/A)	Reserves	Expenditure switching policy
Devaluation	Inflation	Expenditure reduction
Depreciation	Expectations	Rational expectations
Debt service	Indexation	Policy ineffectiveness
Monetary Approach	Tax on money	Populism
Purchasing power parity (PPP)	Dollarization	Adjustment costs
	Central bank independence	Tanzi effect

References

Adelman, I. 1984. Beyond Export-Led Growth. *World Development*, May.

Amsden, A. 1989. *Asia's Next Giant*, Oxford: Oxford University Press.

Alter R. 1991. Lessons from the Export Processing Zone in Mauritius. *Finance & Development*, Dec.

Ariff, M. and H. Hill. 1986. *Export-orientation and Industrialization: the ASEAN Experience.* Allen and Unwin.

Binswanger, H. 1989. "The Policy Response of Agriculture." *Proceedings of the Annual Conference on Development Economics.* World Bank.

Blaug, M., ed. 1968. *Economics of Education.* Baltimore: Penguin Books.

Bleaney, M., and D. Greenaway 1993. Long-Run Trends in the Relative Price of Primary Commodities and in the Terms of Trade of Developing Countries. *Oxford Economic Papers.*

Bauer, P. T. 1971. *Dissent on Development.* London: Weidenfield and Nicolson.

Boserup, E. 1981. *Population Growth and Technological Change.* Chicago, Ill.: Univ. of Chicago Press.

Chenery, H. 1960. Patterns of Growth. *American Economic Review.*

———. 1983. Interaction between Theory and Observation in Development. *World Development*, Oct.

Chenery, H., S. Robinson, and M. Syrquin 1986. *Industrialization and Growth.* Oxford: Oxford University Press.

Chibber, A. 1988. Raising Agricultural Output: Price and Nonprice Factors. *Finance and Development*, June.

Club of Rome. 1972. *The Limits to Growth.* New York: Universe Books.

De Soto, H. 1989. *The Other Path.* New York: Harper and Row.

Dollar, D. 1992. *Exploiting the Advantages of Backwardness: The Importance of Education and Outward Orientation.* World Bank.

Dornbusch, R., F. Sturzenegger and H. Wolf, 1990. *Extreme Inflations: Dynamics and Stabilization.* Brookings Papers on Economic Activity.

Easterly, W., and K. Schmidt-Hebbel, 1993. Fiscal Deficits and Macroeconomic Performance in Developing Countries. *World Bank Research Observer*, July.

The Economist. 1991. A Survey of the IMF and the World Bank, 12 October.

Edwards, S. 1993. Openness, Trade Liberalization, and Growth in Developing Countries. *Journal of Economic Literature,* Sept.

Glewee, P., and G. Hall. 1992. Unorthodox Adjustment and Poverty in Peru. *Finance & Development,* Dec.

Grilli, E., and M. Yang. 1988. Primary Commodity Prices, Manufactured Goods prices, and the Terms of Trade of Developing countries. *World Bank Economic Review,* Jan.

Harberger, A. 1983. The Cost-Benefit Approach to Development Economics. *World Development,* Oct.

———. 1984. Distributional Weights or Basic Needs. *Economic Development & Cultural Change.*

———. 1985. *Economic Policy and Economic Growth.* San Francisco Institute for

Contemporary Studies.

———. 1993. "The Search for Relevance in Economics" *A.E.R. Papers & Proceedings,* May.

Harris, N. 1986. *The End of the Third World.* New York: Penguin Books

Harrison, L. 1992. *Who Prospers?* New York: Basic Books.

Hawkins, J. 1988. The Transformation of Education for Rural Development. *Comparative Education Review.*

Hayek, F. 1981. *Individualism and Economic Order,* Chicago: University of Chicago Press.

Heyman, D., and A. Leijonhufvud. 1994. *High Inflations.* Oxford: Oxford University Press.

Hirschman, A. 1958. *The Strategy of Economic Development* New Haven, Conn.: Yale University Press.

Ingham, B. 1993. The Meaning of Development: Interactions Between "New" and "Old" Ideas. *World Development.*

International Labour Office, "World Labour Report", annual issues Oxford: Oxford University Press.

James, J., and F. Stewart. 1989. New Products: The Welfare Effects of the

Introduction of New Products in Developing Countries. *Oxford Economic Papers.*

Kaplan, R. 1994. *The Coming Anarchy.* Altantic Monthly, Feb.

Kasliwal, P. 1989. "Is India Overborrowed" *Economic Development and World Debt* edited by H. Singer and S. Sharma Macmillan.

Kiguel, M., and N. Liviatan. 1992. When Do Heterodox Stabilizations Work? *World Bank Research Observer,* Jan.

Killick, T. 1981. *Policy Economics: A Textbook of Applied Economics on Developing Countries.* Heinemann.

Kim, J-I., and L. Lau. 1992. *The Sources of Economic Growth of the Newly Industrialized Countries of the Pacific Rim.* Stanford, Calif.: Stanford University.

Klitgaard, R. 1986. *Elitism and Meritocracy in Developing Countries: Selection Policies for Higher Education.* Baltimore, Md.: Johns Hopkins University Press.

———. 1990. *Tropical Gangsters: Development and Decadence in Deepest Africa.* Basic Books.

Kuznets, S. 1981. Modern Economic Growth. New Haven, Conn.: Yale University Press.

Lal, D. 1983. *The Poverty of "Development Economics."* Cambridge, Mass.: Harvard University Press.

———. 1988. *The Hindu Equilibrium.* Oxford: Oxford University Press.

Lal, D., and S. Rajapatirana. 1987. Foreign Trade Regimes and Economic Growth. *World Bank Research Observer* July.

Lau, L., D. Jamison, S. Liu, and S. Rivkin. 1993. Education and Economic Growth: Some Cross-Sectional Evidence from Brazil. *Journal of Development Economics* Vol. 41, Issue 1.

Leamer, E. 1984. *Sources of International Comparative Advantage* Cambridge, Mass.: M.I.T. Press.

Lewis, W. A. 1954. Economic Development with Unlimited Supplies of Labor. Manchester School of Economics and Social Studies. Vol 22 (2).

Maddison, A., and J. van Ark. 1993. "International Comparisons of Real Product and Productivity", *A.E.R. Papers & Proceedings,* May.

Mankiw, N., D. Romer, and D. Weil. 1992. A Contribution to the Empirics of Economic Growth. *Quarterly Journal of Economics,* May.

Massey, D., 1993. Theories of International Migration: A Review and Appraisal. *Population & Development Review,* Sept.

McMahon, W., and Boediono. 1992. Universal Basic Education: An Overall Strategy of Investment Priorities for Economic Growth" *Economics of Education Review,* June.

Morris, C., and Adelman. 1989. Nineteenth Century Development Experience and Lessons for Today. *World Development,* Sept.

Pollak, R., and S. Watkins. 1993. Cultural and Economic Approaches to Fertility *Population & Development Review,* Sept.

Populi, monthly magazine, UN Population Fund, New York.

Psacharopoulos, G. 1985. Returns to Education: A Further International Update. *Journal of Human Resources,* April.

Reidel, J. 1984. Trade as the Engine of Economic Growth in Developing Countries, Revisited. *Economic Journal,* March.

Reynolds, L. 1983. The Spread of Development to the Third World: 1850–1980. *Journal of Economic Literature,* Sept.

Riskin, C. 1994. Chinese Rural Poverty: Marginalized or Dispersed? *American Economic Review,* May.

Robey, B. 1993. The Fertility Decline in Developing Countries. *Scientific American,* Dec.

Robinson, J. 1979. *Aspects of Development and Underdevelopment.* Cambridge: Cambridge University Press.

Romer, P. 1992. "Two Strategies for Economic Development: Using Ideas and Producing Ideas." *Proceedings of the World Bank Annual Conference on Development Economics.*

Rosenzweig, M. 1990. Population Growth and Human Capital Investments: Theory and Evidence. *Journal of Political Economics,* Oct.

Schultz, T. W. Transforming Traditional Agriculture. New Haven, Conn.: Yale University Press.

Sen, A. 1982. Development: Which Way Now? *Journal of Development Economics.*

———. 1993. The Economics of Life and Death. *Scientific American,* May.

Simon, J. 1981. The Ultimate Resource. Princeton, NJ: Princeton University Press.

Singh, N. 1992. Multinationals, Technology and Government Policy. In *Development Policy and Economic Theory*. Oxford, England: Oxford University Press.

Srinivasan, T. N. Human Development: A New Paradigm or Reinvention of the Wheel? *American Economic Review*, May.

Stern, N. 1989. The Economics of Development: A Survey. *Economic Journal*, Sept.

Stiglitz, J. 1976. The Efficiency Wage Hypothesis, Surplus Labour, and the Distribution of Income in LDCs. *Oxford Economic Papers*.

Streeten, P. 1983. Development Dichotomies. *World Development*, Oct.

Sudgen, R. 1993. Welfare, Resources, and Capabilities: A Review of *Inequality Reconsidered* by Amartya Sen, *Journal of Economic Literature*, Dec.

Takacs, W. E. 1994. Domestic Content and Compensatory Export Requirements: Protection of the Motor Vehicle Industry in the Philippines. *World Bank Economic Review*, Jan.

Todaro, M. P. 1969. A Model of Labor Migration and Urban Unemployment in Less Developed Countries. *American Economic Review*.

Torii, T. 1991. Changing the Manfacturing Sector under the New Economic Policy. *Developing Economies*, Dec.

Toye, J. 1985. Dirigisme and Development Economics. *Cambridge Journal of Economics*, Mar.

U.N. Development Program (UNDP), "Human Development Report" Oxford: Oxford University Press, 1991, '92, '93, '94

U.N. 1992. International Fund for Agricultural Development (IFAD), "The State of World Rural Poverty", New York, NY: New York University Press.

Worldwatch Institute, Brown, Lester et al., "State of the World", annual issues. Norton.

World Bank, "World Development Report", annual issues. Washington D.C.

Young, A. 1994. Lessons from the East Asian NICs: A Contrarian View European Economic Review.

Index